Violence

Against Women and Children

Violence

Against Women and Children

NAVIGATING SOLUTIONS

Edited by
**Mary P. Koss,
Jacquelyn W. White,
and Alan E. Kazdin**

Volume 2

American Psychological Association • Washington, DC

HV
6250.4
.W65
V5216
2011
V.2

Published by
American Psychological Association
750 First Street, NE
Washington, DC 20002
www.apa.org

To order
APA Order Department
P.O. Box 92984
Washington, DC 20090-2984
Tel: (800) 374-2721; Direct: (202) 336-5510
Fax: (202) 336-5502; TDD/TTY: (202) 336-6123
Online: www.apa.org/pubs/books
E-mail: order@apa.org

In the U.K., Europe, Africa, and the Middle East, copies may be ordered from
American Psychological Association
3 Henrietta Street
Covent Garden, London
WC2E 8LU England

Typeset in Goudy by Circle Graphics, Inc., Columbia, MD

Printer: Maple-Vail Book Manufacturing Group, York, PA
Cover Designer: Naylor Design, Washington, DC
Cover Art: *All the Little Children*, 1990, oil paints and Cray-Pas, by Dori Jalazo

The opinions and statements published are the responsibility of the authors, and such opinions and statements do not necessarily represent the policies of the American Psychological Association.

Library of Congress Cataloging-in-Publication Data

Violence against women and children / edited by Jacquelyn W. White, Mary P. Koss, and Alan E. Kazdin. — 1st ed.
    p. cm.
 Includes bibliographical references and index.
 ISBN-13: 978-1-4338-0912-5
 ISBN-10: 1-4338-0912-5
 ISBN-13: 978-1-4338-0913-2 (e-book)
 ISBN-10: 1-4338-0913-3 (e-book)
 1. Women—Violence against—United States. 2. Women—Violence against—
United States—Prevention. 3. Children—Violence against—United States.
4. Children—Violence against—United States—Prevention. I. White, Jacquelyn W.
II. Koss, Mary P. III. Kazdin, Alan E.

 HV6250.4.W65V5216 2010
 362.82'920973—dc22

                    2010023861

British Library Cataloguing-in-Publication Data

A CIP record is available from the British Library.

Printed in the United States of America
First Edition

CONTENTS

CONTRIBUTORS

Ileana Arias, PhD, Principal Deputy Director, Centers for Disease Control and Prevention, Atlanta, GA

Tricia B. Bent-Goodley, PhD, School of Social Work, Howard University, Washington, DC

Rebecca Campbell, PhD, Department of Psychology, Michigan State University, East Lansing

Anna I. Coward, MA, Department of Psychology, Fairleigh Dickinson University, Teaneck, NJ

David S. Crampton, PhD, Mandel School of Applied Social Sciences, Case Western Reserve University, Cleveland, OH

John Eckenrode, PhD, Cornell University Family Life Development Center, Cornell University, Ithaca, NY

Katie M. Edwards, PhD candidate, Department of Psychology, Ohio University, Athens

Deborah Epstein, JD, Georgetown University Law Center, Georgetown University, Washington, DC

Kathleen Coulborn Faller, PhD, ACSW, LMSW, School of Social Work, University of Michigan, Ann Arbor

Adeena M. Gabriel, BA, Department of Psychology, Fairleigh Dickinson University, Teaneck, NJ

Christine A. Gidycz, PhD, Department of Psychology, Ohio University, Athens

Lisa A. Goodman, PhD, Department of Counseling and Developmental Psychology, School of Education, Boston College, Chestnut Hill, MA

Alan E. Kazdin, PhD, ABPP, Department of Psychology, Yale University, New Haven, CT

Mary P. Koss, PhD, Mel and Enid Zuckerman College of Public Health, University of Arizona, Tucson

Roger J. R. Levesque, JD, PhD, Department of Criminal Justice, Indiana University, Bloomington

Lindsay M. Orchowski, PhD, Center for Alcohol and Addiction Studies, Brown University, Providence, RI

Debra Patterson, PhD, School of Social Work, Wayne State University, Detroit, MI

Joan Pennell, MSW, PhD, Center for Family and Community Engagement, North Carolina State University, Raleigh

Jeffrey J. Pokorak, JD, Suffolk University Law School, Suffolk University, Boston, MA

Marcus Pope, MEd, Institute on Domestic Violence in the African American Community, University of Minnesota, St. Paul

Robert A. Prentky, PhD, Department of Psychology, Fairleigh Dickinson University, Teaneck, NJ

Johnny Rice II, MS, School of Community Health and Policy, Morgan State University, Baltimore, MD

Paul A. Schewe, PhD, Department of Criminology, Law, and Justice, University of Illinois, Chicago

Ilene Seidman, JD, Suffolk University Law School, Suffolk University, Boston, MA

Susan L. Staggs, PhD, Department of Psychology, University of Wisconsin–Stout, Menomonie

Cris M. Sullivan, PhD, Department of Psychology, Michigan State University, East Lansing

Oliver J. Williams, PhD, Institute on Domestic Violence in the African American Community, University of Minnesota, St. Paul

Jacquelyn W. White, PhD, Department of Psychology, University of North Carolina at Greensboro

FOREWORD

ILEANA ARIAS

Violence against women and children is a prevalent and costly public health problem in the United States. However, medical and social sciences have been able to garner unprecedented levels of the social and political will necessary to support research on the etiology and maintenance of violence against women and children to guide development of prevention and treatment programs and strategies. *Violence Against Women and Children* presents state-of-the-art theoretical and empirical perspectives on the response to violence against women and children. The two volumes, *Violence Against Women and Children, Volume 1: Mapping the Terrain* and *Violence Against Women and Children, Volume 2: Navigating Solutions*, document the tremendous health and economic burden to individuals, families, communities, and society, highlighting the huge disparities related to race, class, and other marginalized dimensions. Empirically based responses of various sectors—criminal justice, health care, mental health—are represented in this book, but, most important, *Violence Against Women and Children* issues a strong call for innovative, interdisciplinary approaches that aim for the primary prevention of violence against women and children, adopting the public health perspective.

Identifying and controlling factors that affect morbidity and mortality across the life span are the objectives of public health. Traditionally, public health practitioners and researchers have focused on infectious diseases in controlling morbidity and mortality. However, the relevance of infectious diseases has decreased over time while the relevance of chronic diseases has increased. Although not considered a traditional public health problem in the past, violence is a priority among public health problems because of its impact on morbidity and mortality, and because like smallpox and many other infectious diseases, it is a problem that can be understood and prevented through the application of epidemiological methods.

Traditionally, the functions of public health in the United States have included assessment of morbidity and mortality trends, causes, and prevention needs; assurance of implementation of legislative mandates and statutory responsibilities; policy development to support individual and community health efforts; and evaluation of effectiveness, accessibility, and quality of population-based health services. In the United States, federal, state, and local governments have had the lead responsibility for these functions because many public health functions require the exercise of authority and because the government is obligated to ensure that the public interest is served by any policy decisions. More recently, a "public health model" that moves beyond the traditional notion of public health as a function of government agencies has focused on assuring and providing individual-level services. This model describes a comprehensive approach to address significant public health problems, placing an increased emphasis on the development and dissemination of interventions at the community level and explicitly encouraging input from others outside the public sector and from multiple disciplines. Specifically, the public health approach begins with the definition and description of the problem and the determination of its scope. Empirical research is supported to identify risk and protective factors. These empirical data guide the development of prevention strategies and interventions. Finally, the public health model disseminates effective prevention strategies and interventions and supports widespread adoption and implementation.

Critical to the success of the public health approach is the inclusion of the various spheres of influence and control of the problem and responses to it. As documented by the work in these volumes, the socioecological model is key to developing and implementing what to do. Violence is a complex issue, and no single variable or sector alone is adequate to explain and prevent it. The socioecological model allows the integration of risk and protective factors from multiple domains of factors that influence violence. It includes and directs attention to variables at the individual, relationship, community, and societal levels, such as individual attitudes about violence, family environment, economic situation, and social policies. The model accommodates the complex interplay among the different levels of risk and protective factors and offers the possibility of a more robust and appropriate approach to prevention. Complexity is not limited to considerations of *what* to do to prevent; it is also central to considerations of *how* to effectively prevent. Traditionally, the focus of violence has been on changing individuals or individual attitudes and behavior through the use of individually focused interventions, such as psychological interventions, arrest and prosecution, or media campaigns. However, the socioecological model points to a wide spectrum of prevention ranging from personal-level change to policy-level change. Attempts to change individual attitudes and behavior may not aggregate to true population change. Likewise, broad contextual changes (e.g., policy change, systems change) are indispensible to support and sustain an individual behavioral change. In addition to changing and strengthening individual knowledge and skills to prevent violence against women and children, we need to create contextual changes by promoting community education, educating providers, fostering coalitions and networks to support change, changing organizational practices, and influencing policy and legislation.

We know through our experience in addressing other public health issues that prevention is possible. Violence prevention is broad and multifaceted, and it requires skills and approaches from many disciplines and areas of expertise. Capitalizing on the strengths of public health, we can prevent violence by promoting efforts to modify or eliminate the individual, relationship, community, and societal influences that result in perpetration, victimization, and bystander attitudes that allow violence to occur. Our efforts need to increasingly target general populations (universal efforts) and those at heightened risk (selected efforts) to ensure that the greatest number of people benefit from the prevention of violence. Advances in our science and attitudes about women, children, and violence suggest that it is time for ending violence against women and children to become a public health priority.

PREFACE

Less violence tops most lists of what would make a better world. Violence-related problems are preeminent on today's health and development agenda. Among the acknowledged realities about violence is the disproportionate amount experienced by women and children in their day-to-day lives at the hands of those who are expected to love and nurture them (Krug, Dahlberg, Mercy, Zwi, & Lozano, 2002).

Violence against women and children is an all-too-frequent outgrowth of historical patterns. Even today, most cultures, despite varying practices, embrace patterns of courtship, marriage, and child rearing that reinforce deeply entrenched traditions that support female and child deference to men and adults, respectively (Henson & Wilson, 2008).

Reducing violence against women and children has been a long-sought goal. Many agendas for reducing violence exist that were formulated on the basis of reviews of empirical research, such as the American Psychological Association report *No Safe Haven: Male Violence Against Women at Home, at Work, and in the Community* (Koss et al., 1994); the National Academy of Sciences volume *Understanding Violence Against Women* (Crowell & Burgess, 1996); the Centers for Disease Control and Prevention's *Injury Research Agenda,*

2009–2018 (National Center for Injury Prevention and Control, 2009); and the World Health Organization's (2009) *Violence Prevention: The Evidence* (see also Burchart, Phinney, Check, & Villavecces, 2004; Krug et al., 2002; National Scientific Council on the Developing Child, 2007; Whitaker, Lutzker, & Shelley, 2005). Universally, these documents conclude that experiencing violence and abuse can have lifelong negative consequences for individuals, communities, nations/states, and the world and that violence is broadly significant across public health, development, and security policy planning. However, Koss and White (2008) observed that these antiviolence agendas typically are expressed in broad language. Analysis of them across time may suggest to the casual reader that little progress has been made because the same items have been included for almost 20 years. The lack of concise summaries of current science and analysis of the gaps and deficits in the evidence constitutes a significant challenge in formulating strategic agendas to reflect the scope of knowledge and its increasing sophistication.

The two volumes *Violence Against Women and Children, Volume 1: Mapping the Terrain* and *Violence Against Women and Children, Volume 2: Navigating Solutions* are part of an ambitious initiative by the American Psychological Association (APA) begun under the leadership of then–APA President Alan E. Kazdin in 2008. Additional activities, described below, helped shape the development of these volumes, and they will in turn serve as a valuable resource as the initiative grows. To begin, the Presidential Summit on Violence and Abuse in Relationships: Connecting Agendas and Forging New Directions was convened. The meeting demonstrated clearly that advocacy groups, nongovernmental organizations, and governmental agencies both nationally and globally have prioritized changing violence-supportive genderized norms and reducing violence, among other goals. As laudatory as these efforts are, however, they are occurring piecemeal. Splintered and self-contained groups have formed within research, practice, and policy communities. And even within these fenced yards, still smaller play areas are delineated where those trained in a single discipline gather together. Although it is true that many do similar work that only superficially appears different due to definitional and methodological preferences, it is not well shared in print because of narrow publication indexing systems. It is also true that disciplines perform services, such as medical or justice, that must remain separate systems but could improve their response through coordination.

To counteract nonproductive duplication of effort, reduced voice, lost potential for innovations stemming from cross-fertilization, and inadequate dissemination of current scholarship in accessible formats, the field is challenged to develop a multifaceted and coordinated set of activities that would at once bring together individuals working on critical issues of interpersonal violence and identify advances, commonalities, and opportunities for synergies. Essential to this work is the recognition of the interconnectedness of various types of interpersonal violence (e.g., child maltreatment, elder abuse, intimate partner violence, sexual assault), disciplines (e.g., criminal justice, public health, medicine, psychology, social work, sociology), and areas of focus (e.g., research, practice, policy, advocacy, services, survivor voices). The presidential summit stimulated a series of meetings that revealed the hunger in the field for a forum to meet, share perspectives and knowledge, forge alliances, build workforce capacity, and plan advocacy and policy initiatives to realize a national, multidisciplinary commitment to end interpersonal violence across the life span. Hence, the National Partnership to End Interpersonal Violence Across the Lifespan was born.

To foster information exchange, APA launched a new journal, *Psychology of Violence*. This journal was conceived to reflect the goals of the initiative that led to its creation by, for example, having research, practice, and policy sections rather than focusing exclusively on knowledge as it is defined within academic, research-oriented disciplines. The present volumes were also commissioned under the presidential initiative with the goal of providing an updated and sound scientific foundation communicated in an accessible format that would interest a broad group of readers. We envisioned the potential readership to include advocates, practitioners, funders, policymakers, and academics trained in a variety of disciplines, such as anthropology, criminology, cultural studies, economics, family studies, gender studies, law, media studies, medicine, nursing, policy, psychology, public health, sociology, theology, and victimology.

The editors' intent with these volumes was to depart from the traditional review format and avoid as much jargon as possible within the overarching goal of communicating usable scientific knowledge. The study of violence against women and children has evolved as independent specialties that focus on one point in the life span, an organizational evolution that fails to capture the reality that multiple forms of violence happen to the same people. Our admittedly imperfect solution to avoid recreating the same problems we have critiqued was to invite diverse contributors who represent the fields of epidemiology; maternal and child health; clinical, social, and community psychology; sociology; social work; and law. These eminent scholars provide a statement of what is known about prevalence, impact, sector response, and prevention of child abuse, domestic violence, and sexual violence. The authors took on the challenge to condense into short formats topics that have been the subject of encyclopedic edited volumes and to nevertheless acknowledge nuances and alternative viewpoints. They direct a spotlight on the lack of clarity regarding definitions, theories, and appropriate methodologies that characterizes work on violence aimed at women and children (Jordan, 2009). The contributors were asked to answer three seemingly simple questions:

- What do we know?
- How do we know it?
- What are the next steps?

Each chapter follows that organization. The editors' intent was to capture the careful study and accumulated knowledge of the recent past and to prod our experts to acknowledge the distance already covered before charting future directions. Because these volumes are focused on communicating science, we recognize that there are other important perspectives that are not represented, most particularly those of the women and children who live surrounded by violence. It is from them that workers across all the fields of violence draw their inspiration and perseverance.

The present volumes serve as a significant feature of the initiative because they archive expertise from many different areas. The volumes convey what has been learned, what the gaps are, and priority areas of work. As a first, the integration of multiple disciplines and the culling of commonalities represent an important step for moving forward. We are grateful to the many who contributed to the volumes as well as the thinking behind them. The contributors, all eminent in their areas, agreed to come together to bring diverse subjects into a common format. The volume editors also appreciate the collaborative and collegial working relationships that we developed with each other and with all the contributors. As we mulled over difficult issues and came to consensus, we are all the more committed to the collaborative process, and we believe that it is the best approach for addressing the complex and important issue of interpersonal violence. Finally, we acknowledge the support of our home institutions, the University of Arizona, the University of North Carolina at Greensboro, and Yale University, for giving us the opportunity to collaborate on this project.

REFERENCES

Burchart, A., Phinney, A., Check, P., & Villavecces, A. (2004). *Preventing violence: A guide to implementing the recommendations of the world report on violence and health*. Geneva, Switzerland: World Health Organization.

Crowell, N. A., & Burgess, A. W. (Eds.). (1996). *Understanding violence against women*. Washington, DC: National Academy Press. doi:10.1037/10204-000

Henson, C. B., & Wilson, S. M. (2008). *Families in a global context*. New York, NY: Routledge.

Jordan, C. E. (2009). Advancing the study of violence against women: Evolving research agendas into science. *Violence Against Women, 15,* 393–419. doi:10.1177/1077801208330692

Koss, M. P., Goodman, L. A., Browne, A., Fitzgerald, L. F., Keita, G. P., & Russo, N. F. (1994). *No safe haven: Male violence against women at home, at work, and in the community.* Washington, DC: American Psychological Association.

Koss, M. P., & White, J. W. (2008). National and global agendas on violence against women: Historical perspective and consensus. *American Journal of Orthopsychiatry, 78,* 386–393. doi:10.1037/a0014347

Krug, E. G., Dahlberg, L. L., Mercy, J. A., Zwi, A. B., & Lozano, R. (Eds.). (2002). *The world report on violence and health.* Geneva, Switzerland: World Health Organization.

National Center for Injury Prevention and Control. (2009). *CDC injury research agenda, 2009–2018.* Atlanta, GA: U.S. Department of Health and Human Services, Centers for Disease Control and Prevention.

National Scientific Council on the Developing Child. (2007). *The science of early childhood development: Closing the gap between what we know and what we do.* Cambridge, MA: Harvard University, Center on the Developing Child. Retrieved from http://www.developingchild.net

Whitaker, D. J., Lutzker, J. R., & Shelley, G. A. (2005). Child maltreatment prevention priorities at the Centers for Disease Control and Prevention. *Child Maltreatment, 10,* 245–259. doi:10.1177/1077559505274674

World Health Organization. (2009). *Violence prevention: The evidence.* Geneva, Switzerland: Author.

Violence
Against Women and Children

INTRODUCTION

MARY P. KOSS, JACQUELYN W. WHITE,
AND ALAN E. KAZDIN

The magnitude of violence against women and children is alarming, and awareness of the problem is the first step toward prevention. People cannot stop something they cannot see or name. Once named, violence against women and children, in its various forms, is no longer socially and culturally invisible. Furthermore, identification of key modifiable risk and protective factors builds the foundation of scientifically sound primary prevention. Simultaneously, description and quantification of psychological, health, behavioral, and economic consequences contribute to design and implementation of best practices in secondary and tertiary prevention. Therefore, *Violence Against Women and Children, Volume 2: Navigating Solutions* focuses on direct services to victims and offenders, justice system responses, and prevention. Eminent scholars representing several disciplines summarize what is currently known about child abuse, sexual violence, and domestic violence, broadly conceptualized. They identify consensus in findings, and, where it does not exist, they delineate competing positions. They also address the importance of understanding methods used in research, gaps in knowledge, and the priorities that emerge from their analyses. The identification of current methods and their strengths and weaknesses provides insight into how to improve definitions, assessment methods, theoretical models, and research methods.

The chapters are selective, not comprehensive, reviews. Furthermore, certain forms of violence against women and children, such as teen dating violence and elder abuse, are only touched on in the context of broader analyses.

TERMINOLOGY

We as editors chose the terms *child abuse and maltreatment*, *sexual violence*, and *domestic violence* to title each section, with some reluctance. Some contributors preferred to use different terms, such as *child victimization*, *child violence*, *sexual assault*, or *intimate partner violence*, each of which represents a slight shift in focus that leads to organizational difficulties. For example, sexual assault includes a spectrum of unwanted sex acts, beginning with those that may lack overt violence. Domestic violence covers a variety of behaviors, including physical, sexual, psychological, and economic abuse. Clearly, this broad definition necessitates some overlap in content with chapters on sexual violence. Nevertheless, omitting forced sex acts from our discussion of domestic violence would be at variance with reality. Subsuming all unwanted sex acts under the heading of domestic violence, on the other hand, would be just as problematic. A Google search reveals that the term *domestic violence* occurs far more frequently than *intimate partner violence*, *woman abuse*, or *partner abuse*. Similarly, *child maltreatment* is an extremely broad term, yet *child abuse* is the most frequently used term. The various terms capture different elements and nuances, but the lack of standard terminology is one of the most evident obstacles in the field of violence against women and children. Neither we as editors nor the individual contributors undertook to recommend the best terms to use.

ATTENTION TO DIVERSITY

Chapters vary in coverage of intersections of violence with ethnicity and with marginalized populations, including lesbian, gay, bisexual, and transgendered or sexual minority individuals and individuals with disabilities. This variability reflects in part the extent to which these interactions have been ignored in research studies, an oversight noted by several authors.

OVERVIEW OF *VIOLENCE AGAINST WOMEN AND CHILDREN, VOLUME 2: NAVIGATING SOLUTIONS*

The chapters in this volume make it abundantly clear that despite extensive localized efforts to better coordinate responses to victims and offenders, many strands are not well connected. For example, although most direct services are provided in the community, the scholarship on best practices is typically conducted in academic centers using highly selected groups of people, tightly controlled methods, and service provision by mental health professionals. This information is frequently not translatable to the community. Thus, many services actually provided are unevaluated, and few methods that have been rigorously tested are implemented in the field. The justice system is highly constrained by constitutional rights and statutes that by their very nature ensure more consideration for offenders than for victims. Although humane in intention, justice processes and outcomes typically are not perceived positively by victims and, moreover, fail to impose sanctions on a sufficient number of offenders to deter violence against women and children at either the individual or community level. Prevention efforts are numerous but may not be well designed for maximal impact; often the focus is disproportionately at the individual level as opposed to broader societal change. Throughout, the experts grapple with strategies to move ahead, noting that despite many areas of consensus on broad goals, much more active debate exists on the means to achieve them.

The book is organized into four sections: Child Abuse and Maltreatment, Sexual Violence, Domestic Violence, and a conclusion. Each section opens with a chapter examining social services and psychological interventions focused on victims, followed by a chapter focusing on responses to offenders. Although mentioned briefly in some chapters, treatment in medical settings and medicoforensic protocols are not systematically reviewed. The third chapter of each section focuses on justice system responses, and the fourth is devoted to prevention. (Although primary prevention might, at first glance, appear to belong as the first chapter in each section, primary prevention efforts are the most recent and most experimental responses to interpersonal violence, with relatively few empirical research studies in support.) To the maximum extent possible, the chapters are organized around three questions: What do we know? How do we know it? What are the next steps? The Conclusion identifies the areas of consensus that emerged from this volume and then charts a course forward based on the contributions of experts to both volumes in the series.

Those authors in each section who examined victim services raise several common themes, including inadequate availability of services, lack of coordination among and within systems that provide different types of services to the same victims, varying quality of available responses (due in part to variability across communities in approach, comprehensiveness, quantity, and quality of services), and the small extent to which services are evaluated and best practices disseminated throughout the United States. All of the authors observe that services are inequitable and that White, heterosexual, nondisabled women and their children are better served than other groups. In Chapter 1, Kathleen Coulborn Faller notes the tension in the field of child maltreatment between rescuing the child and rehabilitating the abuser. The former approach results in many investigations and few removals; the latter is characterized by an array of programs for family support that are only assumed to be helpful. In Chapter 5, Rebecca Campbell and Debra Patterson assess services for victims of sexual violence. The authors conclude, on considering the high rate of posttraumatic stress symptoms among rape survivors, that there is a need for widely available, demonstrably effective mental health services for them. However, most care is provided outside of the formal mental health system, and that system does not effectively collaborate to transfer knowledge to those who deliver the bulk of services. In Chapter 9, Cris M. Sullivan documents that the level of available shelter services and transitional housing is insufficient to accommodate the number of victims of domestic violence and their children. As a result, housing help more often than not comes from informal sources, and there is limited evidence of its effectiveness; the same is true of advocacy and counseling services.

The experts who discuss offender services focus on three very different delivery settings. Child maltreatment is typically addressed within social services; prison is the setting in which the review of services for rapists is based; and domestic violence offender treatment is viewed from the perspective of community-based, court-ordered batterers' treatment programs. Despite these dramatic differences in reference, all authors observe that existing responses have limited impacts and some may actually exacerbate problems. Likewise, they all bring to light disparities in how services are offered and to whom. In Chapter 2, Joan Pennell and David S. Crampton explain that although foster care is undertaken in the interests of the child, it has poor outcomes, including the child's failure to complete high school and subsequent elevated rates of unemployment, homelessness, and mental health problems. They observe a consensus for the need to shift emphasis from investigation and protection as a guiding philosophy to the potential of family-based and family-strengthening approaches to child maltreatment. In Chapter 6, Robert A. Prentky, Adeena M. Gabriel, and Anna I. Coward summarize the many studies that support the conclusion that sex offender therapy in prison reduces the rate of reoffense among those receiving treatment by approximately 6%. They conclude that making sex offender treatment more effective would require a sea change in the conditions under which it is offered. In Chapter 10, Tricia B. Bent-Goodley, Johnny Rice II, Oliver J. Williams, and Marcus Pope describe much that is lacking in current responses to those who commit domestic violence. Most treatment programs are court-ordered, but little is known about effective methods when therapy is coerced. Furthermore, current programs pay inadequate attention to serving men of color, exert little accountability on those who drop out, often after just a few sessions, and have no systematized method for addressing the safety of the battered partners and children of their clients.

Justice responses across forms of violence involve multiple arenas, including criminal and civil systems, juvenile justice, and, for some, mandatory reporting requirements that impact people working in criminal justice, social services, medicine, and education. Authors uniformly identify a very significant number of statutory law and policy changes that have been aimed at increasing offender accountability and victim safety and at decreasing the ways in which justice itself traumatizes people. Because law in each of the areas of violence against women and children is set state by state, there are not only wide variances in practices but also arduous barriers to effecting change. In Chapter 3, Roger J. R. Levesque discusses child maltreatment and lays out the many streams of justice that are charged with responding to it. In particular, he contrasts family courts, criminal justice, and juvenile justice in philosophy regarding and response to child maltreatment. In Chapter 7, Ilene Seidman and Jeffrey J. Pokorak review justice system responses to sexual violence. Their extensive review of statutory and procedural changes won by victim advocates over the past 30 years concludes that victims still have fewer rights than offenders and little chance of having their harm validated by the justice system. Prejudicial stereotypes persist against victims of sexual assault and hurt them at every level of the justice processes, both criminal and civil. In Chapter 11, Lisa A. Goodman and Deborah Epstein cover the same ground from the perspective of domestic violence. They observe the numerous policy victories intended to better protect victims and their children that have fallen short of expectations. For example, although arrest rates have risen, most perpetrators receive no or lenient sentences, despite the increase of domestic homicide that is associated with prosecution.

Among the chapters that focus on prevention, the reader may be struck with an apparent incongruity. In Chapter 4, John Eckenrode writes about prevention of child abuse and focuses on programs directed at adults (parents). In Chapter 12, Susan L. Staggs and Paul A. Schewe address prevention of domestic violence by dismissing programs aimed at adults as ineffective and too late. They emphasize the importance of work with children, consistently and across their educational experience, in age-appropriate coaching for healthy relationships. In Chapter 8, Christine A. Gidycz, Lindsay M. Orchowski, and Katie M. Edwards, in their discussion of sexual assault, illuminate constraints that have to date limited prevention programming to formal schooling, whether primary, middle school, high school, or higher education. Most efforts have been psychoeducational, aimed at changing attitudes and increasing knowledge, and most have demonstrated little or no effect. The authors highlight several promising newer avenues for sexual assault prevention that focus on teaching skills to those not directly involved in responding and preventing.

In sum, the contents of this volume, especially taken in the context of the documented scope and costs of violence against women and children that appear in *Violence Against Women and Children, Volume 1: Mapping the Terrain*, suggest heroic efforts of responders in the face of a maze of systems, barriers to change, and inadequate resources. Volume 2 concludes with a final chapter that charts the next steps to enhance response to violence and to reduce it. Lest readers be left with a sense of hopelessness from the brief overview of this volume, they may rest assured that each expert has offered carefully thought-out plans and concrete steps to move ahead. All of them, like the readers of this volume, take their inspiration from the fact that our work is not abstract. When violence directly affects women and children, we sit with them and are both saddened and inspired. We move forward knowing that this topic is of utmost relevance to building a stronger, safer, and more sustainable human civilization.

I

CHILD ABUSE
AND MALTREATMENT

1

VICTIM SERVICES FOR CHILD ABUSE

KATHLEEN COULBORN FALLER

Child abuse is a social problem addressed within various fields, each with its own definitions as the foundation for the interventions. The medical field took the lead in defining child abuse in the 1960s, when Henry Kempe and colleagues described and coined the term *battered child syndrome* to refer to young children with multiple, nonaccidental injuries at various stages of healing (Kempe, Silverman, Steele, Droegemueller, & Silver, 1962). Medical definitions focus on the type of injury the child sustains and documentation that it is an inflicted, as opposed to an accidental, injury. Injuries may be bruises, cuts, scrapes, burns, fractures, internal organ injuries, or brain injuries. Medical professionals focus on child safety. Medical personnel typically form their opinion about whether an injury is consistent with accidental or non-accidental origin by noting the site of the injury (buttocks, back, back of legs, and face are nonaccidental injury sites), any peculiarities about the injury that indicate how it was caused (e.g., an injury that appears to have been inflicted by a belt, a burn that appears to have been caused by a cigarette or a hot iron, or a brain injury that appears to have been caused by shaking), or whether there are multiple injuries, particularly if they appear to be at differ-ent stages of healing, when the caretaker's explanation does not fit the injury, and/or when there is a delay seeking medical treatment (e.g., Giardino & Alexander, 2005; Reece & Ludwig, 2001).

Like medical professionals, mental health professionals are concerned about injuries resulting from child abuse and long-term physical impairment but also focus on the psychological trauma that children sustain when abused by someone who should be taking good care of them. Psychological harm is manifested in behaviors (e.g., aggression) and emotions (e.g., posttraumatic stress disorder; e.g., Briere, 2004; Cicchetti, Toth, & Maughan, 2000; Crittenden, 1998; Mersky & Reynolds, 2007; Widom, 1997; Willis, 1995). Mental health professionals direct their expertise to ameliorating the impact of child maltreatment.

Professionals in the legal field are concerned with whether a case satisfies the legal definition of maltreatment and therefore warrants state intervention. Legal definitions of child maltreatment can be found in federal legislation, for example, in the Child Abuse Prevention and Treatment Act (CAPTA; 1974), and in state statutes (discussed in Chapter 3, this volume). Briefly, in CAPTA, child abuse and neglect are defined as involving physical or mental injury, sexual abuse, or neglect or mistreatment of a child under age 18 that threatens or harms the child's welfare and is perpetrated by the legally responsible caretaker.

Interventions with victims of child abuse can include physical removal of the child from the abusive environment and delivery of services to the child and family that decrease the risk to the child of reabuse, as well as treatment of the child and caretakers to address the physical and psychological harm caused by the abuse. This treatment may be delivered to children after they are removed from the abusive environment, but current, evidence-based treatments usually involve both children and their caretakers (e.g., National Child Traumatic Stress Network [NCTSN], 2008a, 2008b, 2008c).

WHAT DO WE KNOW?

Historically, there have been two general approaches to child abuse: rescue and rehabilitation. Although rescue remains an important approach, in recent history, rehabilitation, especially evidence-based intervention, has increasingly become a priority.

Rescue

Rescue currently is undertaken by public child welfare workers, although in the past voluntary agencies and associations played a major role in rescue (Myers, 2006). Each state has its own child protection legislation, but such statutes are fairly uniform from state to state because federal legislation requires certain provisions in state child protection laws for states to qualify for federal discretionary funds (CAPTA, 1974). In most states, health care professionals, mental health professionals, and educational professionals are mandated reporters, that is, they are required by law to report cases of suspected child abuse (and neglect, sexual abuse, and emotional abuse) to the public child welfare agency (child protective services; Child Welfare Information Gateway, 2008). Reports were made on over 6 million children in 2006 (U.S. Department of Health and Human Services [DHHS], 2008a). About 40% of these reports are screened out by child protection staff without, and the remaining reports were then investigated by child protective services caseworkers (DHHS, 2008a). Of the cases investigated, about 30% were substantiated by child protection workers in 2006. Physical abuse cases represented 16% of all of the substantiated cases (neglect being the most common type of maltreatment, 64.1%); the most common type of physical abuse that was reported is minor physical injury (DHHS, 2008a).

Currently, only about one fifth of children in substantiated child maltreatment cases are removed from their homes; approximately two thirds of these children were neglected rather than abused. Physically abused children were only 9% of those removed from maltreating households in 2006 (DHHS, 2008a).

Once rescued from the abusive environment, children are placed in a home considered to be safe, usually a foster care placement (about two thirds of the time), or a relative placement (about one third of the time; DHHS, 2008b). A small percentage of children are initially placed in group care facilities, such as shelters and group homes. Although child placement is usually intended to be short-term, while the family is rehabilitated, in reality placement may be long-term and involve multiple moves from one foster home to the next, sometimes into increasingly restrictive placements (Children's Rights, 2006). Children of color are overrepresented in foster care (58%; Children's Rights, 2006; DHHS, 2008b). Children of color remain in out-of-home care longer and are less likely to be adopted, should parental rights be terminated (DHHS, 2008b). Thus, although rescue from an abusive environment usually provides initial safety, it may result in long-term detrimental consequences to children, especially for children of color. Attempts to provide services to children in their own homes, therefore, are preferred when it is safe to do so.

An integral component of service delivery in cases of child abuse is casework. A caseworker may be a case manager, whose primary role is mobilizing services on behalf of the child and the child's caretakers/family. Or the caseworker may be more skilled and both directly address the problems that led to the child abuse and its sequelae, relying on other services for specific needs, for example, substance abuse treatment for the parent and medical treatment for the child. Casework service may be delivered by public sector child welfare workers or voluntary agency caseworkers. A major task of the caseworker is motivating the caretaker or family to address the problems that resulted in the child abuse. However, casework services are also provided to children after they have been removed from the home. The caseworker assists the child in transitions, such as removal from parental care, change in placement, and return home. The caseworker also addresses any behavior problems the child may manifest in placement, adjustment to a new school, and maintaining contact with parents and siblings while in care. In contrast, when child abuse is being addressed while the child remains at home, casework services that focus specifically on the child are not common.

Rehabilitation

Rehabilitation is attempted by providing families and children with services and treatment. These interventions may be delivered while children remain in the home or after they are removed to a safe environment. The services may be concrete, such as emergency funds; supportive—for example, by Parent Aides (i.e., volunteers or paraprofessionals who develop a relationship with and provide support to maltreating parents; Faller, 1981; Kadushin & Martin, 1988); or therapeutic.

Victims of physical abuse are much less likely to receive treatment than victims of sexual abuse because, even today, removal of the child from the unsafe environment and placing the child in a safe one is assumed to be therapeutic in itself (Chaffin & Friedrich, 2004). Furthermore, very few interventions with physically abused children focus primarily on the child. Interventions focus on either the parent, the parent and child as a unit, or the family. Interventions that focus on the parent have been called "trickle down treatment." The theory that undergirds these approaches is that, as the parent improves, he or she will treat the child more appropriately and the child will improve. Programs such as Parent Aides and Parents Anonymous are built on this theory. Interventions that include parent and child may focus on the interaction between parent and child and, in most instances, the parent and child as individuals as well. Family-focused interventions take into account that acts of abuse occur within a family context, may involve more than one child, and do harm to other children present as well as the direct victims.

Until relatively recently, interventions in cases of child abuse were derived from "practice wisdom" and, some would argue, from the child abuse ideology of the moment (Chaffin & Friedrich, 2004). The array of trendy interventions has included both programs and therapies for children or their parents. Illustrative of popular programs are Intensive Family Preservation, including Homebuilders (Family Resource Center, n.d.; Littell, 2001; Schuerman, Rzepnicki, & Littell, 1994) and Healthy Start. Homebuilders involves intensive, short-term (4–6 weeks), in-home services to parents and children. The Homebuilder may meet with the family on a daily basis and be available 24 hr a day, 7 days a week, mobilizing the family to function better, employing a variety of techniques. Healthy Start is a home-visitor program for new parents at risk of abusing their children (and in some communities, known abusive parents). Home visitors may be nurses or paraprofessionals and teach parents skills for addressing the needs of their infants.

Another example of a program that historically has been assumed to be helpful for abusive parents is Parents Anonymous, a support group for abusive and potentially abusive parents (Faller, 1981; Parents Anonymous, Inc., 2008; National Center on Crime and Delinquency, 2008). The initiative dates back to the 1960s and is now worldwide. Its principles include (a) mutual support, (b) parent leadership, (c) shared leadership with sponsoring professionals, and (d) anonymity and confidentiality (Parents Anonymous, Inc., 2008). Historically, the majority of members are voluntary and not required to attend by child protective services or courts (Faller, 1981; National Center on Crime and Delinquency, 2008).

An example of a trendy treatment is rebirthing therapy for reactive attachment disorder (RAD; American Academy of Child and Adolescent Psychiatry, 2008; Mayo Clinic, 2010). Rebirthing therapy is one of a number of treatments developed to address attachment disorders assumed to be consequent of child abuse and associated early deprivation. Rebirthing therapy involves putting the abused child through a simulation of the birthing process. In one case, in 2000, rebirthing therapy led to the death of 10-year-old Candace Newmaker, who was believed by her adoptive mother to have RAD. The incident resulted in the criminal conviction of her two rebirthing therapists (Caldwell, 2001). This tragedy accounts in part for the recent move toward evidence-based practice for child maltreatment (Saunders, Berliner, & Hanson, 2004).

In the past 10 years, there have been a number of initiatives to implement evidence-based treatments with children who have been abused and their caretakers (Hensler, Wilson, & Sadler, 2004). The development of evidence-based practices with victims of abuse is emerging and dynamic. The treatments described in this next section are those with the most clinical acceptance and research evidence. The interventions include play therapy with traumatized children (e.g., Gil, 1991, 1996a, 1998), parent–child interaction therapy (e.g., Chaffin, Silovsky, et al., 2004), multisystemic therapy (MST; Swenson, Henggeler, Taylor, & Addison, 2005), abuse-focused cognitive behavioral therapy (Kolko, 2002), and trauma-focused cognitive behavioral therapy for child traumatic grief (Cohen, Mannarino, & Deblinger, 2006).

These treatments all have theoretical bases related to both the causes and effects of child abuse, have addressed cultural difference in client populations, and include at least some components that are based upon social learning theory. Each of these treatments is briefly described. Evaluation findings are described in the next section.

Trauma-focused play therapy (Gil, 1991, 1996b, 1998) builds on a substantial history of the use of therapeutic play to assist children in distress (e.g., Axline, 1989; Jernberg, 1979). Play therapy assumes that children are more accomplished in play than in verbal communication and more likely to communicate their trauma indirectly, through play. The therapist structures the play so that it will be therapeutic through the careful choice of toys and other media to be used in the play therapy session. As Gil stated, play becomes "a mechanism for allowing abused children to use symbols (toys) to externalize their internal world, project their thoughts and feelings, and process potentially overwhelming emotional and cognitive material from a safe distance" (Saunders, Berliner, & Hanson, 2004, p. 54). The therapist, through observations, interpretations, and cognitive restructuring, assists the child in resolving his or her trauma. This treatment is open-ended; the therapist terminates treatment when the child's functioning improves. Trauma-focused play therapy is unique among the treatments described in this chapter in that it focuses principally on the abused child and its base is the therapist–child interaction. Nevertheless, Gil, who has written the most extensively about play therapy with abused children, also advises parallel work with caretakers and systemic work with children's families (Gil, 1996a; Saunders et al., 2004).

Parent–child interaction therapy (PCIT), as its name suggests, aims at changing negative caretaker–child interactions to positive ones. It is relatively short term (12–20 sessions) and facilitates change through didactic input and coaching the caretaker as he or she interacts with the child. PCIT may be delivered in the home and has been adapted to be culturally sensitive (NCTSN, 2008c). PCIT has two core components. First the caretaker is helped to build better relationship skills by receiving feedback from the therapist through a small ear microphone or some other means while actually interacting with the abused child. Relationship skills include Praise, Reflection, Imitation, Description, and Enthusiasm, or PRIDE. The caretaker who has mastered these skills has acquired positive discipline strategies, which involve clear commands about appropriate behavior, praise or rewards for appropriate behavior, and consistent delivery of acceptable consequences (e.g., time-out, withdrawal of privileges) for inappropriate behavior. An important component of treatment is session-by-session feedback to the parent about performance. This usually involves counting and charting parental behaviors and child responses. As caretakers master the PCIT skills, a program for transfer of these changes from treatment sessions into the child's home environment is implemented (Hembree-Kigin & McNeil, 1995; Hood & Eyberg, 2003; NCTSN, 2008c).

MST is a promising practice. Although it has been used primarily as a treatment alternative to confinement for delinquents with substance abuse and violence problems (U.S. Office of Justice Programs, 2007), a randomized clinical trial of MST is under way for cases of child abuse (Chaffin & Friedrich, 2004). MST has the considerable advantage of taking into account the larger social context in which the abuse occurred, not just the parent–child or family dynamics. MST is delivered in families' homes as a strategy to over-come barriers to service delivery and focuses on empowering caretakers to develop informal helping systems using their social networks (e.g., friends, neighbors, extended family) and assisting caretakers in accessing services in various delivery systems to address child behavior problems. It is a short-term intervention (about 4 months) that employs a team model with 24/7 avail-ability (Swenson, Henggeler, Taylor, & Addison, 2005).

Abuse-focused cognitive behavioral therapy (AF-CBT; Kolko, 2002; Kolko & Swenson, 2002) involves parallel and conjoint cognitive behavioral/family-systems treatment of the physically abusive parent and the child; it has also been delivered in a group context. One of its strengths is that it was developed and has been implemented in a low-income, urban environ-ment and has incorporated input from African American child welfare professionals and community partners (NCTSN, 2008b). The interven-tion is short-term, for 12 to 24 weekly sessions, and divided into three phases: Phase 1—psycho-education and engagement, Phase 2—individual and fam-ily skills training, and Phase 3—family applications. The treatment provides intrapersonal training of cognitive and affective techniques, coping tech-niques, and interpersonal behavioral skills designed to promote the expres-sion of prosocial behavior and discourage the use of coercive/abusive tactics at both the individual and family levels (Kolko & Swenson, 2002).

Finally, trauma-focused cognitive behavioral therapy for child traumatic grief (TG-CBT; Cohen, Mannarino, & Deblinger, 2006) is an adaptation of trauma-focused cognitive behavioral therapy, which has been field tested with sexually abused children and their caretakers at two sites and subjected to a follow-up study (Deblinger, Mannarino, Cohen, & Steer, 2006; Deblinger, Steer, & Lippman, 1999). Cohen and colleagues (2006) described it as a highly relevant treatment for children who have experienced the trauma of child physical abuse. It has particular applicability to physically abused children and their nonabusive caretakers. To date, research on TG-CBT has been con-ducted with children who lost a family member in the September 11, 2001, terrorist attack and their caretakers. Its theoretical underpinnings involve cognitive behavioral, family, and empowerment bases, integrated with grief-focused interventions. Core components are parallel child and caretaker trauma- and grief-focused sessions and conjoint parent-child sessions. TG-CBT is short-term, provided over 12 to 16 sessions; the first eight are typically trauma focused, and subsequent sessions are typically grief focused.

HOW DO WE KNOW IT?

A modest number of studies have evaluated intervention programs and treatment of physically abused children. This discussion is limited to promising practices. Some intervention programs have been the subject of evaluations, for example, intensive in-home interventions, such as Homebuilders (e.g., Schuerman, Rzepnicki, & Littell, 1994) and home visiting programs, such as Healthy Start (Daro & Donnelly, 2002). Although, intuitively, both Homebuilders and Healthy Start make sense and both showed initial promise, more rigorous, controlled studies have not borne out the early positive findings (Daro & Donnelly, 2002; Littell, 2001; Schuerman, Rzepnicki, & Littell, 1994). In Schuerman and colleagues' (1994) critical review of the research on intensive in-home interventions, they determined this approach was not superior to traditional child welfare services in reducing the recurrence of child maltreatment. Similarly, Daro and Donnelly (2002) documented the mixed results of home visiting programs. They pointed out that such mixed results relate somewhat to the variable expertise of the home visitors, but they also reported that such programs do not address underlying problems that play an important role in child maltreatment, parental substance abuse, domestic violence, and mental health problems.

In addition, research has explored the efficacy of and, in some cases, the effectiveness of treatments of abused children and their caretakers. *Efficacy* refers to testing an intervention in an optimal environment, such as in a university-based clinic, where researchers can control extraneous factors and variables. In contrast, *effectiveness* refers to testing whether the intervention works in the real world of practice, where some extraneous factors and variables are not in the control of researchers. Efficacy trials can be thought of as pilot studies; effectiveness trials usually involve multiple sites. Although effectiveness trials should be required for interventions and treatments with most populations, they are especially crucial in situations of child abuse because intervention and treatment typically occur in less than optimal service delivery contexts. There have been three important initiatives to evaluate the accumulated evidence to support treatments (and some intervention programs) for child abuse. Each of these undertakings articulated relevant evidence and used a metric (a scale with ratings from *good* to *bad*) to rate the evidence.

The first initiative was the Office for Victims of Crime (OVC) rating of treatments for physical and sexual abuse (Saunders, Berliner, & Hanson, 2004).

The OVC guidelines evaluated 24 treatments and programs for physically and sexually abused children, their caretakers, and child maltreatment offenders. These interventions were rated on their theoretical underpinnings, clinical literature about their utility, clinical acceptance, potential harm, and empirical support, using a 6-point scale (1 = *well-supported, efficacious treatment;* 2 = *supported and probably efficacious treatment,* 3 = *supported and acceptable treatment,* 4 = *promising and acceptable treatment;* 5 = *innovative or novel treatment;* 6 = *concerning treatment*). Only TF-CBT that had been employed and studied in cases of sexual abuse received the top rating (e.g., Deblinger, Mannarino, Cohen, & Steer, 2006). This model was the foundation from which TG-CBT was developed for traumatized children (Cohen, Mannarino, & Deblinger, 2006). Most of the treatments described and rated in this chapter (PCIT, MST, AF-CBT) received a ranking of 3 (supported and acceptable treatment). Although play therapy is probably the most widely employed treatment with abused children, there were no clinical evaluations extant in 2004 of its efficacy or effectiveness, and it was rated 4 (promising and acceptable treatment), which is less of an endorsement than three other ratings described. Two programs used in cases of physical abuse, Intensive Family Preservation and Parents Anonymous, were also rated 4, and rebirthing therapy was rated as 6, as a treatment raising concerns about its suitability.

Building on this important OVC initiative to inform the professional community about the evidence to support interventions in child abuse and working with member organizations of the NCTSN, the Kauffman Foundation funded and supported further study of evidence-based intervention in child maltreatment (Hensler, Wilson, & Sadler, 2004; Kauffman Best Practices Project, 2004). These professionals identified three cognitive behavioral interventions as meeting their criteria for best practices: TF-CBT, AF-CBT, and PCIT. They noted that these interventions possess the highest level of theoretical, clinical, and empirical support (Hensler, Wilson, & Sadler, 2004, p. 8).

The Kauffman Foundation report (2004) cautions that although three treatments were identified as best practices, the field is dynamic; new interventions are continually being developed and refined. In recognition of the vitality of the child abuse and child trauma intervention field, the National Child Traumatic Network website, at Empirically Supported Practices (NCTSN, 2008a), provides extensive documentation on best practices, and the site is updated on a regular basis. Currently, 32 trauma-focused interventions are listed on the website, a dozen of which are relevant to the treatment of physical abuse. For each intervention, there is a fact sheet that includes (a) treatment description, (b) target population, (c) essential components, (d) clinical and anecdotal evidence, (e) research evidence, (f) pilot and feasibility trials, (g) randomized control trials, (h) outcomes, (i) implementation requirements and readiness, (j) training materials required, (k) pros and cons (qualitative impressions), (l) contact information, and (m) references. All interventions use some standardized measure to assess outcomes. Although play therapy appears to be widely practiced, it is not rated as an empirically supported or promising practice on the NCTSN website.

On the NCTSN website, PCIT has cited six published case studies (Bagner, Fernandez, & Eyberg, 2004; Borrego, Anhalt, Terao, Vargas, & Urquiza, 2006; Borrego, Urquiza, & Rasmussen, 1999; Dombrowski, Timmer & Blacker, 2005; Fricker-Elhai, Ruggiero, & Smith, 2005; Timmer et al., 2006), and one randomized controlled trial ($N = 110$; Chaffin, Silovsky, et al., 2004). The last is the only one of the treatment studies that reported recidivism rates. Of PCIT recipients, 19% were rereported for child maltreatment within a median of 850 days, compared with 49% receiving the customary intervention (Chaffin, Silovsky, et al., 2004). Although this is a comparatively positive outcome, one fifth of families were rereported in a little more than 2 years. TG-CBT offers a book describing its clinical application (Cohen, Mannarino, & Deblinger, 2006), one pilot study ($N = 61$; Cohen, Mannarino, & Knudsen, 2004; Cohen, Mannarino, & Staron, 2006), and one randomized controlled trial ($N = 40$; Brown, Goodman, Cohen, & Mannarino, 2004).

AF-CBT has the most evidence to support it, according the NCTSN website. There was a pilot study conducted in Salt Lake City involving 150 cases and a randomized controlled trial involving 55 cases in Pittsburgh. An ongoing study funded by the National Institute of Mental Health is currently training practitioners as well as implementing the intervention (NCTSN, 2008b).

GAPS IN THE KNOWLEDGE BASE AND SERVICE DELIVERY

There are four major gaps in services for victims of child abuse. The first gap is in knowing what programs help abused children and their families. Most of the evaluation efforts have been of therapy rather than of programs. Violence in abusive families often occurs in a context of community violence, poverty, and intractable parental problems, such as substance abuse and mental health problems. That the programs that have been studied, such as Intensive Family Preservation and Healthy Start, have mixed outcomes probably relates to the lack of a "quick fix" for the larger context that results in child maltreatment. Having supportive services on a short-term basis does not ultimately alleviate chronic problems. Evaluation of interventions that address the multiplicity and complexity of challenges that result in child abuse is costly and requires painstaking work. It is far more feasible to evaluate a treatment program that focuses on discrete behaviors and short-term outcomes.

The second gap is in knowledge about treatment outcomes. Although there are promising beginnings in the development of evidence-based treatment, knowledge about effective therapy remains limited. This is demonstrated by the small number of randomized clinical trials and small numbers of clients in these studies. In addition, to date, follow-up has been short-term, and only one study includes rereports for child maltreatment. A real challenge is whether the positive changes observed in the short term will be sustained over time and what the impact of treatment is on the likelihood of rereports for child maltreatment. For the most part, problems that lead to the abusive caretaker behavior are not addressed, making recidivism over time an important risk.

The third gap is that treatment evaluations to date have primarily involved efficacy trials. Effectiveness trials are still to come, and implementing evidence-based interventions on a widespread basis will be a real challenge. Both the circumstances and the service delivery personnel present potential obstacles. Caseloads may be high and families resistant. The practitioners who deliver services to abused children and their families usually have bachelor's or master's level degrees in human services. They are accustomed to doing treatment intuitively and not according to a manual or fixed sequence of steps. Often they are unaware of evidence-based practices and are resistant to reading and relying on research in their work (Hensler, Wilson, & Sadler, 2004).

The fourth gap is the paucity of resources to implement evidence-based interventions and indeed to provide any treatment whatsoever to physically abused children. While reports have increased exponentially since the passage of CAPTA (1974), intervention resources have grown by a mere fraction (Miller, Cohen, & Wiersema, 1996). Without a change in the will and mandate of the American people, abused children and their families will continue to go without appropriate intervention and treatment.

WHAT ARE THE NEXT STEPS?

Without greater societal recognition, support for parenthood and childhood, and a better safety net, children will continue to be abused and neglected. This chapter has attempted to document the levels of efficacy and effectiveness that have been established for promising practices in the field of child maltreatment. Many limitations of existing knowledge were identified and the gaps described. It should be evident that there is consensus about how to evaluate clinical practices. What is lacking is the substantial resource investment to fill in the gaps by creating materials to train providers in standard methods, conduct efficacy and effectiveness studies, and build a trained workforce able and willing to use proven effective techniques to address the treatment of abused children and their families.

REFERENCES

American Academy of Child and Adolescent Psychiatry. (2008). Reactive attachment disorder. *Facts for Families, 85.* Retrieved from http://www.aacap.org/cs/root/facts_for_families/reactive_attachment_disorder

Axline, V. (1989). *Play therapy.* London, England: Ballantine. (Original work published 1947)

Bagner, D. M., Fernandez, M. A., & Eyberg, S. M. (2004). Parent-child interaction therapy and chronic illness: A case study. *Journal of Clinical Psychology in Medical Settings, 11*(1), 1–6. doi:10.1023/B:JOCS.0000016264.02407.fd

Borrego, J., Anhalt, K., Terao, S. Y., Vargas, E. C., & Urquiza, A. J. (2006). Parent-child interaction therapy with a Spanish-speaking family. *Cognitive and Behavioral Practice, 13,* 121–133. doi:10.1016/j.cbpra.2005.09.001

Borrego, J., Urquiza, A. J., & Rasmussen, R. A. (1999). Parent-child interaction therapy with a family at high risk for physical abuse. *Child Maltreatment, 4,* 331–342. doi:10.1177/1077559599004004006

Briere, J. (2004). Psychological assessment of child abuse effects in adults. In J. Wilson & T. Keane (Eds.), *Assessing psychological trauma and PTSD* (2nd ed., pp. 538–564). New York, NY: Guilford Press.

Brown, E. J., Goodman, R. F., Cohen, J. A., & Mannarino, A. P. (2004, November). *Randomized controlled treatment outcome study for childhood traumatic grief.* Paper presented at Conceptualization, Measurement and Treatment of Childhood Traumatic Grief Symposium, 20th Annual Meeting of the International Society for Traumatic Stress Studies, New Orleans, LA.

Caldwell, C. (2001). *Death by therapy.* Retrieved from http://www.papillonsartpalace.com/deathby.htm

Chaffin, M., & Friedrich, W. N. (2004). Evidence-based treatments in child abuse and neglect. *Children and Youth Services Review, 26,* 1097–1113. doi:10.1016/j.childyouth.2004.08.008

Chaffin, M., Silovsky, J. F., Funderburk, B., Valle, L. A., Brestan, E. V., Balachova, T., . . . Bonner, B. L. (2004). Parent-child interaction therapy with physically abusive parents: Efficacy for reducing future abuse reports. *Journal of Consulting and Clinical Psychology, 72,* 500–510. doi:10.1037/0022-006X.72.3.500

Child Abuse Prevention and Treatment Act (CAPTA; 1974). Pub. L. 93-247. Retrieved from http://www.childwelfare.gov/systemwide/laws%5Fpolicies/federal/index.cfm?event=federalLegislation.viewLegis&id=2

Child Welfare Information Gateway. (2008). *State statutes.* Retrieved from http://www.childwelfare.gov/systemwide/laws_policies/state/

Children's Rights. (2006). *Facts about foster care*. Retrieved from http://www. childrensrights.org/issues-resources/foster-care/facts-about-foster-care/

Cicchetti, D., Toth, S., & Maughan, A. (2000). An ecological-transactional model of child maltreatment. In A. J. Sameroff, M. Lewis, & S. Miller (Eds.), *Handbook of developmental psychopathology* (2nd ed., pp. 689–722). Dordrecht, the Netherlands: Kluwer Academic.

Cohen, J. Goodman, R. F., Mannarino, A. P., & Brown, E. J. (2004). Treatment of childhood traumatic grief: Contributing to a new emerging condition in the wake of community trauma. *Harvard Review of Psychiatry*, *12*, 213–216. doi:10.1080/ 10673220490509543

Cohen, J., Mannarino, A., & Deblinger, E. (2006). *Treating trauma and traumatic grief in children and adolescents*. New York, NY: Guilford Press.

Cohen, J. A., Mannarino, A. P., & Knudsen, K. (2004). Treating childhood traumatic grief: A pilot study. *Journal of the American Academy of Child and Adolescent Psychiatry*, *43*, 1225–1233. doi:10.1097/01.chi.0000135620.15522.38

Cohen, J. A., Mannarino, A. P., & Staron, V. (2006). A pilot study of modified cognitive behavioral therapy for childhood traumatic grief (CBT-CTG). *Journal of the American Academy of Child and Adolescent Psychiatry*, *45*, 1465–1473. doi:10.1097/01.chi.0000237705.43260.2c

Crittenden, P. (1998). Dangerous behavior and dangerous contexts: A 35-year perspective on research on the developmental effects of child physical abuse. In P. Trickett & C. Schellenbach, *Violence against children in the family and the community* (pp. 11–38). Washington, DC: American Psychological Association. doi:10.1037/10292-001

Daro, D., & Donnelly, A. C. (2002). Charting the waves of prevention: Two steps forward and one step back. *Child Abuse & Neglect*, *26*, 731–742. doi:10.1016/ S0145-2134(02)00344-7

Deblinger, E., Mannarino, A., Cohen, J., & Steer, R. (2006). A follow-up study of a multi-site, randomized, controlled trial for children with sexual abuse related PTSD symptoms. *Journal of the American Academy of Child and Adolescent Psychiatry*, *45*, 1474–1484. doi:10.1097/01.chi.0000240839.56114.bb

Deblinger, E., Steer, R., & Lippman, J. (1999). Two-year follow-up study of cognitive behavioral therapy for sexually abused children suffering post-traumatic stress symptoms. *Child Abuse & Neglect*, *23*, 1371–1378. doi:10.1016/S0145-2134(99) 00091-5

Dombrowski, S. C., Timmer, S. G., & Blacker, D. M. (2005). A positive behavioural intervention for toddlers: Parent-Child Attunement Therapy. *Child Abuse Review*, *14*, 132–151.

Faller, K. C. (Ed.). (1981). *Social work with abused and neglected children: A manual of interdisciplinary practice*. New York, NY: The Free Press.

Family Resource Center. (n.d.). *Intensive in-home services*. Retrieved from http:// frcmo.org/IIS.aspx

Fricker-Elhai, A. E., Ruggiero, K. J., & Smith, D. W. (2005). Parent-child interaction therapy with two maltreated siblings in foster care. *Clinical Case Studies*, *4*(1), 13–39. doi:10.1177/1534650103259671

Giardino, A., & Alexander, R. (2005). *Child maltreatment*. St. Louis, MO: G. W. Medical.

Gil, E. (1991). *The healing power of play*. New York, NY: Guilford Press.

Gil, E. (1996a). *Systemic treatment of families who abuse*. San Francisco, CA: Jossey-Bass.

Gil, E. (1996b). *Treating abused adolescents*. New York, NY: Guilford Press.

Gil, E. (1998). *Essentials of play therapy with abused children*. New York, NY: Guilford Press.

Hembree-Kigin, T., & McNeil, C. B. (1995). *Parent-child interaction therapy*. New York, NY: Plenum Press.

Hensler, D., Wilson, C., & Sadler, B. (2004). *Closing the quality chasm in child abuse treatment: Identifying and disseminating best practices. The findings of the Kauffman best practices project*. San Diego, CA: The Chadwick Center.

Hood, K. K., & Eyberg, S. M. (2003). Outcomes of parent-child interaction therapy: Mothers' reports of maintenance three to six years after treatment. *Journal of Clinical Child and Adolescent Psychology*, *32*, 419–429.

Jernberg, A. (1979). *Theraplay*. San Francisco, CA: Jossey-Bass.

Kadushin, A., & Martin, J. (1988) *Child welfare services* (6th ed.). New York, NY: Macmillan.

Kauffman Best Practices Project. (2004). *Closing the quality chasm in child abuse treatment: Identifying and disseminating best practices*. Charleston, SC: National Crime Victims Research and Treatment Center.

Kempe, C. H., Silverman, F., Steele, B., Droegemueller, W., & Silver, H. (1962). The battered-child syndrome. *JAMA*, *181*, 17–24.

Kolko, D. J. (2002). Child physical abuse. In J. E. B. Myers, L. Berliner, J. Briere, C. T. Hendrix, C. Jenny, & T. Reid (Eds.), *APSAC handbook of child maltreatment* (2nd ed., pp. 21–54). Thousand Oaks, CA: Sage.

Kolko, D. J., & Swenson, C. C. (2002). *Assessing and treating physically abused children and their families: A cognitive behavioral approach*. Thousand Oaks, CA: Sage.

Littel, J. (2001). Client participation and outcomes of intensive family preservation services. *Social Work Research*, *25*, 103–114.

Mayo Clinic. (2010). *Reactive attachment disorder*. Mayo Foundation for Medical Education and Research. Retrieved from http://www.mayoclinic.com/health/reactive-attachment-disorder/ds00988

Mersky, J. P., & Reynolds, A. (2007). Child maltreatment and violent delinquency: Disentangling main effects and subgroup effects. *Child Maltreatment*, *12*, 246–258. doi:10.1177/1077559507301842

Miller, T., Cohen, M., & Wiersema, B. (1996). *Victim costs and consequences: A new look*. Washington, DC: National Institute of Justice.

Myers, J. E. B. (2006). *Child protection in America: Past, present and future.* New York, NY: Oxford University Press.

National Center on Crime and Delinquency. (2008). *Parents Anonymous outcome evaluation: Promising findings for child maltreatment reduction.* Retrieved from http://www.parentsanonymous.org/paTEST/NCCDSpecialReport308.pdf

National Child Traumatic Stress Network. (2008a). *Empirically supported practices.* Retrieved from http://www.nctsn.org/nccts/nav.do?pid=ctr_top_trmnt_prom#q4

National Child Traumatic Stress Network. (2008b). *Abuse-focused cognitive behavior therapy (AF-CBT).* Retrieved from http://nctsn.org/nctsn_assets/pdfs/promising_practices/afcbt_general.pdf

National Child Traumatic Stress Network. (2008c). *Parent-child interaction therapy (PCIT).* Retrieved from http://nctsn.org/nctsn_assets/pdfs/promising_practices/pcit_general.pdf

Parents Anonymous, Inc. (2008). *Strengthening families around the world.* Retrieved from http://www.parentsanonymous.org/pahtml/parBene.html

Reece, R., & Ludwig, S. (2001). *Child abuse: Medical diagnosis and management.* Philadelphia, PA: Lippincott Williams & Wilkins.

Saunders, B., Berliner, L., & Hanson, R. (2004). *Child physical and sexual abuse: Guidelines for treatment.* Charleston, SC: National Crime Victims Research and Treatment Center.

Schuerman, J., Rzepnicki, T., & Littell, J. (1994). *Putting families first: An experiment in family preservation.* New York, NY: Aldine de Gruyter.

Swenson, C., Henggeler, S., Taylor, I., & Addison, O. (2005). *Multisystemic therapy and neighborhood partnerships.* New York, NY: Guilford Press.

Timmer, S. G., Urquiza, A. J., Herschell, A. D., McGrath, J. M., Zebell, N. M., Porter, A. L., & Vargas, E. C. (2006). Parent-child interaction therapy: Application of an empirically supported treatment to maltreated children in foster care. *Child Welfare, 85,* 919–939.

U.S. Department of Health and Human Services, Administration for Children and Families. (2008a). *Child maltreatment, 2006.* Retrieved from http://www.acf.hhs.gov/programs/cb/pubs/cm06/

U.S. Department of Health and Human Services, Administration for Children and Families. (2008b). *The AFCARS report.* Retrieved from http://www.acf.hhs.gov/programs/cb/stats_research/afcars/tar/report14.htm

U.S. Department of Justice Office of Juvenile Justice and Delinquency Prevention. *OJJDP model programs guide.* (2007). Retrieved from http://www.dsgonline.com/mpg2.5/TitleV_MPG_Table_Ind_Rec.asp?id=363

Widom, C. (1997). *Child abuse, neglect, and witnessing violence.* Handbook of antisocial behavior (pp. 159–170). Hoboken, NJ: Wiley.

Willis, D. (1995). Psychological impact of child abuse and neglect. *Journal of Clinical Child Psychology, 24,* 2–4.

2

FAMILY SERVICES FOR CHILD ABUSE AND MALTREATMENT

JOAN PENNELL AND DAVID S. CRAMPTON

Within the fields of psychology, social work, and allied professions, there is a growing consensus that reducing and eliminating child maltreatment must include interventions at the parent, family, and community levels. Interventions exclusively delivered at the individual level have limited benefit, particularly over time. One means of improving child outcomes is to change the context in which maltreatment occurs. We are just beginning to learn how to strengthen families and their communities. Ultimately, real progress will require an approach that combines therapeutic interventions with children and their caregivers along with strategies that engage extended family and community members. To make progress, we need to identify the frameworks shaping interventions for parents, examine their intended and unintended consequences, and figure out ways to integrate the contributions of parent, family, and community strengths in forging directions for the future.

Child welfare paradigms influence policy, practice, and evaluation on strategies to address child maltreatment. What we know about these strategies and how we know this are shaped by how we make sense of maltreating parents. The primary emphasis in the United States is on parents as abusing their children and secondarily on parents as themselves in need of support, with the least attention given to these parents as members of their communities.

27

The three perspectives are each embedded in a child welfare paradigm: child protection to dysfunctional parents, family support for parents in need, and community building with isolated parents. Combined, the paradigms encompass practice at three levels—individual, family, and community—and the research suggests that integrating work across the levels is necessary to safeguard children.

In addressing what we know about child welfare services, the chapter begins by reviewing the historical developments that have influenced which interventions are applied to which parents, the paradigms that these interventions reflect, and the current understanding of their outcomes. In addressing how we know this, the chapter turns to two frameworks shaping research in the field, and in examining ways to address gaps, the chapter reviews new data sources for evaluating outcomes for children at different stages of development. In conclusion, next steps for promoting an integrated strategy for protecting and nurturing children and their families are proposed.

WHAT DO WE KNOW?

Under Anglo-American law, parents have both a legal right and obligation to care for their children. Parents who fail to meet normative expectations through acts of commission (abuse), omission (neglect), or incapacity (dependency) are subject to state interventions. The United States and other countries adopting British law specify the state as the *parens patriae*, taking charge of minors whose parents cannot or do not adequately care for them (see Chapter 3, this volume). The manner in which the state intervenes is shaped by how parents whose children are not adequately protected are viewed and, thus, the role that the child welfare system should assume in the lives of these parents and their children. Although the United States has a dominant practice model of child welfare, it evinces a complex mix of approaches that reflect trends inside and outside the country.

Historically, public child welfare in the United States provided for abandoned and orphaned children from poor, White families. It was based on an earlier child-saving approach by churches and community groups that believed they were rescuing children from the corruption of urban life or immoral parents (Trattner, 1999). The first social workers included friendly visitors (later known as *caseworkers*) who went into families' homes and offered information about child rearing and settlement house workers (the precursors to community organizers) who helped change the neighborhoods in which disadvantaged, often immigrant, families resided. Social welfare agencies and juvenile court became avenues for abused women and their children to receive some protection and support (Gordon, 1988). Largely excluded from these services, African Americans developed their own benevolent societies, frequently connected to local churches, to address familial and community needs, and African American social workers used a race lens to analyze issues and encouraged race pride to advance their communities (Carlton-LaNey, 1999).

Child Protection to Dysfunctional Parents

By the 1950s, public child welfare primarily provided foster care and concentrated services on poor families and child neglect. During this period, African American children were incorporated into White child welfare, largely because of Black migration to urban centers, White exodus from inner cities, and the civil rights movement. Not until the 1960s, when physicians identified the battered child syndrome (Kempe, Silverman, Steele, Droegmueller, & Silver, 1962), was public child welfare redirected to responding to reports of child physical abuse and later in the 1980s to child sexual abuse.

The focus on child abuse led to a paradigm shift in public child welfare so that the primary service became child protection (Lindsey & Shlonsky, 2008, p. 376). The perspective here is that maltreating parents are dysfunctional and that without necessary changes their children should be removed from their care. Although substantiated reports of neglect far outstrip those of abuse, the latter serves as the organizing framework for child protection (Cameron, Freymond, Cornfield, & Palmer, 2007, p. 13). One compelling reason from a system perspective is that in cases known to child welfare the agency is considered legally liable when children die or are seriously injured at the hands of their parents.

Because the aim is to protect children from their parents, strategies emphasize forensic investigation, child removal, and foster care. In their capacity as case managers, social workers were primarily expected to monitor the safety of children, and other professionals or the public at large, depending on the state's mandatory reporting law, were required to report cases of suspected child maltreatment. The result was a spiraling upward of reports and narrowing of services to investigations as opposed to supports to struggling families (Kamerman & Kahn, 1997). The net widened as more children entered (at least partially because of the crack-cocaine epidemic) and stayed in foster care for indefinite periods of time, often transferred from placement to placement (Testa, 2008), and the net widened further as children's exposure to domestic violence was defined in some states as a failure to protect (Edleson, 2004).

The outcomes for children have been mixed. Since the mid-1990s, reports of child maltreatment steadily climbed, pointing to more attention to child protection; substantiations of child maltreatment reports fell, particularly for abuse, paralleling declines in related social indicators, such as for youth suicide and violent crime. However, child fatalities related to maltreatment doubled, giving the United States one of the highest rates among developed countries (Trocmé, 2008). Among children placed in foster care, one third of youths do not complete high school or its equivalent, and teen pregnancy has been high; on discharge, young adults often become homeless, have difficulty finding employment, and experience serious mental health issues (Maluccio & Pecora, 2006). More recently, time spent in foster care has been reduced through expediting adoptions by relative or nonrelative caregivers of their foster children (Testa, 2008).

The federal government conducts assessments of children's safety, permanency (i.e., continuity in caring relationships), and well-being as part of the Child and Family Services Reviews mandated by the Adoption and Safe Families Act of 1997. These reviews show that national performance goals are not being met by every state (Berrick, 2009). Overall, child protection has been faulted for five major shortcomings: heavy-handed treatment of families who are low risks, underinclusion of others who are overlooked, lack of capacity to handle the volume of work, fragmentation of service delivery, and a dual and often conflicting mandate of protecting children while trying to keep families together (Waldfogel, 2008). This has pushed U.S. child welfare toward reform and other paradigms for relating to parents.

Family Support for Parents in Need

Other paradigms, although more muted than child protection, are evident in the United States, and their juxtaposition with child welfare systems abroad assists in amplifying their discourses and identifying their features. The Nordic countries are known for applying a family support system that emphasizes "care *of* the family" rather than expectations of "care *in* the family" (italics in original; Hessle, 2000, p. 9). In the United States, this approach appears in efforts to provide in-home supports for rehabilitating families and keeping children with their parents (see Chapter 1, this volume). A rehabilitative perspective permits identifying that the parents themselves have been victimized, whether in their own childhood or in their intimate relations. Within this framework, maltreating parents are perceived as in need of services to help them and improve their care of their children. Case management entails assessing needs and connecting families to services such as mental health counseling, addictions treatment, and domestic violence programs.

One supportive service used to reduce maltreatment of very young children is home visiting for their parents, who are often single, first-time mothers.

The evidence for these programs has been mixed and points to the need to reassess the theory underlying home visitation programs (Marcenko & Staerkel, 2006). Helping parents feel better about themselves or providing parent education and case management may not, on their own, improve parenting. Additionally, attention needs to be given to changing parent-child interactions, increasing resources for impoverished families, and connecting families to an integrated network of informal supports and formal services that fit local conditions and cultures (Marcenko & Staerkel, 2006). Supports are also needed for caregivers beyond the biological parents. Compared with caregivers in the general population, foster parents are more likely to be older, have less education, and live below the poverty level. Moreover, children in foster care have significant developmental and mental heath delays; thus, foster parents need substantial community support in order to raise these children optimally (Barth et al., 2008).

In the United States, a major trend in moving away from a child protection paradigm for all families receiving child welfare services and toward a more customized approach is known as *differential, multiple,* or *alternative response* (Waldfogel, 2008, p. 236). Adopted in over half the U.S. states, differential response has available multiple tracks in order to respond more sensitively to the needs of individual families. Higher risk situations, concerning such matters as child abuse, fatalities, and abandonment, receive a forensic investigation in conformity with the child protection paradigm. Lower risk cases, usually involving child neglect or dependency, are handled through less adversarial family assessments conducted by social workers without involving police investigators, with interviews of children typically held with parents present and without leading to a substantiation of the parent as maltreating and posting of the parent's name on a central registry. In determining assignment of tracks, states typically take into account the age of the child and factors such as histories of parental addictions and child's exposure to domestic violence (Kaplan & Merkel-Holguin, 2008). If indicated by new information, cases can be switched to a different track.

Initially child advocates expressed fears that a family assessment would fail to adequately identify risks and protect children. The evidence built up over more than a decade indicates, to the contrary, that children are not endangered by multiple response systems and that this approach may lessen repeat maltreatment and augment services to families and their satisfaction with these services (Ortiz, Shusterman, & Fluke, 2008; Waldfogel, 2008). For instance, a Minnesota evaluation randomly assigned families eligible for the assessment track to the investigation or assessment tracks and reported that the families in the assessment track received more services and had fewer rereports of maltreatment (Loman & Siegel, 2005). In terms of placement of children outside the home, the results have been mixed: For families receiving an alternative response as opposed to conventional services, the likelihood of removals was lower in Minnesota, higher in Missouri, and unaffected in Washington State (Conley & Berrick, 2008). The varying outcomes may be a function of differences in how states design and implement differential response.

Nevertheless, the unclear impact on child removals points to the limitation of family interventions that do not take into account the neighborhoods in which children live, especially those of children of color. A particularly troubling aspect of child welfare is the disproportionate representation on caseloads of African American, Native American, and other racialized populations (Belanger, Bullard, & Green, 2008). For example, in 2000, although African American children made up only 15% of all children living in the United States, they accounted for 37% of the children in foster care. Other groups, such as Hispanic children, tend to be underrepresented nationally but overrepresented in certain states or counties. Disproportionate representation is not a matter of African American parents mistreating their children more, and once factors such as income and family structure are taken into account, they appear to have significantly lower rates of maltreating their children (Sedlak & Schultz, 2005). The overrepresentation may be a consequence of racial bias in how child welfare agencies handle cases involving minority populations (Dettlaff & Rycraft, 2008). Their overrepresentation would not be of such concern if involvement with child welfare meant better services and outcomes; however, children of color are treated less well with poorer results (Hill, 2006). These disparities signal the need for moving beyond family to community solutions.

In their seminal work *Children of the Storm: Black Children and American Child Welfare*, Billingsley and Giovannoni (1972) earlier documented the failure of private and public child welfare organizations to develop services for African American children in their own homes. It is likely that when Billingsley and Giovannoni used the phrase "in their own home," they did not mean only services in the family's residence; rather, they meant comprehensive support of the family context including their extended family and community. Later, Wulczyn, Barth, Yuan, Jones Harden, and Landsverk (2005) showed that disproportionality is most pronounced for African American infants in poor communities; thus, efforts to reduce disproportionality should include integrated strategies to provide support to young children and their families. Another example is that African American children removed from their homes are more likely to be placed with relatives than are White children. This helps in reducing the trauma of separation and preserving family ties but is also accompanied by greater child behavioral and mental health issues and extended placements. These problematic results are probably the result of child welfare providing fewer resources to kin than nonkin caregivers and of lower incomes in minority communities (Hill, 2008).

Community Building With Isolated Parents

Another paradigm of child welfare is community building that seeks to strengthen the positive connections between isolated parents and their communities. This approach has been encouraged by a range of groups, including feminist, youth, cultural, faith, and consumer (Cameron et al., 2007), and emphasizes preventive strategies (see Chapter 4, this volume). Overcoming isolation may mean severing dangerous or debilitating relationships, reconnecting to cultural traditions, and participating in civic engagement. A closely related child welfare model, adopted in India and South Africa, is developmental social welfare that links economic and social goals (Patel, 2005; Schmid, 2008). In the United States, it appears in efforts to connect economic sufficiency and child welfare to eradicate poverty (Mulroy, Nelson, & Gour, 2005). It is based on social development as "a process of planned social change designed to promote the wellbeing of the population as a whole in conjunction with a dynamic process of economic development" (Midgely, 1995, p. 250). Parents in this paradigm are to be educated, trained, and supported to participate fully in the social, political, and economic life of their communities. In addition to connecting children and their families to needed services, case management here becomes community organizing and involves mobilizing informal and formal supports on their behalf and weaving them into networks to strengthen their own communities.

Within child welfare and other child-serving agencies, an increasingly applied strategy for community building is engaging families and their networks in making and implementing plans (Nixon, Burford, & Quinn, 2005). These plans address concerns identified by child welfare as well as by the family group, that is, the family, its extended family, and other close connections. In the United States, child welfare approaches to family engagement include family group decision making, family team meetings, team decision-making, and child and family teams. Although they vary in their specific procedures, the overall intent is to build partnerships within family groups and among families, community organizations, and public agencies.

An example is an early Canadian trial of family group decision making to address family violence, that is, both child maltreatment and domestic violence in the same family (Pennell & Burford, 1995). Influenced by the family group conferencing model from Aotearoa New Zealand, the intervention emphasized the family group's leadership in developing plans to stop abuse. Three culturally and geographically diverse communities in the eastern provinces of Newfoundland and Labrador agreed to take part in the demonstration project: a northern Inuit community; a rural peninsula with inhabitants of French, English, and Mi'kmaq (aboriginal) heritage; and the capital of St. John's, settled largely by Irish and English.

To adapt family group decision making to these contexts, planning was carried out at the provincial and community levels, and input was sought from cultural, feminist, religious, and professional organizations. In consultation with local planning committees, family group conference coordinators were selected; they were independent from protective services, and thus families were less likely to confuse their role with those of child protection, police, corrections, and so forth. After receiving an agency referral, the coordinators invited the family group to take part in a conference and, on their agreement, prepared the family and service providers, with particular attention devoted to safety measures such as support people. The conferences began with introductions and then moved to information sharing about the concerns to be addressed. Once the family group had sufficient information, the service providers, including the coordinator, left the room so that the family group could deliberate in privacy and formulate their plan. After they had formulated their plan, they invited the coordinator and service providers to return to the room, and together they finalized the plan. Before the plan could go into effect, it had to be approved by the involved protective authorities. During a 1-year period, conferences were held for 32 families with very serious safety issues. Demonstrating that the model involves extensive community organizing, the conferences were attended by 472 participants (384 family group members and 88 service providers).

To evaluate family group decision making, a longitudinal and quasi-experimental design was used. Interviews were held with 115 family members on the impact of conferencing, police files were checked for reoccurrence of domestic violence, and child welfare files of the conferenced families were compared with those of similar families receiving services in the same locales. With corroboration from all data sources, the main findings were that conferencing reduced indicators of child maltreatment and domestic violence, improved child development, and strengthened support networks (Pennell & Burford, 2000). A later North Carolina study found that the conferences used participatory decision-making and succeeded in reengaging fathers or the paternal side of the family in supporting children and youth (Pennell, 2006).

Partnering is facilitated by participatory planning that taps into the cultural practices of families, collaborative and community-based delivery of services, and ongoing monitoring to reinforce a shared responsibility for follow through on plans (Pennell & Anderson, 2005). Engaging in family meetings in itself yields benefits: an increased sense of family togetherness and pride in their own efficacy (Walton, McKenzie, & Connolly, 2005), improved relations between families and their workers (Kemp, 2007), and less adversarial court deliberations (Burford, Pennell, & Edwards, in press). Family group members have been notably generous in volunteering support, including opening their homes to their young relatives (Gunderson, Cahn, & Wirth, 2003; Titcomb & LeCroy, 2005). Kinship care, along with more supports for keeping children with their families or returning them more rapidly, has reduced reliance on nonrelative foster care. As a consequence, family-engagement meetings have lessened the disproportionate placement of African American, Latino, and Native American children into state care (Crampton & Jackson, 2007; Pennell, Edwards, & Burford, 2010; Texas Department of Family and Protective Services, 2006). Participation in the meetings has not substantively endangered children's safety (Berzin, 2006; Sundell & Vinnerljung, 2004) or, more positively, has been accompanied by improvements to their safety (Pennell & Burford, 2000; Sawyer & Lohrbach, 2008).

From a community perspective, retaining family ties is a way to decrease the fragmentation of communities of color. In *Shattered Bonds: The Color of Child Welfare*, Dorothy Roberts (2002) contended that in predominantly African American neighborhoods, "family disintegration leads to community disintegration" (p. 27). Reflecting on the potential benefits and dangers of family-engagement meetings, Roberts (2007) observed that culturally sensitive practice may only "regulate minority families more effectively" (p. 7) and that the litmus test of the cultural competence of the meetings is an actual "change in child welfare decision making" (p. 7) that respects the families' cultural context. Building support around children and their families is one step toward strengthening communities both socially and economically. Local supports mean that caregiving and treatment remain in children's neighborhoods, thereby decreasing their estrangement from family and neighbors and increasing funding for economically deprived communities. Even with these infusions, catching them up to income levels in other communities, though, will remain at issue.

A potentially viable means of reinforcing family-engagement strategies is to embed them within community collaboratives that build partnerships among families, community organizations, and public child welfare. Larger scale efforts in California; Iowa; and Washington, DC, have worked to sustain these partnerships by offering clear practice models, aligning policy and practice, providing training, and evaluating program delivery and outcomes. The collaboratives are able to "build circles of support for struggling parents and integrate agency frontline workers with people from many walks of life" but "community organizing has been a weak spot, and an often difficult concept for social service professionals to embrace" (White, 2008, p. 15). Within any of the child welfare paradigms, integrating work across the individual, family, and community levels continues to be a challenge and will require legislation, funding, policy, education, training, and evaluation to guide and sustain good practice.

HOW DO WE KNOW IT?

Research on the etiology of child maltreatment has evolved from a focus on the individual characteristics of children or their parents to ecological models that highlight the interactions among individuals, families, neighborhoods, and communities. Two major research traditions have influenced the thinking about the relationships between context and child maltreatment: One focuses on social disorganization and the other focuses on ecological–transactional development (Coulton, Crampton, Irwin, Spilsbury, & Korbin, 2007). In terms of the paradigms discussed in this chapter, social disorganization fits into the community-building paradigm, whereas the ecological perspective is rooted in the family-support paradigm. The social disorganization literature has a top-down perspective in which neighborhoods of varying strength are identified and then varying rates of child maltreatment are examined. The ecological perspective has a bottom-up view in which parents with varying levels of maltreatment are identified and then the research examines how their environments differ. Both traditions have their strengths, but progress will require developing research that integrates them as well as the more dominant child-protection paradigm.

The first tradition, developed by sociologists and social workers, examines the relationship between geographic concentrations of social problems and social processes within neighborhoods thought to contribute to social control, such as network ties, shared norms, collective efficacy, institutional resources, and routines (Sampson, Morenoff, & Gannon-Rowley, 2002). Testa and Furstenberg (2002) noted that social workers and sociologists as far back as the early 1900s have repeatedly documented "the tendency for delinquent and neglected children to concentrate geographically in a common set of Chicago neighborhoods" (p. 238). This perspective has led to an interest in how neighborhoods can be strengthened to support families and to reduce child maltreatment (Melton, 2005; U.S. Advisory Board on Child Abuse and Neglect, 1993). The strength of the social disorganization tradition is that it describes some of the specific social structures and processes within neighborhoods that may be related to child maltreatment and provides some explanation as to how social structure and process are related. Social disorganization theory, however, provides little specificity about how these neighborhood characteristics might influence the behaviors and development of children and their families.

The second tradition, led by developmental psychologists, examines how the environment influences child development and parenting (Belsky, 1993; Belsky & Jaffee, 2006; Bronfenbrenner, Moen, & Garbarino, 1984; Cicchetti & Lynch, 1993; Garbarino, 1977). In 1991, the commissioner for children, youth, and families in the U.S. Department of Health and Human Services asked the National Academy of Sciences to convene an expert panel on child maltreatment research (National Research Council, 1993). The panel selected a developmental–ecological–transactional model of the etiology of child maltreatment to review the existing research. This model views child maltreatment within a system of risk and protective factors interacting across four levels: individual or ontogenic, family or microsystem, the exosystem (which includes neighborhoods), and the social or macrosystem. More recently, this model has been used to demonstrate reciprocal relationships among children's exposure to community violence, child maltreatment, and child functioning over time (Cicchetti & Valentino, 2006). The strength of this approach is that it describes some of the specific ways in which the environment may influence the transactions between a parent and child and between a family and the neighborhood. However, the ecological–transactional model provides limited explanation about how neighborhood conditions and social processes influence these transactions and about how and why these neighborhood conditions and processes occur.

WHAT ARE THE NEXT STEPS?

The sociological and developmental traditions, especially when offsetting each other's limitations, have helped research to move away from an individualistic focus to taking into account familial and community contexts. Progress has also been made because of an increase in data sources on child maltreatment. Until fairly recently, child welfare research was severely limited because of the paucity of reliable data on services for children. Much of what we know about the need to address child maltreatment at the parent, family, and community levels is primarily drawn from what we know does not work in the current child welfare system. A widely adopted child welfare text points out that during congressional testimony in 1980, "One witness noted (only partly in jest) that the government kept a better count of benches in our national parks than children in the foster care system" (Pecora, Whittaker, Maluccio, Barth, & Plotnick, 2000, p. 22).

Fortunately, the federal government later sponsored several projects designed to collect information about the children and families served by the child welfare system. Wulczyn, Barth, Yuan, Jones Harden, and Landsverk (2005) synthesized findings from three major child welfare data sets. The

National Child Abuse and Neglect Data System (NCANDS) includes data on official reports of child maltreatment that are voluntarily submitted by the states to the federal government. NCANDS can demonstrate what happens to reports of child maltreatment made to public agencies, but the data obviously do not include what may be a significant amount of unreported maltreatment. The Multistate Foster Care Data Archive (FCDA) is managed by the Chapin Hall Center for Children at the University of Chicago. Like NCANDS, it consists of data drawn from the agencies that administer child welfare programs and covers placement data for children in out-of-home care. The National Survey of Child and Adolescent Well-Being is the first nationally representative longitudinal survey of children served by the child welfare system. Another unique feature of this study is that includes information collected from children, caregivers, and child welfare personnel.

Drawing on these new sources of information, Wulczyn et al. (2005) presented the best evidence for what works and does not work in child welfare services. First, they described how the Adoption and Safe Families Act of 1997 clarified that the goals of child welfare are to promote safety, permanency, and child well-being. Safety, including preventing maltreatment and its recurrence, is a long-term goal of the system. Permanency, including returning children removed from their caregivers or finding the children some permanent family through adoption or other means, has been a clear goal of the system at least since the Adoption Assistance and Child Welfare Act of 1980. Wulcyzn et al. argued that both safety and permanency are guided by a belief that government intervention in family life should be limited to situations in which there is a high risk of child maltreatment. Promoting child well-being is more complex in that it includes providing support to families who may be trying to raise their children in difficult circumstances. Well-being is measured in terms of whether children's needs are met, including educational, health, and mental health needs. The authors suggest that improving child well-being requires combining elements of bioecological, life span, and public health perspectives. Their analysis demonstrates that "the child welfare system in the United States has served three developmentally distinct populations: children starting out, children starting school, and children starting adolescence" (Wulcyzn et al., 2005, p. 171).

The types of maltreatment and the system's response to their maltreatment are distinct for infant, school-age, and adolescent children. Because these three developmental groups have unique needs, responding to child maltreatment requires attention to both child development and the family environment. Attention to the parent, family, and community levels, however, is somewhat different for each of these age groups. Children are most likely to enter the child welfare system as infants and most often for reasons of neglect. According to Wulczyn et al. (2005), when infants enter foster care, they are 60% more likely to be adopted than to be reunited with their parents. They are also at high risk of developmental delay. The child welfare system's response to maltreatment for children starting out must help families learn to parent children with high needs and provide the community support to allow families to provide appropriate care as soon as possible so that developmental delays can be resolved.

Children entering school are at lower risk of child welfare involvement, but when they do come to the attention of the system, it is more often for reasons of physical abuse (although, like other groups, the most frequent concern is neglect). The increase in risk of involvement as children enter school raises the question of whether they are more likely to be maltreated or whether their maltreatment is more likely to be identified. Wuclzyn et al. (2005) suggested that the data are not definitive and that this finding may be due to the detection of long-term child welfare concerns by school personnel. Clearly, for this age group, the child welfare system must learn how to support parents, families, and communities in coordination with schools.

Last, maltreatment of children starting in adolescence has another distinct dynamic. Nearly half of these children who enter care are placed in some sort of group home setting rather than a family setting, and they have elevated levels of child behavioral problems, delinquency, and suicidality (Wulczyn et al., 2005). This suggests that child welfare services for this group must address the behavior and mental health needs of the children as well as services for their parents. Successful exit from the child welfare system for these older children requires helping families parent a child with behavioral issues of their own and providing community support that allows both parents and adolescents to thrive. What is apparent, though, across all three stages of child development is that effective caregiving requires the involvement of familial and community supports. This understanding guides how we can move forward in addressing child maltreatment and increasing our knowledge of successful strategies.

CONCLUSION

From its earliest days, the profession of social work viewed individuals within their social context: Caseworkers started with changing individuals, and community organizers with changing neighborhoods, but both groups sought to address all ecological levels. Their capacity to do so, however, was supported and constrained by the social policies and practice frameworks of their times. In their assessment of person-environment practice, Kemp,

Whittaker, and Tracy (1997) noted that throughout its history, the profession has struggled with balancing person-centered and environmental interventions. Simultaneously promoting individual and social transformation has been derailed by approaches seeking to change either people or communities rather than collaborating with people within local and global networks (Simon, 1994).

Each of the three child welfare paradigms identified in this chapter has an important contribution to make to child welfare. There are dysfunctional parents from whom children must be protected, there are parents who need family supports in order to care for their children, and there are isolated parents who require building or rebuilding their community connections. Often, all three levels need to be strengthened within the same family. Taken together, these three paradigms can lead to a balanced approach that integrates work across the individual, family, and community levels. The difficulty is that U.S. child welfare policy today focuses primarily on changing individuals rather than communities and thus has limited the adoption of innovative practices and more fundamental reconceptualization of practice paradigms. Improving parenting without changing the family context could mean that parenting over time deteriorates if parents are isolated. Nor may improving the context without improving specific parenting skills reduce child maltreatment. Comprehensive family support should include both helping parents develop better parenting skills and strengthening parents' communities to improve the well-being of all family members. Each strategy alone will not be sufficient without the other.

To support a balanced approach, interdisciplinary practice and research are needed that bring together social, psychological, economic, and political perspectives. This will mean developing collaborations that include diverse fields, are informed by family and community participants, test strategies in real world contexts, and have sustained funding to study effects over time. It will also mean strategies that attend to all three levels that comprise comprehensive supports to children and their families and generate data that increase our understanding and enhance person–environment practice. This is the time for moving ahead. Rebalancing child welfare appears all the more feasible in a new era in which the president himself brings an understanding of the importance of community organizing for troubled neighborhoods and changing our national dialogue.

REFERENCES

Adoption Assistance and Child Welfare Act of 1980, Pub. L. No. 96-272 (1980).

Adoption and Safe Families Act of 1997, Pub. L. No. 105-89 (1997).

Barth, R. P., Green, R., Webb, M. B., Wall, A., Gibbons, C., & Craig, C. (2008). Characteristics of out-of-home caregiving environments provided under child welfare services. *Child Welfare, 87*(3), 5–39.

Belanger, K., Bullard, L. B., & Green, D. K. (Eds.). (2008). Racial disproportionality in child welfare [Special issue]. *Child Welfare, 87*(2).

Belsky, J. (1993). Etiology of child maltreatment: A developmental-ecological analysis. *Psychological Bulletin, 114,* 413–434. doi:10.1037/0033-2909.114.3.413

Belsky, J., & Jaffee, S. R. (2006). The multiple determinants of parenting. In D. Cicchetti & D. Cohen (Eds.), *Developmental psychopathology* (2nd ed., pp. 38–85). Hoboken, NJ: Wiley.

Berrick, J. D. (2009). *Take me home: Protecting America's vulnerable children.* New York, NY: Oxford University Press.

Berzin, S. C. (2006). Using sibling data to understand the impact of family group decision-making on child welfare outcomes. *Children and Youth Services Review, 28,* 1449–1458. doi:10.1016/j.childyouth.2006.03.003

Billingsley, A., & Giovannoni, J. M. (1972). *Children of the storm: Black children and American child welfare.* New York, NY: Harcourt Brace and Jovanovich.

Bronfenbrenner, U., Moen, P., & Garbarino, J. (1984). Child, family, and community. In R. Park (Ed.), *Review of child development research* (pp. 283–328). Chicago, IL: University of Chicago Press.

Burford, G., Pennell, J., & Edwards, M. (in press). "A friendlier, less intimidating experience": Family team meetings as principled advocacy. *Journal of Public Child Welfare.*

Cameron, G., Freymond, N., Cornfield, D., & Palmer, S. (2007). Positive possibilities for child and family welfare: Expanding the Anglo-American child protection paradigm. In G. Cameron, N. Coady, & G. R. Adams (Eds.), *Moving toward positive systems for child and family welfare: Current issues and future directions* (pp. 1–77). Waterloo, Ontario: Wilfrid Laurier University Press.

Carlton-LaNey, I. (1999). African American social work pioneers' response to need. *Social Work, 44,* 311–321.

Cicchetti, D., & Lynch, M. (1993). Toward an ecological/transactional model of community violence and child maltreatment: Consequences of children's development. *Psychiatry, 56,* 96–118.

Cicchetti, D., & Valentino, K. (2006). An ecological-transactional perspective on child maltreatment: Failure of the average expectable environment and its influence on child development. In D. Cicchetti & D. Cohen (Eds.), *Developmental psychopathology* (2nd ed., pp. 129–201). Hoboken, NJ: Wiley.

Conley, A., & Berrick, J. D. (2008). Implementation of differential response in ethnically diverse neighborhoods. *Protecting Children, 23*(1&2), 30–38.

Coulton, C. J., Crampton, D. S., Irwin, M., Spilsbury, J. C., & Korbin, J. E. (2007). How neighborhoods influence child maltreatment: A review of the literature and alternative pathways. *Child Abuse & Neglect, 31,* 1117–1142. doi:10.1016/j.chiabu.2007.03.023

Crampton, D., & Jackson, W. (2007). Family group decision making and the over-representation of children of color in foster care: A case study. *Child Welfare, 86*(3), 51–69.

Dettlaff, A. J., & Rycraft, J. R. (2008). Deconstructing disproportionality: Views from multiple community stakeholders. *Child Welfare, 87*(2), 37–58.

Edleson, J. L. (2004). Should childhood exposure to adult domestic violence be defined as child maltreatment under the law? In P. G. Jaffe, L. L. Baker, & A. Cunningham (Eds.), *Protecting children from domestic violence: Strategies for community intervention* (pp. 8–29). New York, NY: Guilford Press.

Garbarino, J. (1977). The human ecology of child maltreatment: A conceptual model for research. *Journal of Marriage and the Family, 39,* 721–735. doi:10.2307/350477

Gordon, L. (1988). *Heroes of their own lives: The politics and history of family violence.* New York, NY: Viking.

Gunderson, K., Cahn, K., & Wirth, J. (2003). The Washington State long-term outcome study. *Protecting Children, 18*(1 & 2), 42–47.

Hessle, S. (2000). Child welfare on the eve of the twenty-first century: What we have learned. In M. Callahan & S. Hessle (Eds.; with S. Strega) , *Valuing the field: Child welfare in an international context* (pp. 3–21). Burlington, VT: Ashgate.

Hill, R. B. (2006). *Synthesis of research on disproportionality in child welfare: An update.* Retrieved from http://www.racemattersconsortium.org/docs/Bob HillPaper_FINAL.pdf

Hill, R. B. (2008). Gaps in research and public policy. *Child Welfare, 87,* 359–367.

Kamerman, S. B., & Kahn, A. J. (Eds.). (1997). *Children & their families in big cities: Strategies for service reform.* New York, NY: Columbia University.

Kaplan, C., & Merkel-Holguin, L. (2008). Another look at the national study on differential response in child welfare. *Protecting Children, 23*(1–2), 5–21.

Kemp, T. (2007). *Family welfare conferences—The Wexford experience: An evaluation of Barnardos family welfare conference project.* Ballincollig, County Cork, Republic of Ireland: Nucleus.

Kemp, S., Whittaker, J. K., & Tracy, E. (1997). *Person–environment practice: The social ecology of interpersonal helping.* New York, NY: de Gruyter.

Kempe, C. H., Silverman, F., Steele, B., Droegmueller, W., & Silver, H. (1962). The battered-child syndrome. *JAMA, 181,* 17–24.

Lindsey, D., & Shlonsky, A. (2008). Closing reflections: Future research directions and a new paradigm. In D. Lindsey & A. Shlonsky (Eds.), *Child welfare research: Advances for practice and policy* (pp. 375–399). New York, NY: Oxford University Press. doi:10.1093/acprof:oso/9780195304961.003.0023

Loman, L. A., & Siegel, G. L. (2005). Alternative response in Minnesota: Findings of the program evaluation. *Protecting Children, 20*(2–3), 79–92.

Maluccio, A. N., & Pecora, P. J. (2006). Foster family care in the USA. In C. McAuley, P. J. Pecora, & W. Rose (Eds.), *Enhancing the well-being of children and families through effective interventions: International evidence for practice* (pp. 187–202). Philadelphia, PA: Jessica Kingsley.

Marcenko, M., & Staerkel, F. (2006). Home visiting for parents of pre-school children in the USA. In C. McAuley, P. J. Pecora, & W. Rose (Eds.), *Enhancing the well-being of children and families through effective interventions: International evidence for practice* (pp. 82–90). Philadelphia, PA: Jessica Kingsley.

Melton, G. B. (2005). Invited commentary: Mandated reporting: A policy without a reason. *Child Abuse & Neglect, 29,* 9–18. doi:10.1016/j.chiabu.2004.05.005

Midgley, J. (1995). *Social development: The developmental perspective in social welfare.* London, England: Sage.

Mulroy, E. A., Nelson, K. E., & Gour, D. (2005). Community building and family-centered service collaboratives. In M. Weil (Ed.), *The handbook of community practice* (pp. 460–474). Thousand Oaks, CA: Sage.

National Research Council. (1993). *Understanding child abuse and neglect.* Washington, DC: National Academy Press.

Nixon, P., Burford, G., & Quinn, A. (with Edelbaum, J.). (2005, May). *A survey of international practices, policy & research on family group conferencing and related practices.* Retrieved from http://www.americanhumane.org/site/DocServer/FGDM_www_survey.pdf?docID=2841

Ortiz, M. J., Shusterman, G. R., & Fluke, J. D. (2008). Outcomes for children with allegations of neglect who receive alternative response and traditional investigations: Findings from NCANDS. *Protecting Children, 23*(1&2), 57–69.

Patel, L. (Ed.). (2005). *Social welfare and social development in South Africa.* Cape Town, South Africa: Oxford University Press Southern Africa.

Pecora, P., Whittaker, J. K., Maluccio, A. N., Barth, R. P., & Plotnick, R. D. (2000). *The child welfare challenge: Policy, practice, and research.* New York, NY: de Gruyter.

Pennell, J. (2006). Restorative practices and child welfare: Toward an inclusive civil society. *Journal of Social Issues, 62,* 257–277.

Pennell, J., & Anderson, G. (Eds.). (2005). *Widening the circle: The practice and evaluation of family group conferencing with children, youths, and their families.* Washington, DC: NASW Press.

Pennell, J., & Burford, G. (1995). *Family group decision making: New roles for "old" partners in resolving family violence: Implementation report* (Vols. I–II). St. John's, Newfoundland and Labrador, Canada: Memorial University of Newfoundland, School of Social Work.

Pennell, J., & Burford, G. (2000). Family group decision making: Protecting children and women. *Child Welfare, 79,* 131–158.

Pennell, J., Edwards, M., & Burford, G. (2010). Expedited family group engagement and child permanency. *Children and Youth Services Review, 32,* 1012–1019. doi: 10.1016/j.childyouth.2010.03.029

Roberts, D. (2002). *Shattered bonds: The color of child welfare.* New York, NY: Basic Books.

Roberts, D. (2007). Toward a community-based approach to racial disproportionality. *Protecting Children, 22*(1), 4–9.

Sampson, R. J., Morenoff, J. D., & Gannon-Rowley, T. (2002). Assessing neighborhood effects: Social processes and new directions in research. *Annual Review of Sociology, 28,* 443–478. doi:10.1146/annurev.soc.28.110601.141114

Sawyer, R. Q., & Lohrbach, S. (2008). *Olmsted County Child and Family Services: Family involvement strategies.* Rochester, MN: Olmsted Country Child and Family Services.

Schmid, J. E. (2008). *The story of South African child welfare: A history of the present.* Unpublished doctoral dissertation. Wilfrid Laurier University, Kitchener, Ontario, Canada.

Sedlak, A., & Schultz, D. (2005). Racial differences in child protective services investigation of abused and neglected children. In D. Derezotes, J. Poertner, & M. Testa (Eds.), *Race matters in child welfare: The overrepresentation of African American children in the system* (pp. 231–241). Washington, DC: Child Welfare League of America Press.

Simon, B. L. (1994). *The empowerment tradition in American social work: A history.* New York, NY: Columbia University Press.

Sundell, K., & Vinnerljung, B. (2004). Outcomes of family group conferencing in Sweden: A 3-year follow-up. *Child Abuse & Neglect, 28,* 267–287. doi:10.1016/j.chiabu.2003.09.018

Testa, M. (2008). New permanency strategies for children in foster care. In D. Lindsey & A. Shlonsky (Eds.), *Child welfare research: Advances for practice and policy* (pp. 108–125). New York, NY: Oxford University Press. doi:10.1093/acprof:oso/9780195304961.003.0006

Testa, M., & Furstenberg, F. F. (2002). The social ecology of child endangerment. In M. K. Rosenheim, F. E. Zimring, D. S. Tanenhaus, & B. Dohrn (Eds.), *A century of juvenile justice* (pp. 237–263). Chicago, IL: University of Chicago Press.

Texas Department of Family and Protective Services. (2006, October). *Family group decision-making: Final evaluation.* Retrieved from http://www.dfps.state.tx.us/Documents/about/pdf/2006-10-09_FGDM_Evaluation.pdf

Titcomb, A., & LeCroy, C. (2005). Outcomes of Arizona's family group decision making program. *Protecting Children, 19*(4), 47–53.

Trattner, W. I. (1999). *From poor law to welfare state: A history of social welfare in America.* New York, NY: Free Press.

Trocmé, N. (2008). Epidemiology of child maltreatment. In D. Lindsey & A. Shlonsky (Eds.), *Child welfare research: Advances for practice and policy* (pp. 15–25). New York, NY: Oxford University Press. doi:10.1093/acprof:oso/9780195304961.003.0001

U.S. Advisory Board on Child Abuse and Neglect. (1993). *Neighbors helping neighbors: Foundations for a new national strategy*. Washington, DC: U.S. Government Printing Office.

Waldfogel, J. (2008). The future of child welfare revisited. In D. Lindsey & A. Shlonsky (Eds.), *Child welfare research: Advances for practice and policy* (pp. 235–241). New York, NY: Oxford University Press.

Walton, E., McKenzie, M., & Connolly, M. (2005). Private family time: The heart of family group conferencing. *Protecting Children, 19*(4), 17–24.

White, A. (2008). *Scale of change: Creating and sustaining collaborative child welfare reform across cities and states*. New York, NY, and Washington, DC: Center for the Study of Social Policy.

Wulczyn, F., Barth, R. P., Yuan, Y.-Y. T., Jones Harden, B., & Landsverk, J. (2005). *Beyond common sense: Child welfare, child well-being, and the evidence of policy reform*. New Brunswick, NJ: AldineTransaction.

3

JUSTICE RESPONSES TO CHILD ABUSE AND MALTREATMENT

ROGER J. R. LEVESQUE

In a single year in the United States alone, child abuse and neglect affect thousands of children. Official estimates published by the National Clearing-house on Child Abuse and Neglect Information (2006) indicate that 3 million children are alleged to be victims of abuse or neglect and receive some form of investigative or intervention services from a state-supported child protection agency. Of these 3 million children, state agencies substantiate approximately 872,000 children as victims of maltreatment.

Although knowledge of child maltreatment has grown, the systems charged with ensuring justice remain quite narrow. Most of us think of law enforcement and the criminal justice system when we think of legal responses to victimization. Yet, justice system responses to child maltreatment are just part of a maze of different systems that society has charged with ensuring the healthy development of individuals. Regulated by their own sets of legal rules, these systems now provide the vast majority of private and state-supported care and services for maltreated children and those deemed at risk of harm. They include the health and mental health care systems, child welfare systems, juvenile justice systems, and educational systems. Together, these systems reveal a massive ability to intervene in families and influence their care of children. Interventions may be intended to directly protect children from harm and even the risk of harm but also to provide support and guide the socialization of children.

This chapter focuses on justice system components of societal responses. First, the key components of legal systems are described, including their significance to children's healthy development, contributions to the prevention of maltreatment, and responses to formal allegations of maltreatment. Next, research that has addressed key decision points in legal responses is examined. The analysis then focuses on necessary steps to address evolving changes in the practice and legal environments. Several controversies emerging from legal developments, within each system as well as across them, are examined.

WHAT DO WE KNOW? THE NATURE OF JUSTICE SYSTEM RESPONSES TO CHILD MALTREATMENT

Child Welfare Systems

There is really no such thing as a single entity called the "child welfare system" or its synonym—the "dependency system." Rather, a wide variety of systems exist, regulated by different rules. All operate at state levels and are ruled by state laws. States define what constitutes child mistreatment within their jurisdictions, and that definition dictates when states will intervene and how they will do so. Each state also has established procedures for investigating reports of potential maltreatment and provides programs and supportive services that are meant to address the needs of children and their families. States also determine when and under what circumstances to remove children from their homes and place them in foster care, reunite children with their families after having removed them, and seek the termination of parental rights. Every state has outlined circumstances that render reports either discretionary or mandatory. Despite potential diversity, all systems operate on the simple principle that they serve children's needs. They evince a preference to assist families in their efforts to care for their children, but they also permit aggressive interventions that could result in severing children's ties with their families.

Any broad overview of laws regulating child welfare necessarily precludes analysis of nuances. Thus, this analysis by necessity focuses on federal law. Federal legislation creates broad mandates that states must follow to receive federal funding, and all states must abide by the U.S. Constitution in their implementation of laws. Among numerous federal statutes, three are particularly important. The first major federal legislation to address child maltreatment is the 1974 Child Abuse Prevention and Treatment Act (CAPTA). CAPTA provides states with federal funding and support for prevention, assessment, investigation, prosecution, and treatment activities. The statute requires states to adopt mandatory child abuse and neglect reporting laws, appoint guardians ad litem, and ensure the confidentiality of records. In addition, CAPTA provides a definition for child abuse and neglect that must be incorporated into state laws as a minimum for substantiating child abuse and neglect. The statute defines abuse and neglect as "any physical act or failure to act on the part of a parent or caregiver, which results in death, serious physical or emotional harm, sexual abuse or exploitation, or an act or failure to act which presents an imminent risk of serious harm" (42 U.S.C. § 5106g). The second important legislation is the 1980 Adoption Assistance and Child Welfare Act (the Child Welfare Act). The Child Welfare Act requires reasonable efforts to avoid unnecessary removals of children from their homes, thus codifying the family preservation movement of the 20th century. The third major piece of federal legislation is the 1997 Adoption and Safe Families Act (the Safe Families Act). This legislation was enacted in response to concerns that children were being placed in foster care indefinitely and moved from one foster home to another. The Safe Families Act established the practice of permanency planning and mandated a timeline specifying when children must be reunited with their families, permanently placed with relatives, or placed for adoption.

Despite the influence of federal acts, each state remains responsible for its own child welfare program. The legal principle that guides a state's authority and responsibility is known as the *parens patriae* power. This principle permits states to intervene on behalf of children deemed in imminent harm. Every state uses a version of the imminent harm standard in its definition of child maltreatment, and child welfare investigators use the definition to substantiate abuse or neglect and whether it warrants state intervention. This standard allows states to focus on certain harms while essentially ignoring others, just as it permits the state to craft certain remedies while ignoring others that may be even more fruitful. Courts can intervene if an allegation of maltreatment fits into a determined category of maltreatment. Initially, a court may provide a temporary custody hearing to evaluate whether probable cause exists to believe that the minor is abused, neglected, or dependent, whether urgent and immediate necessity requires the child's removal, and if the relevant child protection agency has made reasonable efforts to eliminate the necessity of removal by providing appropriate services. If necessary, a court can designate a suitable placement for the child. All states now are federally mandated to be timely when removing children from their families and to place limits on temporary custody.

To retain the child's custody, a court must hold a variety of hearings to ensure appropriate balance between children's rights to protection and their caretakers' rights to relationships. Courts must hold adjudicatory hearings before preset (typically 90-day) windows close. If allegations of abuse or neglect are supported, courts then hold dispositional hearings to determine whether minors' best interests would be served by becoming wards of the court. Courts may commit minors to one of four entities: a suitable relative or other person, the probation department, an agency for care or placement, or the state's child protection agency itself. In making these decisions, courts now seek to prioritize permanency goals for children when they initially are placed and ensure that the services being provided to them and their families focus on achieving that goal. Typically, courts revisit children's cases at least every 6 months to review the service plan. At these hearings, and based on a number of factors that constitute the totality of each child's individual and social circumstances, courts either continue or revise permanency goals. The state maintains control over children as long as they remain minors or until courts determine that permanency has been achieved and the health, safety, and best interests of the children and the public no longer require wardship.

The legal system mandates the types of services that may be available, and those services often can be provided by the state itself or private parties. The child welfare system focuses on child maltreatment committed by family members, and thus it does not focus on maltreatment that may occur in schools, institutions, or even in public places. Families do not necessarily have a right to services; the child welfare system provides services that a court deems appropriate in light of available resources. Although children and families may have important rights when states decide to intervene, many have yet to be developed fully, such as the rights of families during investigation, rights to be free from seizure, and the types of legal representation due families when states litigate claims (for a deeper analysis of the points, see Levesque, 2008).

Criminal Justice Systems

Before the development of modern, state-supported child welfare systems, the criminal justice system served as the dominant legal response to child maltreatment. Well-recognized characteristics differentiate criminal justice and child welfare. In the criminal justice system, victimization constitutes harm against the state, whereas in the child welfare system the harm is against an individual child. Although victimization provides a reason for criminal justice to intervene, it shifts the focus away from the child and toward alleged offenders. Intervention no longer assumes that the state acts benevolently and in their interests. The criminal justice system's responses involve its own investigative army—technical experts, attorneys, judges, and correctional personnel. The state holds the power to incapacitate defendants pending the outcome of litigation, and, if it prevails, it assigns moral blame to them and can deprive them of their liberties. These actions differ from those of the child welfare system, which does not seek to place moral blame or to punish.

The state's power to use criminal law enforcement, however, is not absolute. Our legal system has developed at least two broad kinds of restraints that limit the state's power to identify, adjudicate, punish, and control those deemed offenders. Restraints in the first set are substantive. The law seeks to impose criminal penalties only for conduct, not for status (e.g., one can be arrested for drunk driving but not for being an alcoholic). The conduct must be blameworthy and the legal system must declare it illegal. That declaration must provide potential offenders with notice that their actions, and the penalties for those actions are subject to the law's control. These restraints are quite different from child welfare systems' focus on harm to children and their protection and healthy development. The second broad type of restraints is procedural. Most notably, the criminal justice system requires the government to prove beyond a reasonable doubt that individuals are responsible for alleged actions when they dispute charges and request trials. Finding responsibility on the basis of this high level of certainty requires procedural protections, including the right to confrontation and cross-examination, the right to counsel, and prohibitions against requiring individuals to be witnesses against themselves. In addition, the state may punish only once and it cannot retroactively increase penalties. Rules of evidence regulate the admission of evidence, such as those governing the testimony of experts to ensure presentation of reliable facts to juries rather than junk science. In contrast to criminal processes, responses within the child welfare system reduce the burdens of proof, relax evidentiary standards, limit the right to counsel, and remove rights against self-incrimination.

The rising recognition of child maltreatment, along with the belief that the criminal justice system should be more involved, has led to changes relating to trial procedures for admitting children's testimony and reforms that aim to incapacitate and control offenders. Two sets of examples are illustrative. The first involves the criminal justice system's effort to accommodate some children's special needs by using alternative procedures to provide their testimony. The most common procedural alterations involve videotaping or closed-circuit television rather than (and sometimes in addition to) live testimony. The second involves statutes that seek to incapacitate certain types of sex offenders through civil commitment following completion of their sentences. (For other important exceptions to defendant's rights in child abuse cases, see Coleman, 2005.) Furthermore, the criminal justice system may control family members and prohibit, for example, abuse of controlled substances. Studies reveal increasing efforts to aggressively pursue those who offend against children, especially those with no prior relationship. Offenders imprisoned for crimes against children now make up more than 20% of all prisoners incarcerated for violent crimes; 65% of that number are incarcerated for nonfamilial child sex abuse (Finkelhor & Ormrod, 2001).

Juvenile Justice Systems

From its inception, the juvenile court defined its mission as benevolent, grounded in the state's *parens patriae* authority to assist children whose own parents, for whatever reason, had been unable to provide them with adequate care. It espoused a rehabilitative philosophy, emphasizing the needs of the individual child rather than the circumstances or acts that triggered the court's intervention. Laws envisioned the juvenile court system essentially as a super parent who could assist children and families in need. This system intervenes when minors violate criminal statutes or commit any of a series of infractions collectively referred to as *status offenses*. The range of criminal offenses encompasses misdemeanors and less serious felonies as well as serious or violent felonies. In the case of status offenders, unlike those who have committed crimes (i.e., delinquents), the system permits intervention to support parental authority or to substitute itself for parents perceived as ineffective in controlling children or placing them at risk of increased norm-violating conduct. This mandate essentially straddles delinquency and child welfare jurisdictions. The juvenile court grounds its dependency jurisdiction in state disapproval of parental conduct and grounds its delinquency jurisdiction in the minor's violation of a criminal statute. Status offense jurisdiction combines censure of the minor's misbehavior with disapproval of parental ineffectiveness that accompanies the court's involvement. The juvenile, criminal, and child welfare systems inevitably intersect in mission as well as in practice.

Although juvenile courts typically are not part of reviews of justice system responses to child maltreatment, they are relevant for four major reasons. First, the lines that delineate the systems' jurisdiction may be unclear and may be similar to those of the dependency and criminal justice systems. Minors under jurisdiction of any of these systems could be treated similarly and even in identical facilities. Second, offenders are removed from homes and communities because of familial failure. Child maltreatment rates are disproportionately high among both delinquent youth and status offenders. Third, juveniles themselves are a major source of maltreatment against children. They arguably constitute the largest category of sex offenders against minors. They also commit other common forms of maltreatment against peers (e.g., sexual harassment, bullying). Dependency cases in contrast ignore much of the violence occurring outside of homes. Last, jurisprudential developments in juvenile justice provide important precedents that can transfer to other systems. Significant reforms in juvenile justice systems, as exemplified by *In Re Gault* (1967), were grounded on the failure of the state to act on behalf of children when it was given the responsibility. In a series of landmark cases beginning with *Gault*, the U.S. Supreme Court extended a range of constitutional protections to defendants in juvenile court. Although those rights were more limited than those of adults, they nevertheless may transfer to other state actions on behalf of children, such as in the representation of children and parents in dependency proceedings (see Levesque, 2008). These developments can help challenge notions that the alleged *parens patriae* mission renders traditional due process protections unnecessary.

Medical and Mental Health Care Systems

Social responses to child maltreatment necessarily involve two other highly regulated systems that directly address the needs of children and their families: medical and mental health. A firm legal foundation already links heath care systems to other justice system responses. Health systems are involved in frontline responses to maltreatment. Indeed, the modern recognition of the need to respond to child maltreatment emerged in the medical setting. Health care systems respond to allegations of maltreatment and often are the ones to initiate formal allegations that lead other systems to intervene. For example, medical professionals are among mandated reporters, as are other professionals who offer services to children, such as social workers, school nurses, and others who conduct and provide a wide variety of mental health evaluations of children. Nearly half of children presented for psychiatric hospitalization have been abused or neglected (see, e.g., Boxer & Terranova, 2008). Mental disorders may go undiagnosed in many children, especially if they are poor or lack medical insurance or their families are troubled by the stigma presented by mental health problems.

Health systems also link to child welfare and criminal justice systems to the extent that parents' failure to provide adequate medical and mental health care can itself constitute maltreatment. Despite the variation in terms, all states have laws that include medical neglect as a form of maltreatment. The failure to provide medical care can be deemed maltreating even though it was unintentional, parents lacked resources and access to care, and the caretakers took what they deemed as appropriate steps to provide care (see Levesque, 2002a). Even when children and families are involved in the child welfare system, they may not necessarily have a right to the necessary services to remedy their circumstances, the state may not be obligated to provide them, or a state may be reasonably unable to provide the services (Levesque, 2008).

Even if a variety of health care services may be available to children, other rules may limit access. A widely accepted general rule is that children lack an independent right to access medical care (for a review, see Levesque, 2000). Provision of medical services to children without parental consent may constitute assault and battery by the service provider. As a result, minors typically must defer to their parents' wishes regarding health services. Generally, parents are entitled to make medical decisions for their children unless such decisions place the child's life or society at risk. The needs of parents to provide care for their children, coupled with the legal system's failure to formulate these types of services as positive rights that states must support, has resulted in parents increasingly transferring their children's custody to the state in hopes that they will obtain needed medical care. Parents do so to benefit from the U.S. Supreme Court ruling that once a government acts to take a person into its custody, the Constitution imposes upon it a corresponding duty to assume more responsibility for that person's safety and general well-being, which includes necessary rehabilitative services (Levesque, 2006).

Educational Systems

Educational systems are another set of complex legal systems that relate directly to child maltreatment. Parents' failure to use educational systems may open families to allegations of educational neglect. Schools also gain significance because they have moved beyond traditional educational concerns (Levesque, 2002c). Schools increasingly take on duties that range from addressing the ills of poverty to fostering children's positive mental health (see, e.g., Individuals with Disabilities Education Act, 1990; No Child Left Behind Act, 2001). Given how these laws address what we know constitutes risk factors for maltreatment (e.g., poverty, discrimination, some disabilities), as well as factors that help prevent maltreatment (effective education), these actions could serve as powerful ways to address child maltreatment. Schools also address violence itself, as revealed by efforts to address peer harassment, bullying, and other harms like dating violence. School-based health and mental health services have the greatest likelihood of reaching more of those who need such services. It is not surprising, then, that schools have become important places to recognize, prevent, and respond to child maltreatment.

HOW DO WE KNOW IT? KEY DECISION POINTS

Although facing challenges and sometimes being marked by limitations, existing empirical studies do shed light on the nature, need, and effectiveness of justice system responses to child maltreatment (see Levesque, 2008). To render our analysis manageable, we examine findings that relate to key decision points in justice systems' responses and that highlight lessons for justice system reform.

Identifying Cases of Child Maltreatment

One of the most critical decision points in justice system is identification of potentially maltreating situations. This process continues to attract considerable controversy over whether it results in too many unsubstantiated results, whether mandated reporting results in too many unnecessary intrusions in children and families, whether even the mandated reporting approach still fails to uncover cases that would benefit from intervention, and whether voluntary help-seeking would make better use of resources. If the primary goal of mandatory reporting is to increase the number of cases, requiring professionals and others to report suspicions of maltreatment increases formal identification (Melton, 2005). The best evidence indicates increases with the advent of mandatory reporting, but research continues to find massive underreporting. It may be that entirely voluntary systems would yield similar or even better results. Self-reports of child maltreatment are much higher; an important study found that the incidence of physical abuse determined by maternal self-reports was up to 40 times greater than that of official child physical abuse reports, and the incidence of sexual abuse was 15 times greater (Theodore et al., 2005).

A fair examination of mandated reporting requires that we consider unintended consequences. Mandated reporting renders professionals the largest source of cases, but the majority of cases end in a lack of substantiation (Mathews & Bross, 2008). Better training could reduce reporting of cases that are not substantiated (Drake & Jonson-Reid, 2007). However, research questions whether substantiation should be the standard for measuring effective reporting. Research consistently reveals that substantiated and unsubstantiated cases are more or less similar. Nor does the receipt of services offer a good standard because (a) severe cases of maltreatment may not need services—the ties of family members could be more easily terminated without the provision of services—or (b) the maltreatment is not deemed serious enough to require services; a national probability study of service provision indicated that several rereports are often needed before services are deemed necessary to protect children (Kohl & Barth, 2007). The chances of disrupting treatment needed by abusers are increased by asking professionals to report cases of maltreatment (Levesque, 2002a). Nevertheless, professionals generally endorse mandated reporting laws and report that filing child maltreatment reports does more good than harm to therapeutic processes (Kalichman & Craig, 1991).

A flaw in the existing literature is that these studies have focused more on clinicians, and not, for example, on teachers, who also provide a large percentage of reports. Criticisms of reporting, such as its leading to the inefficient use of resources and unnecessary intrusion in families, actually may have more to do with how the system responds to referrals than how referrals are made to the system. In addition, apparently obvious standards to measure effectiveness may not be particularly useful in light of the complexities of the systems involved. Conclusions like these highlight a central lesson. When we examine research dealing with one decision point, it is important to consider the findings in the contexts of other relevant justice systems as well as those of professions involved in service delivery.

Addressing Children's Needs in Legal Proceedings

A second decision point that generates both research and controversy involves children's roles in the legal system. There are three areas of relevant research, of which the first is the extent to which children can be trusted as reporters of maltreatment and how the system may influence the likelihood of their telling the truth. Research has well documented that, especially in cases involving child sexual abuse, children questioned for the first time are likely to deny abuse and are susceptible to various pressures to recant (Lyon & Dorado, 2008). Research also reveals, however, that effective system responses may overcome children's denials of transgressions and increase the truthfulness of disclosures, including child-friendly versions of the oaths to report the truth increase (Lyon & Dorado, 2008). Researchers also have shown that structured interviews can increase the reliability of children's testimony and that interviewer training could be effective in soliciting more reliable evidence (Lamb, Orbach, Hershkowitz, Esplin, & Horowitz, 2007). Regrettably, both intensive and brief training programs for investigative interviewers may impart knowledge about desirable practices but appear to have little if any effect on the actual behavior of forensic investigators (Lamb et al., 2007). Also regrettably, we do not have comparable data for adults; adults involved in domestic violence are not immune from recanting to avoid assistance from criminal justice systems (Levesque, 2001).

The second area of research involves the rapid spread of child advocacy centers even in the absence of data addressing their effectiveness. These centers are distinctive for taking multijurisdictional approaches to interviewing children, as they include representation from law enforcement, child protective services, legal prosecution, and mental health, medical, and victim advocacy entities, as well as the centers themselves. Although participation from different systems may vary, centers tend to retain similar goals, such as reducing the number of interviews, using more child-sensitive investigations and, more controversially, increasing the number and success of prosecutions. A review of these efforts revealed some benefits but concluded that the centers may not, from the children's perspective, be more child friendly than other approaches and may not lead to more prosecutions (Faller & Palusci, 2007).

However, child advocacy centers vary in their implementation and remain difficult to evaluate.

The third important group of studies involves efforts to make courts more child friendly, including the use of out-of-court testimony through videotapes or closed-circuit television. The legal system has adapted itself to the use of these methods and now, with some restrictions, permits them (see Levesque, 2006). Research reveals that they reduce some harms that would have occurred had children testified live in the presence of juries and defendants, but alternative methods may decrease the credibility of child witnesses and reduce jurors' empathy toward the child—all of which predictably reduces jurors' confidence in defendants' guilt (Goodman et al., 2006).

Providing Services to Maltreating Families

A third decision point that research increasingly addresses involves what to do with families that are deemed to be maltreating. Because a substantial percentage of cases that identify children as maltreated do not result in the provision of services (see Levesque, 2002a), debate exists about whether services should be mandated. Evidence reveals that involuntary services provided through child welfare systems may not be viewed as punitive (Drake & Jonson-Reid, 2007), whereas other evidence indicates that the system may be experienced as punitive if there is potential threat of removing children from their families (Levesque, 2008). Overall, a variety of studies have found that about two thirds to three quarters of child welfare system clients are satisfied with investigative processes and services received; those services rank slightly lower than voluntary services from mental health systems (Drake & Jonson-Reid, 2007). Considerable legal consequences could attach to the finding that from one third to one quarter of families would experience the interventions as intrusive and unsatisfying. That percentage may be unacceptably high in a society concerned with intrusions on family privacy and child protection.

Another important research focus is the effectiveness of treatment, whether mandated or not, in keeping families intact and free from violence. Research reveals that families and their children who participate in court-ordered treatment may be more likely to complete treatment, showing signs of success such as an increased likelihood of remaining together compared with those that accept voluntary plans (see, e.g., MacMahon, 1997). Among the most encouraging research in this area is recent research involving family treatment drug courts. A careful experimental, four-site national study found that children who participated in the programs entered permanent treatment more quickly and were more likely to be united with their parents (Green, Furrer, Worcel, Burrus, & Finigan, 2007). Other studies report similar positive effects on family reunification and reveal the value added of treatment experiences for offenders (Boles, Young, Moore & Beard, 2007). Note, of course, that these studies involve drug offenders and the threat of criminal sanctions, which are permissible because of the criminal justice system's involvement.

Controlling Offenders and Protecting Communities

A fourth decision point involves how to respond to offenders, especially those who are not family members. Research shows that the use of criminal justice system responses is much less frequent than interventions by child welfare agencies. Once in the criminal justice system, however, prosecutions of crimes against children tend not to differ from other cases (Cross, Walsh, Simone, & Jones, 2003). Yet, subsequent to prosecution for crimes against children, offenders seem to again be treated differently by greater efforts to control them, compared with other offenders. Offender registration laws and civil commitment responses in the case of child sexual abuse illustrate well these developments.

One of the foundational rationales for the use of civil commitment is the belief that offenders can be rehabilitated and treated successfully. Yet, even the U.S. Supreme Court cases accepting this rationale have cited research indicating that there actually were no effective treatments for this type of case (see Levesque, 2006). Perhaps equally problematical, the policies often require predictions of dangerousness by clinicians. Although it may be true that emerging assessment tools are increasing in effectiveness, the Supreme Court approved of clinical judgments in predicting dangerousness when it was widely concluded that clinicians were worse than chance in predicting future offending behavior. The legal system permits the use of future dangerousness testimony even when the relevant scientific community's ethical standards would prohibit it.

In terms of offender registration policies, as well as related efforts including community notification, monitoring, and supervision, Cohen and Jeglic (2007) concluded that few studies support these new policies and that studies that do exist portray them as less than promising. The findings demonstrate that these efforts may indeed reach some intended effects, such as controlling offenders, but such effects may emerge at the cost of other important goals, such as the successful community reintegration of offenders (Levenson, D'Amora, & Hern, 2007). Similarly, definitions of effectiveness may well be too narrow. For example, even though we may be dealing with what would appear to be simple, enforceable rules that can be evaluated easily, research may lead to results that remain open to interpretations. Increasingly popular residential restrictions on high-risk offenders are illustrative. An innovative study of the implementation of residential restrictions found that 40% of high-risk offenders resided within 500 feet of a restricted zone as defined by the researchers (it included schools but not parks and other areas that other laws often include; Grubesic, Mack, & Murray, 2007). The ease with which one can travel 500 feet, especially when one is highly motivated, certainly calls into question these increasingly popular initiatives aiming to control offenders and protect society.

It remains quite remarkable how popular reforms often are undertaken and spread without the benefit of evaluations and may well continue and become widespread even though evaluations reveal concerns regarding the policies' collateral consequences or overall ineffectiveness. Perhaps even more disconcerting, the legal system may adopt rules that deliberately run counter to the best empirical evidence and even contradict the ethical standards of service providers. Clearly, empirical findings are but one factor that influences the development and administration of child protection policies.

WHAT ARE THE NEXT STEPS?

Justice system responses to child maltreatment rest on a variety of systems that claim different missions, possess a variety of capacities, and often reveal conflicting agendas. Because legal responses to children's harms emerge from fragmented systems, they generate a steady stream of pleas to ensure collaboration and greater consistency in how society addresses children's needs. The controversies provide a starting point for envisioning reform efforts. We focus on six examples of legal developments that must be addressed to enact successfully the types of systemic reforms championed by advocates and supported by research evaluating social responses to child maltreatment.

Engaging Appropriate Expertise

The study of child maltreatment provides some of the most vivid examples of the power of social science to transform deeply ingrained legal conceptions. The popularization of the battered child syndrome is a testament to the power of persuasive research, as is confirmation of the existence of foster care drift. This type of evidence contributed to reshaping who enters child welfare systems and how they are treated when in them (Levesque, 2008). Of course, research detailing the place of race in state-supported systems also has led to impressive changes in the nature of education, juvenile justice, and mental health systems. The potential role of experts and their evidence is enormous. Regrettably, the legal system is not known for embracing empirical findings, even those that are well accepted throughout the scientific community (Levesque, 2006). And even a cursory look at legal responses to child maltreatment, including the commentaries of legal scholars, reveals no exception to the tendency to resist social science research. For example, empirical research reveals that child neglect is the most prevalent form of maltreatment (Levesque, 2002a). Yet neglect remains neglected: legal responses and commentaries disproportionately focus on child sexual maltreatment. Studies also show how broad social forces—cultural, economic, and religious, among others—contribute to child maltreatment (Levesque, 2001). Yet the everyday life of those administering the legal system tends to focus on individual children, parents, and families. The legal system even allows social factors such as religious beliefs to serve as excuses for what otherwise would be deemed maltreatment. Numerous studies also document well the success of a wide variety of interventions and primary prevention programs. Yet the legal system can mainly focus on maltreatment that already has occurred. Embracing and reforming laws so that they would address these concerns certainly would lead to a radical transformation of our legal system and how we treat children. The limited extent to which research and expertise are used, then, tends to show that the legal system responds best to evidence that addresses practical legal concerns and that legal systems share a restricted ability to respond to situations.

Moving Outside of the Criminal Justice System

The growth of legal systems outside of the criminal justice system (most notably, the child welfare and juvenile justice systems) constitutes the most important development in addressing violence against children. These systems embrace different missions and goals that now buttress and complement the criminal justice system. Most notably, the systems outside of the criminal justice system were meant to focus on victims and risks of harm and to provide services that would enhance human development. The systems even have been transformed as sites meant to ensure broader social justice and healthy development. Rather than focusing on punishing those who have harmed children and seeking to foster general deterrence, the systems have sought and continue to offer assistance to victims as well as those who have harmed or simply were at risk of harming children. The systems also provide broad resources that shape society's social fabric, to the extent that commentators often ignore the significance of these systems for protecting children from harm and for fostering environments that reduce the risk of harm.

The development and use of legal systems outside of the criminal justice system has not escaped controversy. Most notably, their use has been viewed as insufficiently focused on reducing violence against children. Supporting this line of argument is the low percentage of parents who are prosecuted for having killed their children and the low percentage of prosecutions for other crimes against children, compared with prosecutions for similar abuses against adults (see Martell, 2005). In many ways, there appears to be a "family discount" in penalties for a variety of crimes relating to families. There also appears to be a parallel discounting in the civil justice system. Most notably, commentators find it odd that laws can permit parents to discriminate against their children and that the state can support such discrimination, as revealed by some well-established religious and cultural exceptions to child maltreatment (see Levesque, 2001). Similarly, legal systems have been viewed as problematic when they permit parents to control the mental and medical treatment of their children, both in terms of inappropriately providing treatment or not providing it when necessary (Levesque, 2002a). Despite the benefits of moving outside of the criminal justice system, then, the use of other systems, as well as the nature of the systems themselves, still can create unsatisfactory approaches to children's health and development. An important standard against which to evaluate responses to child maltreatment likely includes ensuring that children are being treated fairly even when they are being treated differently from adults.

Retaining Different Views of Rights

Related to different goals and missions, the systems charged with assisting children remain controversial to the extent that they use methods and procedures that rest on different conceptions of rights. The civil systems, most notably, generally involve rights that require reduced protections, an approach that permits the discretion shaping the systems' preventive stance. This discretion permits flexibility, wise decision making, and a more aggressive identification of cases for intervention even when no actual harms have occurred. The discretion reaches widely, from child welfare workers to school personnel and to mental health staff and others who interact with children.

The fundamental challenge of providing the state with more power to intervene in family life—even in the absence of observable harm—is that systems necessarily must reduce the rights of those subjected to interventions. When child welfare services intervene, for example, families have reduced search and seizure rights and may not have the right to counsel, and states have reduced burdens of proof to support invasive interventions. The effects of reduced rights reverberate and contribute to several other limitations that result from using a civil justice–based approach to address children's harms. Although discretion may be necessary to protect some children effectively, discretion does come with costs when it leaves room for considerable bias by those who implement laws. Criticisms of the child welfare system are illustrative. Individuals belonging to certain groups inevitably suffer more intrusions into their personal relationships than do other groups. Although it is important not to generalize across caseworkers, the system as a whole evinces bias against nonmajority racial groups and those living in poverty, as well as other minorities, such as nonheterosexual parents (see Levesque, 2008). Although that bias may be embedded in the laws, the bias continues even when laws do not require differential treatment. Of course, the same charge of biased treatment may be levied against the criminal justice system. However, even those parents not belonging to minority groups have reduced rights when systems other than the criminal justice system respond to allegations of victimization, even though the state's intrusion in their personal affairs can be equally damaging.

Such issues have gained increasing urgency as legal developments support efforts to move outside of traditional legal systems, and their concomitant legal protections, to resolve family dysfunction and offer services. For example, private charities always have played a dominant role in child welfare responses (Myers, 2006). Their role certainly still remains, but it continues to change as they increasingly accept funds from take government-supported sources. Challenges, in this regard, arise to the extent that individuals have rights against state actions; however, their civil rights against private groups remain much murkier, if recognized at all. When private organizations play governmental roles, issues inevitably arise in terms of the rights of individuals who access those services (Levesque, 2002b).

Uniting Multiple Legal Systems

The differences in goals and legal rules have led to significant developments that seek to coordinate responses from multiple systems. By far, the most important development is multidisciplinary teams that seek to coordinate and ensure collaborations in investigations of maltreatment allegations. Typically, these processes occur with investigative professionals (e.g., law enforcement, child welfare workers, prosecutors) and others concerned with children's safety and protection (e.g., victim advocates, mental health professionals). Successful teams cultivate collaborative environments that permit members to benefit from each others' expertise. These efforts do report considerable success (Levesque, 2008), and they are of considerable significance given that many youth served by one system satisfy the legal criteria required to trigger the intervention of others. And, when children are not served appropriately in one system, they cross over to others. These teams clearly reveal the potential for public policies that would combat the lack of coordination among fragmented systems that, on their own, cannot meet the needs of children, their families, and their communities.

Despite potential benefits, important limitations remain that hamper efforts to offer more appropriately comprehensive interventions. The use of teams does not eradicate problems that arise from the distinct system-specific nomenclatures typically used to describe children in need and their eligibility for services, and legal jurisdictions obscure the substantial overlap among the children who fall within these systems' mandates. Problems due to differences in basic definitions are exacerbated by legal mandates that may conflict with those of other systems. Each system still consists of various collections of professionals, facilities, agencies, and organizations operating in both public and private sectors. These collections are all funded by an assortment of local, state, and federal sources and are controlled differently by them.

The different (yet sometimes highly related) systems' missions also are of significance. The multidisciplinary approach has long been used by children's advocacy centers, but it primarily has been limited to cases involving sexual maltreatment and the most egregious cases of physical abuse and neglect. This is unsurprising given that criminal justice systems focus much more on sexual abuse and severe physical abuse allegations than on neglect. As a result, these teams deal only with a minority of the total cases and certainly do not address well those less extreme cases that go unrecognized but could be reached through broader efforts. Collaboration remains challenging to implement and has yet to focus on broader system levels.

Responding to Shifting and Conflicting Legal Landscapes

Shifting legal mandates, especially those that conflict with prior ones, may well be for the better, but they do make it difficult to develop more effective systems. Legally, for example, the development of children's rights actually remains problematic because our legal system generally retains a profound attachment to parental rights. Children increasingly have rights within their homes and outside of them. For example, children now have greater independent rights to services, such as in cases of emergencies, or when they can show that their parents would harm them if they sought their consent, or when they are deemed mature enough. We do not, however, have a consistent jurisprudence of children's rights. It is equally problematic that we no longer have a consistent jurisprudence of parental rights. Most notably, even the long-established simple rule that parents retain their rights as long as they are not abusive becomes quickly unhelpful in practice. How abusive must parents be to forfeit their parental rights? Which rights do they lose? How much of a right do they lose when they lose one? When do they lose different rights? In addition to these complexities, the very foundations on which these rights have been developed still undergo development. Supreme Court cases have revisited the right to privacy, which constitutes one of the most important ways the legal system protects relationships (*Lawrence v. Texas*, 2003); and the Court has revisited the notion of what constitutes children's best interests, the types of relationships a legal system can protect, and when the legal system can seek to protect children's relationships that are, for example, outside of traditionally defined (nuclear) families (*Troxell v. Granville*, 2000). How these recent cases will develop remains to be seen, just as it remains to be determined how these types of cases will influence the way we differentiate the rights of children from those of their parents.

In addition to jurisprudential developments, we have seen important new developments in the federal government's role in children's lives within the child welfare, health, criminal justice, juvenile, and educational systems. There is a widespread need to develop standards, yet states' responses remain challenging to the extent that, in many arenas, state laws continue to conflict with federal mandates. The disparities continue even when states, in theory, are supposed to follow federal mandates or forgo significant amounts of federal funds. Some of the clearest instances of disparities involve the special procedures meant to protect children who provide testimony in criminal proceedings and the development of rules of evidence meant to accommodate children's needs, the different state rules that regulate the case plans child welfare agencies are supposed to develop when they remove children from their homes, and even such basic responses as the definitions of what constitutes child maltreatment. These potential areas of conflict are likely to continue given that states essentially may choose whether and how to respond to federal legislative mandates that themselves may be open to different interpretations. These developments mean that we have a wide variety of legal systems that may or may not work well together and that may actually conflict.

Envisioning Different Systems

Our close look at legal concerns attendant to treating children's harms differently reveals the fundamental limitations of reform proposals offered by leading commentators. Several offer well-received suggestions that, although nuanced, develop common themes. Some suggest that we must draw strict lines between neglect and abuse and then have law enforcement address severe abuse while social workers focus on neglect (Guggenheim, 2005; Lindsey, 2003). Others argue, though, that all investigative and coercive aspects of child welfare systems should be conducted by law enforcement; caseworkers would then be free to respond nonpunitively and better assist troubled families (Pelton, 1989). Some would focus on more aggressive termination of parental rights (Gelles, 1996), whereas others also would do so but highlight the availability of adoption as the most realistic way to deal with current child welfare system crises (Bartholet, 1999). Others champion the need to focus on establishing voluntary, nonpunitive access to help for troubled parents (U.S. Advisory Board on Child Abuse and Neglect, 1993). Still others argue for a differential response, one that would have child protective systems involved but serving less as investigative agencies and more as resources that assess the needs of families and guide them to formal and informal help from private and public agencies, including the criminal justice system (Myers, 2006; Waldfogel, 1998). We do not suffer for lack of proposals.

Although important, none of the suggestions for reform could be undertaken without significant reforms in the legal rules in which they would operate. For example, moving aggressively to sever ties between parents and abused children remains a challenge given the reality that parents have constitutional rights to parent their children as they deem fit and have a right to family privacy that protects them from state intrusions. Similarly, suggesting a response that would remove investigative roles from caseworkers remains problematic because caseworkers inevitably would have relevant evidence that could be useful to law enforcement. Lessening reliance on caseworkers would be problematic because law enforcement's abilities to investigate and respond to allegations are subject to more limitations. Similar concerns arise for voluntary systems, which could raise problematic and complex legal issues when they would confront abusive situations. Focusing on less severe forms of abuse in one system and on more severe forms in another also may be problematic to the extent that maltreatment constitutes a continuum of severity from mild to severe, and such determinations would require, among other things, investigation and legal rules that would be difficult, if not impossible, to develop and implement. Granting some systems increased discretion runs the risk of creating systems marked by biases and invidious discrimination. Any of the serious proposals to reshape social responses to child maltreatment require a close examination of legal rules and principles that reach beyond narrowly defined child welfare systems. Regrettably, a clear understanding of legal rules is difficult to come by. Our legal system is exceedingly nuanced and is undergoing important changes, and our system of laws thrives on diversity and experimentation. Indeed, and as we have seen, the laws regulating this area increasingly result in conflicting and overlapping legal mandates.

CONCLUSION

Great social and legal ambivalence continues to shape state interventions in families and children's lives. Even the Supreme Court itself evinces conflicting views. In some cases, the Court criticizes the legal systems for casting their nets too broadly and for overreaching in children's and families' domains. At the same time, the Court has deemed fit to pronounce the systems as failing to protect adequately children's needs and to foster their healthy development. These criticisms are not new. Since their inceptions, social service delivery institutions have struggled with mixed agendas: providing for the welfare of children by protecting their relationships, health, and safety while still, when necessary, removing them from their homes or otherwise circumventing parental rights claims in the name of children's health and safety. These systems' missions become balancing acts between interfering with parents' venerable right to raise their children as they deem fit and society's compelling obligation to protect vulnerable children. These purposes can either coincide or diverge when put into practice. Clear and permanent lines are not likely to develop; society continues to change and legal systems attempt to adapt to those changes.

Despite ambivalence and persistent change, foundational principles continue to guide legal system responses to children and families. Most notably, the state's *parens patriae* and police power interests in promoting children's welfare continue to justify intervention (both apparent and subtle) in families and their regulation of children's lives. The ways society seeks to serve these principles certainly continues to change, but the rationales that support them do not. The rapid expansion of state services and the infusion of services in our everyday lives simply reflect efforts to respond to those rationales. It remains our obligation to ensure that state responses remain compatible with core legal traditions of valuing parent–child relationships and family integrity, ensuring freedom from unnecessary institutionalization and incarceration, integrating those deemed different into community life, recognizing the need to respond to the best social science available, reducing unwarranted prejudices in the manner society treats children and groups of children and their families, and fostering children's positive development into well-adjusted and constructively contributing members of society. These enduring traditions necessarily must be part of our constantly developing efforts to respond to violence against children.

REFERENCES

Adoption Assistance and Child Welfare Act of 1980. Pub. L. No. 96-272, 94 Stat. 500.

Adoption and Safe Families Act of 1997. Pub. L. No. 105-89, 111 Stat. 2115.

Bartholet, E. (1999). *Nobody's children: Abuse and neglect, foster drift, and the adoption alternative*. Boston, MA: Beacon Press.

Boles, S. M., Young, N. K., Moore, T., & Beard, S. D. (2007). The Sacramento dependency drug court: Development and outcomes. *Child Maltreatment, 12*, 161–171. doi:10.1177/1077559507300643

Boxer, P., & Terranova, A.M. (2008). Effects of multiple maltreatment experiences among psychiatrically hospitalized youth. *Child Abuse & Neglect, 32*, 637–647.

Child Abuse Prevention and Treatment Act of 1974. Pub. L. No. 93-247, 88 Stat. 5, 42 U.S.C. §§ 5101-5107.

Cohen, M., & Jeglic, E. L. (2007). Sex offender legislation in the United States: What do we know? *International Journal of Offender Therapy and Comparative Criminology, 51*, 369–383. doi:10.1177/0306624X06296235

Coleman, D. L. (2005). Storming the castle to save the children: The ironic costs of a child welfare exception to the Fourth Amendment. *William and Mary Law Review, 47*, 413–540.

Cross, T. P., Walsh, W. A., Simone, M., & Jones, L. M. (2003). Prosecution of child abuse: A meta-analysis of rates of criminal justice decisions. *Trauma, Violence & Abuse, 4*, 323–340. doi:10.1177/1524838003256561

Drake, B., & Jonson-Reid, M. (2007). A response to Melton based on the best available data. *Child Abuse & Neglect, 31*, 343–360. doi:10.1016/j.chiabu.2006.08.009

Faller, K. C., & Palusci, V. J. (2007). Children's advocacy centers: Do they lead to positive outcomes? *Child Abuse & Neglect, 31*, 1021–1029. doi:10.1016/j.chiabu.2007.09.001

Finkelhor, D., & Ormrod, R. (2001). *Offenders incarcerated for crimes against juveniles.* Office of Juvenile Justice and Delinquency Prevention, U.S. Department of Justice. Retrieved from http://www.ncjrs.gov/html/ojjdp/jjbul2001_12_3/contents.html

Gelles, R. (1996). *The book of David: How preserving families can cost children's lives.* New York, NY: Basic Books.

Goodman, G. S., Myers, J. E. B., Qin, J., Quas, J., Castelli, P., Redlich, A. D., & Rogers, L. (2006). Hearsay versus children's testimony: Effects of truthful and deceptive statements on jurors' decisions. *Law and Human Behavior, 30*, 363–401. doi:10.1007/s10979-006-9009-0

Green, B. L., Furrer, C., Worcel, S., Burrus, S., & Finigan, M. W. (2007). How effective are family treatment drug courts? Outcomes from a four-site national study. *Child Maltreatment, 12*, 43–59. doi:10.1177/1077559506296317

Grubesic, T., Mack, E., & Murray, A. T. (2007). Geographic exclusion: Spatial analysis for evaluating the implications of Megan's Law. *Social Science Computer Review, 25*, 143–162. doi:10.1177/0894439307298930

Guggenheim, M. (2005). *What's wrong with children's rights.* Cambridge, MA: Harvard University Press.

Individuals with Disabilities Education Act of 1990. Pub. L. No. 101-476, 104 Stat. 1103 (codified as amended at 20 U.S.C. 1400 et seq. [2005]).

In re Gault, 387 U.S. 1 (1967).

Kalichman, S., & Craig, M. (1991). Professional psychologist's decision to report suspected child abuse: Clinician and situation influences. *Professional Psychology, 22*(1), 84–89. doi:10.1037/0735-7028.22.1.84

Kohl, P. L., & Barth, R. P. (2007). Child maltreatment recurrence among children remaining in-home: Predictors of re-reports. In R. Haskins, F. Wulczyn, & M. Bruce Webb (Eds.), *Child protection: Using research to improve policy and practice* (pp. 207–225). Washington, DC: Brookings Institution Press.

Lamb, M. E., Orbach, Y., Hershkowitz, I., Esplin, P. W., & Horowitz, D. (2007). A structured forensic interview protocol improves the quality and informativeness of investigative interviews with children: A review of research using the NICHD Investigative Interview Protocol. *Child Abuse & Neglect, 31*, 1201–1231. doi:10.1016/j.chiabu.2007.03.021

Lawrence v. Texas, 539 U.S. 558 (2003).

Levenson, J. S., D'Amora, D. A., & Hern, A. L. (2007). Megan's Law and its impact on community re-entry for sex offenders. *Behavioral Sciences & the Law, 25,* 587–602. doi:10.1002/bsl.770

Levesque, R. J. R. (2000). *Adolescents, sex, and the law: Preparing adolescents for responsible citizenship.* Washington, DC: American Psychological Association. doi:10.1037/10342-000

Levesque, R. J. R. (2001). *Culture and family violence: Fostering change through human rights law.* Washington, DC: American Psychological Association. doi:10.1037/10432-000

Levesque, R. J. R. (2002a). *Child maltreatment and the law: Foundations in science, policy and practice.* Durham, NC: Carolina Academic Press.

Levesque, R. J. R. (2002b). *Not by faith alone: Religion, adolescence and the law.* New York, NY: New York University Press.

Levesque, R. J. R. (2002c). *Violent adolescents, model adolescents: Shaping the role and promise of education.* New York, NY: Plenum.

Levesque, R. J. R. (2006). *The psychology and law of criminal justice processes.* Hauppauge, NY: Nova Science.

Levesque, R. J. R. (2008). *Child maltreatment and the law: Returning to first principles.* New York, NY: Springer. doi:10.1007/978-0-387-79918-6

Lindsey, D. (2003). *The welfare of children.* New York, NY: Oxford University Press. doi:10.1093/acprof:oso/9780195136715.001.0001

Lyon, T. D., & Dorado, J. S. (2008). Truth induction in young maltreated children: The effects of oath-taking and reassurance on true and false disclosures. *Child Abuse & Neglect, 32*, 738–748. doi:10.1016/j.chiabu.2007.08.008

MacMahon, J. (1997). Perinatal substance abuse: The impact of reporting infants to child protective services. *Pediatrics, 100*, 5, e1.

Martell, D. R. (2005). *Criminal justice and the placement of abused children.* New York, NY: LFB Scholarly Publishing.

Mathews, B., & Bross, D. C. (2008). Mandated reporting is still a policy with reason: Empirical evidence and philosophical grounds. *Child Abuse & Neglect, 32,* 511–516. doi:10.1016/j.chiabu.2007.06.010

Melton, G. B. (2005). Mandated reporting: A policy without reason. *Child Abuse & Neglect, 29,* 9–18. doi:10.1016/j.chiabu.2004.05.005

Myers, J. (2006). *Child protection in America.* New York, NY: Oxford University Press. doi:10.1093/acprof:oso/9780195169355.001.0001

National Clearinghouse on Child Abuse and Neglect Information. (2006). *Summary of key findings*. Washington, DC: U.S. Department of Health and Human Services.

No Child Left Behind Act of 2001. Pub. L. No. 107-110, 115 Stat. 1425 (codified as amended at 20 U.S.C. 6316(b)(1)(E)) (Supp. II 2002).

Pelton, L. (1989). *For reasons of poverty: A critical analysis of the American child welfare system*. Westport, CT: Praeger.

Theodore, A., Chang, J., Runyan, D., Hunter, W., Bangdiwala, S., & Agans, R. (2005). Epidemiologic feature of the physical and sexual maltreatment of children in the Carolinas. *Pediatrics, 115*, e331–337. doi:10.1542/peds.2004-1033

Troxell v. Granville, 530 U.S. 57 (2000).

U.S. Advisory Board on Child Abuse and Neglect. (1993). *Neighbors helping neighbors: A new national strategy for the protection of children*. Washington, DC: U.S. Government Printing Office.

Waldfogel, J. (1998). *The future of child protection*. Boston, MA: Harvard University Press.

4

PRIMARY PREVENTION OF CHILD ABUSE AND MALTREATMENT

JOHN ECKENRODE

Annually, about 1 million children are maltreated in the United States (U.S. Department of Health and Human Services, 2008). Since Kempe's seminal work in the 1960s (Kempe, Silverman, Steele, Droegemueller, & Silver, 1962) on the battered child syndrome, public awareness of this social problem has increased, as have significant federal and state efforts to establish child protective systems to identify maltreated children and respond to their needs. Large-scale epidemiological studies such as the National Incidence Studies (e.g., Sedlak & Broadhurst, 1996) and the National Survey of Child and Adolescent Well-being (Dowd et al., 2008) have described more accurately the scope and nature of the maltreatment problem and associated risk factors. Many private not-for-profit advocacy organizations that promote research, prevention, and treatment (e.g., Prevent Child Abuse America, National Children's Advocacy Center) have emerged, practitioners working with abused and neglected children (e.g., American Professional Society on the Abuse of Children) have become more professionalized, and child maltreatment has become a recognized subspecialty in fields beyond social work, such as psychology and pediatrics.

Although the prevention of child maltreatment has long been advocated, it has gained increased attention in recent years. The purpose of this chapter is to provide an overview of the state of current knowledge with regard to primary prevention efforts of child maltreatment. It complements previous chapters in this volume that focus attention on treatment approaches to victims and offenders as well as justice approaches to these issues.

The multiple approaches to child maltreatment prevention reflect a complex understanding of the risk and protective factors operating at multiple levels of analysis—from the individual parent and child to the larger society (MacMillan et al., 2009; Wolfe, 1999). Most scientifically evaluated prevention efforts have been designed to intervene at the level of the individual (parent, child) or family. Community-level or societal-level interventions are more difficult to implement and evaluate. However, a few community-level interventions are discussed here.

Various frameworks characterize prevention efforts in this field, some descriptive and some more theoretical. Two prominent ones are the developmental–ecological model and the public health model. In the developmental–ecological model (Belsky, 1993; Cicchetti & Lynch, 1993), maltreatment is proposed to result from a complex interaction of risk and protective factors operating at the levels of individuals, families, and communities and within the broader society and culture. This model suggests that narrow interventions, such as parenting classes, that are focused on single risk factors or one aspect of the ecological domain are unlikely to have much impact on community rates of child maltreatment unless combined with other interventions that address the multiple conditions that compromise parents' caregiving ability.

The public health model organizes prevention into primary, secondary, and tertiary efforts. Public health approaches tend to focus on primary prevention. In recent years the primary–secondary–tertiary distinction has been replaced in some writings by the terms *universal*, *selective*, and *indicated* (Kellam & Langevin, 2003; Mrazek & Haggerty, 1994). Universal interventions are directed at whole populations, such as media campaigns. Selective interventions target a smaller portion of the population at somewhat increased risk, such as family support or training programs for low-income parents. Indicated interventions target an even smaller population of those at greatest risk, such as programs aimed at preventing recurrence of maltreatment among parents who have had prior involvement with child protective services.

In addition to identifying and classifying prevention efforts, researchers have been paying more attention to the strength of the evidence for program effectiveness. However, relatively few scientifically rigorous evaluations of primary prevention programs have been conducted, some of which are reviewed subsequently in this chapter.

WHAT DO WE KNOW?

This section summarizes the current state of knowledge about programs with proven efficacy in preventing maltreatment. Priority is given to programs evaluated using randomized controlled trials while recognizing some of the limitations of experimental approaches (McCall & Green, 2004). Space constraints did not allow for the description of other programs that may also prove beneficial in preventing maltreatment, such as the Family Connections program serving low-income parents at risk for child neglect (DePanfilis & Dubowitz, 2005) or Project Safecare, which has shown promise in reducing re-reports of maltreatment among families reported to child protective services (Gershater-Molko, Lutzker, & Wesch, 2002).

Home Visitation for Parents

Perinatal home visitation has received considerable attention as a maltreatment prevention strategy for families with children under the age of 3 years (e.g., Bilukha et al., 2005). The common element of these programs is that services are delivered in the parents' home, but they vary widely in terms of the background and training of the visitors, the frequency and content of the visits, the populations served, and their effectiveness (Guterman, 2001). The goal is to reduce risk factors for maltreatment, such as risky prenatal health behaviors, lack of knowledge and skills, and closely spaced births, and promote sensitive, competent care of the child by providing parents with support, information, teaching, and referrals to community services. The evidence supporting the effectiveness of home visitation has been mixed, reflecting differences in program models and populations addressed (Olds, Sadler, & Kitzman, 2007; Sweet & Appelbaum, 2004). Efforts at disseminating home visiting programs began when the evidence supporting their efficacy was quite limited. To date, few studies of perinatal home visiting using randomized designs have reported evidence for reductions in official state-verified reports of maltreatment or in parent self-reports of behaviors that constitute maltreatment (Olds et al., 2007).

Although the current scientific data would suggest a cautious and incremental approach to the widespread implementation of home visitation programs, policymakers and advocates in the child maltreatment field have widely promoted home visitation programs as a means of preventing child abuse and neglect. Many home visitation efforts supported by states and local communities have adopted programs such as Healthy Families America (Daro & Harding, 1999), the Nurse–Family Partnership program (Olds, Hill,

Robinson, Song, & Little, 2000), and Parents as Teachers (Wagner, Spiker, & Linn, 2002).

The most consistent evidence for the efficacy of perinatal home visiting in preventing child maltreatment comes from the Nurse–Family Partnership program. This program represents a 30-year effort to examine the effectiveness of home visiting by nurses to at-risk pregnant and parenting mothers and their children (Olds et al., 2000). The first randomized trial was conducted in Elmira, New York, the second in Memphis, Tennessee, and the most recent in Denver, Colorado. Initial evaluation of the Elmira study showed that perinatal nurse home visitation resulted in a significant reduction in the rate of verified cases of child maltreatment during the first 2 years of their children's lives among the most at-risk women, those who were poor, unmarried, and teenagers (Olds, Henderson, Chamberlin, & Tatelbaum, 1986).

A follow-up study of the Elmira families conducted when the children were 15 years old confirmed that the early effects of the program in reducing maltreatment were not only sustained but became stronger over time, with nurse-visited families having significantly fewer substantiated child maltreatment reports over that 15-year period (Olds et al., 1997). This study provided the first evidence from a randomized trial for the long-term effects of home visitation on rates of child maltreatment. A subsequent analysis showed that the program was most effective in reducing maltreatment reports for the four fifths of mothers in the study reporting low to moderate levels of domestic violence (Eckenrode et al., 2000).

A replication of the Nurse–Family Partnership program in Memphis did not find treatment effects on official reports of child maltreatment because the rates of confirmed reports in Memphis were too low to permit detection of a treatment effect (Kitzman et al., 1997). However, consistent with the Elmira trial, this study found that children of nurse-visited mothers had fewer and less severe health-related encounters and hospitalizations for injuries and ingestions consistent with inadequate parenting, as well as more positive ratings of the home environment.

Findings from studies evaluating the impact of other home visitation programs, such as Healthy Families America, have shown no or very limited effects on reductions in child maltreatment (Chaffin, 2004; Olds et al., 2007). For example, an evaluation of the Hawaii Healthy Start Program, the predecessor of Healthy Families America (Duggan et al., 2004), reported no effects for confirmed child maltreatment reports, parent's reports of abusive caregiving, or observations of care in the home during the children's first 2 years of life. Mothers did report less neglectful behavior in the first 3 years of the child's life. A more recent evaluation of a randomized trial of the Alaska Healthy Families program showed no effect on state-verified cases of maltreatment, although mothers in the intervention group reported lower rates of milder physical and psychological punishment compared with controls by age 2 (Duggan et al., 2007).

Similarly, a recent randomized trial of the Healthy Families America program in New York State showed no effect on substantiated child protective services reports through age 2, although home-visited parents reported having committed fewer acts of serious physical abuse in the past year than the control group (DuMont et al., 2008). The effects were stronger among first-time teen mothers and women with low psychological resources (lower IQ, low efficacy, more depression), similar to findings for the Nurse–Family Partnership program (Olds et al., 2000). A small randomized study on an enhanced Healthy Families America model (targeting negative attributions for babies' crying) found less self-reported harsh parenting and lower rates of physical abuse compared with the unenhanced version of Healthy Families or a control group (Bugental et al., 2002). This finding suggests that theory-based enhancements to existing models may lead to improved outcomes in future studies.

Parents as Teachers is a popular, nationally disseminated program that works with parents of children under age 3 in their homes and with group meetings (Wagner, Spiker, & Linn, 2002). Its Born to Learn curriculum has been adopted by other home visiting programs, such as Healthy Families America. Three experimental studies have been published: one of a program serving primarily Latino parents, one serving teen parents where the intervention was enhanced with case management, and a larger multisite study (Wagner, Spiker, & Linn, 2002). The only program effect directly related to maltreatment was found in the teen study: No open child protective services cases occurred in the control group, compared with 2.4% in an enhanced treatment group (using case management). This single finding, however, was not corroborated with other findings on parenting or child outcomes, or on observed or reported quality of the home environment.

In sum, home visiting programs vary considerably in terms of staffing, visit protocols, families served, the timing and number of visits, quality controls, and scientific evidence for efficacy. Few experimental studies have directly varied program components, but comparisons across studies suggest that home visiting programs are more likely to be successful in preventing dysfunctional parenting and child maltreatment if they focus on higher risk parents (e.g., low-income, unmarried, or teen mothers; higher risk children), begin visits during pregnancy, use nurses or other professionals as visitors, visit frequently (30 or more times) and over a long period (2 or more years), use a variety of strategies (teaching, modeling, rehearsal, referrals), and address the psychosocial needs of the parent while supporting the child's development.

School-Based Programs

Schools have been an important setting for child maltreatment prevention efforts, especially concerning issues of sexual abuse. Several curricula designed for children have been developed and evaluated that focus on the prevention of sexual abuse and abduction (MacMillan, MacMillan, Offord, Griffith, & MacMillan, 1994). Examples are Body Safety Training (Wurtele, 2007), Talking About Touching (Committee for Children, 2001), and Good-Touch/Bad Touch (Church, 1983). The curricula typically involve some combination of videos, printed matter, and instruction by adults. Some programs have tried to involve parents by including parent education meetings and sending materials home. Through these curricula, children learn about their own bodies; about different kinds of touches (good and bad, safe and unsafe); to say "no"; to leave risky situations; and that secrets about touching can and should be told to a trusted adult (Kenny, Capri, Thakkar-Kolar, Ryan, & Runyon, 2008).

A meta-analysis combining the results of 16 school-based programs evaluated with randomized or quasi-randomized studies was conducted by the Cochrane Collaborative (Zwi et al., 2007). Complementing previous meta-analyses and reviews (e.g., Davis & Gidycz, 2000), this meta-analysis showed that most studies reported (a) significant improvements in knowledge measures, although none of the studies measured knowledge retention beyond 12 months; (b) some positive effects on protective behaviors in simulated risk situations; and (c) stronger effects among 8- to- 13-year-olds than with younger children. Programs that employ concrete concepts, such as behavioral skills, reinforced with different forms of media (e.g., written materials, film, theater) and an interactive experience that includes rehearsal and modeling, appear to have stronger effects. Few studies, including those involving parents, have shown effects on reducing actual incidents of sexual abuse. One national survey showed that exposure to assault prevention programs was not associated with a reduced incidence of victimization or injury, although it was associated with a greater likelihood that children would disclose the victimization and not blame themselves (Finkelhor, Asdigian, & Dziuba-Leatherman, 1995).

There is still much to learn about whether the knowledge gains demonstrated with these programs translate into fewer incidences of sexual abuse in the general population over a long period of time. Questions have also been raised as to the effectiveness of such programs when the perpetrator is known and trusted by the child and whether it is fair to place the responsibility for the prevention of sexual abuse on young children. Programs such as these are not a replacement for adult responsibility and must be viewed alongside other community efforts to ensure child safety (Zwi et al., 2007).

Comprehensive approaches target high-risk children as they enter school and are designed to promote general developmental competencies and actively involve teachers and parents. They are leading the way to future school-based approaches that aim to prevent all forms of child maltreatment. The Chicago Child–Parent Centers program begins in preschool for children in high-poverty neighborhoods and provides a variety of family support services inside and outside the schools (Reynolds, 2000). Particular emphasis is on increasing parental involvement with their children in school and at home. In addition to finding effects on school achievement and reductions in juvenile offenses when these children reached adolescence, long-term evaluations of the program also showed that child participants were less likely to be maltreated, as measured by court petitions and child protective service involvement (Reynolds & Robertson, 2003).

Preschool programs such as Early Head Start also represent an important opportunity for child maltreatment prevention. Though not specifically designed to prevent maltreatment, the program is intended to improve the home environment and parenting practices for low-income families and therefore may indirectly affect maltreatment. A variety of strategies are used, including home visits, child care, case management, parenting education, health care and referrals, and family support. Local programs choose whether to employ a home-based model (primarily using paraprofessionals), a center-based model, or a mix of the two.

A randomized trial of 3,000 families in 17 programs reported results when children were 3 years old (Love et al., 2005). Compared with the control group, Early Head Start parents were rated as having more supportive and safe home environments, were more supportive to their children in play, read more to their children, and reported spanking less. It is noteworthy that the program effects on parenting were stronger in the mixed model than in home visiting alone. However, few Early Head Start programs employed comprehensive home visiting models like the Nurse–Family Partnership, so this evaluation did not provide a robust test of the possible impacts on parenting of a model that combined a strong, theory-driven home visiting component with a center-based service focused on cognitive and social development.

Multilevel Public Health Interventions

Universal prevention efforts such as public education and information campaigns through the media represent important tools for raising public awareness of the problem of child maltreatment, reinforcing community standards regarding the care of children, raising funds for community initiatives, and exerting public pressure on governmental bodies to institute policies and programs to support children (Daro & Donnelly, 2002). Ultimately, effective child maltreatment prevention approaches require a comprehensive community-based strategy that combines universal and more targeted programs. Although public awareness campaigns are potentially a valuable prevention strategy, their effectiveness can be difficult to judge and they are likely to affect only a more motivated subpopulation of the target audience. For individuals who are not literate or who are isolated from the media, other locally based efforts that directly reach parents must be employed. Even the best evidence-based programs aimed at high-risk populations reach only a small portion of eligible parents. To increase the numbers of persons who receive prevention efforts, some programs have attempted to develop multilevel interventions that combine relatively inexpensive approaches that reach large numbers of parents with more targeted and intensive approaches that reach higher risk parents. Two examples of multifaceted programs that are supported by considerable evidence include efforts to prevent shaken baby syndrome and the Triple P program.

Shaken Baby Syndrome

Shaking is a major cause of serious head injury leading to death and neurological problems in children aged 2 years or younger (Keenan et al., 2003). Shaken baby syndrome is often the result of anger triggered by a baby's inconsolable crying (Barr, Trent, & Cross, 2006). Universal primary prevention programs, organized in part by the National Center on Shaken Baby Syndrome (http://www.dontshake.org) have used a variety of strategies to educate the public and individual parents, such as TV and radio public service announcements, educational materials given to health care facilities, and hospital-based programs for new parents. An evaluation of a large-scale program involving a brief hospital-based educational program using print and video materials in 16 hospitals in New York State showed a 47% reduction in the incidence of abusive head trauma cases in the years following the start of the program (compared with previous statewide data and using Pennsylvania as a control; Dias et al., 2005).

More research is needed to confirm the efficacy of such multicomponent approaches. But this work suggests that a simple, inexpensive program with a strong message delivered at a critical period when parents are receptive to receiving information can be effective in preventing this form of physical abuse. A statewide intervention program currently under way in North Carolina, the Period of PURPLE Crying (Runyan, Zolotor, Barr, & Murphy, 2009), combines a hospital-based and health-provider-delivered educational program together with a media campaign designed to influence social norms against shaking. PURPLE is an acronym for characteristics of difficult-to-manage crying episodes. This work builds on two recent experimental studies in Washington state and British Columbia that showed that delivering PURPLE materials in prenatal classes, maternity ward stays, or pediatric visits increased maternal knowledge considered important to shaken-baby prevention and resulted in more mothers sharing this information with others (Barr et al., 2009).

The Triple P Program

One of the few examples of a population-based approach to the prevention of problematic parenting, including child maltreatment, is the Triple P program developed in Australia by Sanders and colleagues (Sanders, Markie-Dadds, & Turner, 2003). Triple P is designed to train parents to increase positive interactions and to use less coercive practices when dealing with behavior problems in children from birth to age 16, and it thus has the potential to prevent maltreatment, especially physical abuse. The program has five levels of intervention, including universal public information campaigns, brief consultations with parents regarding typical child behavior problems, and more intensive multisession interventions with a smaller population of parents of children dealing with more serious child behavior problems.

There is considerable evidence supporting various components of the program. The outcomes in these studies are often not measures of maltreatment per se but of risk factors for maltreatment, such as maternal depression, or of dysfunctional parenting (e.g., Sanders & McFarland, 2000). A recent large, population-based trial, the U.S. Triple P System Population Trial (Prinz, Sanders, Shapiro, Whitaker, & Lutzker, 2009), reported maltreatment outcomes measured at the population level. The first study of its kind in the child abuse prevention field, this trial randomized 18 counties to Triple P or care-as-usual conditions, matched on demographic and baseline child-abuse factors. Existing service providers were trained to deliver the program. Results showed that Triple P counties had lower rates of substantiated child maltreatment cases, out-of-home placements, and emergency department visits for maltreatment than the control group counties, after accounting for baseline rates. These results are impressive, given methodological limitations that work against finding positive effects (e.g., issues of statistical power). It will be important to see if the results of this trial can be maintained over time and if the results can be replicated in other communities, such as more urban settings.

HOW DO WE KNOW WHAT WORKS?

The rapidly increasing number of research articles on child maltreatment prevention, alongside the growing insistence of policymakers, funders, and administrators that only programs that are evidence-based receive public funding, presents a challenge to local, state, and federal decision makers in choosing effective prevention strategies. There are several sources of information about effective prevention programs, including peer-reviewed journal articles reporting evidence for particular interventions, published review articles, meta-analyses, task force and commission reports, and government- or university-sponsored lists and registries. Each source has its strengths and limitations (Substance Abuse and Mental Health Services Administration [SAMHSA], 2007); therefore, it is imperative that conclusions regarding an intervention's efficacy should come from more than one source and be based on multiple methodologies that span qualitative and quantitative studies such as case studies, ethnographic studies, process studies, experimental and quasi-experimental studies, dissemination research in naturalistic settings, and cost–benefit analyses (APA Presidential Task Force on Evidence-Based Practice, 2006; Kazdin, 2008). Lack of consistency across expert lists and registries stems from different interpretations of what constitutes evidence for effectiveness and methods used to select candidate programs, as well as variations in the purpose and scope of the reviews, lists, or reports (Kellam & Langevin, 2003).

There is currently no single list or registry that identifies effective child maltreatment prevention programs. However, some lists or registries that include programs related to abuse or neglect are available:

- The California Evidence-Based Clearinghouse for Child Welfare: http://www.cachildwelfareclearinghouse.org/
- University of Colorado, Blueprints for Violence Prevention: http://colorado.edu/cspv/blueprints/
- SAMHSA National Registry of Evidence-Based Programs and Practices: http://www.nrepp.samhsa.gov/
- The Children's Bureau's Office on Child Abuse and Neglect, Emerging Practices in the Prevention of Child Abuse and Neglect project: http://www.childwelfare.gov/preventing/programs/what works/report/report.pdf
- The Centers for Disease Control and Prevention's Community Guide, related to the topic of violence: http://www.thecommunity guide.org/violence/default.htm

These lists typically use expert panels to identify and rank programs depending on the level of evidence. For example, the California Clearinghouse uses a 6-point scale ranging from *well-supported by research evidence* to *concerning practice*. To obtain the highest ranking, a program would need to show that (a) there is no evidence indicating that the program constitutes a substantial risk of harm to those receiving it, compared to its likely benefits; (b) the program is explicitly described in a manual; (c) the program is supported by least two randomized trials in different settings that report positive program effects in published, peer-reviewed articles; (d) in at least one randomized trial, the program has demonstrated a sustained effect at least 1 year beyond the end of treatment; (e) outcome measures must be reliable and valid, and administered consistently and accurately across all subjects; and (f) if multiple outcome studies have been conducted, the overall weight of the evidence supports the benefit of the practice. This is a fairly high standard that few child maltreatment prevention programs currently meet, but it represents a goal that is consistent with other public health efforts.

In evaluating how we know what we know about the prevention of maltreatment, it is useful to refer to different phases of prevention research and the associated standards of evidence in each, as discussed in the broader field of prevention science (Flay et al., 2005; Kellam & Langevin, 2003). Three general phases of prevention research are efficacy, effectiveness, and dissemination. *Efficacy* research seeks to establish the beneficial effects of a program under optimal conditions of delivery and scientific rigor (usually a randomized trial). Efficacy trials may be conducted by the developers of a program using highly trained and supervised staff under circumstances in which the researcher has control over the implementation of the program. Examples include the three randomized trials conducted to evaluate the Nurse–Family Partnership program (Olds et al., 2000) or the randomized trials testing the Parents as Teachers program (Wagner & Clayton, 1999). The Institute of Medicine outlined a set of standards for the preliminary phases of intervention development prior to launching a full-scale randomized trial (Mrazek & Haggerty, 1994; Olds et al., 2007); these phases include using theory and research to identify risk and protective factors; developing strategies for changing those factors; designing the preliminary program using theory and qualitative research, quasi-experimental studies, and small-scale experimental studies; and assessing the feasibility and acceptability for targeting populations and communities.

Effectiveness research focuses on the next phase, in which the program is tested in more natural conditions. This is usually a step toward scaling up a program to measure and study variations across sites in fidelity to implementing the intervention (Olds, 2002). In the child maltreatment field, the experimental study of the Hawaii Healthy Start Program conducted by Duggan et al. (2004) could be considered an effectiveness trial, given that it evaluated an ongoing, scaled-up program. The lack of positive findings regarding maternal risk factors or actual maltreatment incidents may have been partly due to problems in implementing the program with fidelity and adequately engaging families (Duggan et al., 2004), although it may reflect on the adequacy of the underlying model (Olds et al., 2007).

Not all programs with evidence of efficacy and effectiveness are ready to be disseminated. *Dissemination* research seeks to determine if the training and support structures developed in the effectiveness phase can be sustained and expanded to new communities and populations. For example, a lack of trained personnel may limit the scale and timing of dissemination efforts. Dissemination may also have to wait until the monitoring and technical assistance systems are established to support new efforts and provide feedback to ensure quality improvement.

One potential pitfall of the imperative for programs to become evidence based is that outcome evaluations are conducted prematurely, before adequate process data have been collected. A case example was the federally funded Comprehensive Child Development Program, a precursor to Early Head Start. This large, two-generation demonstration project began in 1989 and adopted a case management model to serve the needs of low-income families with children younger than 1 year of age (St. Pierre, Layzer, Goodson, & Bernstein, 1997). A large-scale evaluation showed few positive effects, causing considerable questions to be raised in the government and media about the efficacy of such comprehensive community approaches. The evaluation was subsequently criticized for both its implementation and methodology (Gilliam, Ripple, Zigler, & Leiter, 2000), suggesting that this large-scale study occurred before the necessary formative research was conducted.

Likewise, the disappointing results of randomized trials for some home visiting programs such as Healthy Families America have led some researchers (e.g., Chaffin, 2004) to question the wisdom of widespread dissemination of this model until stronger evidence is in place. The initial trials did reveal information that could inform later trials intended to test improved or enhanced program models. Prevention research is often described as a cyclical process of continuous quality improvement in which one generation of research improves the next (Kellam & Langevin, 2003). In their evaluation of the Hawaii Healthy Start Program, Duggan et al. (2004) reported that home visitors often encountered family risks for maltreatment, such as poor parent mental health, substance use, and domestic violence, but that the training program devoted little time to these topics and the visitors felt unprepared to address them. This suggests areas of program improvement that might inform a new generation of trials.

Similarly, the Elmira Nurse–Family Partnership trial showed that program effects on maltreatment prevention were less for women reporting the highest levels of domestic violence (Eckenrode et al., 2000). This informed the subsequent Denver trial of the Nurse–Family Partnership, in which nurses gave more attention to issues of partner communication and domestic violence, and the results showed that nurse-visited women reported less domestic violence than control group women (Olds et al., 2004). These examples suggest the need for a culture of experimentation, refinement, and reexperimentation in the child maltreatment prevention field before programs are deemed ready for wide-scale dissemination. It also suggests that a final judgment, positive or negative, should not be made about programs based on a single randomized trial, however well designed.

WHAT ARE THE NEXT STEPS?

A substantial community-level reduction in child maltreatment is an attainable goal. There has been no lack of creativity, passion, commitment, and effort directed at this social problem. Progress has been slow and incremental, however, in part because the emphasis on establishing systems to detect and treat maltreated children and maltreating parents has at times diverted scarce resources away from primary prevention strategies focused on providing support and assistance to families who are at risk for parenting problems (Melton & Barry, 1994).

Also, early prevention efforts were more advocacy driven than science based (Chaffin, 2004). Although advocacy was crucial in mobilizing communities and building public support for prevention efforts, it did not generally advance the science of child maltreatment prevention. We are now in an era of accountability in which policymakers are demanding that public funds be spent on evidence-based and cost-effective approaches. The field of prevention research has also matured, with clearer guidelines for what is considered evidence of effectiveness and how prevention studies should be conducted (Flay et al., 2005; Kellam & Langevin, 2003; Mrazek & Haggerty, 1994). Advances in the prevention of child maltreatment are likely to come from improvements to the scientific base supporting each phase of prevention research—from efficacy through effectiveness through dissemination. To date, there are still relatively few rigorous evaluations of maltreatment prevention efforts. Some of the remaining gaps and associated recommendations are listed below.

Developments in Theory and Research

The foundation of a successful prevention effort is research that identifies the risk and protective factors that are linked to elevated rates of maltreatment. (For reviews of this research and assessments of gaps in the knowledge base, see Chapters 2 and 3 in *Violence Against Women and Children, Volume 1: Mapping the Terrain;* White, Koss, & Kazdin, 2011.) This research should not only establish the strength of the relationship between various risk and protective factors and maltreatment but also determine how prevalent these factors are in the population of interest and how amenable they are to change.

The best targets for prevention efforts are risk or protective factors that are prevalent in the population, have the strongest association with maltreatment, and are shown to be modifiable with reasonably priced interventions (Klevens & Whitaker, 2007).

Some categories of risk have typically been the focus of maltreatment prevention efforts, such as parenting knowledge or attitudes. Other high-prevalence risk factors, such as teen pregnancy, poverty, or partner abuse, have received much less attention. This is in part due to segmentation within fields of research, practice, and policy. For example, the fields of child maltreatment and partner abuse have historically developed separately despite their seeming relevance to each other, evidence for co-occurrence within families, and common risk factors (O'Leary & Woodin, 2006). Similarly, the child maltreatment field has developed separately from the fields of mental health and substance use. It was noted previously that issues of mental health, substance use, and partner violence have been discussed as crucial contextual factors in the design and execution of home visiting programs. This is just one example of how program development for child maltreatment prevention would benefit from collaborative partnerships that involve research and practice traditions outside the immediate maltreatment field.

Advances in the Science of Prevention

There have been significant gains in the rigor with which child maltreatment prevention programs have been evaluated. However, much is left to do to meet the standards set for the field of prevention science more generally (Flay et al., 2005; Olds et al., 2007). This includes developing interventions using formative research and pilot testing prior to testing them with randomized trials. This initial work entails developing a clear theory that identifies the specific risk and protective factors the intervention targets, specifying and pilot testing the methods proposed to influence these factors, and conducting qualitative research on the feasibility of the approach within the proposed populations and community settings.

Once pilot work is completed and a randomized trial is designed, there remain many challenges that threaten the integrity of such trials, such as selection bias in terms of who participates in trials, a biased assignment process, lack of statistical power, and diffusion of the treatment into the control group, among others (McCall & Green, 2004). The science of conducting experiments continues to develop, as does the science of conducting non-experimental or quasi-experimental studies. The best strategy for the prevention field would be to combine the best of both methodological traditions to achieve a coherent picture of the effects of a program approach within community settings.

Integration of Prevention Programs

There is considerable variation in the child maltreatment prevention field in terms of how universal or indicated is the approach, the risk or protective factors involved, the type of maltreatment targeted, the methods used to effect change, and the participants in the program (e.g., whether the parents or the children). In addition to conducting more rigorous evaluations of prevention programs focused on specific issues and subgroups (e.g., assault prevention in school-aged children, shaken baby syndrome prevention among new parents), there is a need to build integrated approaches that address multiple targets (risks, people, communities) and use multiple change methods. Similar challenges exist in other fields, such as public health and behavioral medicine, where attempts have been made since the 1970s to move beyond interventions focused on single risk factors, such as smoking, diet, or physical activity, to multifactorial approaches designed to alter several risk behaviors at once (Prochaska, Spring, & Nigg, 2008). These studies have met with mixed success, but the child maltreatment field might learn from these efforts and from the theoretical and methodological advances coming out of those fields.

The lack of integration is also evident across service delivery systems. Despite evidence that family income and other indicators of socioeconomic status strongly relate to child maltreatment risk (e.g., Slack, Holl, McDaniel, Yoo, & Bolger, 2004), programs that address family financial resources, such as those offering cash assistance, are rarely coordinated with programs that seek to address parenting knowledge or behaviors (Berger & Brooks-Gunn, 2005). A comprehensive approach to the prevention of maltreatment will require coordinated efforts across these and other sectors.

Moving From Research to Implementation

The prevention research process leads from research on risk and protective factors, to the design and testing of interventions, to wide-scale dissemination. Each of these steps presents challenges to the researcher and the practitioner seeking to bring science and practice together to prevent child maltreatment. These include technical assistance to practitioners who seek access to the best available evidence, consistent high-quality training to support prevention activities, a prevention infrastructure to build capacity for prevention efforts, and more scientific study to improve the implementation process (Saul et al., 2008). To focus more clearly on these challenges and provide a framework for addressing them, the Division of Violence Prevention at the Centers for Disease Control and Prevention has developed the Interactive Systems Framework for Dissemination and Implementation as applied to the fields of child maltreatment and youth violence prevention (Wandersman et al., 2008).

The framework has three parts: the Prevention Synthesis and Translation System, which describes activities related to the synthesis of existing evidence on effectiveness and its translation for use by practitioners; the Prevention Support System, which focuses on building capacities in organizations through training, technical assistance, and coaching; and the Prevention Delivery System, which focuses on activities crucial to the implementation of prevention programs in practice settings.

In each of these systems, multiple issues must be addressed to build an effective prevention system in child maltreatment. For example, more attention and more research should be devoted to obstacles encountered in the implementation of evidence-based programs, including the tension that exists between whether to implement a program exactly as developed or to adapt it to local needs (Saul et al., 2008). Adaptation to local conditions and culture may have benefits in terms of recruitment and retention of families in programs and in provider acceptance (Kumpfer, Alvarado, Smith, & Bellamy, 2002), but other research suggests that maintaining high fidelity leads to higher effectiveness in terms of outcomes (Fixsen, Naoom, Blase, Friedman, & Wallace, 2005). One approach to this issue is that adaptation should not occur until high fidelity has first been demonstrated and that adaptations should not be adopted in a haphazard manner but should be evidence based as well.

Federal and state agencies and private foundations can do much to help stimulate the development of the systems necessary to add to the knowledge base and disseminate best practices through allocation of funding, requests for proposals that reflect the most pressing priorities, encouragement of multisite and collaborative studies, provision of technical assistance and dissemination of research, and programmatic support materials and tools. Such systems may prove crucial in moving the science of child maltreatment prevention into community-based practice settings.

REFERENCES

APA Presidential Task Force on Evidence-Based Practice. (2006). Evidence-based practice in psychology. *American Psychologist, 61*, 271–285. doi:10.1037/0003-066X.61.4.271

Barr, R. G., Rivara, R. P., Barr, M., Cummings, P., Taylor, J., Lengua, L. J., & Meredith-Benitz, M. (2009). Effectiveness of educational materials designed to change knowledge and behaviors regarding crying and shaken baby syndrome in mothers of newborns: A randomized controlled trial. *Pediatrics, 123*, 972–980. doi:10.1542/peds.2008-0908

Barr, R. G., Trent, R. B., & Cross, J. (2006). Age-related incidence curve of hospitalized Shaken Baby Syndrome cases: Convergent evidence for crying as a trigger to shaking. *Child Abuse & Neglect, 30*, 7–16. doi:10.1016/j.chiabu.2005.06.009

Belsky, J. (1993). Etiology of child maltreatment: A developmental-ecological analysis. *Psychological Bulletin, 114*, 413–434. doi:10.1037/0033-2909.114.3.413

Berger, L. M., & Brooks-Gunn, J. (2005). Socioeconomic status, parenting knowledge and behaviors, and perceived maltreatment of young low-birth-weight children. *The Social Service Review, 79*, 237–266. doi:10.1086/428957

Bilukha, O., Hahn, R., Crosby, A., Fullilove, M., Liberman, A., Moscicki, S., . . . Briss, P. A. (2005). The effectiveness of early childhood home visitation in preventing violence: A systematic review. *American Journal of Preventive Medicine, 28*(2, Suppl. 1), 11–39. doi:10.1016/j.amepre.2004.10.004

Bugental, D. B., Ellerson, P. C., Lin, E. K., Rainey, B., Kokotovic, A., & O'Hara, N. (2002). A cognitive approach to child abuse prevention. *Journal of Family Psychology, 16*, 243–258. doi:10.1037/0893-3200.16.3.243

Chaffin, M. (2004). Is it time to rethink Healthy Start/Healthy Families? *Child Abuse & Neglect, 28*, 589–595. doi:10.1016/j.chiabu.2004.04.004

Church P. (1983). Good-Touch/Bad-Touch Program [Copyrighted curriculum]. Childhelp, Inc.

Committee for Children. (2001). *Talking about touching.* Seattle, WA: Committee for Children.

Cicchetti, D., & Lynch, M. (1993). Toward an ecological/transactional model of community violence and child maltreatment: Consequences for children's development. *Psychiatry, 56*, 96–118.

Daro, D., & Donnelly, A. C. (2002). Child abuse prevention: Accomplishments and challenges. In J. E. B. Myers, L. Berliner, J. Briere, C. T. Hendrix, C. Jenny, & T. A. Reid (Eds.), *The APSAC handbook on child maltreatment* (2nd ed., pp. 431–448). Thousand Oaks, CA: Sage.

Daro, D. A., & Harding, K. (1999). Healthy Families America: Using research to enhance practice. *The Future of Children, 9*, 152–176. doi:10.2307/1602726

Davis, M. K., & Gidycz, C. A. (2000). Child sexual abuse prevention programs: A meta-analysis. *Journal of Clinical Child Psychology, 29*, 257–265. doi:10.1207/S15374424jccp2902_11

DePanfilis, D., & Dubowitz, H. (2005). Family Connections: A program for preventing child neglect. *Child Maltreatment, 10*, 108–123. doi:10.1177/1077559505275252

Dias, M. S., Smith, K., deGuehery, K., Mazur, P., Li, V., & Shaffer, M. L. (2005). Preventing abusive head trauma among infants and young children: A hospital-based, parent education program. *Pediatrics, 115*, e470–e477. doi:10.1542/peds.2004-1896

Dowd, K., Kinsey, S., Wheeless, S., Thissen, R., Richardson, J., Suresh, R., . . . Biemer, P. (2008). National Survey of Child and Adolescent Well-being (NSCAW) Waves 1–5 [Data set]. Retrieved from National Data Archive on Child Abuse and Neglect website, http://www.ndacan.cornell.edu

Duggan, A., Caldera, D., Rodriguez, K., Burrell, L., Rohde, C., & Crowne, S. S. (2007). Impact of a statewide home visiting program to prevent child abuse. *Child Abuse & Neglect, 31*, 801–827. doi:10.1016/j.chiabu.2006.06.011

Duggan, A., McFarlane, E., Fuddy, L., Burrell, L., Higman, S. M., Windham, A., & Sia, C. (2004). Randomized trial of a statewide home visiting program: Impact in preventing child abuse and neglect. *Child Abuse & Neglect, 28,* 597–622. doi:10.1016/j.chiabu.2003.08.007

DuMont, K., Mitchell-Herzfeld, S., Greene, R., Lee, E., Lowenfels, A., Rodriguez, M., & Dorabawila, V. (2008). Healthy Families New York (HFNY) randomized trial: Effects on early child abuse and neglect. *Child Abuse & Neglect, 32,* 295–315. doi:10.1016/j.chiabu.2007.07.007

Eckenrode, J., Ganzel, B., Henderson, C., Smith, E., Olds, D., & Powers, J. (2000). Preventing child abuse and neglect with a program of nurse home visitation: The limiting effects of domestic violence. *JAMA, 284,* 1385–1391. doi:10.1001/jama.284.11.1385

Finkelhor, D., Asdigian, N., & Dziuba-Leatherman, J. (1995). Victimization prevention programs for children: A follow-up. *American Journal of Public Health, 85,* 1684–1689. doi:10.2105/AJPH.85.12.1684

Fixsen, D. L., Naoom, S. F., Blase, K. A., Friedman, R. M., & Wallace, F. (2005). *Implementation research: A synthesis of the literature.* Tampa, FL: University of South Florida, Louis de la Parte Florida Mental Health Institute, The National Implementation Research Network.

Flay, B. R., Biglan, A., Boruch, R. F., Castro, F. G., Gottfredson, D., Kellam, S., . . . Ji, P. (2005). Standards of evidence: Criteria for efficacy, effectiveness and dissemination. *Prevention Science, 6,* 151–175. doi:10.1007/s11121-005-5553-y

Gershater-Molko, R. M., Lutzker, J. R., & Wesch, D. (2002). Using recidivism data to evaluate Project Safecare: Teaching bonding, safety and healthcare skills to parents. *Child Maltreatment, 7,* 277–285. doi:10.1177/1077559502007003009

Gilliam, W. S., Ripple, C. H., Zigler, E. F., & Leiter, V. (2000). Evaluating child and family demonstration initiatives: Lessons from the Comprehensive Child Development Program. *Early Childhood Research Quarterly, 15,* 41–59. doi:10.1016/S0885-2006(99)00041-1

Guterman, N. B. (2001). *Stopping child maltreatment before it starts: Emerging horizons in early home visitation services.* Thousand Oaks, CA: Sage.

Kazdin, A. E. (2008). Evidence-based treatment and practice. *American Psychologist, 63,* 146–159. doi:10.1037/0003-066X.63.3.146

Keenan, H. T., Runyan, D. K., Marshall, S. W., Nocera, M. A., Merten, D. F., & Sinal, S. H. (2003). A population-based study of inflicted traumatic brain injury in young children. *JAMA, 290,* 621–626. doi:10.1001/jama.290.5.621

Kellam, S. G., & Langevin, D. (2003). A framework for understanding "evidence" in prevention research and programs. *Prevention Science, 4,* 137–153. doi:10.1023/A:1024693321963

Kempe, C. H., Silverman, F. N., Steele, B. F., Droegemueller, W., & Silver, H. K. (1962). The battered child syndrome. *JAMA, 181,* 17–24.

Kenny, M. C., Capri, V., Thakkar-Kolar, R. R., Ryan, E. E., & Runyon, M. K. (2008). Child sexual abuse: From prevention to self-protection. *Child Abuse Review, 17*(1), 36–54. doi:10.1002/car.1012

Kitzman, H., Olds, D. L., Henderson, C. R., Hanks, C., Cole, R., Tatelbaum, R., . . . Barnard, K. (1997). Effects of prenatal and infancy home visitation by nurses on pregnancy outcomes, childhood injuries, and repeated childbearing: A randomized controlled trial. *JAMA, 278,* 644–652. doi:10.1001/jama.278.8.644

Klevens, J., & Whitaker, D. J. (2007). Primary prevention of child physical abuse and neglect: Gaps and promising directions. *Child Maltreatment, 12,* 364–377. doi:10.1177/1077559507305995

Kumpfer, K. L., Alvarado, R., Smith, P., & Bellamy, N. (2002). Cultural sensitivity and adaptation in family-based prevention interventions. *Prevention Science, 3,* 241–246. doi:10.1023/A:1019902902119

Love, J. M., Kisker, E. E., Ross, C., Raikes, H., Constantine, J., Boller, K., . . . Vogel, C. (2005). The effectiveness of early head start for 3-year-old children and their parents: Lessons for policy and programs. *Developmental Psychology, 41,* 885–901. doi:10.1037/0012-1649.41.6.885

MacMillan, H. L., MacMillan, J. H., Offord, D. R., Griffith, L., & MacMillan, A. (1994). Primary prevention of child sexual abuse: A critical review. Part II. *Journal of Child Psychology and Psychiatry, and Allied Disciplines, 35,* 857–876. doi:10.1111/j.1469-7610.1994.tb02299.x

MacMillan, H. L., Wathen, C. N., Barlow, J., Fergusson, D. M., Leventhal, J. M., & Taussig, H. N. (2009). Interventions to prevent child maltreatment and associated impairment. *The Lancet, 373,* 250–266. doi:10.1016/S0140-6736(08)61708-0

McCall, R. B., & Green, B. L. (2004). Beyond the methodological gold standards of behavioral research: Considerations for practice and policy. Society for Research in Child Development. *Social Policy Report, 18*(2), 1–20.

Melton, G. B., & Barry, F. D. (1994). *Protecting children from abuse and neglect.* New York, NY: The Guilford Press.

Mrazek, P. J., & Haggerty, R. J. (Eds.). (1994). *Reducing risks for mental disorders: frontiers for preventive intervention research.* Washington, DC: National Academy Press.

Olds, D. L. (2002). Prenatal and infancy home visiting by nurses: From randomized trials to community replication. *Prevention Science, 3,* 153–172. doi:10.1023/A:1019990432161

Olds, D. L., Eckenrode, J., Henderson, C. R., Kitzman, H., Powers, J., Cole, R., . . . Luckey, D. (1997). Long-term effects of home visitation on maternal life course and child abuse and neglect: 15-year follow-up of a randomized trial. *JAMA, 278,* 637–643. doi:10.1001/jama.278.8.637

Olds, D. L., Henderson, C. R., Chamberlin, R., & Tatelbaum, R. (1986). Preventing child abuse and neglect: A randomized trial of nurse home visitation. *Pediatrics, 78,* 65–78.

Olds, D. L., Hill, P., Robinson, J., Song, N., & Little, C. (2000). Update on home visiting for pregnant women and parents of young children. *Current Problems in Pediatrics, 30,* 109–141. doi:10.1067/mps.2000.105091

Olds, D. L., Robinson, J., Pettitt, L., Luckey, D. W., Holmberg, J., Ng, R. K., . . . Henderson, C. R. (2004). Effects of home visits by paraprofessionals and by nurses: Age 4 follow-up results of a randomized trial. *Pediatrics, 114,* 1560–1568. doi:10.1542/peds.2004-0961

Olds, D. L., Sadler, L., & Kitzman, H. (2007). Programs for parents of infants and toddlers: Recent evidence from randomized trials. *Journal of Child Psychology and Psychiatry, and Allied Disciplines, 48,* 355–391. doi:10.1111/j.1469-7610.2006.01702.x

O'Leary, K. D., & Woodin, E. M. (2006). Bringing the agendas together: Partner and child abuse. In J. R. Lutzker (Ed.), *Preventing violence: Research and evidence-based intervention strategies* (pp. 239–258). Washington, DC: American Psychological Association. doi:10.1037/11385-010

Prinz, R. J., Sanders, M. R., Shapiro, C. J., Whitaker, D. J., & Lutzker, J. R. (2009). Population-based prevention of child maltreatment: The U.S. Triple P system population trial. *Prevention Science, 10,* 1–12. doi:10.1007/s11121-009-0123-3

Prochaska, J. J., Spring, B., & Nigg, C. R. (2008). Multiple health behavior change research: An introduction and overview. *Preventive Medicine, 46,* 181–188. doi:10.1016/j.ypmed.2008.02.001

Reynolds, A. J. (2000). *Success in early intervention: The Chicago Parent-Child Centers.* Lincoln: University of Nebraska Press.

Reynolds, A. J., & Robertson, D. L. (2003). School-based early intervention and later child maltreatment in the Chicago Longitudinal Study. *Child Development, 74,* 3–26. doi:10.1111/1467-8624.00518

Runyan, D. K., Zolotor, A. J., Barr, R. G., & Murphy, R. A. (2009.) The period of PURPLE crying: Keeping North Carolina babies safe. In K. A. Dodge & D. Coleman (Eds.), *Community-based prevention of child maltreatment* (pp. 102–118). New York, NY: Guilford Press.

Sanders, M. R., Markie-Dadds, C., & Turner, K. M. T. (2003). Sanders, M. R., Markie-Dadds, C., & Turner, K. M. T. (2003). Theoretical, scientific and clinical foundations of the Triple P-Positive Parenting Program: A population approach to the promotion of parenting competence. *Parenting Research and Practice Monograph, 1,* 1–21. Retrieved from http://www.pfsc.uq.edu.au/papers/Monograph_1.pdf

Sanders, M. R., & McFarland, M. (2000). Treatment of depressed mothers with disruptive children: A controlled evaluation of cognitive behavioral family intervention. *Behavior Therapy, 31,* 89–112. doi:10.1016/S0005-7894(00)80006-4

Saul, J., Duffy, J., Noonan, R., Lubell, K., Wandersman, A., Flaspohler, P., . . . Dunville, R. (2008). Bridging science and practice in violence prevention: Addressing ten key challenges. *American Journal of Community Psychology, 41,* 197–205. doi:10.1007/s10464-008-9171-2

Sedlak, A., Broadhurst, D. D., & National Center on Child Abuse and Neglect. (1996). *Third national incidence study of child abuse and neglect: Final report*. Washington, DC: U.S. Department of Health and Human Services, Administration for Children and Families, Administration on Children, Youth and Families, National Center on Child Abuse and Neglect.

Slack, J. S., Holl, J., McDaniel, M., Yoo, J., & Bolger, K. (2004). Understanding the risks of child neglect: An exploration of poverty and parenting characteristics. *Child Maltreatment, 9*, 395–408. doi:10.1177/1077559504269193

St. Pierre, R. G., Layzer, J. I., Goodson, B. D., & Bernstein, L. (1997). *National impact evaluation of the Comprehensive Child Development Program: Final report*. Cambridge, MA: Abt Associates.

Substance Abuse and Mental Health Services Administration. (2007). *Identifying and selecting evidenced-based interventions*. Washington, DC: Department of Health and Human Services. Retrieved from http://download.ncadi.samhsa.gov/csap/spfsig/Final_SPFGuidance_Jan04_2007.pdf

Sweet, M. A., & Appelbaum, M. I. (2004). Is home visiting an effective strategy? A meta-analytic review of home visiting programs for families with young children. *Child Development, 75*, 1435–1456. doi:10.1111/j.1467-8624.2004.00750.x

U.S. Department of Health and Human Services, Administration on Children, Youth and Families. (2008). *Child Maltreatment 2006*. Washington, DC: U.S. Government Printing Office.

Wagner, M. M., & Clayton, S. L. (1999). The Parents as Teachers program: Results from two demonstrations. *The Future of Children, 9*(1), 91–115.

Wagner, M., Spiker, D., & Linn, M. I. (2002). The effectiveness of the Parents as Teachers program with low-income parents and children. *Topics in Early Childhood Special Education, 22*(2), 67–81. doi:10.1177/02711214020220020101

Wandersman, A., Duffy, J., Flaspohler, P., Noonan, R., Lubell, K., Stillman, L., . . . Saul, J. (2008). Bridging the gap between prevention research and practice: The interactive systems framework for dissemination and implementation. *American Journal of Community Psychology, 41*, 171–181. doi:10.1007/s10464-008-9174-z

White, J. W., Koss, M. P., & Kazdin, A. E. (Eds.). (2011). *Violence against women and children, Vol. 1: Mapping the terrain*. Washington, DC: American Psychological Association.

Wurtele, S. K. (2007). *The body safety training program: A personal safety program for parents to teach their children*. Colorado Springs, CO: Wurtele.

Wolfe, D. A. (1999). *Child abuse: Implications for child development and psychopathology* (2nd ed.). Thousands Oaks, CA: Sage.

Zwi, K. J., Woolfenden, S. R., Wheeler, D. M., O'Brien, T. A., Tait, P., & Williams, K. W. (2007). School-based education programmes for the prevention of child sexual abuse. *Cochrane Database of Systematic Reviews, 3*, CD004380.

II

SEXUAL VIOLENCE

5

SERVICES FOR VICTIMS OF SEXUAL VIOLENCE

REBECCA CAMPBELL AND DEBRA PATTERSON

The purpose of this chapter is to review the literature on sexual assault victims' postassault help-seeking experiences with the medical and mental health systems (see Chapter 7, this volume, regarding victims' experiences with the legal system). It is beyond the scope of this chapter to delve into the literatures on secondary or tertiary mental health intervention research. By way of introduction, we begin by defining the key terms used in this chapter. Consistent with the definitions put forth by Koss and Achilles (2008), *rape* refers to an unwanted act of oral, vaginal, or anal penetration committed through the use of force, threat of force, or when incapacitated; *sexual assault* refers to a broader range of contact and noncontact sexual offenses, up to and including rape. The focus of this review is sexual assault, but it is important to note that many studies on community services sampled only rape survivors, thereby underrepresenting the experiences of victims of nonpenetration sexual assault. The terms *victim* and *survivor* are used interchangeably in this chapter. The term *survivor* conveys the strength of those who have been raped; the term *victim* reflects the criminal nature of this act. *Medical services* refers to acute care for sexual assault victims, typically obtained within 72 to 96 hours postassault. Although survivors may seek medical care weeks, months, or even years after the assault, there is scant empirical research on later medical care to be included in this review. *Mental health services* refers to either short-term or long-term counseling that victims may seek in private or community or other public settings at any point postassault. Finally, *advocacy services* refers to the assistance provided by rape crisis center staff and volunteers, which includes helping survivors obtain medical and mental health services as well as helping them negotiate the criminal justice system.

WHAT DO WE KNOW?

Victims' Experiences With the Medical System

Sexual assault victims have extensive postassault medical needs, including injury detection and care, medical forensic examination, screening and treatment for sexually transmitted infections (STIs), and pregnancy testing and emergency contraception. Although most victims are not physically injured to the point of needing emergency care (Ledray, 1999), traditionally, police, rape crisis centers, and social service agencies have advised victims to seek treatment in hospital emergency departments for a medical forensic exam (Martin, 2005). The survivor's body is a crime scene, and because of the invasive nature of rape, a medical professional is needed to collect the evidence for a *rape kit* (i.e., forensic evidence collection of biological evidence taken from a victim's body). The rape kit, or rape exam, usually involves plucking head and pubic hairs; collecting loose hairs by combing the head and pubis; swabbing the vagina, rectum, and/or mouth to collect semen, blood, or saliva; and obtaining fingernail scrapings in the event the victim scratched the assailant. Blood samples may also be collected for DNA, toxicology, and ethanol testing (Martin, 2005).

Victims often experience long waits in hospital emergency departments because sexual assault is rarely an emergent health threat, and during this wait victims are not allowed to eat, drink, or urinate so as not to destroy physical evidence of the assault (Ledray, 1999). When victims are finally seen, they get a cursory explanation of what will occur, and it often comes as a shock that they must have a pelvic exam immediately after such an egregious, invasive violation of their bodies (Martin, 2005). Many victims describe the medical care they receive as cold, impersonal, and detached (Campbell, 2005, 2006). Furthermore, the exams and evidence collection procedures are often performed incorrectly (Martin, 2005). Most hospital emergency department personnel lack training in sexual assault forensic exams, and those who are trained usually do not perform exams frequently enough to maintain proficiency (Plichta et al., 2006).

Forensic evidence collection is often the focus of hospital emergency department care, but sexual assault survivors have other medical needs, such as information on the risk of STIs/HIV and prophylaxis (i.e., preventive medications to treat any STIs that may have been contracted through the assault). The American Medical Association (1995) and the Centers for Disease Control and Prevention (2002) have recommended that all sexual assault victims receive STI prophylaxis and HIV prophylaxis (i.e., repeated testing for or preventive medications to treat any STIs that may have been contracted through the assault) on a case-by-case basis after risk assessment. However, analyses of hospital records have shown that only 34% of sexual assault patients are treated for STIs (Amey & Bishai, 2002). Yet, data from victims suggest much higher rates of STI prophylaxis: 57% to 69% of sexual assault victims have reported that they received antibiotics during their hospital emergency department care (Campbell, 2005, 2006; Campbell, Wasco, Ahrens, Sefl, & Barnes, 2001; National Victim Center, 1992). But not all victims are equally likely to receive STI-related medical services. Even though knowing the assailant does not mitigate one's risk, victims of nonstranger sexual assault are significantly less likely to receive information on STIs/HIV or STI prophylaxis (Campbell et al., 2001). In addition, one study found that Caucasian women were significantly more likely to get information on HIV than ethnic minority women (Campbell et al., 2001).

Postassault pregnancy services are also inconsistently provided to sexual assault victims. Only 40% to 49% of victims receive information about the risk of pregnancy (Campbell et al., 2001; National Victim Center, 1992). The AMA (1995) and the American College of Obstetricians and Gynecologists (1998) have recommended emergency contraception for victims at risk of pregnancy, but only 21% to 43% of sexual assault victims who need emergency contraception actually receive it (Amey & Bishai, 2002; Campbell, 2005, 2006; Campbell et al., 2001). Espey and colleagues' (2009) survey of hospitals in a state with a mandated emergency contraception law found that only 52% of the responding emergency departments routinely provide emergency contraception to sexual assault patients. To date, no studies have found systematic differences in the provision of emergency contraception as a function of victim or assault characteristics, but Catholic hospitals are significantly less likely to provide emergency contraception (Smugar, Spina, & Merz, 2000).

In addition to the challenges they face obtaining needed services, sexual assault victims also encounter substantial victim blaming from medical system personnel. In the process of the forensic exam, STI services, and pregnancy-related care, physicians and nurses may sometimes ask victims about their prior sexual history; sexual response during the assault; what they were wearing; and, inexcusably, what they did to cause or provoke the assault (Campbell, 2005).

Medical professionals may view these questions as necessary and appropriate, but sexual assault survivors find them upsetting. For example, Campbell (2005) found that as a result of their contact with emergency department physicians and nurses, most sexual assault survivors stated that they felt bad about themselves (81%), depressed (88%), violated (94%), distrustful of others (74%), and reluctant to seek further help (80%). Only 5% of victims in Ullman's (1996) study rated physicians as a helpful source of support, and negative responses from formal systems, including medical, significantly exacerbate victims' posttraumatic stress disorder (PTSD) symptomatology (Campbell, Sefl, et al., 1999; Ullman & Filipas, 2001). Victims who do not receive basic medical services rate their experiences with the medical system as more hurtful, which has been associated with higher PTSD levels (Campbell et al., 2001). Specifically, victims of nonstranger sexual assault who received minimal medical services but encountered high victim blaming appear to be the most at risk: These women had significantly higher levels of PTSD symptoms than victims who did not seek medical services at all (Campbell, Sefl, et al., 1999).

To address these shortcomings in postassault medical care for sexual assault victims, rape crisis centers have been instrumental in advocating on behalf of individual victims as well as creating broader systemic change (Martin, 2005). Since the 1970s, rape crisis centers have been leading efforts to create standardized rape kits and providing volunteer medical advocates on a 24-7 basis to help victims in hospital emergency departments (Macy et al., 2009; Martin, 2005). Unfortunately, not all hospitals work with rape crisis centers, which may compromise victim care. In a quasi-experimental study, Campbell (2006) compared victims' medical forensic exam experiences in two hospitals that were highly similar (e.g., number of victims served per year, patient sociodemographic characteristics), except that one had a policy of paging rape crisis center advocates to assist victims and the other did not work with advocates. Victims who had the assistance of an advocate were significantly more likely to receive comprehensive care and less likely to experience victim blaming treatment from medical system personnel. Although these differences cannot be attributed solely to the efforts of the rape crisis center advocates, this study suggests that victims may benefit from some assistance to navigate the chaos of hospital emergency departments.

Alternatively, it may be more effective to change the postassault medical care delivery system entirely, which was the founding premise of Sexual Assault Nurse Examiner (SANE) programs. SANE programs were created by the nursing profession in 1970s and grew in rapid numbers during the 1990s (Campbell, Patterson, & Lichty, 2005). These programs were designed to circumvent many of the problems of traditional hospital emergency department care by having specially trained nurses, rather than physicians, provide

24/7 crisis intervention and medical care to sexual assault victims in either hospital emergency department or community clinic settings. Influenced by psychiatric and community mental health nursing, SANE programs place strong emphasis on treating victims with dignity and respect in order to decrease postassault psychological distress. Many SANE programs work with their local rape crisis centers so that victim advocates can also be present for the exam to provide emotional support, combining the potential benefits of both service programs.

The medical forensic exam performed by SANE programs is more thorough than what victims receive in traditional emergency department care. Most SANE programs use specialized forensic equipment (e.g., colposcope), which allows for the detection of microlacerations, bruises, and other injuries (Ledray, 1999). With respect to STI/HIV and emergency contraception care, national surveys of SANE programs find service provision rates of 90% or higher (Campbell et al., 2006). As with traditional emergency department medical care, SANE programs affiliated with Catholic hospitals are significantly less likely to conduct pregnancy testing or offer emergency contraception (but do so at higher rates than non-SANE, Catholic-affiliated emergency departments; Campbell et al., 2006). In a quasi-experimental longitudinal study, Crandall and Helitzer (2003) compared medical service provision rates 2 years before with rates 4 years after the implementation of a hospital-based SANE program and found significant increases in STI prophylaxis care (from 89% to 97%) and emergency contraception (from 66% to 87%).

Victims' experiences in receiving postassault medical care in SANE programs are markedly different from what they undergo in traditional hospital emergency departments. For example, qualitative studies of Canadian specialized sexual assault services (which are similar to American SANE programs) have found that patients feel respected, safe, reassured, in control, and informed throughout their crisis period (Du Mont, White, & McGregor, 2009; Ericksen et al., 2002). Similarly, Campbell, Patterson, Adams, Diegel, and Coats's (2008) evaluation of services with 52 sexual assault patients in a Midwestern SANE program found that survivors felt very supported, respected, believed, and well cared for by their SANE nurses. In a qualitative follow-up study with the same SANE program, survivors noted that they appreciated the joint efforts of both the SANE nurse and the rape crisis center victim advocate (Campbell, Bybee, Ford, Patterson, & Ferrell, 2009). Victims noted that the nurses and advocates worked well together as a team to provide comprehensive psychological support to them as well as their families. However, as Cole and Logan (2008) documented, there can be some tension and conflict between SANEs and rape crisis center advocates around negotiating responsibilities, but collaboration between SANE programs and advocacy organizations is important to ensure that victims' needs are being met.

Victims' Experiences With Mental Health Services

Given the tremendous negative impact of sexual assault on women's psychological well-being, sexual assault victims are quite likely to need mental health services. Between 17% and 65% of women with a lifetime history of sexual assault develop PTSD, 13% to 51% meet diagnostic criteria for depression, 73% to 82% experience fear and/or anxiety, 12% to 40% develop generalized anxiety, 13% to 49% become dependent on alcohol, 23% to 44% have suicidal ideation, and 2% to 19% may attempt suicide (Campbell, Dworkin, & Cabral, 2009; Koss, Bailey, Yuan, Herrera, & Lichter, 2003). These sequelae are largely due to the trauma of the sexual assault itself, but, as noted previously, victim blaming responses from social systems can exacerbate victims' distress. Despite victims' high need for mental health services, there has been comparatively less research on what services they actually receive and whether that care improved their psychological health. Survivors may obtain mental health services in myriad ways, and their experiences vary considerably as a function of treatment setting.

First, some victims receive mental health services by participating as research subjects in randomized controlled trial treatment outcome studies (e.g., Resick et al., 2008). This option is available only to sexual assault survivors who live in communities where such research is being conducted and who fit eligibility criteria. However, this kind of research is not intended to provide large-scale services; the goal is to establish empirically supported treatments that can then be disseminated for wider scale benefit (American Psychological Association Presidential Task Force on Evidence-Based Practice, 2006; McHugh & Barlow, 2010). The results of these studies suggest that cognitive behavioral therapies, such as cognitive processing therapy and prolonged exposure, are effective in alleviating PTSD symptoms (Foa, Keane, & Friedman, 2000; Vickerman & Margolin, 2009). The victims who participate in these trials receive high-quality treatment, but theirs is not the experience of the typical sexual-assault victim seeking postassault mental health services (Koss et al., 2003).

A second, and more typical, way in which victims receive postassault mental health services is community-based care provided by psychologists, psychiatrists, or social workers in private or public clinic settings. More victims receive mental health services in these settings than in treatment outcome studies, but clinics are still highly underutilized and have serious accessibility limitations. Most victims who seek traditional mental health services, for example, are Caucasian (Starzynski, Ullman, Townsend, Long, & Long, 2007). Ethnic minority women are more likely to turn to informal sources of support (e.g., friends, family) and may not necessarily place the same value on formal psychotherapy (Bletzer & Koss, 2006). Victims without health insurance are also significantly less likely to obtain mental health services (Koss et al., 2003; Starzynski et al., 2007).

When victims do receive community-based mental health services, it is unclear whether practitioners are consistently using empirically supported treatments. Two statewide random sample studies of practitioners have suggested that it is unlikely. Campbell, Raja, and Grining's (1999) survey of licensed mental health professionals in a Midwestern state found that most (52%) reported using cognitive behavioral methods with victims of violence (including but not limited to sexual assault victims). Almost all practitioners stated that they rarely used a single approach and that they intentionally combined multiple therapeutic orientations and treatments. Sprang, Craig, and Clark's (2008) study of mental health practitioners in a Southern state also found high use of cognitive behavioral interventions with trauma victims (including but not limited to sexual assault survivors), but again, practitioners did not use these interventions exclusively. Exposure therapy, a cognitive behavioral therapy approach with strong empirical support (Foa et al., 2000), was rarely cited as a preferred treatment. These studies suggest that cognitive behavioral therapy approaches are often used by community practitioners, but without in-depth evaluation of how the services were implemented, it would be a stretch to conclude that most victims receive empirically supported care in community-based mental health services. It can take quite a while for evidence-based practice to become standard care (Kazdin, 2008). In the typical efficacy–effectiveness–dissemination research cycle, multiple efficacy studies are conducted (often in highly controlled settings/contexts) to examine whether a treatment works, followed by multiple effectiveness studies to determine whether the results are replicable in real-world practice and community settings. This process can take several years before the findings are disseminated to practitioners.

Few studies have examined if and how victims benefit from community-based mental health services. In general, victims tend to rate their experiences with mental health professionals positively and characterize their help as useful and supportive (Campbell et al., 2001; Ullman, 1996). Whether positive satisfaction results in demonstrable mental health benefit is largely unknown. However, in one study Campbell, Sefl, et al. (1999) found that community-based mental health services were particularly helpful when victims had had negative experiences with the legal and/or medical systems (e.g., blamed for the assault, asked about their sexual histories). Victims who encountered difficulty in obtaining needed services and experienced substantial victim blaming from the legal and medical systems had high PTSD symptomatology, but among this high-risk group of survivors, those who had been able to obtain mental health services had significantly lower PTSD, suggesting that there may have been some benefit from receiving such services. In this same sample, however, 25% of women who received postassault mental health services rated this contact as hurtful (with 19% characterizing it as severely hurtful; Campbell et al., 2001). Indeed, some mental health practitioners have expressed concern about whether their own profession works effectively with sexual assault victims: In a statewide study, 58% of practitioners felt that mental health providers engage in practices that would be harmful to victims and questioned the degree to which victims benefit from services (Campbell & Raja, 1999).

A third setting in which victims may obtain mental health services is advocacy service organizations, such as rape crisis centers and domestic violence shelter programs. Rape crisis centers help victims negotiate their contact with the legal and medical systems, and they also provide individual and group counseling (Martin, 2005). These agencies are perhaps the most visible and accessible sources for mental health services for sexual assault victims (Koss et al., 2003), as they provide counseling free of charge and do not require health insurance. As with traditional mental health services, there is still evidence of racial differences in service utilization as Caucasian women are significantly more likely to utilize rape crisis center services than are ethnic minority women (Wgliski & Barthel, 2004).

Little is known about the therapeutic orientations and treatment approaches used in rape crisis centers, but current data indicate a strong feminist and/or empowerment theoretical orientation (e.g., shared goal setting, focus on gender inequalities, identification of sexual assault not only as a personal problem but also as a social problem; Edmond, 2006; Ullman & Townsend, 2008). In a national survey of rape crisis centers and domestic violence shelters, approximately 70% of the agencies reported using cognitive behavioral methods in combination with other methods (e.g., client centered and feminist; Edmond, 2006). With respect to counseling outcomes, Wasco et al. (2004) compared self-reported PTSD symptoms pre- and postcounseling among victims receiving rape crisis center counseling services; they found significant reductions in distress levels and self-blame over time and increases in social support, self efficacy, and sense of control. Because these studies did not examine the content of services or include comparison groups, it is unclear whether these improvements are attributable to the services provided.

HOW DO WE KNOW IT?

In sexual violence research, victim services are an understudied topic. To date, sexual assault researchers have concentrated primarily on prevalence/incidence, risk factors for perpetration and victimization, mental health sequelae, physical health effects, and prevention. As a result, there are very few studies with national random samples regarding victims' experiences in seeking community services. Older studies, such as the National Victim Center's *Rape in America* project led by Kilpatrick and colleagues (1992), provided reasonably comprehensive information about victims' experiences with services. Unfortunately, more recent national-scale projects, such as the National Violence Against Women Survey (Tjaden & Thoennes, 1998), did not capture much detail about postassault community services. Regionally based survivor samples (e.g., Campbell et al., 2001; Ullman & Filipas, 2001) or statewide service provider samples (e.g., Plichta et al., 2006) are more typical in this area of inquiry. Therefore, there is a pressing need for national-scale research on victims' experiences in seeking community services and the impact of that assistance (or lack thereof) on their recovery.

Few prospective longitudinal research studies have explicitly examined community help-seeking. Such designs advance our understanding of the complex process of help seeking and can help disentangle how different kinds of services and patterns of service received affect survivors' health outcomes. However, prospective research could require recruiting victims very soon after the assault, mostly likely at some initial point of system entry (e.g., medical forensic exam, hotline call to a rape crisis center). This is a very fragile, vulnerable time for survivors—and for their service providers, who are concerned that research could interfere with service delivery and jeopardize their tentative relationship (Campbell, Adams, & Patterson, 2008). To address this issue, it may be useful to develop collaborative relationships with community organizations to codevelop recruitment protocols that are responsive to the needs of both survivors and service providers (Campbell, Patterson, et al., 2008). Making longitudinal research on victim services more commonplace will require input, participation, and buy-in from social system personnel. However, it is important to note that immediate postassault recruitment may not be necessary for all studies.

Most research on victim services relies on retrospective, self-report data. Typically, survivors are recruited to participate in research through a variety of community-based strategies (e.g., media, mass mailings, community postings; for a review, see Campbell, Sefl, Wasco, & Ahrens, 2004). The methodology of these techniques has advanced so that convenience sampling can be avoided and more sophisticated time-space sampling methods can be used (Stueve et al., 2001). In addition, there is a growing literature on how and why sexual assault survivors decide to participate in research (see Rosenbaum & Langhinrichsen-Rohling, 2006). The literature suggests that retrospective methods will likely remain a mainstay in this field because many survivors are reluctant to discuss (either in interviews or in surveys) the assault with researchers until they are further along in their recovery (Campbell & Adams, 2009).

Retrospective designs also raise questions about the accuracy of victims' accounts because data are often collected well after the assault and community help-seeking. In general, memories of traumatic experiences are "reasonably accurate and well-retained for very long periods, but are not completely indelible" (Koss, Tromp, & Tharan, 1995, p. 111). Typically, survivors can accurately recall the rape with vivid, sensory-rich details, but some aspects of the assault context may be less clear (Koss, Figueredo, Bell, Tharan, & Tromp, 1996; Peace, Porter, & Brinke, 2008). With respect to the accuracy of survivors' postassault help-seeking experiences, Campbell (2005) interviewed a sample of survivors who had postassault contact with the legal and medical systems about what services they received and how they were treated by social system personnel. Parallel interviews were also conducted with the doctors, nurses, and police officers with whom these survivors interacted. There was remarkably high, statistically significant agreement between the accounts offered by victims and service providers: Both tended to agree when there were positive service experiences, and both sides readily acknowledged when there were gaps in services and victim-blaming treatment. Taken together, the results of these studies indicate that retrospective data may not be as compromised as feared. Nevertheless, reliance on retrospective, self-report survivor data for the study of victim services limits our understanding of this phenomenon because such methods cannot provide any insight into the underlying motivations of the service providers themselves.

One of the most promising ideas to have emerged for victim services has been the development of truly coordinated community response interventions whereby all service providers from the medical, legal, medical health, and advocacy systems work together to assist sexual assault survivors. Often termed *sexual assault response teams* (SARTs), such interventions are currently being developed and implemented throughout the United States. Most SARTs strive to follow a victim-centered model, which means that the rights, wishes, and decisions of victims and survivors should be respected and social system personnel must tailor their responses to fit the individualized needs of victims and survivors (National Sexual Violence Resource Center [NSVRC], 2006). SARTs differ in how they organize their community's initial response to victims, but the overarching goal is complete coordination so that victims receive comprehensive care no matter where they first present. Some SARTs have a SANE (or emergency department physician) perform the medical forensic exam first, and then the victim/survivor meets separately with police, prosecutors, and other team members. Other SARTs have a group response model whereby SANEs, police, and prosecutors work simultaneously for joint survivor interviews. In addition to these case-level activities, most SARTs have monthly or quarterly meetings of key stakeholders to review progress in individual cases and/or develop protocols and policies for the community response to sexual assault (NSVRC, 2006).

SART interventions are growing in rapid numbers: County- and state-level data suggest there was a 17% to 20% increase in SART activations in the early 2000s (Campbell, 2008). Yet there are virtually no evaluative data to guide their development. SARTs seem like a good idea—it's hard to argue that coordinated, comprehensive care is a bad idea. On the other hand, it is unclear how such diverse stakeholders, who traditionally have had such conflicted relationships (Martin, 2005), can work together to focus first and foremost on the needs of survivors. There are multiple factors that could contribute to the dissonance among stakeholders. For example, each stakeholder has its own unique terminology and varying degrees of knowledge of the laws (e.g., victims' rights, legal protections of defendants), potentially contributing to miscommunication. Further, the goals of one stakeholder's work with survivors can be in opposition to another stakeholder's goals (e.g., victim advocates' goal is to support the survivor, whereas law enforcement's goal is to investigate, which requires the survivor to disclose even when she feels unready or uncomfortable). Cole and Logan (2010) found that alcohol-related sexual assaults may be particularly likely to invoke conflict and disagreement among SART members. In light of these issues, there is a pressing need for empirical research on these intervention models.

WHAT ARE THE NEXT STEPS?

Sexual assault victims have extensive postassault mental health needs, which unfortunately are all too often compounded by negative experiences with other social systems. Moreover, many survivors never receive any help to work through the trauma of the assault (Ullman, 2007). To address this problem, the community response to sexual assault must change. As noted previously, there are several new intervention models, such as SANE programs and SARTs, that merit further study to determine whether widespread implementation is warranted and if so, to identify the critical ingredients needed for programmatic success. In addition, much more can be done to respond to victims' mental health needs. Here we consider two key recommendations, one focused on improving victims' access to trained mental health professionals immediately postassault and the other on enhancing the quality of longer term counseling services.

First, the model of mental health care for sexual assault survivors remains frustratingly antiquated: When victims obtain mental health services it is usually after emotional problems have surfaced, and psychologists and allied professionals are largely absent in the immediate, postassault community response to sexual assault. Bringing trained mental health professionals in earlier could make a significant difference in victims' well-being, and psychological first aid (PFA) is a promising, empirically informed model of early intervention. Based on years of research on crisis intervention techniques, PFA was developed for working with victims of disasters, violence, and other trauma in their immediate aftermath (Ruzek et al., 2007). The goal of PFA is to accelerate recovery and promote mental health through eight core goals and actions: (a) initiate contact in a nonintrusive, compassionate, helpful manner; (b) enhance safety and provide physical and emotional comfort; (c) calm and orient emotionally distraught survivors; (d) identify immediate needs and concerns and gather information; (e) offer practical help to address immediate needs and concerns; (f) reduce distress by connecting to primary support persons; (g) provide individuals with information about stress reactions and coping; and (h) link individuals to services and inform them about services they may need in the future (Ruzek et al., 2007).

Ruzek and colleagues' (2007) review highlights how each of these eight principles has empirical support in the literature. Focusing on psychological and physical safety can interrupt the biological mechanisms of posttrauma stress reactions and can challenge cognitive beliefs about perceived dangerousness. Grounding techniques, which are coping strategies (e.g., deep breathing) that focus individuals on the relative safety of the environment they are now in, can also be effective in interrupting conditioned learning processes that begin to link nonthreatening persons, places, and things to the original trauma event. Trying to calm victims can significantly decrease the likelihood that their immediate anxiety will generalize to other situations and can reduce high arousal levels, which, if prolonged, can lead to acute stress disorder (and later PTSD) as well as significant somatic symptoms. Mobilizing resources to respond to victims' immediate needs and linking them to services in the community has been found to reduce distress and increase long-term quality of life. Providing information about effective coping strategies can foster self-efficacy, which can help victims set realistic expectations for the long-term recovery process. Strengthening social support and coping can help with material resource and other practical needs, but it also provides additional outlets for emotional processing of the traumatic events.

PFA was purposively designed for simple, practical administration wherever trauma survivors are, including hospitals, shelters, and police departments (Brymer et al., 2006). PFA can be performed by mental health professionals, but another role for psychologists and allied professionals is to provide training to health care professionals and legal system personnel to expand capacity for psychological first aid (Parker, Barnett, Everly, & Links, 2006). Mental health professionals could work with hospital emergency departments, SANE programs, and police departments, either as providers of PFA or as training consultants. Similarly, because the medical and legal advocacy provided by rape crisis centers includes crisis intervention, mental health professionals could partner with these centers to ensure that advocates are trained in all PFA core competencies.

Although PFA may be a promising model for postassault care of sexual assault survivors, it is important to note that this approach has not been empirically validated with this trauma population. Because there is always the risk of unintended consequences that may worsen psychological distress, any model of crisis intervention should be rigorously evaluated prior to broad-based adoption and dissemination. In that vein, Resnick and colleagues (Resnick, Acierno, Amstadter, et al., 2007; Resnick, Acierno, Waldrop, et al., 2007) developed a different approach for bringing mental health services to sexual assault victims much more quickly—and their intervention was rigorously evaluated in a randomized controlled trial. They developed a two-part educational video that can be shown to sexual assault victims when they present in hospital emergency departments for medical forensic exams. The video content was informed by decades of research substantiating the utility of brief cognitive behavioral therapeutic approaches with sexual assault victims. The video intervention distilled critical treatment elements in an effort to minimize anxiety and discomfort about the exam itself, and also to prevent longer term psychological distress and substance use. Their results indicated that the video intervention was successful in reducing postassault substance use (among women who used prior to the assault) and postassault psychological distress, particularly among women who had prior histories of sexual assault. This video intervention offers a cost-effective—and easy-to-implement—approach for bringing mental health services to victims in the critical hours immediately following the assault.

Second, when victims do seek mental health services later on in their recovery process, it is imperative that they receive empirically supported treatments. Several researchers/practitioners have called for increased use of evidence-based practice in rape crisis centers and other community-based mental health services settings (Edmond, 2006; Sprang et al., 2008). Making training available for frontline community providers on how to deliver empirically supported treatments is a necessary first step (Sprang et al., 2008), but knowledge is rarely sufficient for innovation adoption (Miller & Shinn, 2005). Changing existing practice requires that individuals and organizations have the training, expertise, and funding to adopt the innovation. Training may be a particularly salient resource because most direct-service mental health professionals do not receive adequate instruction on working with victims (Ullman, 2007). In response to this gap, several national/federal research agendas on interpersonal violence have called for more training of mental health workers and community providers (e.g., medical and criminal justice personnel; Koss, 2008). Ullman (2007) argued that such training must focus on teaching professionals how to inquire in a sensitive manner about women's histories of victimization. Survivors may be reluctant, understandably so, to disclose abuse, and yet the underlying reason for their distress may be a history of victimization (e.g., physical and sexual violence). Training is an important first step in ensuring that mental health professionals are responding appropriately to the needs of victimized women.

Even with adequate training and resources, however, Miller and Shinn's (2005) review indicates that practitioners, whether based in community service centers or in the formal mental health system, can be resistant to evidence-based practice if they perceive that the innovation is incongruent with their values and practice beliefs. In the context of mental health services for sexual assault victims, this seems quite possible, given that rape crisis centers' roots are in the antirape social movement, which arose in a historical context markedly different from that of the mental health profession. The limited empirical data on rape crisis centers' mental health services suggest a strong value of feminist, empowerment-focused approaches (Edmond, 2006; Ullman & Townsend, 2008), which could be perceived as incongruent with therapeutic approaches that do not emphasize the broader social context of sexual assault. Similarly, mental health practitioners who are not affiliated with rape crisis centers specifically favor integrating multiple therapeutic orientations and approaches (Campbell, Raja, & Grining, 1999; Sprang et al., 2008), which could be viewed as antithetical to the adoption of manualized interventions (i.e., a standardized approach to obtaining optimal outcomes). Kazdin (2008) noted that mental health practitioners' skepticism of evidence-based practice may run even deeper. Participant samples and treatment success are often narrowly defined in efficacy research, leaving clinicians to question whether such treatments can create meaningful improvement in clients' everyday life functioning. Research on clinical decision making is clearly warranted to understand how the beliefs and values of rape crisis center counselors and other community-based mental health providers shape their choice and implementation of treatment approaches.

However, none of these challenges to the adoption and implementation of empirically supported treatments is insurmountable. Many empirically supported treatments do indeed have strong feminist roots and also integrate successful approaches across multiple therapeutic models (e.g., Resick's intervention model, among others). Perhaps, then, the challenge is one of mutual buy-in: practitioners willing to learn about and try new intervention models and researchers willing to examine how indigenous knowledge from practice may complement their intervention models. There is a well-documented bias among social scientists who believe that evidence-based practice and empirically supported treatments are more beneficial than indigenous practices. However, many indigenous practices have not been studied and indeed may yet prove effective if studied (Rogers, 2003). In other words, it is entirely possible that the mental health services provided by rape crisis centers and other community-based programs are effective in alleviating victims' symptoms and helping them heal and recover from the trauma of sexual assault. This is an empirical question that needs further examination. Improving mental health care for sexual assault survivors does not necessarily mean promoting the adoption of methods created by researchers in clinical trial/treatment outcome research, although it could. Miller and Shinn (2005) advocated for more research that seeks to understand what is being offered in community settings, to identify indigenous strategies that are effective, and to capture local knowledge and expertise, because closing the research–practice gap requires partnerships with the "agencies, organizations, and associations that are the lifeblood of the community" (p. 179). In that vein, translational research projects with rape crisis centers and other community-based mental health services are needed to evaluate current services, assess the need for adoption of empirically supported treatments, and disseminate effective practices.

REFERENCES

American College of Obstetricians and Gynecologists. (1998). Sexual assault (ACOG educational bulletin). *International Journal of Gynaecology and Obstetrics, 60,* 297–304. doi:10.1016/S0020-7292(98)90089-3

American Medical Association. (1995). *Strategies for the treatment and prevention of sexual assault.* Chicago, IL: Author.

American Psychological Association Presidential Task Force on Evidence-Based Practice. (2006). Evidence-based practice in psychology. *American Psychologist, 61,* 271–285. doi:10.1037/0003-066X.61.4.271

Amey, A. L., & Bishai, D. (2002). Measuring the quality of medical care for women who experience sexual assault with data from the National Hospital Ambulatory Medical Care Survey. *Annals of Emergency Medicine, 39,* 631–638. doi:10.1067/mem.2002.123357

Bletzer, K. V., & Koss, M. P. (2006). After rape among three populations in the Southwest: A time for mourning, a time for recovery. *Violence Against Women, 12,* 5–29. doi:10.1177/1077801205277352

Brymer, M., Layne, C., Jacobs, A., Pynoos, R., Ruzek, J., Steinberg, A., . . . Watson, P. J. (2006). *Psychological first aid: Field operations guide* (2nd ed.). Los Angeles, CA: National Child Traumatic Stress Network and National Center for PTSD.

Campbell, R. (2005). What really happened? A validation study of rape survivors' help-seeking experiences with the legal and medical systems. *Violence and Victims, 20*, 55–68. doi:10.1891/vivi.2005.20.1.55

Campbell, R. (2006). Rape survivors' experiences with the legal and medical systems: Do rape victim advocates make a difference? *Violence Against Women, 12*, 30–45. doi:10.1177/1077801205277539

Campbell, R. (2008). *Multidisciplinary responses to sexual violence crimes: A review of the impact of SANE and SARTs on criminal prosecution.* Washington, DC: National Institute of Justice.

Campbell, R., & Adams, A. E. (2009). Why do rape survivors volunteer for face-to-face interviews? A meta-study of victims' reasons for participating in research. *Journal of Interpersonal Violence, 24*, 395–405. doi:10.1177/0886260508317192

Campbell, R., Adams, A. E., & Patterson, D. (2008). Methodological challenges of collecting evaluation data from traumatized clients/consumers: A comparison of three methods. *The American Journal of Evaluation, 29*, 369–381. doi:10.1177/1098214008320736

Campbell, R., Bybee, D., Ford, J. K., Patterson, D., & Ferrell, J. (2009). *A systems change analysis of SANE programs: Identifying the mediating mechanisms of criminal justice system impact.* Final report for grant 2005-WG-BX-0003. Washington, DC: National Institute of Justice.

Campbell, R., Dworkin, E., & Cabral, G. (2009). An ecological model of the impact of sexual assault on women's mental health. *Trauma, Violence & Abuse, 10*, 225–246. doi:10.1177/1524838009334456

Campbell, R., Patterson, D., Adams, A. E., Diegel, R., & Coats, S. (2008). A participatory evaluation project to measure SANE nursing practice and adult sexual assault patients' psychological well-being. *Journal of Forensic Nursing, 4*, 19–28. doi:10.1111/j.1939-3938.2008.00003.x

Campbell, R., Patterson, D., & Lichty, L.F. (2005). The effectiveness of sexual assault nurse examiner (SANE) program: A review of psychological, medical, legal, and community outcomes. *Trauma, Violence, & Abuse: A Review Journal, 6*, 313–329.

Campbell, R., & Raja, S. (1999). The secondary victimization of rape victims: Insights from mental health professionals who treat survivors of violence. *Violence and Victims, 14*, 261–275.

Campbell, R., Raja, S., & Grining, P. L. (1999). Training mental health professionals on violence against women. *Journal of Interpersonal Violence, 14*, 1003–1013. doi:10.1177/088626099014010001

Campbell, R., Sefl, T., Barnes, H. E., Ahrens, C. E., Wasco, S. M., & Zaragoza-Diesfeld, Y. (1999). Community services for rape survivors: Enhancing psychological well-being or increasing trauma? *Journal of Consulting and Clinical Psychology, 67*, 847–858. doi:10.1037/0022-006X.67.6.847

Campbell, R., Sefl, T., Wasco, S. M., & Ahrens, C. E. (2004). Doing community research without a community: Creating safe space for rape survivors. *American*

Journal of Community Psychology, 33, 253–261. doi:10.1023/B:AJCP.00000 27010.74708.38

Campbell, R., Townsend, S. M., Long, S. M., Kinnison, K. E., Pulley, E. M., Adames, S. B., & Wasco, S. M. (2006). Responding to sexual assault victims' medical and emotional needs: A national study of the services provided by SANE programs. *Research in Nursing & Health, 29*, 384–398. doi:10.1002/nur.20137

Campbell, R., Wasco, S. M., Ahrens, C. E., Sefl, T., & Barnes, H. E. (2001). Preventing the "second rape:" Rape survivors' experiences with community service providers. *Journal of Interpersonal Violence, 16*, 1239–1259. doi:10.1177/088626 001016012002

Centers for Disease Control and Prevention. (2002). Sexual assault and STDs— Adults and adolescents. *Morbidity and Mortality Weekly Report, 51*(RR-6), 69–71.

Cole, J., & Logan, T. (2010). Interprofessional collaboration on sexual assault response teams (SART): The role of victim alcohol use and a partner-perpetrator. *Journal of Interpersonal Violence, 25*, 336–357. doi:10.1177/0886260509334406

Cole, J., & Logan, T. (2008). Negotiating the challenges of multidisciplinary responses to sexual assault victims: Sexual assault nurse examiner and victim advocacy programs. *Research in Nursing & Health, 31*, 76–85. doi:10.1002/nur.20234

Crandall, C., & Helitzer, D. (2003). *Impact evaluation of a Sexual Assault Nurse Examiner (SANE) program* (Document No. 203276). Washington, DC: National Institute of Justice.

Du Mont, J., White, D., & McGregor, M. J. (2009). Investigating the medical forensic examination from the perspectives of sexually assaulted women. *Social Science & Medicine, 68*, 774–780. doi:10.1016/j.socscimed.2008.11.010

Edmond, T. (2006, February). *Theoretical and intervention preferences of service providers addressing violence against women: A national survey.* Paper presented at the Council on Social Work Education Conference, Chicago, IL.

Ericksen, J., Dudley, C., McIntosh, G., Ritch, L., Shumay, S., & Simpson, M. (2002). Client's experiences with a specialized sexual assault service. *Journal of Emergency Nursing, 28*, 86–90. doi:10.1067/men.2002.121740

Espey, E., Ogburn, T., Leeman, L., Buchen, E., Angeli, E., & Qualls, C. (2009). Compliance with mandated emergency contraception in New Mexico emergency departments. *Journal of Women's Health, 18*, 619–623. doi:10.1089/jwh.2008.0919

Foa, E. B., Keane, T. M., & Friedman, M. J. (Eds.). (2000). *Effective treatments for PTSD: Practice guidelines from the International Society for Traumatic Stress Studies.* New York, NY: Guilford Press.

Kazdin, A. E. (2008). Evidence-based treatment and practice: New opportunities to bridge clinical research and practice, enhance the knowledge base, and improve patient care. *American Psychologist, 63*, 146–159. doi:10.1037/0003-066X.63.3.146

Kilpatrick, D. G., Edmunds, C. N., & Seymour, A. (1992). *Rape in America: A report to the nation.* Arlington, VA: National Victim Center.

Koss, M. P. (2008, February). *Interpersonal violence agendas: Past and future*. Paper presented at the American Psychological Association Summit on Violence and Abuse in Relationships, Bethesda, MD.

Koss, M., & Achilles, M. (2008). *Restorative justice responses to sexual assault*. Retrieved from http://www.vawnet.org

Koss, M. P., Bailey, J. A., Yuan, N. P., Herrera, V. M., & Lichter, E. L. (2003). Depression and PTSD in survivors of male violence: Research and training initiatives to facilitate recovery. *Psychology of Women Quarterly, 27*, 130–142. doi:10.1111/1471-6402.00093

Koss, M. P., Figueredo, A. J., Bell, I., Tharan, M., & Tromp, S. (1996). Traumatic memory characteristics: A cross-validated meditational model of response to rape among employed women. *Journal of Abnormal Psychology, 105*, 421–432. doi:10.1037/0021-843X.105.3.421

Koss, M. P., Tromp, S., & Tharan, M. (1995). Traumatic memories: Empirical foundations, forensic, and clinical implications. *Clinical Psychology: Science and Practice, 2*, 111–132. doi:10.1111/j.1468-2850.1995.tb00034.x

Ledray, L. E. (1999). *Sexual assault nurse examiner (SANE) development & operations guide*. Washington, DC: Office for Victims of Crime, U.S. Department of Justice.

Macy, R. J., Giattina, M., Sangster, T. H., Crosby, C., & Montijo, N. J. (2009). Domestic violence and sexual assault services: Inside the black box. *Aggression and Violent Behavior, 14*, 359–373. doi:10.1016/j.avb.2009.06.002

Martin, P. Y. (2005). *Rape work: Victims, gender, and emotions in organization and community context*. New York, NY: Routledge.

McHugh, R. K., & Barlow, D. H. (2010). The dissemination and implementation of evidence-based psychological treatments: A review of current efforts. *American Psychologist, 65*, 73–84. doi:10.1037/a0018121

Miller, R. L., & Shinn, M. (2005). Learning from communities: Overcoming difficulties in dissemination of prevention and promotion efforts. *American Journal of Community Psychology, 35*, 169–183. doi:10.1007/s10464-005-3395-1

National Sexual Violence Resource Center. (2006). *Report on the national needs assessment of sexual assault response teams*. Harrisburg, PA: Author.

National Victim Center. (1992). *Rape in America: A report to the nation*. Arlington, VA: Author.

Parker, C. L., Barnett, D. J., Everly, G. S., & Links, J. M. (2006). Expanding disaster mental health response: A conceptual training framework for public health professionals. *International Journal of Emergency Mental Health, 8*, 101–109.

Peace, K. A., Porter, S., & Brinke, L. (2008). Are memories for sexually traumatic events "special"? A within-subjects investigation of trauma and memory in a clinical sample. *Memory, 16*, 10–21. doi:10.1080/09658210701363583

Plichta, S. B., Vandecar-Burdin, T., Odor, R. K., Reams, S., & Zhang, Y. (2006). The emergency department and victims of sexual violence: An assessment of preparedness to help. *Journal of Health and Human Services Administration, 29*, 285–308.

Resick, P. A., Galovski, T. E., Uhlmansiek, M., Scher, C. D., Clum, G. A., & Young-Xu, Y. (2008). A randomized control trial to dismantle components of cognitive processing therapy for posttraumatic stress disorder in female victims of interpersonal violence. *Journal of Consulting and Clinical Psychology, 76,* 243–258. doi:10.1037/0022-006X.76.2.243

Resnick, H. S., Acierno, R., Amstadter, A., Self-Brown, S., & Kilpatrick, D. (2007). An acute post-sexual assault intervention to prevent drug use: Updated findings. *Addictive Behaviors, 32,* 2032–2045. doi:10.1016/j.addbeh.2007.01.001

Resnick, H., Acierno, R., Waldrop, A. E., King, L., King, D., Danielson, C., . . . Kilpatrick, D. (2007). Randomized controlled evaluation of an early intervention to prevent post-rape psychopathology. *Behaviour Research and Therapy, 45,* 2432–2447. doi:10.1016/j.brat.2007.05.002

Rogers, E. M. (2003). *Diffusion of innovations* (5th ed.). New York, NY: The Free Press.

Rosenbaum, A., & Langhinrichsen-Rohling, J. (2006). Meta-research on violence and victims: The impact of data collection methods on findings and participants. *Violence and Victims, 21,* 404–409. doi:10.1891/vivi.21.4.404

Ruzek, J. I., Brymer, M. J., Jacobs, A. K., Layne, C. M., Vernberg, E. M., & Watson, P. J. (2007). Psychological first aid. *Journal of Mental Health Counseling, 29,* 17–49.

Smugar, S. S., Spina, B. J., & Merz, J. F. (2000). Informed consent for emergency contraception: Variability in hospital care of rape victims. *American Journal of Public Health, 90,* 1372–1376. doi:10.2105/AJPH.90.9.1372

Sprang, G., Craig, C., & Clark, J. (2008). Factors impacting trauma treatment practice patterns: The convergence/ divergence of science and practice. *Journal of Anxiety Disorders, 22,* 162–174. doi:10.1016/j.janxdis.2007.02.003

Starzynski, L. L., Ullman, S. E., Townsend, S. M., Long, D. M., & Long, S. M. (2007). What factors predict women's disclosure of sexual assault to mental health professionals? *Journal of Community Psychology, 35,* 619–638. doi:10.1002/jcop.20168

Stueve, A., O'Donnell, L. N., Duran, R., San Doval, A., & Blome, J. (2001). Methodological issues in time-space sampling in minority communities: Results with Latino young men who have sex with men. *American Journal of Public Health, 91,* 922–926. doi:10.2105/AJPH.91.6.922

Tjaden, P., & Thoennes, N. (1998). *Full report of the prevalence, incidence, and consequences of violence against women: Findings from the National Violence Against Women Survey.* Washington, DC: National Institute of Justice.

Ullman, S. E. (1996). Do social reactions to sexual assault victims vary by support provider? *Violence and Victims, 11,* 143–157.

Ullman, S. E. (2007). Mental health services seeking in sexual assault victims. *Women & Therapy, 30,* 61–84. doi:10.1300/J015v30n01_04

Ullman, S. E., & Filipas, H. H. (2001). Predictors of PTSD symptom severity and social reactions in sexual assault victims. *Journal of Traumatic Stress, 14,* 369–389. doi:10.1023/A:1011125220522

Ullman, S. E., & Townsend, S. M. (2008). What is an empowerment approach to working with sexual assault survivors? *Journal of Community Psychology, 36,* 299–312. doi:10.1002/jcop.20198

Vickerman, K. A., & Margolin, G. (2009). Rape treatment outcome research: Empirical findings and state of the literature. *Clinical Psychology Review, 29,* 431–448. doi:10.1016/j.cpr.2009.04.004

Wasco, S. M., Campbell, R., Howard, A., Mason, G., Schewe, P., Staggs, S., & Riger, S. (2004). A statewide evaluation of services provided to rape survivors. *Journal of Interpersonal Violence, 19,* 252–263. doi:10.1177/0886260503260246

Wgliski, A., & Barthel, A. K. (2004). Cultural differences in reporting of sexual assault to sexual assault agencies in the United States. *Sexual Assault Report, 7,* 92–93.

6

TREATMENT FOR PERPETRATORS OF SEXUAL VIOLENCE

ROBERT A. PRENTKY, ADEENA M. GABRIEL, AND ANNA I. COWARD

This chapter addresses the question of treatment efficacy with sex offenders, a specialized group for whom treatment has been mandated and implemented over the past half century but with whom treatment remains largely disappointing with respect to effectiveness. Extensive research spanning several decades on the effectiveness of psychotherapy, broadly conceived, leads to the general conclusion that therapy works. The average treated individual improves as much as 80% over the average untreated individual (Lambert & Ogles, 2004).

We know substantially less, however, about the effectiveness of psychotherapy with specialized populations. This is a matter of some concern because applying a broadly based treatment model to groups with specialized treatment needs could result in a loss of efficacy if the model fails to take into account unique demands of that specialized population. Focusing on incarcerated offenders, a group that includes predominantly rapists and child molesters, the chapter examines the effectiveness of prison-based treatment, the application of broadly derived treatments to the specialized environment of prison, and the ways in which we might achieve a feasible and more effective treatment program for this specialized population. This chapter does not address the equally important subject of treatment of sex offenders in the community.

WHAT DO WE KNOW?

Legal Context

Before examining the effectiveness of treatment for sex offenders, it is helpful to place these programs in a legal context. Beginning in 1990, with the passage of the first sexually violent predator (SVP) law in the state of Washington (cf. Boerner, 1992; Governor's Task Force on Community Protection, 1989; Fujimoto, 1992), an unprecedented number of state and federal laws intended to curb sexual violence have been passed. No fewer than nine pieces of federal legislation have been approved that seek to reduce sexual violence by managing the "most dangerous" through civil commitment and controlling those returned to the community through registration and public notification.[1]

Although the civil commitment laws recognize a role for treatment, the nature of the role is unclear. Prentky and Burgess (2000) noted,

> The Court apparently envisioned a (limited) role for treatment even in *Hendricks* . . . The Court seemed to adopt a middle-ground position, indicating that the state may be obliged to provide treatment that is *"available"* for disorders that are *"treatable"* (cf. Janus, 1998). By the same token, the Court clearly rejected the proposition that *effective* treatment is required to justify civil commitment." (p. 153)

Despite the aforementioned ambiguity from the Supreme Court (see *Kansas v. Hendricks*), states have generally placed a high priority on treatment. Ruling on five consolidated cases including *Turay v. Seling et al.*, Judge Dwyer observed, for instance, that

> nothing compels a state to adopt a statute of this nature in the first place and many states have not done so, but a state that chooses to have such a program must make adequate mental health treatment available to those committed. (p. 16)

---

[1]Federal legislation has included the Violence Against Women Act of 1994 (VAWA); the expanded VAWA legislation in 2000 (Pub. L.106-386, 18 U.S.C. 2261); the Wetterling Act, passed in 1994 as part of the Violent Crime Control and Law Enforcement Act (42 U.S.C. 14071); the amended Wetterling Act of 1996, known as "Megan's Law" (Pub. L. 104-145); the amended Federal Rules of Evidence, in 1995, to include prior sex crimes; the Pam Lynchner Sexual Offender Tracking and Identification Act (42 U.S.C. 14072) in 1996; the Wetterling Improvements Act of 1997 (Pub. L. 105-119); the Victims of Trafficking and Violence Prevention Act of 2000; and the Adam Walsh Child Protection and Safety Act of 2006 (Pub. L. No. 109-248, 42 U.S.C. 16901).

Although *adequate* has never been operationalized, all states with sex offender civil commitment statutes provide for some form of sex offender–specific treatment. Indeed, forensic treatment of sex offenders, whether in prison or in the community, has evolved into a niche of clinical practice that employs a significant number of practitioners. The largest professional organization, the Association for Treatment of Sexual Abusers (ATSA), has an estimated 2,049 clinical members, and that number clearly does not reflect the numerous therapists who treat sex offenders and do not belong to ATSA (e.g., between 50% and 60% of those who attend ATSA conferences are nonmembers). It is reasonable to conclude that sex offender treatment has become a salient niche of clinical practice.

In this chapter, we tackle several straightforward questions regarding the efficacy of treatment for sex offenders: (a) What does extant empirical research tell us about the efficacy of sex offender treatment? (b) What does the literature say about the underlying factors that are most strongly associated with treatment efficacy in *general* clinical practice? (c) What may we infer from the application of these factors to the practice of treating sex offenders? (d) What are the basic principles of evidence-based *general* clinical practice? and (e) How might we apply (and achieve) evidence-based practice in treatment of sex offenders?

Rationale for Treating Sex Offenders

The rationale for treating sex offenders has been described as *pro bono publico*—"for the good of the public" (Prentky, 1995). That is, the most compelling reason for treating sex offenders is reducing the likelihood that those offenders will reoffend and create additional victims. The primary goal of sex offender treatment is not to cure sex offenders or to make them feel better but (a) to reduce the risk that they will reoffend, and (b) to assist with the optimal management of those sex offenders who are in the community. Therefore, sex offender–specific treatment invariably targets problems that are risk-relevant. Beyond that fact, sex offender treatment is much like treatment of other behavior problems. The commonly accepted modality is cognitive behavior therapy. Techniques used include relapse prevention, aimed at averting recidivism through the identification of precursors, and cognitive behavioral techniques, intended to influence problematic emotions and behaviors. These techniques were developed for the general population and have been adapted for use with sex offenders. By and large, the major differences between standard mental health treatment and sex offender–specific treatment lie in the conditions and circumstances of treatment, not the treatment itself. In the standard mental health model, an underlying assumption is that clients voluntarily seek help, prompted by a personal crisis or personal distress. By contrast, it is most often the case that sex offenders have not freely chosen to be in treatment. They are placed in treatment by the court as part of an agreement to avoid going to prison, as part of a prison-based treatment program or civil commitment program, or as part of a release condition after serving their sentence. Although offenders may "volunteer" for a prison-based treatment program, with the understanding that such participation will be looked upon favorably by the court and/or the parole board, such participation is often prompted by motives other than the desire to be in treatment. Civilly committed sex offenders will be placed in a treatment program, with the implied understanding that their progress in treatment is tied to the timing of their release. It is rare that these offenders step forward and volunteer for treatment out of a genuine desire to change their behavior. The net result is that sex offenders are a captive population of "clients" who, for the most part, enter treatment with little or no desire to be there. Moreover, sex offender treatment is rarely, in any true sense, confidential. Since sex offenders are expected to "come clean" and disclose all sexually deviant behavior, whether those behaviors are known to the criminal justice system or not, they are placed in a bind. If they comply, what they disclose may be used against them in future legal proceedings. If they do not comply, their noncompliance and their failure to meet treatment goals may be used against them. Sex offenders obviously are aware of this predicament, a condition that encourages "partial truths" and partial disclosures.

HOW (WELL) DO WE KNOW IT?

Because the principal goal of sex offender treatment is to reduce future sex offending, the rate of reoffending, or recidivism, is typically used to measure the impact of interventions. Differences in sexual recidivism rates across studies may be attributable to offender characteristics or program characteristics (e.g., differences in the amount and quality of treatment provided, differences in the conditions under which treatment was provided, and differences in posttreatment supervision), as well as differences in how the studies were conducted, such as length of follow-up, sources of data used to estimate recidivism, and the definition of what constitutes recidivism (Prentky, Lee, Knight, & Cerce, 1997). These differences should be regarded as a cautionary note when drawing conclusions about the following outcome research.

In an early meta-analytic study, Hall (1995) combined 12 studies of treated sex offenders for a total sample of 1,313 men. Hall found a small but significant overall decrease in sexual recidivism as a function of treatment. The recidivism rate for treated sex offenders was 19%, compared with the recidivism rate of 27% for untreated sex offenders. For those studies that used cognitive behavior therapy or antiandrogen medication (drugs that lower the level of testosterone, reducing the frequency and intensity of sexual urges), the decrease resulting from treatment was more than 8%.

A Canadian study followed 296 treated and 283 untreated offenders for an average of 6 years (Nicholaichuk, Gordon, Gu, & Wong, 2000). This study provided convincing evidence of the efficacy of treatment, with conviction rates of 15% for treated sex offenders and 33% for untreated sex offenders. However, the researchers did note the obvious fact that the statistical difference between the two groups was attributable to the high sexual recidivism rate for the matched comparison group of untreated offenders, not the lower recidivism rate for the treated offenders.

The Collaborative Outcome Data Project on the Effectiveness of Psychological Treatment for Sex Offenders (Hanson et al., 2002) used meta-analysis to combine and collectively examine the effect of treatment in 43 studies with a total of 9,454 sex offenders (5,078 offenders had received some form of treatment, and 4,376 offenders received none). Averaged across all studies, the percentage of offenders who reoffended was approximately 12% for treated and 17% for untreated subjects. When Hanson et al. (2002) considered only studies examining treatments in effect after 1980 (presumably those that used the relapse prevention model), the sexual recidivism rates were approximately 10% for treated and 17% for untreated offenders. The largest meta-analysis to date, collapsed across 69 studies with a total sample size of 22,181 sex offenders (Lösel & Schmucker, 2005), found a 6% reduction in sexual recidivism with treatment.

Zgoba and Simon (2005) compared sex offenders drawn from New Jersey's state prison for sex offenders, where treatment is provided to sex offenders from the general prison population. Of the total sample, 14% committed a new sexual offense within the 7-year follow-up. There were no statistically significant differences in sexual recidivism rates between treated and nontreated offenders: Treatment reduced recidivism by roughly 4% for the rapists and 5% for child molesters.

The gold standard for program evaluation is the randomized clinical trial (RCT), which involves the random assignment of study participants to different conditions. The only RCT of treatment that has been conducted with adult sex offenders (relapse prevention) was California's Sex Offender Treatment and Evaluation Project (hereafter referred to as California's Treatment Project; Marques, Day, Nelson, & West, 1993; Marques, Nelson, Alarcon, & Day, 2000). The volunteers in the California Treatment Project, operating from 1985 to 1995, were randomly assigned to either the treatment condition (the Treatment Group) or to the no-treatment condition (the No-Treatment, Volunteer Control Group). In addition, assuming that willingness to participate might portend a better outcome, the investigators also included a randomly selected group of sex offenders who did not volunteer (the No-Treatment, Non-Volunteer Control Group). At the end of the study, with follow-up ranging from 5 to 14 years, the sexual reoffense rates were 22% for the Treatment Group; 20% for the No-Treatment Volunteer Control Group; and 19% for the No-Treatment, Non-Volunteer Control Group (Marques, Wiederanders, Day, Nelson, & van Ommeren, 2005). There were no significant group differences for either rapists or child molesters.

All three meta-analytic studies yielded similar results: a treatment benefit of approximately a 6% to 8% reduction in sexual reoffending. Because of the large sample sizes, minor differences in rates among the studies can reach statistical significance but may fail to be large enough to have practical significance. The Zgoba and Simon (2005) study, with a much smaller sample, yielded a reduction in recidivism of 4% to 5%, which was not statistically significant. Only one study reported a large reduction (18%) in sexual reoffense rates (Nicholaichuk et al., 2000). Barbaree (1997) observed that the base rates (incidence) of sexual recidivism in most studies range from .10 to .40 and that sample sizes in most studies are relatively small, rarely more than 200 offenders. With a low incidence of sexual recidivism and a small sample, the treatment effect would have to be very large (greater than .50) for differences between treated and nontreated offenders to be statistically significant. As Barbaree (1997) demonstrated, it is unlikely that conventional treatment outcome studies, such as Zgoba and Simon's (2005), could yield a significant treatment effect. This is why we are seeing relatively small, but nonetheless significant, treatment effects from the meta-analyses, which amass very large samples.

Given the consistency of these findings, it is tempting to conclude that treatment can reduce sexual recidivism by roughly 4% to 8%. In doing so, however, we must ignore the results of California's Treatment Project, which used state-of-the-art scientific practices, including use of the RCT design. How to place in perspective the disconcerting findings from the California Treatment Project has itself become a matter of controversy (Marshall & Marshall, 2007, 2008; Seto et al., 2008). Ignoring what is generally regarded as the gold standard is hazardous. As Marques et al. (2005) pointed out, "the most important safeguard against misleading results . . . remains a randomized design" (p. 103). We would go one step further. We would argue that it is pointless to debate the superiority of the RCT design in the abstract without acknowledging that reliable findings on efficacy of prison-based sex offender treatment are compromised by innumerable methodological problems. Marshall and Marshall (2008) appear to be making this point when referring to "the very important process issues of how treatment is delivered" (p. 257). Paradoxically, however, the California Treatment Project was far more rigorously controlled and run and closer to expectation of how treatment in general should be delivered than the prison-based civil commitment programs elsewhere.

TREATMENT MODELS FOR SEX OFFENDERS

Jails and prisons have become the largest institutional repositories for the mentally ill (Huffman, 2006), and in 20 states, sex offenders have become the largest designated group of so-called mentally ill criminals to be civilly committed to prison. Statutory management strategies aimed at sex offenders have created a cottage industry out of treatment programs and therapists targeting this subgroup of criminals. As mentioned previously, despite the significant effects of psychotherapy as a whole, research suggests that no one form of therapy is superior to any other (Smith & Glass, 1977; Wampold et al., 1997); if indeed all modes of therapy are comparably effective, there must be common elements that account for the therapeutic effect when present and that account for the lack of an effect when absent. These commonly identified elements include, but are not limited to, voluntariness of treatment, confidentiality, prevention of dual-role relationships, and similarity in therapist and client values.

Sex offenders have their own treatment model, an adaptation of relapse prevention (e.g., Laws, 1989, 1995; Laws, Hudson, & Ward, 2000; Pithers & Gray, 1996; Pithers, Marques, Gibat, & Marlatt, 1983; Prentky, 2003; Schwartz & Cellini, 1995, 1997). The relapse prevention (RP) model was designed specifically for people with alcoholism (Marlatt, 1985) and has subsequently been used with other addictive behaviors (cf. Brownell, Marlatt, Lichtenstein, & Wilson, 1986). Although sexually aggressive behavior may, in selected cases (e.g., highly repetitive offenses with a clear paraphilic element), conform to an addiction model, there is no evidence that all, or even most, sexual offenders are sexual "addicts." We would argue that sexually aggressive behavior, in its marked heterogeneity, derives from a more complex amalgam of factors than most addictive disorders. Nonetheless, the widely accepted use of the adapted RP model suggests principles that are, at least theoretically, similar to the addictions model (e.g., the notion of compulsivity and irresistibility). Before designing a treatment plan, clinicians must first identify those factors that are most importantly related to the relapsing behavior. *Relapse* refers, in this case, to a new sexual offense, and the focus of the model is a unique *offense cycle* (tailored to an individual) that identifies the many emotional and behavioral precursors leading to relapse *for that individual*. Once the full offense cycle is developed, the offender learns intervention strategies for "breaking" the cycle once it begins.

Although sex offenders have an adapted RP treatment model, the common elements deemed critical for therapeutic efficacy across most domains of clinical practice should apply equally to them. Stated otherwise, there is no reason to believe that sex offenders are so utterly unique with respect to their core treatment issues that the therapeutic process that appears to work for everyone else does not apply to them. Although the beneficiaries of clinical intervention are typically referred to as *patients* or *clients*, incarcerated offenders are *inmates*. We next explore how the therapeutic process applies to this group of inmates.

Voluntariness

Elementary components of the therapeutic process that clinicians take for granted in general practice are weak to nonexistent in prison-based sex offender treatment programs. A great deal of emphasis has been placed on this aspect of the therapeutic process because "the patient's capacity and willingness to participate in the therapy interaction are among the most important determinants of improvement" (Gomes-Schwartz, 1978). Patient involvement correlates significantly with outcome (Windholz & Silberschatz, 1988) and predicts overall improvement (O'Malley, Suh, & Strupp, 1983).

This basic tenet is frequently unmet when sex offenders are placed in treatment. Although some sex offenders undoubtedly welcome the opportunity to be in therapy, many do not, either because they feel they do not require treatment or because participation comes at too high a price (i.e., disclosures in treatment may be used against them in court to justify continued incarceration). In any case, for the majority of sex offenders in prison, treatment is not elective.

The literature has supported this notion. Expressed desire for treatment among incarcerated sex offenders began to decline in the 1980s, and the decline has continued into the 2000s; there has also been a decline in the number of inmates who receive treatment for any length of time (Langevin, 2006). Only half of the offenders surveyed expressed a desire for treatment, fewer were actually treated, and fewer still completed even a short course of treatment (Langevin, 2006). Because of this paucity of interest in therapy among inmates, therapy in prison is typically not voluntary (Mitford, 1973; Wright, 1973). As a result, compliance (which typically consists of treatment attendance, active participation in treatment, and willingness to disclose personal and offense-related information during sessions) tends to be poor, ranging from approximately 46% (Miner & Dwyer, 1995) to 53% (Geer et al., 2001).

Confidentiality

The courts have acknowledged the importance of confidentiality for psychotherapy to be effective, noting that "the mere possibility of the disclosure of facts, emotions, memories, and fears, i.e. of confidential communications, may impede development of the relationship necessary for successful treatment" (*Jaffee v. Redmond*, 1996, quoting *United States v. Trammel*, 1980). When the guarantee of confidentiality is broken or understood to be partial, trust is undermined and with it the assumption of complete and veridical disclosure. Yet confidentiality is fully understood to be, at most, partial in the prison-based treatment programs for sex offenders.

Three levels of confidentiality theoretically exist in a prison setting: (a) between the therapist and inmate, (b) between the therapist and the institution, and (c) among inmates. Therapists' files can be read by prison staff at any time, and the prison has the authority to release records to the courts, to the prosecuting attorney's office, or to other interested parties whenever it is deemed necessary, effectively destroying both therapist/inmate and therapist/ institution privileges (Schlesinger, 1979). Sex offenders typically are required to sign an informed consent statement acknowledging the potential release of such disclosures to the criminal justice system. If treatment disclosures are deemed partial or incomplete, the offender may be classified noncompliant by the therapist. If disclosures include previously unknown victims or unknown inappropriate or coercive sexual behavior, those disclosures will be documented in the progress notes and thus become part of the permanent institutional record that will weigh heavily in future determinations of risk.

As a result, inmates are reluctant to disclose in treatment (Schlesinger, 1979) and often do not trust prison therapists, seeing them as members of the prison staff (Goffman, 1961) rather than as individuals whose only consideration is the inmate's best interests. Although approximately 90% of inmates receiving treatment in the 1960s admitted to their therapists that they had committed the offenses for which they had been incarcerated, this rate declined steadily beginning in the 1980s and dropped to only 50% by the 2000s (Langevin, 2006). The less an inmate reveals in therapy about his history of sexual crimes, the less likely that incriminating information will become public and be used against him. Inmate subculture, moreover, derives its structure from identifying and exploiting weaknesses in other inmates (Schrag, 1973); the less an individual's fellow inmates know, the safer he is likely to be.

This steady decline both in taking responsibility and in willingly engaging in treatment is coincident with the advent of the new wave of civil commitment laws, beginning in 1990. Participation in treatment includes the expectation of full disclosure of all sexually "deviant" behavior, whether known to the criminal justice system or not. Sex offenders are placed in a double bind. Anything less than what is deemed to be "full" disclosure will be assessed unfavorably in progress reports and labeled as noncompliance. On the other hand, all disclosures considered to be clinically significant are likely to be documented, become part of the inmate's permanent record, and used in court to justify continued detention.

Dual Roles

The American Psychological Association's "Ethical Principles of Psychologists and Code of Conduct" (2002) protects clients by prohibiting their therapists from engaging in dual-role relationships. However, no such protection applies to prisoners. In the criminal justice system, therapists often perceive that they have multiple duties: not only to their client/inmate but also to the prison in which they operate. As a result, therapists may find themselves acting as de facto informants. Their duty to the prison is to help ensure the safety of the custodial environment by alerting custody staff about potentially volatile situations. Because of the "special" relationship that therapists have with inmates, the amount of "down time" that therapists may spend with inmates (particularly on units designed to be therapeutic communities), and the presumptive training that therapists receive to identify escalating emotions, therapists are frequently seen as allies of the custody staff. Therapists may also have a perceived duty to protect society by testifying in court about the progress, or lack thereof, of clients in treatment. The offender is sitting in the courtroom, so he hears firsthand what his therapist is saying about him. Given the adversarial nature of the proceeding, what the therapist says may not be flattering and may contribute to a finding that the inmate has not made adequate progress in treatment and thus remains at high risk. It is abundantly clear that the duties and roles of a therapist in a prison context are more complex than those of a therapist in the conventional context. Conflicting duties and blurred roles "go with the territory" for many prison-based therapists.

Values

A *value* has been defined as "an enduring belief that a specific mode of conduct or end state of existence is personally or socially preferable to an opposite or converse mode of conduct or end-state of existence" (Rokeach, 1973). Shaping of patient values can be beneficial. Mental health values (e.g., depression is bad) can and should be influenced by therapists not only because values reflect their expertise but also because shaping of values is a basic goal of the therapeutic process (Tjeltveit, 1999). Therapy is rarely value free, however, where sexuality is concerned. Therapists tend to value sex as an expression of love and commitment and value fidelity and monogamy (Ford & Hendrick, 2003). In addition, therapist characteristics can influence value similarity. Working with clients who possess differing values can affect a therapist's degree of comfort in working with that client, which may in turn influence treatment outcome.

As a result of such differences between general clinical practice and prison-based therapy, it is necessary to consider whether methods that have been proven effective in inpatient and outpatient settings will also be effective in a prison setting. Given that inmates most often have not sought therapy, are not voluntary participants, and frequently are, at best, grudging participants, what can be done to improve the quality, and ultimately the efficacy, of treatment services for sexual offenders?

ESTABLISHING EVIDENCE-BASED PRACTICE

Because of the limitations on treatment provided in prisons, it is impossible to determine if reduced efficacy is the result of the treatment itself or the restrictions being applied to its provision. That being the case, it may be useful to evaluate such treatment in a community, rather than prison, context. The elements of therapy, such as confidentiality and the treatment alliance, are more easily controlled and assured in a community setting, which may have a positive impact on the effectiveness of treatment. We have elsewhere commented that

> the most promising short-term solution to assessing the effectiveness of treatment involves the examination of within-treatment changes (i.e., changes occurring within a group of individuals all receiving the same treatment) on variables that are designed to reflect change in risk status. (Prentky, 2003, 13-7)

This goal, however admirable, is out of reach for prison-based treatment as a result of the patently suboptimal conditions under which such treatment is conducted.

Moreover, applying one formulaic intervention to a markedly heterogeneous group will inevitably yield suboptimal results. This point was underscored in a recent meta-analysis that examined the reduction in sexual reoffense when the principles of R/N/R (Risk/Need/ Responsivity; cf. Andrews & Bonta, 1998; Bonta & Andrews, 2007) are applied to treatment of sex offenders (Hanson, Bourgon, Helmus, & Hodgson, 2009). Programs that adhered to R/N/R evidenced the largest reductions in both sexual and general recidivism. Indeed, program effectiveness increased as the total number of R/N/R principles adhered to increased. The R/N/R model proposes that the most intense treatment services be reserved for those at greatest risk (the Risk part), that treatment programs target those *criminogenic needs* with empirical support (the Need part), and that programs use only techniques with demonstrated *responsivity* (i.e., techniques that sex offenders are known to respond to; the Responsivity part). Modern RP-based treatment programs adhere primarily to the Responsivity component at the expense of the Needs component, reflecting what is arguably the most serious Achilles' heel of contemporary programs.

Remarkably little has changed over the past 20 years or more since Weiner (1985) outlined four fundamental psycholegal issues in sex offender treatment: (a) the ability of the sex offender to give truly informed consent, (b) the voluntariness of the consent, (c) the offender's right to treatment, and (d) the offender's right to refuse treatment. To these seeming core issues, we would add several more articulated in this chapter: (e) the right to engage in treatment free of coercion, including the right to refuse medication and to refuse psychotherapy; (f) the right to maximum confidentiality that can be afforded such individuals; (g) the right to expect that treatment providers remain impartial and not adversarial witnesses in legal proceedings; and (h) the right to expect that the conditions of treatment will be adequate and that the provision of services will be prioritized and safeguarded against unnecessary changes and alterations by custodial personnel.

Overall, sex offender treatment violates two major canons of practice. Treatment modalities that are empirically supported with other clinical populations, such as relapse prevention with alcoholics, and that are imported into sex offender-specific treatment programs must be used as implemented and evaluated in past clinical studies to claim that the sex offender–specific application is an evidence-based treatment. Many treatment approaches, most notably RP, have been modified for use with sex offenders, as is clearly appropriate. To preserve the evidence-based seal of approval, however, the core of the model must be applied as originally tested. Stated otherwise, if RP, or any other modality, has been shown to be clinically effective, it must be implemented as it has been shown to work in clinical trials, not as an altered and possibly less effective version applied to sex offenders in prison. A second overarching violation is the practice itself. The practice of sex offender treatment in prison settings cannot be assumed to adhere, even remotely, to the basic principles underlying treatment efficacy that we have discussed. Determinations about what constitutes effective, evidence-based practice for incarcerated sex offenders are severely undermined by currently prevailing prison-based practice.

Reliable evaluation of the efficacy of treatment services for sex offenders in a prison environment is undermined by the following factors: (a) treatment is subordinated to security, with the inevitable consequence that institutional priorities will always place security above therapy; (b) conditions for therapy are suboptimal (e.g., severe space limitations that often require relying on part-time staff, limited scheduling options, adapting to the ever-changing conditions of a prison environment [which may require canceling groups or other treatment activities on a moment's notice], and maintaining staff morale in an environment that is often unsupportive of or even hostile to treatment); (c) physical safety of prisoners is threatened when they are known in the population as sex offenders, rendering therapy goals dependent on disclosure at odds with physical survival; (d) confidentiality cannot be assumed or ensured; (e) offenders are reluctant "customers"; (f) therapists often are inadequately trained and supervised; (g) program-related resources are limited and often restricted (e.g., therapists may be unable to provide desired interventions, such as behavior therapy or antiandrogen medication); and (h) the environment after release is determined not by individualized considerations but by a complex legal process that may impose sanctions such as sex offender registration and restrictions on work and leisure activities, making the task of examining the efficacy of treatment services for sex offenders exceedingly difficult. Such control strategies, moreover, may have the reverse effect of aggravating reoffense risk by imposing insurmountable obstacles to normal reintegration through forced social isolation, unemployment or underemployment, harassment and social ostracism, and adverse stress and negative effects on whatever social and familial supports may exist (e.g., Logan, 2003). The Wisconsin study is a noteworthy example of such problems (Zevitz & Farkas, 2000).

It should be clear that under these conditions, it would be a serious mistake to draw definitive conclusions about the efficacy, or inefficacy, of prison-based sex offender treatment. As Marques et al. (2005) would undoubtedly agree, research of uncompromising quality that examines the types of treatments being used in prison settings and how they are being implemented is critical. Research alone, however, cannot solve many of the problems enumerated here. Those problems can only be addressed through policy changes that restructure and reprioritize treatment in prisons. Ultimately, effective treatment will serve the implicit purpose of civil commitment and the explicit purpose of public safety. Ineffective treatment serves neither.

We must also recognize the low-base-rate problem articulated by Barbaree (1997) as a serious potential impediment to demonstrating treatment efficacy. Studies more recent than the Hall (1995) study cited previously have found that the base rates for sexual recidivism, irrespective of treatment, are low, around 13% to 14% over 5 years (Hanson & Bussiere, 1998; Hanson & Morton-Bourgon, 2005). When the 5-year base rate for nontreated offenders hovers around 15%, a significant treatment effect would have to reduce reoffense rates to about 5%.

Reducing sexual reoffense rates to 5% might be realized if sex offender treatment programs were brought in line with modern evidence-based guidelines for effective treatment, rather than being grudging afterthoughts to ensure statutory compliance. Hanson (1997) commented that the California Treatment Project study "was exceptionally well designed, but its methodology has one important failing: it is almost impossible to replicate" (p. 133). The reason, of course, is lack of political will (Hanson, 1997), which translates to lack of monetary support. As we have sought to emphasize, however, political will is not just about money. It is about the architecture and the trappings of the treatment program. As Marshall and Marshall (2008) noted, treatment programs must have external as well as internal validity. The key features of effective treatment that we have addressed in this chapter can be applied to sex offenders if there is a will to do so. Thus far, it appears that treatment serves only a secondary function, establishing the legitimacy of civil commitment.

WHERE DO WE GO FROM HERE?

Sexual violence cannot be mitigated by secondary intervention alone. Sexual violence is truly a public health problem and can best be tackled by embracing a public health prevention model (cf. Becker, 2000; English, Pullen, & Jones, 1996; McMahon, 2000; Mercy, 1999; Prentky, 2003; Prentky & Burgess, 2000; see also Chapter 8, this volume). However, because our focus in this chapter has been on secondary intervention, we will end with treatment-specific recommendations.

We begin with one broad conclusion: Application of an evidence-based metric to assess treatment of sex offenders in prison yields underwhelming results. The results are underwhelming principally because of (a) markedly suboptimal treatment conditions and (b) failure to be empirically responsive—to demonstrate the "evidence" part of evidence-based practice. It is not our contention that it is impossible, or indeed even difficult, to provide good treatment in a prison environment. It is our contention that, for treatment to be effective in a prison environment, there must be a firewall separating the treatment program from security-related and court-related concerns.

We offer an example of what that firewall might look like. Either the prison should be co-run by superintendents representing security and mental health, or the superintendent should be a neutral party (e.g., an attorney) with no allegiance to the departments of mental health (the state DMH) or corrections (the state DOC), served by two deputies, one from the DMH and one from the DOC. Treatment services should be provided by an independent vendor that reports to the state DMH, not to the DOC. Clinicians hired by the vendor must be insulated from all security-related and court-related demands. Treatment and clinical progress notes written by vendor therapists should be reviewed by vendor DMH supervisors within the prison and archived with DMH, not placed in the inmate's prison file. In the event that notes include disclosures deemed by the supervisor to be potentially critical to security, the notes are passed along for review by an internal board in the prison that includes the director of security and the clinical director (or their designees). Clinicians should not be asked to appear before any boards, internal or external, that make determinations of dangerousness, and clinicians should appear in court only under subpoena. With the exception of clear, unambiguous threats to security, all disclosures in therapy should be deemed confidential. Treatment should not, moreover, be coerced. Although most offenders will not have readily and eagerly volunteered for treatment, we can expect that many will welcome treatment under conditions of confidentiality. Those who do not participate constructively should be removed, temporarily or permanently. Those who have little ability for or no interest in engaging in treatment will only undermine those who do.

The second point concerning the "evidence" part of evidence-based practice is relatively straightforward. The treatment program must adhere, in every way that is doable given the prison-based nature of the program, to the minimal expectations of evidence-based practice. As we have stated elsewhere, "programs must establish objective, measurable, obtainable treatment goals. Absent clear goals, it is impossible to draw reliable conclusions about the risk-relevant impact of treatment" (Prentky et al., 2006, p. 385). In addition, there must be a comprehensive intake assessment that leads to individualized treatment goals and an individualized treatment plan with a clear pathway to completion. When all treatment goals have been met and the endpoint of the pathway has been reached, clinicians must be free to report that.

The vast majority of sex offenders, whether they are civilly committed or not, return to the community. Treatment does not stop at discharge. Programs must include reintegration components that facilitate offenders' transition back into society. Viable aftercare programs are essential to risk reduction and maintenance in the community. We suggest something along the lines of the Texas Model (Texas Health and Safety Code-841). The Texas SVP statute mandates community-based treatment and specialized supervision for released sex offenders. The conditions of release are strict, and violation of those conditions can result in a felony conviction and return to prison. The underlying assumption of this model is that sex offenders can be effectively controlled and managed in the community, and if an offender violates the conditions of his release, he will be dealt with by the criminal justice system.

The Texas model places the burden of prosocial reintegration squarely on the offender while maintaining a sufficiently tight leash to minimize the chance of further victimization. Those who are reoffense prone (engaging in high-risk behaviors) will be flagged by virtue of their behavior and returned to prison. For the others, those who presumably are *desisters*, the community-based model is a far less expensive, and arguably more effective, method of management. As we have warned, however, even this model is vulnerable to the charge of pretextuality if the conditions of release are impossible to satisfy (Prentky et al., 2006).

Sex offender treatment, alone, will never effectively mitigate sexual violence. Sexual violence is a serious public health problem. As we have noted,

> The branches of this pervasive problem insinuate themselves into, and directly affect, all aspects of society. The problem is not confined to the handful of offenders who spend time in prison and are offered some limited exposure to treatment. By merely reducing the risk of those who have already turned to sexual violence, we will never achieve the ultimate aim of making society a safer place. (Prentky & Schwartz, 2006, p. 6)

Restoration of the rights to sexual autonomy for women and children requires a public health policy that drives a comprehensive public health plan to address all factors that promote all expressions of unwanted sexual behavior.

REFERENCES

American Psychological Association. (2002). Ethical principles of psychologists and code of conduct. *American Psychologist, 57,* 1060–1073. doi:10.1037/0003-066X.57.12.1060

Andrews, D. A., & Bonta, J. (1998). *The psychology of criminal conduct* (2nd ed.). Cincinnati, OH: Anderson Press.

Barbaree, H. E. (1997). Evaluating treatment efficacy with sexual offenders: The insensitivity of recidivism studies to treatment effects. *Sexual Abuse, 9,* 111–128.

Becker, J. V. (2000). Editorial. *Sexual Abuse, 12,* 1. doi:10.1177/107906320001200101

Boerner, D. (1992). Confronting violence: In the act and in the word. *University of Puget Sound Law Review, 15,* 525–77.

Bonta, J., & Andrews, D. A. (2007). *Risk-need-responsivity model for offender assessment and rehabilitation* (Corrections Research User Rep. No. 2007-06). Ottawa, Ontario, Canada: Public Safety Canada.

Brownell, K. D., Marlatt, G. A., Lichtenstein, E., & Wilson, G. T. (1986). Understanding and preventing relapse. *American Psychologist, 41,* 765–782.

English, K., Pullen, S., & Jones, L. (Eds.). (1996). *Managing adult sex offenders in the community: A containment approach*. Research in Brief. Washington, DC: National Institute of Justice.

Ford, M. P., & Hendrick, S. S. (2003). Therapists' sexual values for self and clients: Implications for practice and training. *Professional Psychology: Research and Practice, 34*(1), 80–87. doi:10.1037/0735-7028.34.1.80

Fujimoto, B. K. (1992). Sexual violence, sanity, and safety: Constitutional parameters for involuntary civil commitment of sex offenders. *University of Puget Sound Law Review, 15,* 879–911.

Geer, T. M., Becker, J. V., Gray, S. R., & Krauss, D. (2001). Predictors of treatment completion in a correctional sex offender treatment program. *International Journal of Offender Therapy and Comparative Criminology, 45,* 302–313. doi:10.1177/0306624X01453003

Goffman, E. (1961). *Asylums: Essays on the social situation of mental patients and other inmates*. New York, NY: Anchor Books.

Gomes-Schwartz, B. (1978). Effective ingredients in psychotherapy: Prediction of outcome from process variables. *Journal of Consulting and Clinical Psychology, 46,* 1023–1035. doi:10.1037/0022-006X.46.5.1023

Governor's Task Force on Community Protection. (1989). *Task force on community protection: Final report*. Olympia: Washington State Department of Social and Health Services.

Hall, G. C. N. (1995). Sexual offender recidivism revisited: A meta-analysis of recent treatment studies. *Journal of Consulting and Clinical Psychology, 63,* 802–809. doi:10.1037/0022-006X.63.5.802

Hansen, N. B., Lambert, M. J., & Forman, E. M. (2002). The psychotherapy dose-response effect and its implications for treatment delivery services. *Clinical Psychology: Science and Practice, 9,* 329–343. doi:10.1093/clipsy/9.3.329

Hanson, R. K. (1997). How to know what works with sexual offenders. *Sexual Abuse: A Journal of Research and Treatment, 9,* 129–145.

Hanson, R. K., Bourgon, G.L., Helmus, L., & Hodgson, S. (2009). *A meta-analysis of the effectiveness of treatment for sexual offenders: Risk, need and responsivity*. Corrections User Report 2009-01. Ottawa, Ontario, Canada: Public Safety Canada.

Hanson, R. K., & Bussiere, M. T. (1998). Predicting relapse: A meta-analysis of sexual offender recidivism studies. *Journal of Consulting and Clinical Psychology, 66,* 348–362. doi:10.1037/0022-006X.66.2.348

Hanson, R. K., Gordon, A., Harris, A. J. R., Marques, J. K., Murphy, W., Quinsey, V. L., & Seto, M. C. (2002). First report of the collaborative outcome data project on the effectiveness of psychological treatment for sex offenders. *Sexual Abuse, 14,* 169–194. doi:10.1177/107906320201400207

Hanson, R. K., & Morton-Bourgon, K. (2005). The characteristics of persistent sexual offenders: A meta-analysis of recidivism studies. *Journal of Consulting and Clinical Psychology, 73,* 1154–1163. doi:10.1037/0022-006X.73.6.1154

Hansson, L. & Berglund, M. (1992) Stability of therapeutic alliance and its relationship to outcome in short-term inpatient psychiatric care. *Scandinavian Journal of Social Medicine*, 20, 45–50.

Huffman, E. G. (2006). Psychotherapy in prison: The frame imprisoned. *Clinical Social Work Journal*, 34, 319–333. doi:10.1007/s10615-005-0022-4

Jaffee v. Redmond, 518 U.S. 1 (1996), 516 U.S. 930 (1995), 51 F.3d 1346 (7th Cir. 1995), 142 F.3d 409 (7th Cir. 1998).

Janus, E. S. (1998). Hendricks and the moral terrain of police power civil commitment. *Psychology, Public Policy, and Law*, 4, 297–322. doi:10.1037/1076-8971.4.1-2.297

Kansas v. Hendricks, 521 U.S. 346 (1997).

Lambert, M. J., & Ogles, B. M. (2004). The efficacy and effectiveness of psychotherapy. In M. J. Lambert (Ed.), *Bergin and Garfield's handbook of psychotherapy and behavior change* (5th ed., pp. 139–193). New York, NY: Wiley.

Langevin, R. (2006). Acceptance and completion of treatment among sex offenders. *International Journal of Offender Therapy and Comparative Criminology*, 50, 402–417. doi:10.1177/0306624X06286870

Laws, D. R. (Ed.). (1989). *Relapse prevention with sex offenders*. New York, NY: Guilford Press.

Laws, D. R. (1995). A theory of relapse prevention. In W. O'Donohue & L. Krasner (Eds.), *Theories of behavior therapy* (pp. 445–473). Washington, DC: American Psychological Society. doi:10.1037/10169-016

Laws, D. R., Hudson, S. M., & Ward, T. (2000). *Remaking relapse prevention with sex offenders: A sourcebook*. Thousand Oaks, CA: Sage.

Logan, W. A. (2002–2003). Jacob's legacy: Sex offenders registration and community notification laws, practice, and procedure in Minnesota. *William Mitchell Law Review*, 29, 1287–1341.

Lösel, F., & Schmucker, M. (2005). The effectiveness of treatment for sexual offenders: A comprehensive meta-analysis. *Journal of Experimental Criminology*, 1, 117–146. doi:10.1007/s11292-004-6466-7

Marlatt, G. A. (1985). Relapse prevention: Theoretical rationale and overview of the model. In G. A. Marlatt & J. R. Gordon (Eds.), *Relapse prevention: Maintenance strategies in the treatment of addictive behaviors* (pp. 3–70). New York, NY: Guilford Press.

Marques, J. K., Day, D. M., Nelson, C., & West, M. A. (1993). Findings and recommendations from California's experimental treatment program. In G. C. Nagayama Hall, R. Hirschman, J. R. Graham, & M. S. Zaragoza (Eds.), *Sexual aggression: Issues in etiology, assessment, and treatment* (pp. 197–214). London, England: Taylor & Francis.

Marques, J. K., Nelson, C., Alarcon, J.-M., & Day, D. M. (2000). Preventing relapse in sex offenders: What we have learned from SOTEP's experimental treatment program. In D. R. Laws, S. M. Hudson, & T. Ward (Eds.), *Remaking relapse prevention with sex offenders: A sourcebook* (pp. 321–339). Thousand Oaks, CA: Sage.

Marques, J. K., Wiederanders, M., Day, D. M., Nelson, C., & van Ommeren, A. (2005). Effects of a relapse prevention program on sexual recidivism: Final results from California's sex offender treatment and evaluation project (SOTEP). *Sexual Abuse, 17,* 79–107. doi:10.1177/107906320501700108

Marshall, W. L., & Marshall, L. E. (2007). The utility of the random controlled trial for evaluating sexual offender treatment: The gold standard or an inappropriate strategy. *Sexual Abuse, 19,* 175–191. doi:10.1177/107906320701900207

Marshall, W. L., & Marshall, L. E. (2008). Good clinical practice and the evaluation of treatment: A response to Seto et al. *Sexual Abuse, 20,* 256–260. doi:10.1177/1079063208323839

McMahon, P. M. (2000). The public health approach to the prevention of sexual violence. *Sexual Abuse, 12,* 27–36. doi:10.1177/107906320001200104

Mercy, J. A. (1999). Having new eyes: Viewing child sexual abuse as a public health problem. *Sexual Abuse, 11,* 317–321. doi:10.1177/107906329901100407

Miner, M., & Dwyer, M. (1995). Analysis of dropouts from outpatient sex offender treatment. *Journal of Psychology & Human Sexuality, 7*(3), 77–93.

Mitford, J. (1973). *Kind and usual punishment: The prison business.* New York, NY: Knopf.

Nicholaichuk, T., Gordon, A., Gu, D., & Wong, S. (2000). Outcome of an institutional sexual offender treatment program: A comparison between treated and matched untreated offenders. *Sexual Abuse, 12,* 139–153. doi:10.1177/1079063 20001200205

O'Malley, S. S., Suh, C. S., & Strupp, H. H. (1983). The Vanderbilt Psychotherapy Process Scale: A report on the scale development and a process-outcome study. *Journal of Consulting and Clinical Psychology, 51,* 581–586. doi:10.1037/0022-006X.51.4.581

Pithers, W. D., & Gray, A. S. (1996). Utility of relapse prevention in treatment of sexual abusers. *Sexual Abuse, 8,* 223–230.

Pithers, W. D., Marques, J. K., Gibat, C. C., & Marlatt, G. A. (1983). Relapse prevention with sexual aggressive: A self-control model of treatment and maintenance of change. In J. G. Greer & I. R. Stuart (Eds.), *The sexual aggressor: Current perspectives on treatment* (pp. 214–239). New York, NY: Van Nostrand Reinhold.

Prentky, R. A. (1995). A rationale for the treatment of sex offenders: Pro bono publico. In J. McGuire (Ed.), *What works: Reducing reoffending. Guidelines from research and practice* (pp. 155–172). Chichester, England: Wiley.

Prentky, R. A. (2003). Remediation of coercive sexual behavior. In B. K. Schwartz (Ed.), *Correctional psychology: Practice, programming, and administration* (pp. 13-1–13-33). Kingston, NJ: Civic Research Institute.

Prentky, R. A., & Burgess, A. W. (2000). *Forensic management of sexual offenders.* New York, NY: Kluwer Academic/Plenum.

Prentky, R. A., Janus, E., Barbaree, H., Schwartz, B., & Kafka, M. (2006). Sexually violent predators in the courtroom: Science on trial. *Psychology, Public Policy, and Law, 12*, 357–393. doi:10.1037/1076-8971.12.4.357

Prentky, R. A., Lee, A. F. S., Knight, R. A., & Cerce, D. (1997). Recidivism rates among child molesters and rapists: A methodological analysis. *Law and Human Behavior, 21*, 635–659. doi:10.1023/A:1024860714738

Prentky, R. A., & Schwartz, B. K. (with Burns-Smith, G.). (2006, December). *Treatment of adult sex offenders*. Retrieved from http://www.vawnet.org/Assoc_Files_VAWnet/AR_SexOffendTreatment.pdf

Rokeach, M. (1973). *The nature of human values*. New York, NY: Free Press.

Schlesinger, S. E. (1979). Therapy on a treadmill: The role of the prison psychotherapist. *Professional Psychology, 10*, 307–317. doi:10.1037/0735-7028.10.3.307

Schrag, C. (1973). *Crime and justice: American style*. Washington, DC: National Institute of Mental Health.

Schwartz, B. K., & Cellini, H. R. (1995). *The sex offender: Corrections, treatment, and legal practices* (Vol. 1). Kingston, NJ: Civic Research Institute.

Schwartz, B. K., & Cellini, H. R. (1997). *The sex offender: New insights, treatment innovations and legal developments*. Kingston, NJ: Civic Research Institute.

Seto, M. C., Marques, J. K., Harris, G. T., Chaffin, M., Lalumiere, M. L., Miner, M. H., . . . Quinsey, V. L. (2008). Good science and progress in sex offender treatment are intertwined: A response to Marshall and Marshall (2007). *Sexual Abuse: A Journal of Research and Treatment, 20*, 247–255. doi:10.1177/1079063208317733

Sherman, J. J. (1998). Effects of psychotherapeutic treatments for PTSD: A meta-analysis of controlled clinical trials. *Journal of Traumatic Stress, 11*, 413–435. doi:10.1023/A:1024444410595

Smith, M. L., & Glass, G. V. (1977). Meta-analysis of psychotherapy outcome studies. *American Psychologist, 32*, 752–760. doi:10.1037/0003-066X.32.9.752

Tjeltveit, A. C. (1999). *Ethics and values in psychotherapy*. Florence, KY: Taylor & Frances/Routledge. doi:10.4324/9780203360453

Turay v. Seling et al. Findings of Fact, Conclusions of Law, and Order re Motion Heard October 19–21, 1999. U.S. District Court, Western Court of Washington at Seattle, No. C91-664WD.

United States v. Trammel, 445 U.S. 40 (1980).

Walsh, R. A. (1995). The study of values in psychotherapy: A critique and call for an alternative method. *Psychotherapy Research, 5*, 313–326.

Wampold, B. E., Mondin, G. W., Moody, M., Stich, F., Benson, K., & Ahn, H. (1997). A meta-analysis of outcome studies comparing bona fide psychotherapies: Empirically, "all must have prizes." *Psychological Bulletin, 122*, 203–215. doi:10.1037/0033-2909.122.3.203

Weiner, B. A. (1985). Legal issues raised in treating sex offenders. *Behavioral Sciences & the Law, 3*, 325–340.

Windholz, M. J., & Silberschatz, G. (1988). Vanderbilt Psychotherapy Process Scale: A replication with adult outpatients. *Journal of Consulting and Clinical Psychology, 56*, 56–60. doi:10.1037/0022-006X.56.1.56

Wright, E. O. (1973). San Quentin Prison as seen by the prisoners. In E. O. Wright (Ed.), *The politics of punishment* (pp. 103–151). New York, NY: Harper & Row.

Zevitz, R. G., & Farkas, M. A. (2000). The impact of sex-offender community notification on probation/parole in Wisconsin. *International Journal of Offender Therapy and Comparative Criminology, 44*, 8–21.

Zgoba, K. M., & Simon, L. M. J. (2005). Recidivism rates of sexual offenders up to 7 years later: Does treatment matter? *Criminal Justice Review, 30*, 155–173. doi:10.1177/0734016805284146

7

JUSTICE RESPONSES TO SEXUAL VIOLENCE

ILENE SEIDMAN AND JEFFREY J. POKORAK

Sexual assault is a pervasive problem in the United States, victimizing one in six women (Kilpatrick, Resnick, Ruggiero, Conoscenti, & McCauley, 2007). Although the specific definition of sexual assault, including rape, differs among jurisdictions, all agree that the attempted or actual nonconsensual penetration or contact with the mouth, vagina, or anus of a victim is the core act of sexual assault. The legal response to sexual assault historically focused on the criminal prosecution of perpetrators, seeking accountability through punishment of offenders. The needs of victims, who were often left injured physically, emotionally, financially and in their community standing, were not generally the goals of the legal system. Further, because the primary legal concern has historically been the protection of the person charged with a crime, the victim's honesty and chastity were always challenged, and requirements of proof of utmost resistance by the victim and of "non-consent" made successful prosecutions difficult. Because of these constraints on prosecution, and because the criminal process offered no remedies for the victim, many were warned and convinced that the negative consequences of participation in the criminal process outweighed the advantages of perpetrator accountability and punishment.

Primarily in response to the gender equality movement in the 1970s, the judicial and legislative treatment of crimes of violence against women underwent radical change. The historic single-minded focus on offender accountability through criminal punishment in rape cases increasingly turned to victim-centered protections and remedies in both the criminal and civil law realms. Reforms succeeded in revising antiquated, gender-biased laws regarding the prosecution of sexual assault in every state in the nation. While these reforms were not precisely the same in each state, they all can be described as belonging to one of four general categories: (a) redefining the offenses of sexual assault (including repealing of total spousal immunity and abolishing specific gender designations); (b) evidentiary reforms (elimination of corroboration requirements, enactment of rape shield statutes, and admissibility of fresh complaints); (c) reforms in statutory age requirements for both offenders and perpetrators; and (d) reforms in grading of offenses according to severity of force, use of weapons, and resulting injuries.

In addition, legislatures enacted measures intended to prevent the legal system from perpetrating what commentators have referred to as the "second rape." These protections include the so-called rape shield statutes, which prohibit the introduction of the victim's prior sexual conduct as evidence of consent; the extension of privilege protections to mental health and rape crisis counseling records; reconsideration of the long-held absolute exclusion of marital rape; repeal of evidentiary corroboration requirements, which essentially eliminated the possibility of prosecution in "he said, she said" cases; and the repeal in many states of utmost resistance requirements, which often dimmed the likelihood of conviction absent severe personal injury or clear evidence that the victim physically resisted throughout the entire attack.

Although these reforms represent an important evolution in the legal response to rape, many commentators conclude that they have not translated into meaningful results. Much of the data suggest that the reform of rape laws failed to significantly deter sexual assaults, increase rates of arrest and prosecution, or produce measurable improvements in conviction rates (see Futter & Mebane, 2001; Seidman & Vickers, 2005; Spohn & Horney, 1992). According to a national study published in 2007 (Kilpatrick, Resnick, Ruggiero, Cognoscenti, & McCauley, 2007), just 16% of rapes are reported and the rate falls to 12% among college students, far below the reporting for physical and domestic violence (78%). There are many reasons for the contrast between the high hopes of reform legislation and the low number of positive, measurable outcomes in the legal response to rape. The most likely cause is that the key decision makers in the criminal justice system at every point of outcome measure (arrest, prosecution, conviction) still hold the same antiquated views that the laws were intended to reform. While rape laws changed, fundamental social attitudes toward those who rape, and even particularly toward those who are raped, have not changed dramatically. As a result, victims of non-stranger assault today face many of the same hurdles in the legal system that victims faced before these reforms.

This chapter surveys some of the most vexing issues in the criminal justice system's response to rape as well as the failure of the civil justice system to adequately respond to the pressing needs of rape victims. It also proposes systemic changes to address rape victims' immediate legal needs, provide long-term structural support for victims in society, and enable such victims to access the legal system to assist them as they heal and recover from the trauma of rape.

WHAT DO WE KNOW ABOUT THE CRIMINAL JUSTICE SYSTEM?

Rape is not only an underreported crime, it is also underprosecuted. One in six, or roughly 17.7 million, women have been victims of attempted or completed rape in the United States. Of these victims, only 40% are ever brought to the attention of law enforcement, either through victim reporting or third-party (including health care provider) reports. Out of the 40% of reported sexual assaults, just over half, 50.8%, result in an arrest. Out of the cases in which an arrest is made, 20% are abandoned before formal criminal charges are filed to commence the prosecution (see Rennison, 2002; Reynolds, 1999).

Of this already reduced number of prosecutions, only 58% result in convictions. If a perpetrator is convicted of a felony sexual assault, there is a 69% chance of incarceration. Therefore, viewed in toto, in the 39% of reported rapes, there is only a 16% chance of offender accountability through incarceration. Factoring in the unreported rapes, the chances of incarceration punishment for perpetrators is only 6%, meaning that 15 out of 16 sexual assault victims can expect no significant perpetrator accountability from the criminal justice system (see Pokorak, 2007; Rennison, 2002; Reynolds, 1999).

The prosecutor's first duty is to seek what the prosecutor defines as justice, which leaves him or her in a unique representational role. The prosecutor does not represent the victim but, rather, the citizens of the jurisdiction. Prosecutors are therefore not constrained by fealty or fiduciary obligation to any client in the traditional sense (Caplow, 1998). Although victims of sexual assault may reasonably believe that the prosecutor is representing them, in fact, legally and ethically, the prosecutor cannot. The relationship between prosecutor and victim is further complicated by the prosecutor's unique legal and ethical duties to the defendant as well as to the prosecution and punishment of the guilty. The combination of ethical rules, discovery statutes, procedural rules, and constitutional due process requirements obligate prosecutors to monitor their cases with an eye toward possible exoneration of the charged defendant. Chief among these duties is the prosecutor's

be raped (Kramer, 1994). However, in cases in which the perpetrator administers drugs or alcohol to the victim, prosecutors can use the act of facilitation as evidence of criminal intent, making conviction more likely.

Unconsciousness caused by intoxication is generally recognized as creating an inability to consent. Some jurisdictions still require the perpetrator to have administered the alcohol or drugs with the intent of rendering the victim compliant or incompetent for nonconsent to be presumed. There is no legal consensus regarding when victim intoxication negates the ability to consent or demonstrates nonconsent. For instance, a 14-year-old girl in Kansas who drank two beers was presumed too intoxicated to give consent to sex, whereas a 16-year-old girl in California who drank 5 ounces of bourbon on an empty stomach was found not intoxicated enough to negate her ability to consent to repeated assaults (Mindlin et al., 2007). It is not surprising that alcohol and drugs are frequently the weapons of choice for sexual assault perpetrators.

Rape Shield and Victim Character

Historically, victims' chastity, conduct, appearance, and reputation were the focal points of sexual assault trials. If the victim had previously engaged in any consensual sexual activity, it was argued that she likely consented to the charged sexual conduct with the accused. As part of the reform movement, federal legislatures adopted rape shield statutes to control the invasion of sexual assault victims' privacy (Fialkow, 2006). These statutes prohibit presentation of evidence about a victim's sexual history, previous sexual behavior, or predisposition for sexual conduct at trial (Fialkow, 2006; Mindlin et al., 2007). Nonetheless, trials still focus heavily on the victim's behavior, dress, and character rather than on the defendant's actions (Althouse, 1992) and do not prevent all character attacks on the victim (Anderson, 2004). Further, even when rape shield statutes keep evidence regarding the complainant's sexual behavior out of trial, there is nothing to stop the media from obtaining and distributing information about a complainant's sexual history (Haddad, 2005). The public release of such information can lead to the very embarrassment, humiliation, and salacious public scrutiny that rape shield laws aim to prevent (Haddad, 2005).

Privacy Violations

A common defense strategy in rape prosecution is to suggest that the victim's state of mental health raises concerns that the report is false (Smith, 2000). Though most mental status evidence is inadmissible at trial, records of mental health professionals and rape crisis counselors are vulnerable to discovery by the defense. *Privileges* are rules that protect the verbal and written communications with certain professionals when privacy is an expectation, for example, with psychiatrists and other licensed mental health professionals, lawyers, priests, and others. Almost every state has adopted some form of privileges for patient–psychotherapist and other mental health communication (Nelkin, 2000). However, rules may allow otherwise privileged information to be introduced at trial if the judge finds it relevant to the defense case. In such decisions, the defendant's liberty interest is often found to outweigh the victim's privacy interest.

Some state courts and legislatures are beginning to address the individual role that victims should have in criminal cases in protecting their personal privacy. To that end, some courts (Massachusetts, Arizona, and Colorado, among others) are now allowing victims to appear represented by their own counsel for the purpose of protecting the victim's privacy interests before a rape trial begins. The expansion of this right is vital for victims as they seek productive and private lives after the prosecution ends (Kanter, 2005; Seidman & Vickers, 2005).

Marital Rape

Historically, courts were nearly unanimous that a husband could not be convicted of rape of his wife because marriage alone created a woman's ongoing consent to sexual intercourse with her husband (Walsh, 1983). By 1993, all states had made some form of marital rape a crime (Siegel, 1995). Although approximately half of all states still endorse restrictions on spouse prosecutions, current laws are moving toward recognition that marital rape is indistinct from rape between strangers or acquaintances (Harless, 2003). These reforms, however, have not removed the belief among many prosecutors, judges, and jurors that what goes on between a husband and wife in the bedroom is for them alone and not subject to state laws and restrictions (Hasday, 2000).

Racial Disparities and System Outcome Bias

The race of victim disparities in prosecutions continues to be a significant barrier to more complete offender accountability. For most of our nation's history, it was not a crime in practice to rape a Black woman. In the few places where the rape of a Black woman was technically criminalized, rules of procedure prevented Black women from testifying about their victimization. Prosecutorial discretion to decline prosecution completed the decriminalization of raping a Black woman (e.g., Roberts, 1997). Although prosecution rates for rape of minority woman have increased, an identifiable prosecution pattern exists whereby White women victims are overvalued and women of color are undervalued. At every phase of initial criminal prosecution—charge, plea, and trial—prosecuting attorneys enjoy the constitutionally protected power of discretionary decision making. Results from numerous studies of such discretion have uncovered disturbing patterns of racial bias (e.g., Death Penalty Sentencing, 1990; Rennison, 2001). In 1991, Frohmann looked at the practice of prosecutors when making charging and dismissal decisions. Starting with the widely held belief that stranger rapes are more aggressively prosecuted than acquaintance rapes, she documented how prosecutors employ their power in the face of deviations from a normative rape narrative. She characterized the prototypical rape as the kidnapping and forcible penetration of one White woman by a Black male stranger (Frohmann, 1991, p. 219). Frohmann concluded that prosecutors hold a fixed idea of what constitutes the set of facts most likely to lead to a rape conviction. This idea is not only a product of the prosecutor's independent repertoire of knowledge and stereotypes but also on their attempts to measure the impact that stereotypes and myths about the paradigmatic rape will have on judges and jurors.

Frohmann divided the mythical rape paradigm into four subtypes in which victim behavior could differ from prosecutor's beliefs: (a) the victim's version of what happened (e.g., victim was sexually attracted to perpetrator prior to assault), (b) postincident interaction (e.g., she had consensual sexual intercourse with the suspect following the alleged incident), (c) reporting (e.g., victim failed to make a prompt report, and her reasons for late reporting are inconsistent with officially acknowledged and legitimate reasons), and (d) victim's demeanor (e.g., facial expression, mannerisms, and body language suggest she or he is not telling the truth; Spohn, Beichner, & Davis-Frenzel, 2001, p. 210). Prosecutors consider any deviations to be reasons for case rejection. In a recent follow-up study of victim-reported assaults, Frohmann (1997) examined the ways in which class and race and stereotypes regarding neighborhoods impacted prosecutorial discretion. Frohmann found most rape victims are from lower class, racially mixed, or minority communities. Most jurors, however, tend to come from more culturally homogeneous, predominantly White, middle- and upper middle–class communities. Although these class, race, and culture differences are legally insignificant, they lead prosecutors to fear that jurors might not understand the cultural context and will fail to convict. Prosecutors are also preoccupied with concerns other than justice, such as the likelihood that allocation of their limited resources to a case will produce a conviction. Frohmann used the term *downstreaming* with regard to this trend, but it is more accurately labeled *system outcome bias* (Pokorak, 2006).

Among that small percentage of rapes that are prosecuted, most are resolved by dismissal or plea bargain before trial. In the very small percentage of cases that are tried, most victims will testify (Pokorak, 2007; Seidman &

Vickers, 2005). In some jurisdictions, victims also have the opportunity to provide, during the sentencing phase of a case, victim impact statements whereby they can inform a judge or jury of the harm the defendant has caused them. For some victims, this participation will provide a sense of closure, some relief, and the opportunity for healing. For others, this process will be another painful exposure and no benefit will accrue. From a victim standpoint, the criminal process offers little support and little opportunity to remedy the effects of assault on their lives.

WHAT DO WE KNOW ABOUT THE CIVIL JUSTICE SYSTEM?

The impact of sexual assault on victims' lives is devastating and includes harm to their physical, psychological, economic, and social well-being (Yuan, Koss & Stone, 2006). Even if the criminal justice process could operate at an aspirational level, its emphasis on offender accountability would preclude its providing remedies to stem the potential long-term economic and social harms to victims. It is therefore essential to employ and expand victim-centered remedies found in the civil justice system. These remedies may assist victims in preserving their privacy and in ensuring economic and social stability as well as healing. This section describes current efforts to provide remedies to sexual assault victims in the civil and restorative justice systems that are coextensive or independent of outcomes in the criminal justice process.

Tort Remedies

The most widely available and used alternative to criminal justice remedies is tort litigation, in which a victim sues a perpetrator in civil court. A *tort* is an intentional or negligent wrong (other than a breach of contract) that the law recognizes as a harm that can be compensated. Rape itself is not a tort. However, victims may seek relief under a variety of general tort law claims, including assault and battery, infliction of emotional distress, invasion of privacy, and professional malpractice (Bublick, 2006). Tort suits in rape cases may be pursued in parallel to a prosecution or may be used by victims as a direct substitute for the criminal process. The primary remedy available in tort actions is monetary awards for damages. These suits potentially provide victims with a complementary relief system that can be accessed whether criminal prosecution was successful, failed, or not pursued (Bublick, 2006).

The prevalence of tort cases filed by sexual assault victims has significantly increased over the past decades. From January 1, 2000, through December 31, 2004, the highest appellate courts in the 50 states issued opinions in over 100 tort cases filed by sexual assault victims (Bublick, 2006). Thirty years earlier, over a similar 4-year period from January 1, 1970, through December 31, 1974, those courts issued fewer than 10 opinions in such cases (Bublick, 2006). This number of high court opinions does not accurately represent the total actions filed, as 95% of all civil cases settle before trial and therefore result in no appeal for a high court to consider. Moreover, of those cases that do go to trial, few lower court judgments are appealed (Bublick, 2006). The increasing frequency of appeal to higher courts can, in part, be attributed to the widening understanding that third parties who are not perpetrators sometimes have a legal responsibility to prevent a sexual assault. *Third parties* are people, such as landlords or parking garage owners, and institutions, such as hotels, and universities, that, because of a relationship to the victim (e.g., as a tenant, a customer, user of a service, or guest) have a duty to protect her from foreseeable harm. Allowing suits against both the assailant and legally responsible third parties gives the victim the opportunity to achieve a variety of objectives through the civil tort system. In suits against the assailant, the objectives include perpetrator accountability, compensation, deterrence, apology, or orders intended to increase the continuing safety of the victim, such as transfer of the assailant to a new job, housing facility, or school (Bublick, 1999; Bublick, 2006). In third-party suits, courts award money damages to victims to deter responsible parties from creating or ignoring safety hazards. Such damage awards also encourage these parties to take precautions to protect others to whom they owe a duty of safety (Bublick, 1999).

Many of the barriers that victims face in the criminal justice system, including rape stereotypes, predisposition to question victim credibility, and overemphasis on victim behaviors, similarly exist in the civil law. Yet even in the face of attitudinal barriers, civil remedies offer sexual assault victims certain advantages over criminal prosecution. Civil actions require a lesser burden to prevail, proof by a *preponderance of the evidence* rather than the *beyond a reasonable doubt* standard required in criminal prosecution (Bublick, 2006). Therefore, sexual assault victims can file civil suits regardless of the outcome or existence of a criminal case (Bublick, 2006). Additionally, civil courts do not afford as many procedural advantages in favor of the accused because the defendant's constitutional rights (e.g., the right to remain silent) are generally applicable in civil suits only when a criminal case is pending (Bublick, 2006). In civil suits, victims can compel the other side and third parties to produce documents and other evidence that might help their case, and unlike in criminal cases, the defendant is not entitled to free legal representation (Bublick, 2006). For all these reasons, civil suits put the victim and assailant on more of an equal footing and allow victims the opportunity to choose the forum and the remedies that best suit their individual needs (Bublick, 2006).

Like every legal remedy, however, tort actions present their own set of limitations. As private legal matters, tort suits do not achieve the goal of offender accountability. A negative consequence of pursuing a tort action is that the victim may lose even more of her privacy through invasive discovery procedures and broader evidence production, as there are few statutory rape-shield evidence restrictions in civil cases (Bublick, 2006). As a result, the victim's identity will be known, and evidence of her prior sexual conduct or health history may become public in tort suits through the discovery process.

An additional concern raised by the civil tort system is the legal concept of *comparative fault* embraced by many state courts. Comparative fault allows defendants to argue that a victim's behavior was in whole or in part a legal cause for that victim's rape (Bublick, 1999). Although most jurisdictions do not allow the assailants to raise this defense, third parties are free to base their defense on such a concept (Bublick, 1999). Finally, tort remedy is effective only against perpetrators who have the financial resources to pay such awards, making its usefulness extremely limited. Even if an assailant is found liable in a tort suit, his financial resources are often insufficient to cover the victim's actual damages and legal fees (Koss, 2006). Because of the very limited number of cases that result in an actual monetary payment, tort actions are hardly likely to create a deterrent effect on either perpetrators or third parties.

Other Civil Law Remedies

The psychologist Abraham Maslow's (1954) theory of a hierarchy of human needs offers a vantage point from which to reconceptualize a legal response to rape. In this conceptualization, the basic needs for emotional security, physical safety, shelter, and economic and social stability take precedence over criminal justice remedies that, at best, may offer satisfaction of higher needs, such as vindication and self-actualization. Access to civil law and non-traditional remedies can help restore what the victim lost or is threatened with losing as a result of the assault. These remedies may be available in very specialized settings that allow victims to gain assistance or relief in housing, employment, health care, education, immigration, and other critical areas of the victim's life. Until recently, these diverse sources of legal remedies for rape victims remained unexplored and today are still underutilized. Furthermore, promising alternatives to the criminal and civil litigation systems that offer nonadversarial avenues to engage perpetrators in accountability to victims and communities, known as *restorative justice programs*, have only recently become available to a limited number of victims. This section explores some of the specific substantive areas of civil law that can be made responsive to sexual assault victims, and alternative methods of justice that are designed to maximize both victim healing and perpetrator accountability.

Safety

Sexual assault shatters a victim's sense of safety. The ubiquitous availability of civil protective orders may alleviate some of this harm. Protective orders are designed to offer a quick and relatively easy method for court intervention to protect victims from further contact with or abuse by a perpetrator. Although the criminal justice process may offer enforceable stay-away orders against a defendant in a rape case, that remedy is available only to the few victims whose cases include an arrest or prosecution (see Goodman & Epstein, 2008). However, civil protective orders were designed largely to protect victims of domestic violence; thus, many protective order statutes require a domestic or significant preexisting relationship between the parties that does not fit the casual acquaintance profile of many sexual assaults. A majority of jurisdictions do not offer civil protective orders for victims of such assaults, leaving them vulnerable to unwanted contact, threats, intimidation, or retaliation from known perpetrators or their associates. Legislative efforts to extend civil protection orders to rape victims, regardless of their relationship to the offender, are a simple yet necessary reform to help protect victims after assault.

Housing

Many sexual assaults occur in or near the victim's residence. The result may be an immediate need to terminate a lease, move to a different dorm, return to a family residence, or be given priority status for public housing relocation. For the most part, courts have not protected victims from lease termination actions, nor have they recognized the failure of public housing authorities to address the urgency of the secure housing needs of tenants who are victims of assault. The courts have begun recently to recognize that sexual assault victims may be legally considered as persons with disabilities because of the physical or mental health effects of the assault, including anxiety, depression, or posttraumatic stress. As a person with a disability, a victim is entitled to reasonable accommodation in housing, such as apartment transfers and/or additional security measures. Access to safe housing and relocation assistance are essential remedies for victims immediately postassault and throughout their healing process.

Employment

Employment may be disrupted after sexual assault if victim absenteeism measurably increases and productivity significantly decreases. An assault by a coworker or supervisor triggers even more serious threats to employment, either in the form of retaliation or the inability of the victim to maintain preassault working habits or conditions of employment. Legal interventions to help a victim maintain employment may be necessary, such as requiring workplace accommodations (e.g., shift change, job relocation) or requiring an employer to terminate a perpetrator. Disability pay or unemployment compensation may also be pursued if the ability to work is significantly disrupted. Some employment remedies are available to victims through the Family and Medical Leave Act (Mindlin & Vickers, 2007; Seidman and Vickers, 2005), including a postleave right to return to one's job. Limited legal rights to disability pay or accommodations are likewise available under the Americans with Disabilities Act and similar state laws. There are also civil rights protections from employer retaliation under Title VII and state antidiscrimination laws. Additionally, sexual assault in the workplace may constitute sexual harassment in violation of state and federal law, allowing other forms of redress to the victim.

Education

The incidence of sexual assault at universities and high schools is extraordinarily high. The United States Department of Justice estimates that 35 out of every 1,000 undergraduate females are sexually assaulted each year (Fisher, Cullen, & Turner, 2000, p. 11). The figures are even more staggering for students of high school age, as approximately 100 of every 1,000 girls of high-school age report being victimized each year (see Youth Risk Behavior Survey, 2001). These incident rates represent a significant barrier to access to education for young victims.

There are three significant laws that create various civil obligations for educational institutions to protect students from campus assault and to effectively respond should an assault occur. Title IX of the Educational Amendments of 1972 (20 U.S.C. Sec. 168) requires equal access to participation in and benefits of education and provides for actions against schools that display deliberate indifference to hostile conditions on campus. The Clery Act (20 U.S.C. Sec. 1092 (f)) provides for campus protections and notification to college communities of sexual assaults. Finally, the Family Education Rights and Privacy Act (20 U.S.C. Sec. 1232g) stipulates privacy protections for, among others, victims of sexual assault on campus. Sadly, universities have largely failed to address the issues caused by the presence of student perpetrators on campus, either through their institutional disciplinary procedures or police intervention. Courts have in turn largely failed to enforce those university obligations. This has led to a nationwide failure to make or maintain educational environments as safe places free from conditions in which sexual assault is a common event. Both schools and courts must increase their efforts and exercise their responsibilities through education, support, and enforcement to help stem this tide of assault against young learners.

Immigration Status

Immigrants face higher rates of sexual assault than most in U.S. society (see Tjaden & Thoennes, 1998). This is consistent with the higher rates of rape experienced by members of all vulnerable or isolated populations, including the disabled, those institutionalized, and members of disenfranchised communities such as Native American women on reservation land (Mindlin et al., 2007). Immigrants expect and experience greater barriers to justice and view the court system primarily as a government institution to be avoided. Courts are seen as more punitive than helpful and as institutions that will likely lead to unwanted scrutiny. For similar reasons, immigrants are less likely to seek assistance from law enforcement or even health care providers if that contact might lead to police involvement. Among the serious impacts that can result from a reported assault is the chance that a victim may lose her legal status to remain in the country. An employment or student visa may be lost if the victim cannot maintain adequate attendance or productivity at her workplace or school postassault. Immigrants without adequate legal documentation risk deportation if they become too visible to the legal system. Legislative attempts to support immigrant victims, such as the immigration provisions in the federal Violence Against Women Act (1994) are little used because they are difficult to access, are inconsistently applied among jurisdictions, and do not address the real concerns of victims regarding intrusive questioning about their status. These remedies are also limited in that many are available only to those who participate fully in a prosecution. To protect this particularly vulnerable community, immigrant women must have avenues of redress outside of the criminal system that will allow them to obtain or maintain legal status and seek supportive civil legal remedies without threat of retaliation or deportation.

Privacy

Loss of privacy is a pervasive issue for all sexual assault victims. This is particularly true in small enclosed communities, such as college campuses, where sexual victimization is not uncommon yet is considered deeply shameful. One explanation for the low reporting rate of assault on college campuses, estimated to be as low as 5%, is that the devastating impact of campus gossip on victim complainants and the fear of retaliation within the community promote victim silence (Fisher et al., 2000). Once an assault is reported to law enforcement, a victim reasonably can expect the release of details regarding the assault as well as other confidential information. Even if the victim's name is withheld from the public, in small communities the victim's identity is quickly learned and spread. As civil or criminal cases progress, the media may disseminate information related to prior sexual conduct, psychiatric care, history of prior assault(s), history of drug or alcohol use, and other private health information such as HIV status. Publication of this information may be the result of the legal process itself (a defense attorney subpoena to a treating hospital), intentional leaks by any of the many people involved, or error by court or medical personnel. The growing legislative and judicial expansion of victims' ability to challenge the revelation of their private records during the course of a criminal prosecution, as discussed earlier, is an essential element of continuing reform in the legal response to sexual assault.

Restorative Justice Alternatives to Adversarial Methods

Restorative justice programs offer a response to crime different from those available in the traditional criminal or civil justice system. The traditional criminal justice system treats crime as an act committed against the state, giving the state the sole responsibility to fashion an offender punishment. Restorative justice programs recognize that crimes are acts committed against communities as well as individuals (Umbreit, Vos, Coates, & Lightfoot, 2005). The goal is therefore not punishment of the wrongdoer but rather a process of accountability through which the wrongdoer becomes part of a restoration of those affected communities and individuals (Koss & Achilles, 2008). Restorative justice programs recognize three groups affected by the crime: (a) the victim and the victim's family and friends, (b) community members who experience a loss in safety within the community, and (c) the offender together with his family and friends (Koss & Achilles, 2008).

Restorative justice programs aim to minimize the retraumatization and attrition that may develop within the criminal and civil justice process. *Retraumatization* (sometimes called *the second rape*) refers to the behavior of the personnel who respond to sexual violence, including physicians, police officers, nurses, and prosecutors, which often enhances rather than eases a victim's distress by emphasizing the shame that often results from victimization (Campbell, 2005, 2006; Koss & Achilles, 2008). *Attrition* refers to the number of cases in which validation of the victim and punishment of the offender ultimately occur (Koss & Achilles, 2008). Restorative justice programs provide an opportunity for the victim to tell her story and ask the offender questions while, at the same time, offering the offender a chance to accept responsibility and demonstrate remorse (Koss, 2006; Koss & Achilles, 2008). By providing a source of support for both the victim and the offender, restorative justice programs seek to repair the harm caused to the victim, impose accountability and rehabilitation in a humane context on the offender, and create opportunity to constructively address the damage to the trust and security of citizens at large (Koss, 2006; Koss & Achilles, 2008).

Restorative justice systems have always existed in the United States, most notably within Native American tribes (Koss & Achilles, 2008; Umbreit et al., 2005). Those communities recognized the broader impact of crime. The oral tradition of sharing stories and experiences within their society was a way of creating a shared history in which everyone was an important part of the society and no one, including wrongdoers, was considered an outsider (Deer, 2004). Formal modern versions of restorative justice programs began to emerge in the mid-1970s, primarily in New Zealand and Australia (Umbreit et al., 2005). By the mid-1990s, these programs became more common in the United States, where they now exist in some form in every state (Umbreit et al., 2005). These programs operate parallel to, or independent of, the criminal justice system (Koss & Achilles, 2008). Various methods of restorative justice are available. *Victim/offender dialogue* or mediation is a direct meeting of the victim and the offender in which a facilitator initiates a dialogue between the parties. This dialogue is predetermined by the victim and is intended to answer the victim's questions for the offender, discuss the impact of the crime, and seek recognition of responsibility from the offender (Koss & Achilles, 2008, Umbreit et al., 2005). *Sentencing circles* bring a large group of people together to establish a plan for the offender. These circles involve victims, offenders, family members and friends of affected parties, law enforcement officials, and other community members; they allow each person to speak and present his or her views on how to repair the harm caused by the crime (Koss & Achilles, 2008; Umbreit et al., 2005). *Conferencing* involves the victim, the offender, the family and friends of each, and other community members. The meetings are prepared and often scripted so that the goals of the victim (e.g., explaining the impact of the crime and accepting an apology from the offender), the goals of the offender (e.g., making amends with the victim, expressing remorse, and undertaking personal changes), and the goals of society (e.g., creating a plan to repair the harm and rehabilitate the offender for entrance back into the community) are all met (Koss & Achilles, 2008; Umbreit et al., 2005). For a number of years, a successful conferencing program known as RESTORE in Pima County, Arizona, has been a valuable, victim-driven process used to achieve accountability for crimes within a community through rehabilitation rather than punishment (Koss, Bachar, & Hopkins, 2003).

Although these methods of restorative justice have received a great deal of praise, there is still resistance to them in the traditional justice system. Critics observe that participation in these programs may be forced on victims, that victims may suffer revictimization during this process, that rehabilitation is emphasized over punishment, and that this response to sexual assault and gender-related crimes minimizes and conceals the crime itself (Curtis-Fawley & Daly, 2005; Koss, 2006). Many advocates of restorative justice believe it will be most successful if employed in conjunction with traditional criminal and civil justice systems, as a means to establish a balance in addressing and responding to crime (Koss, 2006).

WHAT ARE THE NEXT STEPS?

The promise of rape law reform has not been fully realized. Rape mythology, victim blaming, and misconceptions about perpetrators continue to plague both the criminal and civil justice systems, keeping offender accountability and victim remedies out of reach in most assaults. To achieve meaningful and lasting improvements, the current proof requirements associated with nonconsent and force must be further improved, drugs and alcohol must be understood as weapons in sexual assault rather than a benign fact of social or sexual interaction, and prosecutors must reexamine the assumptions and biases that contribute to prosecutorial judgments and decision making. Sexual assault victims should be understood to suffer from a host of severe consequences to their civil well-being. The legal system should move toward recognizing these consequences and supporting victim-centered remedies in alternative forums.

Further, we must commit ourselves to more detailed research and study of rape in our society, including community impact as well as disparate impacts on diverse communities. A federally financed and organized research agenda, including outcome studies of the criminal, civil, and restorative justice systems, would create the information needed to reform laws and challenge legal practices and myth-based attitudes held by judges, lawyers, prosecutors, jurors, and the media.

Only a holistic approach to offender accountability, victim remedies, and community healing offers an opportunity for victims to use the legal system to fight the many consequences of assault. Although this approach is not prevalent, some organizations have begun to represent victims in this holistic manner. For example, the Victim Rights Law Center in Boston is dedicated to providing civil legal services to sexual assault victims. These services are designed to assert every victim's right to safety, education, employment, reasonable accommodation, government benefits, medical care, housing, and preservation of immigration status after assault, as well as privacy in the criminal justice process.

Sexual assault victims face enormous substantive, procedural, and attitudinal barriers in the legal system. Through the replication of holistic representation services for victims, continuing demands for accountability of the various justice systems, and further research about and availability of alternative justice remedies, we must continue to demand justice for sexual assault victims.

REFERENCES

Althouse, A. (1992). Thelma and Louise and the law: Do rape shield rules matter? *Loyola of Los Angeles Law Review, 25,* 757–772.

Anderson, M. J. (2004). Time to reform rape shield laws: Kobe Bryant case highlights holes in the armor, *Criminal Justice, 19,* 14–19.

Brady v. Maryland, 373 U.S. 83, 86–87 (1963).

Bublick, E. M. (1999). Citizen no-duty rules: Rape victims and comparative fault. *Columbia Law Review, 99,* 1413–1490.

Bublick, E. M. (2006). Tort suits filed by rape and sexual assault victims in civil courts: lessons for courts, classrooms, and constituencies. *SMU Law Review, 59,* 55; 96–97.

Campbell, R. (2005). What really happened? A validation study of rape survivors' help-seeking experiences with the legal and medical systems. *Violence and Victims, 20,* 55–68.

Campbell, R. (2006). Rape survivors' experiences with the legal and medical systems: Do rape victim advocates make a difference? *Violence Against Women, 12*(1), 30–45.

Caplow, S. (1998). What if there is no client? Prosecutors as "counselors" of crime victims. *Clinical Law Review, 5,* 1–45.

Curtis-Fawley, S., & Daly, K. (2005). Gendered violence and restorative justice: The views of victim advocates. *Violence Against Women, 11,* 603–638.

Death Penalty Sentencing Research indicates pattern of racial disparities. (1990). Hearing before the Subcommittee on Civil and Constitutional Rights of the House Committee on the Judiciary, 101st Cong. 5 (as released by U.S. Gen. Acct. Off., GAO/T-GGD-90-37, May 3, 1990).

Deer, S. (2004). Toward an indigenous jurisprudence of rape. *Kansas Journal of Law and Public Policy, 14*(Fall), 121–154.

Duncan, M. J. (2007). Sex crimes and sexual miscues: The need for a clearer line between forcible rape and nonconsensual sex. *Wake Forest Law Review, 42,* 1087; 1095–1108.

Family and Medical Leave Act (FMLA), 29 U.S.C. Sec. 2601.

Fialkow, D. E. (2006). The media's first amendment right and the rape victim's right to privacy: When does one end and the other begin? *Suffolk University Law Review, 39,* 745–772.

Cullen, F. T., & Turner, M. G. (2000). *The sexual victimization of college women* (NCJ 182369). Washington, DC: U.S. Department of Justice, Bureau of Justice Statistics and National Institute of Justice. Retrieved from http://www.ncjrs.org/pdffiles1/nij/182369.pdf

Frohmann, L. (1991). Discrediting victims' allegations of sexual assault: prosecutorial accounts of case rejection. *Social Problems, 38,* 213–226.

Frohmann, L. (1997). Convictability and discordant locales: reproducing race: Class and gender ideologies in prosecutorial decision-making. *Law & Society Review, 31,* 531–555.

Futter, S., & Mebane, W. R. (2001). The effects of rape law reform on rape case processing. *Berkeley Women's Law Journal, 16,* 72; 83–85.

Goodman, L. A., & Epstein, D. (2008). *Listening to battered women: A survivor-centered approach to advocacy, mental health, and justice*. Washington, DC: American Psychological Association. doi:10.1037/11651-000

Haddad, R. I. (2005). Shield or sieve? People v. Bryant and the rape shield law in high-profile cases. *Columbia Journal of Law and Social Problems, 39*, 185–221.

Harless, S. M. (2003). From the bedroom to the courtroom: The impact of domestic violence law on marital rape victims. *Rutgers Law Journal, 35*, 305–343.

Hasday, J. (2000). Contest and consent: A legal history of marital rape. *California Law Review, 88*, 1373–1505. doi:10.2307/3481263

Kanter, L. H. (2005). Invisible clients: Exploring our failure to provide civil legal services to rape victims. *Suffolk University Law Review, 38*, 253–290

Kilpatrick, D. G., Resnick, H. S., Ruggiero, K. J., Conoscenti, K. M., & McCauley, J. (2007). *Drug facilitated, incapacitated, and forcible rape: A national study* (NCJ 21981). Report submitted to the National Institute of Justice, U.S. Department of Justice. Retrieved from: http://www.ncjrs.gov/pdffiles1/nij/grants/219181.pdf

Koss, M. P. (2006). Restoring rape survivors justice, advocacy, and a call to action. *Annals of the New York Academy of Sciences, 1087*, 206–236. doi:10.1196/annals.1385.025

Koss, M., & Achilles, M. (2008). *Restorative justice responses to sexual assault*. National Online Research Center on Violence Against Women. Retrieved from http://new.vawnet.org/category/Main_Doc.php?docid=1231

Koss, M. P., Bachar, K. J., & Hopkins, C. Q. (2003). Restorative justice for sexual violence: Repairing victims, building community, and holding offenders accountable. *Annals of the New York Academy of Sciences, 989*, 384–396.

Kramer, K. M. (1994). Rule by myth: The social and legal dynamics governing alcohol-related acquaintance rapes. *Stanford Law Review, 47*, 115–160.

Kyles v. Whitley, 514 U.S. 419, 437 (1995).

Little, N. J. (2005). From no means no to only yes means yes: The rational results of an affirmative consent standard in rape law. *Vanderbilt Law Review, 58*, 1321–1364.

Maslow, A. (1954). *Motivation and personality*. New York, NY: Harper.

Mindlin, J. E., Vickers, S. H. (Eds.). (2007). *Beyond the criminal justice system: Using the law to help restore the lives of sexual assault victims: A practical guide for attorneys and advocates*. Boston, MA: Victim Rights Law Center, Inc.

Mohler-Kuo, M., Dowdall, G., Koss, M. P., & Wechsler, H. (2004). Correlates of rape while intoxicated in a national sample of college women. *Journal of Studies on Alcohol 65*(1), 37–45.

Napue v. Illinois, 360 U.S. 264, 271 (1959).

Nelkin, M. (2000). The limits of privilege: The developing scope of federal psychotherapist-patient privilege law. *The Review of Litigation, 20*, 1; 8–9.

Pineau, L. (1989). Date rape: A feminist analysis. *Law and Philosophy, 8*, 217–243. doi:10.1007/BF00160012

Pokorak, J. J. (2006). Rape as a badge of slavery: The legal history of, and remedies for, prosecutorial race-of-victim charging disparities. *Nevada Law Journal, 7*, 1–54.

Pokorak, J. J. (2007). Rape victims and prosecutors: The inevitable ethical conflict of de facto client/attorney relationships. *South Texas Law Review, 48*, 695–732.

Rennison, C. (2001). *Violent victimization and race, 1993–1998*. Washington, DC: U.S. Department of Justice.

Rennison, C. (2002). *Rape and sexual assault: Reporting to police and medical attention, 1992–2000*. Washington, DC: Bureau of Justice Statistics. Retrieved from http://www.ojp.usdoj.gov/bjs/pub/pdf/rsarp00.pdf

Reynolds, M. O. (1999). *Crime and punishment in America: National Center for Policy Analysis Policy Report No. 229*. Retrieved from http://www.ncpa.org/pdfs/st229.pdf

Roberts, D. (1997). *Killing the Black body: Race, reproduction, and the meaning of liberty*. Indianapolis, IN: Pantheon Books.

Schulhofer, S. J. (1998). *Unwanted sex: The culture of intimidation and the failure of the law*. Cambridge, MA: Harvard University Press.

Schuller, R. A., & Wall, A.-M. (1998). The effects of defendant and complainant intoxication on mock jurors' judgments of sexual assault. *Psychology of Women Quarterly, 22*, 555–573.

Seidman, I., & Vickers, S. (2005). The second wave: an agenda for the next thirty years of rape law reform. *Suffolk University Law Review, 38*, 467–491.

Siegel, L. W. (1995). The marital rape exemption: Evolution to extinction. *Cleveland State Law Review, 43*, 351–378.

Smith, W. J. (2000, March 28). *Focusing on damages to win the case* (American Bar Association Continuing Legal Education, ALI-ABA Course of Study). Philadelphia, PA: American Law Institute.

Spohn, C., Beichner, D., & Davis-Frenzel, E. (2001). Prosecutorial justifications for sexual assault case rejection: Guarding the "gateway to justice." *Social Problems, 48*, 206; 210.

Spohn, C., & Horney, J. (1992). *Rape law reform: A grassroots revolution and its impact*. New York, NY: Plenum Press.

Tjaden, P., & Thoennes, N. (1998). *Prevalence, incidence, and consequences of violence against women: Findings from the National Violence Against Women Survey*. Washington, DC: U.S. Department of Justice, National Institute of Justice.

Umbreit, M, S., Vos, B., Coates, R. B., & Lightfoot, E.(2005). Restorative justice in the twenty-first century: A social movement full of opportunities and pitfalls. *Marquette Law Review, 89*, 251–304.

United States v. Bagley, 473 U.S. 667, 676 (1985).

Violence Against Women Act (VAWA). (1994). Title IV, sec. 40001-40703 of the Violent Crime Control and Law Enforcement Act of 1994, HR 3355, Pub. L. No. 103-322.

Walsh, M. G. (1983). Annotation, Criminal responsibility of husband for rape, or assault to commit rape, on wife. 24 A.L.R. 4th 105.

Youth Risk Behavior Surveillance—United States, 2009. (2010). *Morbidity and Mortality Weekly Report, Surveillance Summaries*, 59, SS-5. Retrieved from http://www.cdc.gov/mmwr/pdf/ss/ss5905.pdf

Yuan, N. P., Koss, M. P., & Stone, M. (2006). *The psychological consequences of sexual trauma*. Harrisburg, PA: VAWnet, a project of the National Resource Center on Domestic Violence/Pennsylvania Coalition Against Domestic Violence. Retrieved from http://www.vawnet.org

8

PRIMARY PREVENTION OF SEXUAL VIOLENCE

CHRISTINE A. GIDYCZ, LINDSAY M. ORCHOWSKI,
AND KATIE M. EDWARDS

Sexual violence is considered to be a major public health problem (see Centers for Disease Control and Prevention [CDC], 2004) with far-reaching consequences for both victims and society. The *primary prevention* of sexual violence involves a variety of efforts (e.g., programming, institutional policies, changing societal inequalities) aimed at preventing first-time perpetration or initiatives that take place prior to the occurrence of sexual violence (Valle et al., 2007).

Utilizing a public health framework for prevention of sexual violence dictates that we first have a well-defined problem with identified risk and protective factors (CDC, 2004). Currently, sexual violence is best conceptualized as a worldwide problem that exists on a continuum of severity and across the life span. The CDC's definition of sexual violence includes a range of acts forced against someone's will that encompasses attempted and completed rape, abusive sexual contact e.g., intentional touching of the genitalia, anus, groin, breast, inner thigh, or buttocks), and noncontact sexual abuse (e.g., voyeurism, exhibitionism, behavioral sexual harassment; Basile & Saltzman, 2002). Estimates in the United States reveal that across various samples (community and college), 18% to 25% of women report experiencing either an attempted or completed rape in their lifetimes (Fisher, Cullen, & Turner, 2000; Tjaden & Thoennes, 2000). It is further well documented that the majority of sexual assaults are perpetrated by someone known to the victim (e.g., romantic partner, friend) and that many women are assaulted repeatedly (Rich, Gidycz, Warkentin, Loh, & Weiland, 2005) and remain in the abusive relationships (Edwards, Gidycz, & Murphy, in press). The CDC uses an ecological framework to organize the individual, relationship, community, and societal risk factors that contribute to sexual violence in U.S. society (Valle et al., 2007).

After nearly 40 years of researching the epidemiology and risk factors associated with sexual violence, the scientific community has begun to identify and evaluate potential primary prevention initiatives. These initiatives, for the most part, are predicated on what the scientific community knows about the epidemiology and risk factors for sexual violence. Rigorous evaluation of the effectiveness of prevention initiatives is, problematically, less common. Program evaluations are often limited by small sample sizes, nonrandom assignment to program and control groups, lack of a control-group comparison, or short-term follow-up periods (Gidycz, Rich, & Marioni, 2002). Evidence to support the effectiveness of sexual violence prevention programming is also limited (for a review, see Anderson & Whiston, 2005). Programming must also be careful to decrease the potential for having an iatrogenic effect, for example, increasing self-blame among survivors of violence.

Although the primary prevention of sexual violence involves interventions across various levels and includes programming with groups of individuals as well as policy and societal reforms, the focus of this chapter is primarily on programming efforts aimed at producing individual-level change, emphasizing the scientific evidence behind the practice. Individual-level programming efforts attempt to produce attitude and behavior change among participants and are generally administered in a group-based format. The chapter concludes with a discussion of broader level initiatives and the need to address and evaluate sexual violence prevention across various domains.

WHAT DO WE KNOW?

Program Format and Content

Prevention initiatives are commonly orchestrated through community-based agencies, nonprofit organizations, or academic settings (e.g., elementary, middle school, high school, college). Programs aim to evoke community change by raising individuals' awareness regarding the prevalence of sexual victimization (i.e., awareness-based programs) and its consequences (i.e., empathy-based programs), by encouraging individuals to question and challenge the gender-based norms that promulgate violence against women (i.e., social norms–based programs), or by teaching individuals specific skills to decrease risk factors for violence (i.e., skills-based programs) or the assertiveness strategies to intervene when they witness violence within the community (e.g., bystander intervention programs). Awareness-based, skills-based, and bystander intervention programs have been deployed for all-male, all-female, and mixed-sex target audiences, whereas empathy-based and social norms–based programs are commonly administered to all-male audiences. How these programming approaches function within prevention initiatives across the developmental life span is detailed further below.

Broadly, program protocols that are interactive, include multimedia presentations, role-play or other methods of actively modeling, and practicing and rehearsing skills are likely to be most effective in changing attitude and beliefs among participants (Weisz & Black, 2001). Didactic formats, such as a health education class, in which an expert provides psychoeducation on violence prevention, are currently less emphasized as effective formats for prevention efforts. Rather, peer-led programs that target a single-gender audience are conducted in smaller groups (ideally, intact peer groups, e.g., athletic teams, or dormitories) and include multiple program sessions are likely to be most salient for participants (Brecklin & Forde, 2001).

Prevention efforts may be most effective when program content is tailored to the target audience. It is important to consider cultural diversity when designing preventive interventions as well as when adapting interventions for implementation across diverse communities. Theoretical models that aim to increase the salience of educational material can be used to increase the likelihood of producing long-term attitude and behavior change. One such approach is the elaboration likelihood model (ELM; Petty & Cacioppo, 1986). According to the ELM, central route processing, in which an individual finds a message personally relevant and engages in issue-relevant thinking, is associated with more stable and long-term attitude change. In fact, programs that maximize central route processing of program information are more successful in influencing the behavior of participants (see Heppner, Neville, Smith, Kivlighan, & Gershuny, 1995).

Types of Prevention Initiatives

Awareness-Based Programming

Awareness-based programming represents an indirect environmental change strategy in that programming does not focus on providing participants with specific skills to reduce sexual violence perpetration or victimization. Educational institutions—ranging from elementary schools to colleges and universities—often hire public speakers to discuss personal experiences of sexual violence, provide background on rates of violence, or encourage individuals to get involved in violence prevention efforts. These programs are frequently adapted for several audiences. For example, the integrated public education campaign developed by Men Can Stop Rape (MCSR; 2008) utilizes multiple forms of educational materials to mobilize boys and men to prevent gender-based violence and has been deployed across high school, college, and community settings. This organization is unique because it also delivers awareness-based workshops such as Linking Oppressions: Racism and Rape (MCSR, 2008) and provides training for community advocates and educators. Other awareness-based campaigns deployed in community and academic settings, such as Take Back the Night, are focused more specifically on the needs of girls and women in violence prevention.

Whereas awareness campaigns and public speakers play an important role in community consciousness raising, they fail to provide participants with active practice in skills to recognize, resist, or intervene as a third party against a potential sexual assault. Lack of empirical evaluation of awareness-based initiatives precludes knowing how these efforts result in changing rape-promoting attitudes and beliefs or in reducing incidence of violence. Therefore, they represent only a part of effective sexual violence prevention efforts and are best used in tandem with programs that more directly target environmental change.

Sexual Abuse Prevention Strategies With Children

Broadly, sexual violence prevention is needed across the life span (e.g., middle school, high school, university and post-university levels) to reduce risk factors for victimization later in development, as well as subsequent revictimization. Given that true prevention of child sexual abuse rests with the perpetrators, prevention programs that educate children on how to respond to potentially dangerous situations (e.g., recognizing good touches vs. bad touches, understanding how to respond to strangers) are only one component of a multilevel effort (Reppucci, Land, & Haugaard, 2001). Programs for children operate under a similar theoretical framework as programs for women. Specifically, while we are waiting for the perpetrators of violence to stop its occurrence, vulnerable populations—such as women and children—must be provided with the awareness and ability to fight back. Sexual violence prevention efforts with children function with the dual goals of (a) protecting children from violence by empowering them to recognize coercion and respond to coercive situations and (b) providing children with foundational skills and attitudes for the formation of healthy violence-free relationships later in life (Krug et al., 2002).

Sexual abuse prevention programs with children are commonly administered in a multisession format in the context of a curriculum that addresses other forms of violence, such as bullying behavior (Sidebotham, 2001). Programs aim to empower children through group-based instruction on personal safety, and they vary in content as well as the level of training of the instructor (Becker & Reilly, 1999). Common program components include (a) differentiating between good and bad touching, (b) saying "no" to inappropriate touching, (c) teaching of physical resistance strategies (i.e., yelling, running away), (d) discussing the need to report inappropriate experiences to a trusted adult even if they are instructed not to, and (e) providing resources available for recovery. The majority of programs are developed and conducted by community-based organizations and nonprofit groups; however, some research documents program efforts developed through academic researchers.

The multilevel causes of child abuse and interpersonal violence hold researchers and program developers accountable for developing interventions that span individual, family, community, and societal levels (Little & Kantor, 2002). Programs conducted by nonprofit organizations often teach parents, caregivers, school staff members, and community members strategies for integrating sexual abuse prevention into their work and home lives. Programs that address childhood sexual abuse prevention by working with adults and educators aim to teach them how to talk with children about sexuality and sexual violence, and they empower adults to intervene to stop violence within the community.

Program developers face an array of challenges when implementing a sexual abuse prevention program for children. Challenges include general discomfort in talking to children about sexuality, as well as problems with collaborating with school personnel (Daro, 1994). Prevention programs may be more readily accepted into hesitant communities when they are developed and facilitated in collaboration with already established practitioners in the community, such as nurses within elementary school settings.

The most effective child sexual abuse prevention programs take into account the developmental level of the child, as well as their gender, environment, and family environment (Little & Kantor, 2002). More specifically, however, whereas more than 40 child sexual abuse prevention programs with children have received empirical evaluation through application of a quasi-experimental design or random assignment of children to program and control groups, there are few data regarding the efficacy of such programs in decreasing rates of child sexual abuse (Daro, 1994). Meta-analytic reviews suggest that participants evidence modest changes in knowledge of sexual abuse, the acquisition of self-protective skills, such as "saying no" (Rispens, Aleman, & Goldena, 1997), and social confidence (Taal & Edelaar, 1997).

Sexual Violence Prevention Strategies With High-School Adolescents

Sexual violence prevention programming with high-school age adolescents is often addressed as part of programming combating a continuum of dating violence, including psychological, physical, and sexual abuse (Irwin & Rickert, 2005). Programming often focuses on how to develop healthy dating relationships (Weisz & Black, 2001). Common program components include (a) definitions of date and acquaintance rape; (b) discussion of types of sexual harassment; (c) discussion of stalking; (d) identification of characteristics of healthy dating relationships; (e) identification of personal limits and preferences in dating; (f) provision of strategies for responding to coercive dating relationships; (g) discussion of aftereffects of sexual violence; (h) education about how to report sexual violence; and (i) discussion of medical needs, resources for survivors, and the recovery process.

The vast majority of programs include theatrical presentations, speeches from survivors of domestic violence or sexual violence, classroom discussions, or psychoeducational curriculums. Most programs are administered by community-based organizations or nonprofit groups and are conducted in a mixed-sex audience in health or wellness classrooms (Hilton, Harris, Rice, Krans, & Lavigne, 1998) or community settings. However, some academic-based programming efforts developed by researchers in university settings are also documented. For example, Foshee and colleagues' (1998, 2000) nine-session high school curriculum that includes a play about dating abuse, *Safe Dates*, which is administered over 4 months, engages eighth- and ninth-grade male and female students in didactic and interactive classroom activities as well as a poster contest. Further, innovative video-based program formats have been used to engage adolescent audiences. For example, Pacifici, Stoolmiller, and Nelson (2001) used a video of a "virtual date" to encourage participants to generate ways to address unwanted sexual advances.

The most effective prevention programs for adolescent audiences generally include clear messages about personal responsibilities and boundaries, delivered in a nonblaming manner (Dryfoos, 1991). Discussion and interactive formats also appear to be more effective than lecture-based formats. However, prevention programs focused on adolescent populations have received significantly less research than programs for college populations (Pacifici et al., 2001). Data suggest that adolescents demonstrate an interest in learning about dating relationships and gain awareness about their personal boundaries as a function of program participation. Further, 4-year follow-up data from the Safe Dates program (Foshee et al., 2004) suggest that adolescents who participated in the program evidenced significantly less physical and sexual violence perpetration and victimization. Thus, clearly the Safe Dates program is a promising intervention specifically targeting teen violence.

Bystander Intervention Programs

Bystander intervention programs operate under the belief that all members of a community are affected by violence (Edwards, Jumper-Thurman,

Plested, Oetting, & Swanson, 2000). Therefore, members of the community must be engaged in an ongoing dialogue to debunk the social norms that sustain and condone violence against women, be assertive in taking action to interrupt inappropriate social and dating situations, and be proactive in providing support services to survivors (see Banyard, Plante, & Moynihan, 2004). According to Berkowitz (2004), bystander intervention programs expand upon prevention programs that focus on skills or gaining empathy for survivors by aiming to change the community culture that tolerates violence against women.

Some bystander intervention programs are media-based. For example, the Stop It Now program engages the community in the prevention of violence through the administration of a mass media campaign aimed at decreasing child sexual abuse by increasing adults' knowledge and awareness of the problem (Chasan-Taber & Tabachnick, 1999). More recently, Rheingold et al. (2007) evaluated the Darkness to Light program, which includes a combination of public service announcements, pamphlets, and web-based materials aimed at increasing parents' and children's awareness about child sexual abuse. Skills-based bystander intervention programs have been conducted in high school and college settings, for all-male, all-female, and mixed-sex audiences. The majority of bystander intervention programs have been administered with groups of men (Berkowitz, 2003) and maintain a more specific focus on empowering men to question and challenge the hypermasculine dating norms (Berkowitz, 2004). For example Katz's (1994) Mentors in Violence Prevention program addresses sexual violence in the context of other forms of gendered-based violence and bullying behavior that often occur in a school context by educating students to take an active role in changing their educational climate. The curriculum's *Playbook*, which is specifically tailored either to men and boys or women and girls, includes a range of role-play scenarios that trained peer-mentors use to help participants develop a repertoire of potential responses to various forms of sexual abuse ranging from sexual harassment to sexual violence. The program's initial focus was on male and female athletes; however, the program has been expanded to high school, college, and military populations.

Often bystander intervention programs are jointly administered to single-sex groups of men and women, ostensibly to decrease defensiveness among program participants. For example, the bystander education program developed by Banyard, Moynihan, and Plante (2007) is jointly administered to single-sex groups of college-age men and women. The program consists of discussion, role-play, and didactic instruction on the prevalence, causes, and aftereffects of sexual assault, the role of community members in observing sexual assault, and the types of assertiveness skills that can be used to intervene when witnessing a risky social or dating situation. The program is administered across one to three 90-min sessions and a booster-session review, which is led by trained peer-leaders.

Because bystander interventions are a relatively new approach to sexual violence prevention, only a few have undergone empirical evaluation (e.g., Banyard et al., 2004; Banyard et al., 2007). Initial data suggest that these programs evidence promise for increasing prosocial bystander behaviors and potential to both increase awareness of sexual violence and provide individuals with skills to intervene when they witness coercive dating behaviors.

Sexual Violence Prevention for College Students—Mixed-Sex Audiences

Curriculum-based sexual violence prevention programs for college students were originally administered to mixed-sex audiences. Mixed-sex programming initiatives use interactive, didactic, and multimedia formats to discuss factors related to violence against women with groups of men and women (Gidycz, Layman, et al., 2001). Although the vast majority of sexual violence prevention programs are conducted for college populations, it should be noted that many of the program components overlap with prevention initiatives across developmental time periods. Common program components include discussions of (a) societal attitudes toward violence against women, (b) gender role socialization, (c) local and national definitions of sexual assault, (d) prevalence of sexual assault, (e) consent for sexual activity, (f) resistance tactics and safety precautions, (g) aftereffects of sexual victimization, and (h) resources for survivors of sexual assault. What seems to differentiate curriculum-based programs for college audiences from those for high school audiences is the former's narrower focus on risk factors for sexual assault, as opposed to the broader context of healthy dating relationships.

Programs for mixed-sex college audiences achieved early popularity for their ease of administration and low cost. However, there is considerable debate regarding the ethics of administering a curriculum focused on risk factors for sexual assault to a mixed-sex audience. Program content regarding women's self-protective dating strategies may be harmful to discuss in a mixed-sex audience that could contain potential perpetrators (Gidycz, Rich, & Marioni, 2002). Second, men's and women's needs in programming are different (Gidycz et al., 2002). Thus, curriculum-based programs for mixed-sex audiences may not be as salient or relevant to participants as programs for single-sex audiences. Mixed-sex programs may also incite defensiveness in participants; for example, when women are present, fears of embarrassment may make it difficult for men to openly discuss their attitudes (Berkowitz, 2004).

Several didactic prevention programs for mixed-sex college audiences document changes in rape myth acceptance over a short interim; however, these changes are not maintained over longer follow-up periods (for a review, see Gidycz et al., 2002). Research by Gidycz, Layman, et al. (2001) is currently the only study that evaluated the effectiveness of a didactic program for a mixed-sex audience in reducing rates of sexual victimization among women and perpetration of sexual aggression in men. The program failed to show reductions in rates of either victimization or perpetration (Gidycz, Layman, et al., 2001).

Program developers have responded to ethical criticisms and lack of empirical support by administering *dual-pronged* programs, which concurrently administer men's and women's programs that aim to provide women with risk reduction skills amid concomitant prevention efforts geared toward encouraging men to take responsibility for ending sexual violence. An innovative examination of a dual-pronged sexual violence prevention and risk reduction program was administered by the Laboratory for the Study and Prevention of Sexual Assault at Ohio University (Gidycz & Orchowski, 2009). The research team examined the potential synergistic effects of providing a dual-pronged prevention program to men and women living in the same 1st-year dormitory on campus. The findings suggest that such an approach is promising, and numerous positive outcomes for both men and women were noted, including decreases in rates of self-reported sexual aggression for men who participated in the program relative to the control group participants.

Sexual Violence Risk Reduction Programs for College Women

Programs for women to reduce the risk of sexual assault operate under the belief that until men take responsibility for ending violence against women, women must be provided with strategies to fight back (for a review, see Gidycz et al., 2002). Common program components include a discussion of (a) local and national definitions of sexual victimization, (b) prevalence of sexual assault, (c) societal factors that underlie violence against women, (d) situational risk factors for sexual assault, (e) characteristics of perpetrators of sexual aggression, (f) the role of alcohol and drugs as risk factors for sexual assault, (g) the importance of assessing and acknowledging risky dating situations, (h) self-protective behaviors, (i) assertive sexual communication strategies, (j) verbal and physical resistance strategies, (k) personal experiences of survivors of sexual assault, and (l) the aftereffects of sexual victimization and resources available to survivors.

The framework currently guiding the majority of risk-reduction programs is Rozee and Koss's (2001) "AAA" strategy for reducing risk for victimization. The strategy consists of (a) assessing whether a social or dating experience is potentially dangerous, (b) acknowledging and labeling that a situation is potentially threatening when it is so, and (c) assertively and forcefully taking action via increasingly more assertive verbal and physical resistance strategies.

Self-defense programs are often administered in tandem with the risk-reduction program to provide women with specific practice in resistance techniques (Gidycz, Rich, Orchowski, King, & Miller, 2006; Orchowski, Gidycz, & Raffle, 2008). When conducting programs with women to reduce the risk of sexual assault, program administrators must be aware that their audience will most likely contain a number of survivors (Gidycz et al., 2002). As a result, several programs have been tailored to include information relevant to women with histories of sexual victimization, such as recovery issues and strategies to minimize self-blame (Marx, Calhoun, Wilson, & Meyerson, 2001).

Most evaluations of these risk-reduction programs occur on college campuses. Although rape crisis centers implement some forms of risk-reduction program—through education, outreach, or awareness campaigns—such programs are less frequently evaluated (Campbell, Baker, & Mazurek, 1998). A growing body of evidence suggests that programming to reduce the risk of sexual assault is associated with positive gains, including increases in assertiveness, general levels of self-esteem, perception of control, use of self-protective dating behaviors, competence in self-defense, and deceased use of risky dating behaviors and fear of sexual victimization (Anderson & Whiston, 2005). Programs that include a self-defense component appear to be especially efficacious in increasing women's skills in responding to potential attackers. Less commonly, programs document decreases in victimization rates following program participation (see Hanson & Gidycz, 1993; Orchowski et al., 2008).

The Ohio University Sexual Assault Risk Reduction Program (Gidycz, Lynn, et al., 2006) has undergone consistent, systematic revision over the past 15 years. Successive revisions and program evaluations document reduction in risk of sexual victimization for women without a history of sexual assault (Hanson & Gidycz, 1993) as well as reduction in revictimization rates (Gidycz, Lynn, et al., 2001). In more recent program evaluations, revised program protocols were paired with a self-defense component and a booster session. Results demonstrated increases in participants' use of self-protective dating behaviors (Gidycz, Rich, et al., 2006) as well as a 50% decrease in incidence of rape among program participants compared with the control group (Orchowski et al., 2008)

Empathy-, Social Norms–, and Skills-Based Sexual Assault Prevention for College Men

Because men perpetrate the vast majority of sexual assaults, prevention programs for men operate with the understanding that it is men's responsibility to end sexual violence (see Berkowitz, 2004). Prevention programs specifically tailored to men are commonly conducted in a single-session format, although some programs include a booster session to promote further discussion of program material. Common program components include discussions of (a) prevalence of violence against women, (b) definition of sexual assault, (c) gender role ideology, (d) rape myths, (e) obtaining consent, and (f) how to support a survivor of sexual assault. Although most programs are tailored to college men, similar program content has been used in groups of high school boys.

Empathy-based programs aim to decrease men's rape-supportive attitudes, and subsequent proclivity to rape, by educating men on the aftereffects of sexual assault and encouraging them to support survivors (Berg, Lonsway, & Fitzgerald, 1999). Social norms–based programs address men's tendency to underestimate the positive, prosocial attitudes and behaviors of other men and overestimate other men's undesirable, hypermasculine norms (Berkowitz, 2004). Skills-based programs extend the aims of empathy-based programs by asking men to take responsibility for their interactions with others and to learn skills such as communication strategies, anger management, and negotiating consent in romantic relationships (Berkowitz, 2004). Other programs focus more extensively on men's socialization processes, such as Katz and Earp's (1999) Tough Guise program, which uses a video-based curriculum to question and debunk socialized masculine norms.

Alarmingly, although men perpetrate the vast majority of sexual assaults, Morrison, Hardison, Mathew, and O'Neil's (2004) review revealed that only 8% of sexual assault education programs target men. Prevention programs for men show some evidence for positive change in rape-supportive attitudes and beliefs among college men. This includes changes in men's self-reported likelihood to rape, rape-myth acceptance, and attitudes and beliefs regarding rape (Bachar & Koss, 2001). However, there is very little evidence that prevention programs with college men actually reduce rates of sexual aggression (Foubert, Newberry, & Tatum, 2007). Often data are limited to consumer satisfaction; for example, participants rate how much they learned as a result of participation in the program. Further, the program evaluation designs for men's programs tend to be significantly less rigorous than those used to evaluate women's sexual assault risk reduction programming. Thus, although there are several compelling hypotheses as to how to conduct prevention programming with men, as well as several persuasive arguments as to methods for influencing men's dating behavior, there is very little evidence to suggest that these programming strategies actually work.

These data evade the primary issue: Why is the field of sexual assault prevention from the standpoint of the perpetrator lagging behind sexual assault prevention with children and women in methodologically rigorous program evaluation? One hypothesis is the tendency for men's prevention programming to be conducted in a theatrical format, whereby groups of trained students or professional speakers are hired by a university to provide a speech or dramatic presentation. When nonuniversity personnel are hired by a university to administer programming, a formal evaluation of the program may not be integrated into the design of the program. It is important not only to conduct evaluations but also to raise awareness among higher education that, regardless of the format used to attempt prevention, a paid presenter should be expected to provide evidence of the efficacy of the program.

HOW DO WE KNOW IT?

Program Evaluation Methodology

Only a small number of studies meet standards for rigorous program evaluation. Research is also plagued by small sample sizes and relatively short-term follow-up periods. Best practices involve methodologies and evaluation designs that allow researchers to reliably understand how a program influences attitude and behavior change among participants. Best practices include use of quasi-experimental designs and random assignment of participants to control and program groups, as well as the use of longitudinal follow-up evaluations across an adequate interim and a comprehensive array of measures of attitudinal and behavioral change of the effectiveness of program participation (see Breitenbecher, 2000). Program development is further improved when program modification and evaluation is an ongoing process, involving continued revision and evaluation of program protocol according to feedback from program participants and various theoretical models and data from previous evaluation.

An important future direction for the field of sexual assault prevention is to improve upon the validity of research designs, which often fail to randomly assign participants and also often fail to administer an active treatment or program among the control group. When control group participants only complete questionnaires, they may be less invested in study participation, which may bias comparison study results. Instead, program developers should consider random assignment of participants to control and program groups and engage control-group participants in another theoretically driven health intervention. This research design (i.e., summative evaluation design) may equalize investment in the study between program and control-group participants, leading to a more valid comparison between groups.

As the field progresses, it is vital that individuals engaged in program development and administration emphasize sound evaluation methodology as a fundamental component of their prevention efforts. Conducting research to ensure that prevention programs are actually decreasing rates of sexual violence is not only good science but also an ethical responsibility of program developers. Given that sexual assault is an endemic problem and that rates of sexual assault have not shown a decline over the past 30 years, those engaged in prevention work must be confident that they are putting their strongest effort forward in the fight to end sexual violence. Consistent with a public health approach to prevention, promising programs should be expanded.

Measurement of Behavioral Outcomes

Researchers assess the benefits of participating in a sexual assault prevention program by administering surveys to participants. To assess change as a result of program participation, reliable and valid survey measures should be completed by program participants prior to program participation and at multiple follow-up sessions. Survey measures that are completed at both a short-term and a long-term follow-up period allow program developers to understand how the program is related to both immediate and sustained changes in attitudes and behaviors. Most program evaluations include assessment of attitude and behavior change through self-report measures. For example, participants may complete measures of dating behaviors, attitudes toward women, gender role beliefs, adherence to rape-myth ideology, level of blame ascribed to sexual assault survivors, as well as knowledge of sexual assault. Frequently, the assessments used may be too subtle to detect the effects of an intervention or may not survey relevant constructs of behavior change (Breitenbecher, 2000). Measures of actual experiences, including perpetration of sexual aggression or experience of sexual victimization, are less commonly utilized to evaluate the effectiveness of the program. However, such measures are essential in understanding program influences on rates of sexual assault.

Self-report measures may be influenced by demand characteristics—cues that make participants aware of what those who offer the program seek to find and how participants are expected to behave, which can lead participants to conform to the experimenters' expectations. For this and other reasons, assessments may not reflect lasting ideological change (Gidycz et al., 2002). Behaviorally oriented assessments of attitude and behavior change, which provide an observation of participants' behavior, are an innovative approach to examine the effectiveness of program participation (Yeater & O'Donohue, 1999). For example, the ongoing evaluation of the Community Programming Initiative (Gidycz, 2006) involves the administration of a phone survey following participation, in which participants are asked if they would be in support of allocating university funding to sexual assault prevention efforts on campus. Such behaviorally oriented assessments address some of the limitations of relying on self-report measures, which may be potentially influenced by the response biases of participants, who may feel pressured to report their behavior in a socially appropriate way.

WHAT ARE THE GAPS AND WEAKNESSES IN EXISTING KNOWLEDGE?

Despite the efforts of the past several decades of research on sexual violence, the rates of sexual violence remain alarmingly high. Furthermore, meta-analytic results (Anderson & Whiston, 2005) suggest that current sexual assault programming does not lead to reductions in rates of gendered violence. Moreover, the vast majority of sexual assault research has been conducted with college students, which, it has been argued, can potentially limit the generalizability of programmatic findings (Morrison et al., 2004). However, it is possible that many of the components of college-student programs would transfer or be applicable to community programming efforts.

The majority of prevention efforts are what is referred to as *universal* in the public health model. Universal interventions target everyone in the population as opposed to individuals with differing levels of risk for the perpetration or victimization of sexual violence. Universal programming campaigns pose challenges to detection of program efficacy (see Cuijpers, 2003), but they also may have unknown and possibly negative effects on the sizable portion of an all-female audience who identify as survivors of sexual victimization and are at significantly higher risk of experiencing subsequent assault (Daigle, Fisher & Guthrie, 2007). Whereas universal approaches are useful, more selective approaches to prevention aimed at targeting those most at risk are potentially most cost-effective. However, one major problem (as argued by Knight & Sims-Knight, 2009, in Chapter 2, Volume 1) involved in specifically tailoring programs to high-risk groups is that the data linking specific causal factors to sexual aggression are very limited. Once the research has developed to the point where early risk factors for sexual aggression can be demonstrated to play a causal role in sexual aggression and programs can target these causal factors, the programs should hypothetically be more effective. Further, violence against women is a societal and community issue (Casey & Lindhorst, 2009). Thus, individual-based programming alone is insufficient in addressing this problem. However, the vast majority of psychological research and evaluation efforts have focused on individual-level programming. Finally, rather than conducting the evaluation of preventive efforts as an afterthought, it should be viewed as a necessary component of programming that is just as critical as the program itself. To date, the field is lacking in terms of well-designed program evaluation studies that are rigorous in nature.

WHAT ARE THE NEXT STEPS?

There remain two broad areas in which major advances are needed: (a) improving the development, evaluation, and dissemination of individual-level prevention and risk-reduction programs and (b) broadening prevention efforts beyond the individual level to engender community and societal change.

Individual-level prevention programming research needs greater focus on gender-specific and theory-driven programs. This work would be facilitated by working collaboratively across disciplines and sites to evaluate those components of the existing interventions that are transportable to diverse communities. Doing so requires that researches and community members be proactive in communicating existing programming efforts, collaborate when preparing funding proposals, and be open to taking a bottom-up approach toward developing innovative and integrative prevention initiatives (as opposed to sticking with whatever has been done in the past). Further, there is a pressing need to develop culturally competent programming as well as programming tailored to high-risk groups. Specifically, diversity should be more broadly defined to address programming needs for individuals of various ages, races, sexual orientations, and socioeconomic statuses. Moreover, concerted effort is required to initiate individual-level prevention efforts early in development, as research suggests these programs are more effective in reducing relational violence than programs beginning later in life (Butchart et al., 2004). Future risk-reduction programming efforts should expand upon existing programs developed for high-risk audiences, such as survivors of sexual assault, high-risk drinkers, and members of athletic teams, for example. Given that many college campuses administer large-scale programming to reduce high-risk drinking, this venue may be ideal for future collaboration between health educators and sexual assault prevention advocates on college campuses.

Additionally, we need to change how program evaluation is often viewed. Discussions with key partners should be conducted so that there is buy-in up front, before programming initiatives are implemented. Integrating evaluation and program delivery requires that everyone involved have some familiarity with concepts and methods of program evaluation. Partnerships between community advocates—who commonly administer programs for childhood and adolescent audiences—and individuals working on college campuses, where program evaluation is more common, may be useful in increasing the rigor of evaluations of community-based program efforts. Furthermore, there is a great need for more collaboration between those who deliver programs and those who evaluate them, even on college campuses, given that most of the college-based evaluations have been conducted by academicians, not the practitioners who deliver the programs.

In the current climate of resource scarcity, the field must advocate for the importance of evaluation of programs that contribute to continuous quality improvements so that incentives for innovation are maintained. Achieving this goal requires that advocacy for sound science. Although we believe that there are theoretically sound programs available for men, the evaluation of such programs is often quite limited or lacking methodological rigor. A recent publication by the CDC is an excellent program evaluation guide (Valle et al., 2007).

Public health approaches to prevention dictate that in addition to individual and relational approaches to prevention, which were previously reviewed in this chapter, efforts geared toward broad community-level change are needed. Community and societal change involves transforming the social norms—not just social norms related to sexual violence but also those related to the broader context of gender inequality (Casey & Lindhorst, 2009). Changing social norms at the broader societal level involves policy change, legislative initiatives, and community-wide and institution-wide activism and intervention. Theories of community readiness have largely been ignored in the sexual prevention literature. One such theory is social diffusion (Gladwell, 2002; Rogers, 1995), which suggests that social change comes about when the most socially influential individuals ally with a specified cause. There is growing empirical support for this macrolevel theory within the health prevention literature (i.e., substance abuse, HIV/AIDS; Edwards et al., 2000; Kelly et al., 1991).

Despite research suggesting that social attitudes toward interpersonal violence have changed in recent years and people are now more aware and disapproving of such acts (Klein, Campbell, Soler, & Ghez, 1997), there is no systemic evaluation of prevention efforts based on societal factors. We are not aware of any evaluation of the effectiveness of community-level prevention efforts (e.g., implementation of community safety measures such as lighting, rallies/protests, police training) in changing attitudes or reducing rates of sexual victimization. Although it is much more difficult to evaluate the effectiveness of community-level initiatives, we must begin to document, ideally using multiple measurement points across sufficient time, change in attitudes and rates of sexual assault perpetration and victimization (both reported and unreported). One of the most promising venues of social change could be media-facilitated awareness campaigns such as Men Against Rape, which currently lacks systemic evaluation.

Over the past 30 years, researchers and advocates have learned a great deal about the causes of sexual victimization and how to intervene. Scientific study has also allowed us to examine what is working and what is not working in the primary prevention of sexual assault. As rates of sexual violence have yet to decline, it is clear that advocates must enhance the strength of their preventive efforts and continue to integrate best practices in research to strengthen programming and campaigns to end violence against women.

REFERENCES

Anderson, L. A., & Whiston, S. C. (2005). Sexual assault education programs: A meta-analytic examination of their effectiveness. *Psychology of Women Quarterly, 29,* 374–388. doi:10.1111/j.1471-6402.2005.00237.x

Bachar, K., & Koss, M. P. (2001). From prevalence to prevention: Closing the gap between what we know and what we do. In C. M. Renzetti, J. L. Edleson, & R. K. Bergen (Eds.), *Sourcebook on violence against women* (pp. 117–142). Thousand Oaks, CA: Sage.

Banyard, V. L., Moynihan, M. M., & Plante, E. G. (2007). Sexual violence prevention through bystander education: An experimental evaluation. *Journal of Community Psychology, 35,* 463–481. doi:10.1002/jcop.20159

Banyard, V. L., Plante, E. G., & Moynihan, M. M. (2004). Bystander education: Bringing a broader community perspective to sexual violence prevention. *Journal of Community Psychology, 32,* 61–79. doi:10.1002/jcop.10078

Basile, K. C., & Saltzman, L. E. (2002). *Sexual violence surveillance: Uniform definitions and recommended data elements* (Version 1). Atlanta, GA: Centers for Disease Control and Prevention, National Center for Injury Prevention and Control.

Becker, J. V., & Reilly, D. W. (1999). Preventing sexual abuse and assault. *Sexual Abuse, 11,* 267–278. doi:10.1177/107906329901100403

Berg, D. R., Lonsway, K. A., & Fitzgerald, L. F. (1999). Rape prevention education for men: The effectiveness of empathy induction techniques. *Journal of College Student Development, 40,* 219–234.

Berkowitz, A. D. (2003). Applications of social norms theory to other health and social justice issues. In W. Perkins (Ed.), *The social norms approach to preventing school and college age substance abuse: A handbook for educators, counselors, and clinicians* (pp. 259–279). San Francisco, CA: Jossey-Bass.

Berkowitz, A. D. (2004). *Working with men to prevent violence against women: Program modalities and formats (Part Two).* Violence Against Women Network, Applied Research Forum, National Electronic Network on Violence Against Women. Retrieved from http://www.vawnet.org/Assoc_Files_VAWnet/AR_MenPreventVAW2.pdf

Brecklin, L. R., & Forde, D. R. (2001). A meta-analysis of rape education programs. *Violence and Victims, 16,* 303–321.

Breitenbecher, K. H. (2000). Sexual assault on college campuses: Is an ounce of prevention enough? *Applied & Preventive Psychology, 9,* 23–52. doi:10.1016/S0962-1849(05)80036-8

Butchart, A., Phinney, A., Check, P., & Villaveces, A. (2004). *Preventing violence: A guide to implementing the recommendations of the World Report on Violence and Health.* Geneva, Switzerland: Department of Injuries and Violence Prevention, World Health Organization.

Casey, E. A., & Lindhorst, P. (2009). Toward a multilevel, ecological approach to the primary prevention of sexual assault: Prevention in peer and community contexts. *Trauma, Violence & Abuse, 10*, 91–114. doi:10.1177/152483800 9334129

Campbell, J. C., Baker, C. K., & Mazurek, T. L. (1998). Remaining radical? Organization predictors of rape crisis centers' social change initiatives. *American Journal of Community Psychology, 26*, 457–483. doi:10.1023/A:1022115322289

Centers for Disease Control and Prevention. (2004). *Sexual violence prevention: Beginning the dialogue*. Atlanta, GA: Author.

Chasan-Taber, L., & Tabachnick, J. (1999). Evaluation of a child sexual abuse prevention program. *Sexual Abuse, 11*, 279–292.

Cuijpers, P. (2003). Examining the effects of prevention programs on the incidence of new cases of mental disorders: The lack of statistical power. *American Journal of Psychiatry, 160*, 1385–1391. doi:10.1176/appi.ajp.160.8.1385

Daigle, L., Fisher, B. S., & Guthrie, P. (2007). Victims of crime. In R. C. Davis, A. J. Lugio, & S. Herman (Eds.), *The recurrence of victimization: What researchers know about its terminology, characteristics, causes, and prevention* (pp. 211–232). Thousands Oaks, CA: Sage Publishers.

Daro, D. A. (1994). Prevention of childhood sexual abuse. *The Future of Children, 4*, 198–223. doi:10.2307/1602531

Dryfoos, J. G. (1991). Adolescents at risk: A summation of work in the field—programs and policies. *Journal of Adolescent Health, 12*, 630–637. doi:10.1016/1054-139X(91)90011-L

Edwards, R. W., Jumper-Thurman, P., Plested, B. A., Oetting, E. R., & Swanson, L. (2000). Community readiness: Research to practice. *Journal of Community Psychology, 28*, 291–307. doi:10.1002/(SICI)1520-6629(200005)28:3<291::AID-JCOP5>3.0.CO;2-9

Edwards, K. M., Gidycz, C. A., & Murphy, M. J. (in press). College women's stay/leave decisions in abusive relationships: A prospective analysis of an expanded investment model. *Journal of Interpersonal Violence*.

Fisher, B. S., Cullen, F. T., & Turner, M. G. (2000). *The sexual victimization of college women* [Research report]. Washington, DC: National Institute of Justice. Retrieved from http://www.ncjrs.org/txtfiles1/nij/182369.txt

Foshee, V. A., Bauman, K. E., Arriaga, X. B., Helms, R. W., Koch, G. G., & Linder, G. F. (1998). An evaluation of Safe Dates, an adolescent dating violence prevention program. *American Journal of Public Health, 88*, 45–50. doi:10.2105/AJPH.88.1.45

Foshee, V. A., Bauman, K. E., Ennett, S. T., Linder, F., Benefield, T., & Suchindran, C. (2004). Assessing the long-term effects of the Safe Dates program and a booster session in preventing and reducing adolescent dating violence victimization and perpetration. *American Journal of Public Health, 94*, 619–624. doi:10.2105/AJPH.94.4.619

Foshee, V. A., Bauman, K. E., Greene, W. F., Koch, G. G., Linder, G. F., & MacDougall, J. E. (2000). The Safe Dates program: 1-year follow-up results. *American Journal of Public Health, 90,* 1619–1622. doi:10.2105/AJPH.90.10.1619

Foubert, J. D., Newberry, J. T., & Tatum, J. L. (2007). Behavior differences seven months later: Effects of a rape prevention program on first-year men who join fraternities. *NASPA Journal, 44,* 728–749.

Gidycz, C. A. & Orchowski, L. M. (2009). *Preventing sexual assault on college campuses* (5 R49/ CE 000923-03). Report submitted to the Centers for Disease Control and Prevention.

Gidycz, C. A., Layman, J. M., Rich, C. L., Crothers, M., Bylys, J., Matorin, A., & Jacobs, C. D. (2001). An evaluation of an acquaintance rape prevention program: Impact on attitudes, sexual aggression, and sexual victimization. *Journal of Interpersonal Violence, 16,* 1120–1138. doi:10.1177/088626001016011002

Gidycz, C. A., Lynn, S. J., Rich, C. L., & Loh, C. Marioni, N. L., & Orchowski, L. M. (2006). *The Ohio University Sexual Assault Risk Reduction Program (The Community Programming Initiative Program Protocol).* Unpublished manuscript.

Gidycz, C. A., Lynn, S. J., Rich, C. L., Marioni, N. L., Loh, C., Blackwell, L. M., . . . Pashdag, J. (2001). The evaluation of a sexual assault risk reduction program: A multi-site investigation. *Journal of Consulting and Clinical Psychology, 69,* 1073–1078. doi:10.1037/0022-006X.69.6.1073

Gidycz, C. A., Rich, C. L., & Marioni, N. L. (2002). Interventions to prevent rape and sexual assault. In J. Petrak & B. Hedge (Eds.), *The trauma of adult sexual assault: Treatment, prevention, and policy* (pp. 235–260). New York, NY: Wiley.

Gidycz, C. A., Rich, C. L., Orchowski, L., King, C., & Miller, A. (2006). The evaluation of a sexual assault self-defense and risk-reduction program for college women: A prospective study. *Psychology of Women Quarterly, 30,* 173–186. doi:10.1111/j.1471-6402.2006.00280.x

Gladwell, M. (2002). *The tipping point: How little things can make a big difference.* Boston, MA: Little, Brown.

Hanson, K. A., & Gidycz, C. A. (1993). Evaluation of a sexual assault prevention program. *Journal of Consulting and Clinical Psychology, 61,* 1046–1052. doi:10.1037/0022-006X.61.6.1046

Heppner, M. J., Humphrey, C. F., Hillenbrand-Gunn, T. L., & Debord, K. A. (1995). The differential effects of rape prevention programming on attitudes, behavior and knowledge. *Journal of Counseling Psychology, 42,* 508–518. doi:10.1037/0022-0167.42.4.508

Hilton, N. Z., Harris, G. T., Rice, M. E., Krans, T. S., & Lavigne, S. E. (1998). Antiviolence education in high schools: Implementation and evaluation. *Journal of Interpersonal Violence, 13,* 726–742. doi:10.1177/088626098013006004

Irwin, C. E., & Rickert, V. I. (2005). Editorial: Coercive sexual experiences during adolescence and young adulthood: A public health problem. *Journal of Adolescent Health, 36,* 359–361. doi:10.1016/j.jadohealth.2005.03.001

Katz, J. (1994). *Mentors in Violence Prevention (MVP) trainer's guide*. Boston, MA: Northeastern University's Center for the Study of Sport in Society.

Katz, J., & Earp, J. (1999). *Tough Guise teacher's guide online: A companion to the college and high school versions of the video*, Tough Guise: Violence, Media, and the Crisis in Masculinity. Northampton, MA: Media Education Foundation.

Kelly, J. A., St. Lawrence, J. S., Diaz, Y. E., Stevenson, L. Y., Hauth, A. C., Brasfield, T. L., . . . Andrew, M. E.. (1991). HIV risk behavior reduction following intervention with key opinion leaders of population: An experimental analysis. *American Journal of Public Health, 81*, 168–171. doi:10.2105/AJPH.81.2.168

Klein, E., Campbell, J., Soler, E., & Ghez, M. (1997). *Ending domestic violence: Changing public perceptions/halting the epidemic*. Thousand Oaks, CA: Sage.

Knight, R. A., & Sims-Knight, J. (2009). Risk factors for sexually coercive behavior against women. In M. Koss & J. White (Eds.), *Violence against women and children* (Vol. 1, pp. 290–306). Washington, DC: American Psychological Association.

Krug, E. G., Dahlberg, L. L., Mercy, J. A., Zwi, A. B., & Lozano, R. (Eds.). (2002). *World report on violence and health*. Geneva, Switzerland: World Health Organization.

Little, L., & Kantor, G. K. (2002). Using ecological theory to understand intimate partner violence and child maltreatment. *Journal of Community Health Nursing, 19*, 133–145.

Marx, B. P., Calhoun, K. S., Wilson, A., & Meyerson, L. A. (2001). Sexual revictimization prevention: An outcome evaluation. *Journal of Consulting and Clinical Psychology, 69*, 25–32. doi:10.1037/0022-006X.69.1.25

Men Can Stop Rape. (2008). *Campus strength: Engaging men on campus*. Retrieved from http://www.mencanstoprape.org/usr_doc/Campus_Strength.pdf

Morrison, S., Hardison, J., Mathew, A., & O'Neil, J. (2004). *An evidence-based review of sexual assault preventive intervention programs*. Washington, DC: National Institute of Justice.

Orchowski, L. M., Gidycz, C. A., & Raffle, H. (2008). Evaluation of a sexual assault risk reduction and self-defense program: A prospective analysis of a revised protocol. *Psychology of Women Quarterly, 32*, 204–218. doi:10.1111/j.1471-6402.2008.00425.x

Petty, R. E., & Cacioppo, J. T. (1986). *Communication and persuasion: Central and peripheral routes to attitude change*. New York, NY: Springer-Verlag.

Pacifici, C., Stoolmiller, M., & Nelson, C. (2001). Evaluating a prevention program for teenagers on sexual coercion: A differential effectiveness approach. *Journal of Consulting and Clinical Psychology, 69*, 552–559. doi:10.1037/0022-006X.69.3.552

Reppucci, N. D., Land, D., & Haugaard, J. J. (2001). Child sexual abuse prevention programs that target young children. In P. K. Trickett & C. Schellenbach (Eds.), *Violence against children in the family and the community* (pp. 317–337). Washington, DC: American Psychological Association.

Rheingold, A. A., Campbell, C., Self-Brown, S., de Arellano, M., Resnick, H., & Kilpatrick, D. (2007). Prevention of child sexual abuse: Evaluation of a community media campaign. *Child Maltreatment, 12,* 352–363. doi:10.1177/1077559507305994

Rich, C. L., Gidycz, C. A., Warkentin, J. B., Loh, C., & Weiland, P. (2005). Child and adolescent abuse and subsequent victimization: A prospective study. *Child Abuse and Neglect, 29,* 1373–1394. doi:10.1016/j.chiabu.2005.07.003

Rispens, J., Aleman, A., & Goldena, P. (1997). Prevention of child sexual abuse victimization: A meta-analysis of school programs. *Child Abuse & Neglect, 21,* 975–987. doi:10.1016/S0145-2134(97)00058-6

Rogers, E. M. (1995). *Diffusion of innovations* (4th ed.). New York, NY: The Free Press.

Rozee, P. D., & Koss, M. P. (2001). Rape: A century of resistance. *Psychology of Women Quarterly, 25,* 295–311. doi:10.1111/1471-6402.00030

Sidebotham, P. (2001). An ecological approach to child abuse: A creative use of scientific models in research and practice. *Child Abuse Review, 10,* 97–112. doi:10.1002/car.643

Taal, M., & Edelaar, B. (1997). Positive and negative effects of a child sexual abuse prevention program. *Child Abuse & Neglect, 21,* 399–410. doi:10.1016/S0145-2134(96)00179-2

Tjaden, P., & Thoennes, N. (2000). *Full report of the prevalence, incidence, and consequences of violence against women.* Retrieved from http://www.ncjrs.gov/txtfiles1/nij/183781.txt

Valle, L. A., Hunt, D., Costa, M., Shively, M., Townsend, M., Kuck, S., . . . Baer, K. (2007). *Sexual and intimate partner violence prevention programs evaluation guide.* Atlanta, GA: Centers for Disease Control and Prevention, National Center for Injury Prevention and Control.

Weisz, A. N., & Black, B. M. (2001). Evaluating a sexual assault and dating violence prevention program for urban youths. *Social Work Research, 25,* 89–102.

Yeater, E. A., & O'Donohue, W. (1999). Sexual assault prevention programs: Current issues, future directions, and the potential efficacy of interventions with women. *Clinical Psychology Review, 19,* 739–771. doi:10.1016/S0272-7358(98)00075-0

III

DOMESTIC VIOLENCE

9

VICTIM SERVICES FOR DOMESTIC VIOLENCE

CRIS M. SULLIVAN

It is somewhat difficult to believe today that services for victims of intimate partner violence were virtually nonexistent just 30 years ago. The serious problem of domestic violence was first recognized and named in the United States in large part because of the women's liberation movement but in conjunction with the civil rights movement and the antipoverty movement. Feminists, other community activists, and survivors of domestic violence were instrumental in opening the first emergency shelters created specifically for battered women (Schechter, 1982). These first shelters were often no more sophisticated than women opening their homes to other women, but as public awareness of this problem increased, shelters and other services proliferated throughout the country, so that today there are thousands of domestic violence programs across the United States.

From the beginning of the battered women's movement it was understood that "woman battering" involves a pattern of behavior, generally committed by men against women, that results in the perpetrator gaining an advantage of power and control in the relationship (Dobash, Dobash, Wilson, & Daly, 1992; Johnson, 1995; Stark, 2007). *Battering* includes physical violence and the continued threat of such violence, but it also includes psychological torment designed to instill fear and/or confusion in the victim. The pattern of abuse also often includes sexual and economic abuse, social isolation, and threats against loved ones (Bancroft, 2002; Pence & Paymar, 1993).

The first domestic violence–focused interventions were, by necessity, targeted toward ensuring victims' immediate safety from abuse. Women who were abused often had nowhere to turn, and few laws or policies were in place to protect them or help them stay in their homes safely. Lack of public awareness in general regarding the causes and consequences of this problem led to inadequate or even harmful responses to women's formal and informal help seeking (Gondolf, 1988; Sullivan, 1991). It was never assumed, however, that emergency shelter would be enough by itself to end this widespread social problem. Interventions continued to be created not only to address victims' immediate safety needs but also to address their emotional, economic, health-related, educational, spiritual, and longer term safety needs. There was also an understanding that domestic violence would continue until batterers were held accountable for their actions and prevented from repeating their offenses (National Research Council, 1996). Finally, many efforts were focused on educating the general public about this issue and creating systems change, with the recognition that society as a whole must oppose intimate partner violence if it is ultimately to be prevented.

As our understanding of the dynamics of intimate partner violence has increased, so too have the types of community-based programs for survivors. Empirical studies that have involved listening to survivors themselves have reported that, whether seeking help to end the violence while maintaining the relationship or seeking help to end the relationship as well as the violence, women turn to a variety of community systems to protect themselves and their children. Women turn to informal help sources such as family and friends, and also to formal sources such as the police, health care professionals, religious leaders, and the social service system (Abu-Ras, 2007; Allen, Bybee, & Sullivan, 2004; Bui, 2003; Gordon, 1996; Morrison, Luchok, Richter, & Parra-Medina, 2006; Wright & Johnson, 2009). Unfortunately, women have often been unsuccessful in obtaining help from the very agencies and institutions designed to provide it (Baker, Cook, & Norris, 2003; Donnelly, Cook, Van Ausdale, & Foley, 2005; Gordon, 1996; Postmus, Severson, Berry, & Yoo, 2009; Zweig, Schlichter, & Burt, 2002).

No single book chapter can adequately describe the spectrum of services currently being offered to assist victims of intimate partner violence. This chapter, then, focuses on providing an overview of the most commonly offered victim services found throughout the United States. Where such services have been systematically evaluated, empirical results are presented. The next section includes the two most common crisis-oriented services for domestic violence survivors: shelter and first response teams. Following that are longer term services, including transitional housing, counseling, support groups, advocacy, services for children, and visitation centers. The chapter concludes with a discussion of gaps in our existing knowledge and suggestions for next steps.

WHAT DO WE KNOW?

Crisis-Oriented Services: Shelters and First Response Teams

Domestic Violence Shelter Programs

Although the earliest shelter programs offered little more than beds and short-term support, today community-based shelter programs are likely to provide emergency shelter, 24-hr crisis lines, support groups, counseling services, advocacy, and programs for children. Unfortunately, the number of programs available is still much lower than the number of women in need. Because shelter programs are expensive to operate and maintain, they are primarily located in more populated urban areas rather than in rural, frontier, or Native American reservation communities. However, even in urban areas, the few shelters that exist continue to operate at or above capacity, and all have procedures in place to accommodate women when they are full (generally involving hotel vouchers or referrals to other emergency shelters).

Shelter programs have been found to be among the most supportive, effective resources for women with abusive partners, according to the residents themselves (Bennett, Riger, Schewe, Howard, & Wasco, 2004; Sullivan, O'Halloran, & Lyon, 2008; Tutty, Weaver, & Rothery, 1999). While no woman wants to uproot her children or leave her home for a communal living setting unless she has no other options, shelters remain an important resource for a significant number of women and their children. In addition to immediate safety, women report receiving helpful information, support, advocacy, and safety planning during their stay in shelter. Positive outcomes from staying in a domestic violence shelter include knowing more about one's rights and options, knowing more about community resources, having more safety strategies to call upon, and feeling more hopeful about the future (Sullivan et al., 2008).

First Response Teams

Another intervention that involves providing immediate safety and support at the time of the violent incident is the *first response team*, which generally consists of trained advocates and/or social workers accompanying police officers on domestic violence calls (or shortly after a domestic violence arrest is made). The goal of such teams is twofold: to send abusers the message that there are legal consequences for their violent behavior and to inform victims of community services and resources available to them. Limited evaluations of this intervention suggest it may be meeting its intended goal of providing supportive services and information to survivors of domestic violence. One of the most rigorous evaluations of this service utilized an experimental design and took place in a public housing complex in New York City (Davis & Taylor, 1997). This 6-month longitudinal study found that although those receiving follow-up contact did not report any less abuse over time, victims were more willing to call the police if violence occurred. Similarly, when Stover, Berkman, Desai, and Marans (2010) interviewed women 1 year after they received first response services, they found that women were more likely than those in the control condition to call the police for nonphysical domestic abuse and were more likely to use court-based services and to seek mental health services for their children.

Longer Term Victim Services

While first response teams and shelters focus on providing crisis intervention and immediate safety to victims, as well as informing them of their rights and options, a number of longer term domestic violence victim service programs are available across communities as well. This is in response to the reality that domestic violence is a pattern that too often spans years (Stark, 2007) and frequently continues even after the relationship ends (Fleury, Sullivan, & Bybee, 2000).

Transitional Housing Programs

Batterers often use finances as a means of controlling women during and after the relationship. Some batterers deny their victims access to money or prevent them from working outside the home (Adams, Sullivan, Bybee, & Greeson, 2008). Others harass their victims at work until they are fired (Fawole, 2008), or they damage their homes, causing women to be evicted (Baker, Cook, & Norris, 2003).

One result of these tactics is that some battered women either have no credit or their credit is so badly impaired that it represents too large a risk to landlords. The long-term results for many battered women include being unable to secure and maintain permanent, affordable housing, independent of their abusers. Transitional housing programs for survivors of domestic violence were designed to offer an important alternative to living with an abusive partner, and they are a vital resource for many low-income battered women striving to become free from abuse (Davis & Srinivasan, 1995; Melbin, Sullivan, & Cain, 2003). Although still few in number, transitional housing programs for battered women exist in every state in the nation. All offer women housing in which they can live for a set period of time (usually 1 to 2 years) or until they can obtain permanent housing. Women often pay a small percentage of their income for rent, and most transitional housing programs also include support services such as counseling, housing assistance, and employment assistance (National Council of Juvenile and Family Court Judges, 1998).

Melbin and colleagues (2003) interviewed women who had participated in any of six different transitional housing programs in a Midwestern state. Many women noted that had the transitional housing program not been available, they would have either returned to their assailants, been homeless, resorted to prostitution, or been incarcerated. Given the scarcity of low-income housing across the nation and the continued danger many women face from their assailants even after they end the relationship, transitional housing programs hold great promise for enhancing economic stability for women with abusive ex-partners. The lack of longitudinal studies examining the impact of such services on women's lives, however, limits our understanding of the extent to which transitional housing impacts women's economic stability, psychological well-being, or safety over time.

Counseling Services

The vast majority of domestic violence victim service programs offer counseling (individually or within groups) as one of their core services. Typically, programs engage in *empowerment counseling,* a process through which one party helps the other gain or regain her sense of personal power (Gutiérrez & Lewis, 1999; Parsons, 2001). Experiencing domestic abuse frequently results in a loss of trust as well as a loss of one's sense of control. Empowerment counseling involves helping women recover their personal sense of power and control. It can also be useful to women to learn about the typical dynamics endemic in domestic abuse, which can help women feel less isolated by their experience.

Not all domestic violence counseling services are empowerment based, of course, and many also incorporate a variety of therapeutic approaches (e.g., cognitive behavioral, solution- focused, art therapy) tailored to the individual needs and desires of clients. To date, there have been few evaluations of domestic violence counseling services, and those that exist tend to involve examining client change over time without benefit of comparison or control groups. However, these limited evaluations are at least promising in that they have found improved well-being and coping (Howard et al., 2003; McNamara, Tamanini, & Pelletier-Walker, 2008) as well as increased self-esteem and self-efficacy (Mancoske, Standifer, & Cauley, 1994). One study involving abused women with posttraumatic stress disorder (PTSD) reported decreases in PTSD, depression, and anxiety 3 months after the women received counseling services (Foa, Zoellner, & Feeny, 2006). Taken together, these studies suggest that short-term, trauma-focused counseling may be helpful in alleviating some of the mental health sequelae that typically result from domestic violence.

Support Groups

Support groups were initially created by shelter programs to provide women with a supportive atmosphere in which to discuss their experiences and to share information about resources with other survivors, but such groups have expanded in breadth and scope over time. Now many groups are available that either target specific populations of abused women (e.g., African American women) or that focus on particular circumstances (e.g., groups for women still in the relationship or for women who are no longer being abused but who still seek support in dealing with the aftereffects). Evaluations of such groups have been quite limited, but there is some evidence that they are helpful to women. For example, Tutty, Bidgood, and Rothery (1993) evaluated 12 closed (i.e., not open to new members once begun) support groups for survivors. A common type of group offered to survivors, the closed support group lasts from 10 to 12 weeks and typically focuses on safety planning, offering mutual support and understanding, and discussion of dynamics of abuse. Tutty et al.'s (1993) evaluation involved surveying 76 women before, immediately after, and 6 months following the group. Significant improvements were found in women's self-esteem, sense of belonging, locus of control, and overall stress over time; however, fewer than half of the original 76 women completed the 6-month follow-up assessment ($n = 32$), and there was no control or comparison group for this study.

Tutty et al.'s (1993) findings were corroborated by a more recent study that used an experimental design (Constantino, Kim, & Crane, 2005). In that study, an 8-week group was led by a trained nurse and focused on helping women increase their social support networks and access to community resources. At the end of the 8 weeks, the women who had participated in the group showed greater improvement in psychological distress symptoms and reported higher feelings of social support. They also showed less health care utilization than did the women who did not receive the intervention.

Advocacy Services

To redress the often inadequate or ineffective community responses that women with abusive partners often experience, many community-based programs engage in various forms of advocacy on women's behalf (Peled & Edleson, 1994). Systems-level advocacy efforts are generally targeted at changing public policy or improving institutionalized practices within the criminal justice system, the health care system, the welfare system, and other such institutions. Individual-level advocacy efforts generally involve paraprofessionals, working collaboratively and respectfully with individual survivors, who guide the focus of the intervention to meet their specific needs and desires. Activities identified by programs as being individual-level advocacy have ranged from helping a woman locate housing to accompanying women through the court process. Although individual-level advocacy services are a core component of most domestic violence victim service programs, the belief in their effectiveness was originally predicated largely on anecdotal evidence. In response to the dearth of empirical evidence of the effectiveness of advocacy for women with abusive partners, the author designed and experimentally evaluated a community-based advocacy intervention for women after they exited a domestic violence shelter program (Allen, Bybee, & Sullivan, 2004; Bybee & Sullivan, 2002; Sullivan, 2000; Sullivan & Bybee, 1999). The Community Advocacy Project involved providing advocates to work one-on-one with women who had recently exited a domestic violence shelter, working in their communities with them 6 to 8 hr a week over 10 weeks. Advocates were trained in helping women obtain a variety of community resources, including housing, employment, legal assistance, transportation, education, child care, health care, material goods and services, financial assistance, services for the children (e.g., tutoring, counseling), and social support (e.g., making new friends, joining clubs or groups).

A true experimental design was used to evaluate the impact of the Community Advocacy Project, through which women were randomly assigned to either the intervention group or the control group (services-as-usual). All 278 women, regardless of group assignment, were interviewed preintervention, 10 weeks later (postintervention for those in the experimental group), and again every 6 months over 2 years. Ninety-four percent or more of the women were located and interviewed at each time point.

Women who worked with advocates experienced less violence over time, reported higher quality of life and social support, and had less difficulty obtaining community resources over time. One out of four (24%) of the women who worked with advocates experienced no physical abuse, by the original assailant or by any new partners, across the 24 months of postintervention follow-up. Only one out of 10 (11%) women in the control group remained completely free of violence during the same period. This low-cost, short-term intervention using unpaid advocates appears to have been effective not only in reducing women's risk of reabuse but also in improving their overall quality of life. It is important to remember, however, that although the provision of advocates reduced the risk of further violence by a partner or ex-partner, many women (76% who worked with advocates; 89% who did not) were abused at least once over the 2-year time span. No single intervention will be a panacea for this complex social problem, and many abusive men continue their violence in spite of the strategies women use to protect themselves. In contrast to the broad-based advocacy services described above, many domestic violence advocacy programs focus on working within one particular system (e.g., welfare, housing, criminal legal). Welfare and housing advocacy services are rarer and have yet to be evaluated.

Legal Advocacy Services

The most common type of advocacy offered throughout the country is *legal advocacy*, which can help survivors navigate through civil legal procedures (e.g., divorce, visitation, custody) or criminal cases (e.g., misdemeanor domestic violence). Legal advocacy encompasses a variety of supportive services related to either civil or criminal matters. Whether offered over the telephone or in person, trained advocates provide survivors with both information and support while also advocating on women's behalf with prosecutors, police, probation officers, and other court-related personnel. A common role for legal advocates is to help women obtain protection orders, and many will also accompany women through all phases of the court process as needed.

The only evaluation of a legal advocacy program to date is Bell and Goodman's (2001) quasi-experimental study conducted in Washington, DC. Their research found that women who had worked with advocates reported decreased abuse 6 weeks later, as well as marginally higher emotional well-being compared with women who did not work with advocates. Their qualitative findings also supported the use of paraprofessional legal advocates. All of the women who had worked with advocates talked about them as being very supportive and knowledgeable, and the women who did not work with advocates mentioned wishing they had had that kind of support while they were going through this difficult process.

Children's Services

Today, most domestic violence victim service programs include separate services for the children in the family, as they have also been adversely affected by the abuse perpetrated against their mothers. These services most commonly include counseling, safety planning, and support and education groups, but they may also include advocacy on the child's behalf. The only published evaluations of children's services to date are those focused on support and education groups. Such groups typically run 10 to 12 weeks, and the curriculum is age-appropriate. Sessions include serious topics as well as fun activities and snacks, and children learn about labeling feelings, dealing with anger, and honing their safety skills. One evaluation of such a program revealed that children learned strategies for protection in times of emergencies and regarded their parents in a more positive light. Mothers also reported a positive change in their children's behavioral adjustment (Jaffe, Wilson, & Wolfe, 1988). Gruszinski, Brink, and Edleson (1988) conducted a similar study based on 371 children who attended a program over a 4-year period. They found that children improved their self-concepts, understood that violence in the home was not their fault, became more aware of protection planning, and learned new ways of resolving conflict without resorting to violence. While neither of these early studies included comparison groups, a later randomized control trial also found that children who attended support and education groups reported more appropriate anger responses as well as diminished sense of responsibility for the abuse over time (Wagar & Rodway, 1995).

Visitation and Exchange Centers

Unfortunately, for many women the abuse does not end when the relationship ends. One way that some batterers continue their abusive and controlling tactics is through access to the children they have in common with the survivor (Beeble, Bybee, & Sullivan, 2007). Perpetrators are often legally entitled to visit with their children, and they can then use those visits as opportunities to harass and abuse their ex-partners. In response to this ongoing safety risk, a number of domestic violence programs have opened visitation and exchange centers through which they can minimize contact between the parents and offer protection to the women and children (Park, Peterson-Badali, & Jenkins, 1997). Such centers often have separate entrances for the custodial and noncustodial parents, and typically they have security cameras not only within the building but covering the surrounding parking lot as well. This center can be used by parents needing to exchange children for unsupervised visits; it can also be used to facilitate court-ordered supervised visits. When a noncustodial parent has supervised visits with the children, a trained staff member monitors the interactions and ideally can prevent the abuser from behaving inappropriately with the children (either by behaving abusively toward them, saying negative things about the other parent, or asking the children for personal information about their mothers). Although such visitation centers appear promising, the issues around custody and visitation are complex (including the reality that some abused women become noncustodial parents and are ordered into supervised visitation), and they are in need of systematic evaluation.

HOW DO WE KNOW IT?

Much of what we believe we know about the effectiveness of domestic violence victim services is based on anecdotal reports, conventional wisdom, and lived practice. While valuable information can be drawn from personal practice and experience, systematic and rigorous evaluation is also needed to better understand whether programs are effective, in what ways they are effective, and for whom they are effective.

In 1998, the National Research Council identified evaluation of domestic violence interventions as "one of the most critical needs of this field" (p. 59). Unfortunately, a great deal of the existing research and evaluation has suffered from a variety of methodological problems, including but not limited to small sample sizes and samples with limited generalizability (e.g., shelter samples, predominantly White samples, exclusively impoverished samples), nonexperimental designs, cross-sectional designs that preclude identifying causal relationships, and measures lacking established validity and reliability. More funds, as well as larger designations of funds per study, are needed in order for more rigorous research to be conducted on the effectiveness of current interventions and programs. Conducting research that involves safely locating and interviewing battered women and includes longitudinal designs is time, resource, and personnel intensive. Only by funding additional large-scale, rigorous evaluations will our knowledge base considerably increase.

WHAT ARE THE NEXT STEPS?

The past 35 years have borne witness to an explosion of interventions designed to address and eliminate intimate partner violence. Although domestic violence victim service programs strive to be effective resources to all survivors, the reality is that not all services are equally accessible, available, or relevant across different populations of women. Programs that are not culturally diverse and culturally competent can lack relevance for large groups of women and may even do more harm than good (Bent-Goodley, 2005; Gillum, 2009; Yoshioka & Choi, 2005). For example, many domestic violence programs promote women's autonomy and independence as the underlying framework guiding their service delivery. While this focus may resonate for many middle-class Anglo women (who, not coincidentally, are still most likely to be in leadership positions within domestic violence organizations), it may not speak to the core beliefs of women from more collectivist cultures, who value interdependence and collective well-being over self-reliance and individual gain. Many women, therefore, refuse or abandon services if they feel pressured to make decisions that go against these values or that result in their losing access to family or community.

Women with mental health problems, cognitive disabilities, substance abuse disorders, and/or criminal histories are sometimes denied various domestic violence services (Zweig et al., 2002), and other women experience significant practical barriers to receiving help (e.g., women who do not speak

English as a first language, women with physical disabilities; Baladerian, 2009). For most if not all survivors of domestic violence, the abuse is not the only (or even the most) pressing concern in their lives. Many service programs are now recognizing this complexity and working harder to take a more holistic response to women's needs. National efforts are also under way to help domestic violence victim service programs with this charge. For example, the National Training and Technical Assistance Center on Domestic Violence, Trauma and Mental Health (NTTAC), funded by the U.S. Department of Health and Human Services Administration on Children, Youth and Families, is focused on providing the technical assistance and tools needed to respond effectively to battered women's trauma-related or mental health concerns. The National Network to End Violence Against Immigrant Women is committed to building organizational capacity to handle complex immigration issues and to understand the cultural needs of various immigrant communities. A number of state domestic violence coalitions have prioritized helping local programs respond more appropriately to women with a wide range of disabilities. These are just a sampling of state and national efforts designed to make domestic violence services relevant and accessible to all women.

Although gains continue to be made, a great deal more work must be done. For example, domestic violence shelters were originally viewed as a temporary measure, needed until laws and policies changed so that women could stay in their homes free of violence and abuse. The laws have vastly improved in the past 35 years, but the reality remains that it is often the victim who is forced to flee her home. The bureaucratization of domestic violence programs over time has also recently come under increased scrutiny and debate (Lehrner & Allen, 2009; Macy, Giattina, Parish, & Crosby, 2010). Not all programs now work from a sociopolitical perspective or see themselves as part of a social change movement.

There is some empirical evidence to suggest that at least some of the programs and interventions being offered to survivors of intimate partner violence are resulting in positive change. Unfortunately, there is still much more that we do not know about what works, how it works, and for whom it works. Since the Violence Against Women Act (P.L. 103-322) was enacted in 1994, a considerable influx of dollars has entered communities. It is essential that programs and policies be guided by sound empirical evidence in order for those funds to be best utilized. However, given the complexity of this issue, research and evaluation should be conducted in collaboration with practitioners, survivors, and advocates who are most knowledgeable about it.

It is also important to focus research and evaluation in communities of color, conducted by knowledgeable researchers from within these communities. Many of the published studies to date lack adequate representation of people of color, sometimes but not always reflecting the services currently being provided. Much more work is required to ensure that culturally competent and culturally relevant research guides our programmatic efforts. Similarly, more work is needed to understand the effectiveness of interventions for lesbians and gay men, for immigrants and refugees, for those with disabilities or multiple needs, and for other traditionally marginalized groups (Lightfoot & Williams, 2009).

As knowledge about the complex issue of domestic violence has grown, as funding has increased, and as more community members are accepting responsibility for ending intimate male violence against women and children, community-based services have developed that reflect this growth. Today, most communities have at least some programs available for survivors and their children. Efforts have improved to ensure that services are culturally appropriate and respectful of the complex obstacles facing women with abusive partners. However, no community can be said to be doing enough. Too many survivors are still receiving insufficient help, and too many communities are providing uncoordinated or inadequate assistance.

Services for victims of domestic violence have clearly come a long way, but the journey is far from over. These services will continue to develop and expand to meet the changing needs of women and children. At the same time, advocates nationwide eagerly anticipate the day when such support services for women and their children are no longer necessary.

REFERENCES

Abu-Ras, W. (2007). Cultural beliefs and service utilization by battered Arab immigrant women. *Violence Against Women, 13*, 1002–1028.

Adams, A. E., Sullivan, C. M., Bybee, D., & Greeson, M. (2008). Development of the Scale of Economic Abuse. *Violence Against Women, 14*, 563–588.

Allen, N. E., Bybee, D. I., & Sullivan, C. M. (2004). Battered women's multitude of needs: Evidence supporting the need for comprehensive advocacy. *Violence Against Women, 10*, 1015–1035.

Baker, C. K., Cook, S. L., & Norris, F. H. (2003). Domestic violence and housing problems: A contextual analysis of women's help-seeking, received informal support, and formal system response. *Violence Against Women, 9*, 754–783.

Baladerian, N. J. (2009). Domestic violence and individuals with disabilities: Reflections on research and practice. *Journal of Aggression, Maltreatment & Trauma, 18*, 153–161.

Bancroft, L. (2002). *Why do they do that? Inside the minds of angry and controlling men.* New York, NY: Putnam.

Beeble, M., Bybee, D., & Sullivan, C. M. (2007). Abusive men's use of children to control their partners and ex-partners. *European Psychologist, 12*(1), 54–61.

Bell, M. E., & Goodman, L. A. (2001). Supporting battered women involved with the court system: An evaluation of a law school–based advocacy intervention. *Violence Against Women, 7,* 1377–1404.

Bennett, L., Riger, S., Schewe, P., Howard, A., & Wasco, S. (2004). Effectiveness of hotline, advocacy, counseling and shelter services for victims of domestic violence: A statewide evaluation. *Journal of Interpersonal Violence, 19,* 815–829.

Bent-Goodley, T. B. (2005). Culture and domestic violence: Transforming knowledge development. *Journal of Interpersonal Violence, 20,* 195–203.

Bui, H. N. (2003). Help-seeking behavior among abused immigrant women. *Violence Against Women, 9,* 207–239.

Bybee, D. I., & Sullivan, C. M. (2002). The process through which a strengths-based intervention resulted in positive change for battered women over time. *American Journal of Community Psychology, 30,* 103–132.

Constantino, R., Kim, Y., & Crane, P. A. (2005). Effects of a social support intervention on health outcomes in residents of a domestic violence shelter: A pilot study. *Issues in Mental Health Nursing, 26,* 575–590.

Davis, L. V., & Srinivasan, M. (1995). Listening to the voices of battered women: What helps them escape violence. *Affilia: Journal of Women & Social Work, 10,* 49–69.

Davis, R. C., & Taylor, B. G. (1997). A proactive response to family violence: The results of randomized experiment. *Criminology, 35,* 307–333.

Dobash, R. P., Dobash, R. E., Wilson, M., & Daly, M. (1992). The myth of sexual symmetry in marital violence. *Social Problems, 39*(1), 71–91.

Donnelly, D. A., Cook, K. J., Van Ausdale, D., & Foley, L. (2005). White privilege, color blindness, and services to battered women. *Violence Against Women, 11,* 6–37.

Fawole, O. I. (2008). Economic violence to women and girls: Is it receiving the necessary attention? *Trauma, Violence & Abuse, 9,* 167–177.

Fleury, R. E., Sullivan, C. M., & Bybee, D. I. (2000). When ending the relationship doesn't end the violence: Women's experiences of violence by former partners. *Violence Against Women, 6,* 1363–1383.

Foa, E. B., Zoellner, L. A., & Feeny, N. C. (2006). An evaluation of three brief programs for facilitating recovery after assault. *Journal of Traumatic Stress, 19,* 29–43.

Gillum, T. L. (2009). Improving services to African American survivors of IPV: From the voices of recipients of culturally specific services. *Violence Against Women, 15,* 57–80.

Gondolf, E. W. (1988). *Battered women as survivors: An alternative to learned helplessness.* Lexington, MA: Lexington Books.

Gordon, J. S. (1996). Community services for abused women: A review of perceived usefulness and efficacy. *Journal of Family Violence, 11,* 315–329.

Gruszinski, R. J., Brink, J. C., & Edleson, J. L. (1988). Support and education groups for children of battered women. *Child Welfare, 67,* 431–444.

Gutiérrez, L. M., & Lewis, E. A. (1999). *Empowering women of color.* New York, NY: Columbia University Press.

Howard, A., Riger, S., Campbell, R., & Wasco, S. (2003). Counseling services for battered women: A comparison of outcomes for physical and sexual assault survivors. *Journal of Interpersonal Violence, 18,* 717–734.

Jaffe, P., Wilson, S. K., & Wolfe, D. (1988). Specific assessment and intervention strategies for children exposed to wife battering: Preliminary investigation. *Canadian Journal of Community Mental Health, 7,* 157–163.

Johnson, M. P. (1995). Patriarchal terrorism and common couple violence: Two forms of violence against women. *Journal of Marriage and the Family, 57,* 283–294.

Lehrner, A., & Allen, N. E. (2009). Still a movement after all these years? Current tensions in the domestic violence movement. *Violence Against Women, 15,* 656–677.

Lightfoot, E., & Williams, O. (2009). Critical issues in researching domestic violence among people of color with disabilities. *Journal of Aggression, Maltreatment & Trauma, 18,* 200–219.

Macy, R. J., Giattina, M. C., Parish, S. L., & Crosby, C. (2010). Domestic violence and sexual assault services: Historical concerns and contemporary challenges. *Journal of Interpersonal Violence, 25,* 3–32.

Mancoske, R. J., Standifer, D., & Cauley, C. (1994). The effectiveness of brief counseling services for battered women. *Research on Social Work Practice, 4,* 53–63.

McNamara, J. R., Tamanini, K., & Pelletier-Walker, S. (2008). The impact of short-term counseling at a domestic violence shelter. *Research on Social Work Practice, 18,* 132–136.

Melbin, A., Sullivan, C. M., & Cain, D. (2003). Transitional supportive housing programs: Battered women's perspectives and recommendations. *Affilia: Journal of Women and Social Work, 18,* 445–460.

Morrison, K. E., Luchok, K. J., Richter, D. L., & Parra-Medina, D. (2006). Factors influencing help-seeking from informal networks among African American victims of intimate partner violence. *Journal of Interpersonal Violence, 21,* 1493–1511.

National Council of Juvenile and Family Court Judges. (1998). *Family Violence: Emerging programs for battered mothers and their children.* Reno, NV: National Council of Juvenile and Family Court Judges.

National Research Council. (1996). *Understanding violence against women.* Washington, DC: National Academy Press.

National Research Council. (1998). *Violence in families: Assessing prevention and treatment programs.* Washington, DC: National Academy Press.

Park, N. W., Peterson-Badali, M., & Jenkins, J. M. (1997). An evaluation of supervised access I: Organizational issues. *Family and Conciliation Courts Review, 35*(1), 37–50.

Parsons, R. J. (2001). Specific practice strategies for empowerment-based practice with women: A study of two groups. *Affilia: Journal of Women & Social Work, 16,* 159–179.

Peled, E., & Edleson, J. L. (1994). Advocacy for battered women: A national survey. *Journal of Family Violence, 9,* 285–296.

Pence, E., & Paymar, M. (1993). *Education groups for men who batter: The Duluth model*. New York, NY: Springer.

Postmus, J. L., Severson, M., Berry, M., & Yoo, J. A. (2009). Women's experiences of violence and seeking help. *Violence Against Women, 15*, 852–868.

Schechter, S. (1982). *Women and male violence*. Boston, MA: South End Press.

Stark, E. (2007). *Coercive control: How men entrap women in personal life*. New York, NY: Oxford University Press.

Stover, C. S., Berkman, M., Desai, R., & Marans, S. (2010). The efficacy of a police-advocacy intervention for victims of domestic violence: 12-month follow-up data. *Violence Against Women, 16*, 410–425.

Sullivan, C. M. (1991). Battered women as active helpseekers. *Violence Update, 1*, 1; 8; 10–11.

Sullivan, C. M. (2000). A model for effectively advocating for women with abusive partners. In J. P. Vincent & E. N. Jouriles (Eds.), *Domestic violence: Guidelines for research-informed practice* (pp. 126–143). London, England: Jessica Kingsley.

Sullivan, C. M., & Bybee, D. I. (1999). Reducing violence using community-based advocacy for women with abusive partners. *Journal of Consulting and Clinical Psychology, 67*, 43–53.

Sullivan, C. M., O'Halloran, S., & Lyon, E. (2008, September). *What women wanted and what they received from shelter: Findings from the United States and Ireland*. Keynote address presented at the First World Congress of Women's Shelters, Edmonton, Alberta, Canada.

Tutty, L. M., Bidgood, B. A., & Rothery, M. A. (1993). Support groups for battered women: Research on their efficacy. *Journal of Family Violence, 8*, 325–343.

Tutty, L. M., Weaver, G., & Rothery, M. (1999). Residents' views of the efficacy of shelter services for assaulted women. *Violence Against Women, 5*, 898–925.

Wagar, J. M., & Rodway, M. R. (1995). An evaluation of a group treatment approach for children who have witnessed wife abuse. *Journal of Family Violence, 10*, 295–306.

Wright, C. V., & Johnson, D. M. (2009). Correlates for legal help-seeking: Contextual factors for battered women in shelter. *Violence and Victims, 24*, 771–785.

Yoshioka, M. R., & Choi, D. Y. (2005). Culture and interpersonal violence research: Paradigm shift to create a full continuum of domestic violence services. *Journal of Interpersonal Violence, 20*, 513–519.

Zweig, J. M., Schlichter, K. A., & Burt, M. R. (2002). Assisting women victims of violence who experience multiple barriers to service. *Violence Against Women, 8*, 162–180.

10

TREATMENT FOR PERPETRATORS OF DOMESTIC VIOLENCE

TRICIA B. BENT-GOODLEY, JOHNNY RICE II,
OLIVER J. WILLIAMS, AND MARCUS POPE

Addressing the needs of domestic violence perpetrators is complex. Many would like to place the perpetrator in jail and forget about him. Yet survivors of domestic violence often maintain a connection with the perpetrator for many reasons: Perhaps they have children together, she may not want the relationship to end as much as she wants the abuse to stop, they may live in the same community and see each other often, or they may find themselves at community and family gatherings that place them in proximity to each other (Tubbs & Williams, 2007). In addition, even if the man is no longer involved with the woman against whom he has perpetrated violence, he will likely move on to another relationship and potentially place other women at risk. Consequently, failing to provide early, effective treatment services for perpetrators of abuse imposes a high toll on individual women, children, and society. The ways in which we consider and engage perpetrators of abuse are critically important and a vital element of responding to and reducing violence against women and girls. This chapter provides a critical examination of what we know about batterers' intervention programs (BIPs) and emerging issues and challenges, and offers recommendations to advance the work.

WHAT DO WE KNOW?

BIPs are designed to address the abusive thoughts and behaviors of perpetrators of abuse (Gondolf, 2002). When BIPs began in the late 1970s, they were more closely affiliated with battered women's programs and were focused on using feminist analyses of patriarchal power in relationships as a foundation to ground efforts to end men's violence against women. At that time, men often sought services and attended voluntarily via informal systems. Today, of those who receive BIP services, more than 80% have been mandated to attend by the criminal justice system (Bent-Goodley & Williams, 2008; Healey, Smith & O'Sullivan, 1998; Jackson et al., 2003).

What Treatment for Whom?

BIP efforts are now focused primarily on providing education or treatment through a group setting for perpetrators. They can also include other treatment modalities, such as case management and individual counseling services. These programs typically focus on challenging rigid sex-role perceptions, developing the necessary skills to be nonviolent and nonabusive in a relationship, and exploring the social and emotional backdrop of violent actions to control the behaviors of the victim. These programs emphasize the importance of holding the perpetrator accountable for his behavior and maintaining the safety of the victim, particularly if the relationship is still ongoing (Healey, Smith, & O'Sullivan, 1998). Typologies of perpetrators have been developed to inform treatment decisions, to provide a way of recognizing different types and levels of perpetration, and to better understand the behaviors of individuals who perpetrate violence (Bender & Roberts, 2007; Chiffriller & Hennessy, 2007; Holtzworth-Munroe & Stuart, 1994; Lohr et al., 2005; Saunders, 1992). These typologies are important to pursue and refine; however, they have limits in their ability to account for the variability among perpetrators of abuse. Typologies can be used as a guide but are not a singular way of identifying a perpetrator of violence because a person can still be a batterer and not fit a standard profile. Typologies have also not yet delivered on their promise to function as grounds on which to match intervention approaches to batterer characteristics to maximize effectiveness. Currently, BIPs must find ways to address the needs of these different types of perpetrators within a treatment context that integrates them.

To best work with men who batter, one has to believe that the person has the capacity to change (Bent-Goodley, 2005a). Although violence has multiple causes, to a substantial extent battering is a learned behavior, and batterers lack incentive to change if society does little to truly sanction the abuse of women. Although there are laws in place that clearly articulate that violence against women is wrong, images in movies, music, and television and socially reinforced, rigid sex-role perceptions continue to fuel this learned behavior. If the behavior is learned, then the perpetrator has the capability to unlearn those behaviors and change his perceptions of the use of violence to control his partner (Aymer, 2008; Bennett & Williams, 2001). When perpetrators receive the message that the practitioner does not believe they can change, their willingness to fully engage in the treatment program may be diminished. At the same time, the perpetrator must be committed to change and must acknowledge that his behavior is wrong, unjustified, and unacceptable. There must be a genuine commitment to change that is rooted in challenging his thoughts about women and what it means to be in a healthy relationship, and the commitment must be practiced on a daily basis. One cannot diminish or discount the fact that perpetrators make a choice to use violence and abuse, nor can one downplay the importance of the perpetrator's choice to desist from violence.

Service Delivery System Response

The service system response to domestic violence is fragmented and does not necessarily serve any one group optimally. The current system offers needed emergency shelters, victims' and children's support and services, legal services, and transitional housing for women and children. There are several challenges in developing services for men who have perpetrated abuse. Some men have the perception that men who receive counseling are weak, and as a consequence they do not seek services (Campbell, Neil, Jaffe, & Kelly, 2010). Social service systems are often not designed to engage and retain men in services, either because the provider does not know how to best engage men in services or does not fully understand the unique challenges that men face and how they translate into service needs (Aymer, 2008; Powell, 2008). Moreover, the number of male service providers is small. As a result, for a man who would prefer to work with a male provider, that option is very limited. All of these factors carry weight in the context of a larger system already challenged with how to best engage and retain men in counseling services. (Aymer, 2008; Bent-Goodley & Williams, 2008; Williams, 1999). These provider systems for men—both BIPs and other programs—could be more proactive in providing services to men and boys before domestic abuse occurs. Although primary prevention programs exist, few are available and focused on teaching boys and men about healthy relationship skills, parenting, and strategies to promote violence-free homes. Likewise, secondary prevention services may not be available to men interested in receiving help to address their issues. Consequently, the context of service provision for men is important to consider both within and outside of BIPs.

Culture and BIPs

Many scholars in the field of domestic violence have called for more attention to culture in serving men of color who are perpetrators of domestic violence (Bell & Mattis, 2000; Bent-Goodley, 2005b; Carrillo & Tello, 2008; Gondolf & Williams, 2001; Hancock & Siu, 2009; Williams, Oliver, & Pope, 2008). The necessary blended perspective emphasizes the importance and benefits of the core elements of BIPs, such as holding the perpetrator accountable for his behavior, but including more attention to themes of concern for men of color (Williams, 2008). These themes are often related to racism, poverty, cultural nuances, and living in hostile environments. Facilitators of traditional batterers' groups are often uncomfortable and threatened by such discussions and may see them as unrelated to men's violence toward their partner (Williams, 1999). Yet they are critical to understanding how men of color receive and experience BIPs.

Issues that are especially overlooked include those related to biases within the criminal justice system and racism experienced by men of color (Bent-Goodley, 2005b; Carrillo & Tello, 2008). When group members raise these topics, the facilitator is trained to redirect their attention to their violence toward their partners and how their actions led to their current situation. This practice is consistent with the feminist perspective on which BIPs, which typically use a feminist analysis to explain battering, have been built. These programs emphasize the influence of patriarchy, sexism, and male privilege on men's behavior toward women (Aymer, 2008; Healey, Smith, & O'Sullivan, 1998). Group facilitators consistently confront men about the power and control tactics they use to dominate their partners. Given the manipulative tendencies of batterers and the risk of collusion between male group facilitators and batterers, unresolved and emergent issues indirectly related to their violence can be overlooked as facilitators stay on message. The lack of attention and the redirection around themes of racial oppression can be viewed as an inability or unwillingness to acknowledge the unique experiences of men of color. The decision to not incorporate the cultural experiences of men is problematic, given that racial oppression is a central component of the lived experiences of many men of color (Bent-Goodley, 2001; Bent-Goodley & Williams, 2008; Powell, 2008). Racism and oppression often lead to feelings of anger and powerlessness. Consequently, men of color may displace their anger and frustration about racism toward their partners through violence (Williams, 1999). The field is left with two challenging questions: (a) How do you acknowledge the lived experiences of men of color? (b) How can we simultaneously address the cultural context and confront men regarding the violence they have perpetrated?

A practitioner employing a blended perspective, confronting men regarding their history of violence and abusive tactics, understands how issues of power and control are centralized in a sexist society but also knows when to acknowledge themes related to racial oppression. Therefore, the practitioner confronts the man regarding male dominance and sexism but also engages him regarding authentic issues that emerge around oppression. For example, if a client introduces an experience or scenario in which he felt discriminated against by the criminal justice system, the facilitator using a blended perspective may allow this discussion and use the scenario to underscore issues of oppression. The facilitator could then help the client understand the destructive nature of his behavior by drawing connections between the racial oppression he experienced and the gender oppression he has inflicted on his partner. Furthermore, engaging issues of racism can give clients more effective tools and problem-solving skills for responding to racism, so anger and bitterness are not displaced on his partner.

To successfully blend traditional batterer intervention methods with culturally responsive methods, group facilitators need to be well trained and knowledgeable about the different populations they serve in a group setting. A sign of a skillful and culturally congruent practitioner is the ability to discern when it is appropriate to engage a group member around a particular theme from when it is not. "A culturally competent worker and group member would know when to acknowledge the racism, when to confront what is not racism, and when to confront violent and abusive behavior" within that context (Williams, 1999, p. 233). Additionally, practitioners who use a blended perspective must continuously engage in self-examination and reflection, given the level of engagement and interaction with the client that a blended perspective demands.

Culturally congruent counseling allows for practitioners to provide services that are specific to the population, show an awareness of key issues that warrant attention, and activate methods to fully engage the participants—by getting them to actively participate and invest in the intervention process. The cultural context is not abstract; it is centered on using forms of cultural expression and strengths while recognizing the barriers to developing programs, services, and responses that take all aspects of cultural diversity into account. There is diversity both within and outside of different cultural groups. Current consensus on best practices in BIPs is that culture matters in improving the effectiveness of BIPs. Yet there continues to be an overwhelmingly one-size-fits-all approach to BIP services.

Intersections With Fatherhood

We cannot take an approach that promotes fatherhood at all costs; however, it is possible that some men may feel compelled to stop abusive behaviors because of the impact on their children. BIP services have seldom examined the role of fatherhood among perpetrators of abuse (Arean & Davis, 2007). Yet it is important to remember that many men who batter remain in the lives of their children even after the couple's relationship ends (Salisbury, Henning, & Holdford, 2009). Consequently, understanding the major elements—fathers, domestic violence, and parenting—after separation is critical in treating male batterers. Battered women may fear having to maintain a parental relationship with the abusive partner for fear of continued violence (Tubbs & Williams, 2007). Some abusive men use the parental arrangement to continue to manipulate, intimidate, and harass their former partners (Peled, 2000; Williams, Boggess, & Carter, 2001). Others use the children to monitor the woman's daily actions and behavior, seeing them as an opportunity to continue the psychological and emotional bondage of the abuse. Many battered women who understand the difficulty of escaping the abuse still see continuance of the relationship with the father as being in the child's best interest (Tubbs & Williams, 2007). As a result, they attempt to navigate the risks and allow the relationship with the children, despite their own fear and insecurity regarding safety. Children are often confused, fearful, anxious, in pain, and resentful toward the abusive father, yet they also long to maintain a relationship with him (Peled, 2000). Abusive fathers may view having a relationship with the child as a right, but they tend to use the same techniques as parents that they use when interacting with their partners. Many batterers are rigid and controlling parents, neglectful of the children, and limited in their involvement unless they are receiving outside recognition or some incentive (Bancroft & Silverman, 2002). Thus, connections with fatherhood and parenting with BIP are increasingly being recognized as critical to providing contemporary BIP services.

Child Custody Issues

Practitioners and advocates of treatment for domestic violence support termination of the man's custodial arrangement if he is terrorizing, manipulating, or harassing the survivor through the children. Most judges attempt to determine the best interest of the child in deciding visitation and custody cases. Levin and Mills (2003) examined child custody laws in each state and the District of Columbia. Ten states deny custody to parents who were abusive toward a partner. Thirty-four states use domestic violence as one factor in assessing custody of the child, and four states do not mention domestic violence at all. Fathers' rights groups have emerged to advocate for joint or sole custody by arguing that children need their father's presence in their lives. In essence, determining child custody when domestic violence has occurred is largely uneven across the states, with the majority of states either not recognizing domestic violence or acknowledging domestic violence as just one of a myriad of factors in deciding child custody. Equally dismaying is how child welfare and criminal justice systems respond in cases of femicide in which the killer's family may want joint or shared custody with the victim's surviving family (Bent-Goodley & Brade, 2007). These instances, while certainly not as prevalent as cases involving child custody between separating parents, require child welfare agencies to assess what arrangements would be in the best interest of children. Other complex case management situations involving battering occur when perpetrators seek to manipulate their kin and punish the victim by challenging her for custody (Bent-Goodley & Brade, 2007). These emerging issues warrant critical and diligent attention as they continue to be discussed in the field.

Intersections With the Prisoner Reentry Movement

Many men being released from prison have histories of perpetrating intimate partner violence, but they are rarely provided with any BIP services while incarcerated and are often released from prison without a plan for reducing intimate partner violence as part of their reentry into society (Oliver & Hairston, 2008). An incarcerated batterer may continue to manipulate and abuse his partner and force her, through threats and intimidation, to tell the parole officer that she wishes to have the batterer live with her after release as a condition of his parole. Parole officers may neglect to ask an abuser's partner if the relationship with the perpetrator has been violent. As a result, the woman is placed at risk from a person who has, most likely, received no treatment in prison and may in fact have become even more violent as a result of his incarceration. These women are often silent about a range of fears, including a perpetrator's abuse and violence, fear of the criminal justice system, and fear of formal provider systems. It is critical that BIPs be a part of the service plan requirements for those men before their release, as a condition of their release, and after their release from prison.

HOW DO WE KNOW IT?

Despite all that BIPs are charged to do, three primary questions arise in connection with them: (a) Do perpetrators of abuse have the capacity to change? (b) Do BIPs work? and (c) Are women safe once their partner is participating in a BIP? One of the major challenges affecting these programs is the lack of consistency across interventions and state requirements (Gondolf, 2004; Healey, Smith, & O'Sullivan, 1998). States vary in the required lengths of treatment, screening criteria, and referral processes. Interventions can range from no specific program length in some states to 5 years in other states.

However, the average length of treatment is 26 weeks and typically between 16 and 52 weeks. Additionally, there is significant variation across states and within local provider systems as to the focus of the intervention and types of services required. Some states use screening criteria to determine the perceived readiness of the perpetrator and/or use a standardized lethality assessment on first contact. Some providers consider the substance abuse, mental health, and psychiatric history of the perpetrators, and others do not (Bennett & Williams, 2003). These inconsistencies make it challenging to effectively evaluate treatment strategies for perpetrators across settings.

There are multiple challenges when trying to evaluate the extent to which BIPs actually keep women safe. Most BIP services focus on having the perpetrator take responsibility for his actions, skill building in nonviolence and nonthreatening behaviors, developing safe and respectful forms of communication, attitudes toward women and the impact of these attitudes on behavior, and how domestic violence affects women and children (Williams & Becker, 1994). Some programs use a psychoeducational approach, and others adopt a cognitive behavioral approach to intervention. However, there are several central issues across these programs. First, long-term follow-up may be complicated if the relationship ends. One study found that 21% of perpetrators had new partners at their 30-month follow-up (Gondolf, 1997). Second, it is often difficult to ascertain if the perpetrator is using nonphysical tactics of abuse in an effort to intimidate or maintain silence. Third, selecting a measure of success is complex. Rearrest rates are misleading because those who complete these programs are often White, middle-class, employed men who are least likely to interact with the criminal justice system and thus could be abusive without being caught (Dutton, Bodnarchuk, Kropp, Hart, & Ogloff, 1997). Fourth, there is an average 50% attrition rate in BIPs, making it difficult to ascertain the actual effectiveness of the intervention versus the impact of self-selection on program outcomes. Consequently, there are mixed findings as to the effectiveness of BIP services and their ability to keep women safe. In an examination of four major BIP evaluations, the studies evidenced some or all of the following problems: low sample sizes, high attrition, and exclusion of key types of perpetrators, such as men who were also substance abusers, unmarried, or unemployed, or had a previous criminal record. And, as is often true with compromised study designs, they did not produce strong findings to suggest that the programs were highly effective (Bennett & Williams, 2001). BIPs have the potential to impact the decision making of perpetrators, but there is not one model that works across all groups, there is still more to learn about what works and what does not work, and there are still considerable challenges to assessing and testing the effectiveness of these models.

WHERE DO WE GO FROM HERE?

How we provide services for perpetrators of abuse is of critical importance to ending violence against women and girls. Moving forward, it is imperative to build culturally congruent services, ensure that services are coordinated and comprehensive, enhance the effectiveness and evaluation of BIPs, create opportunities for communities and men to engage in violence prevention, and foster greater advocacy efforts to work toward stopping violence.

Enhancing Culturally Focused BIP Services

As the field moves forward, the role of culture cannot be limited to one session or one activity; it has to be infused throughout the philosophy, structure, and activities of the project. A practitioner need not be a member of a particular group to offer culturally congruent services, but that individual needs to be clear about his or her biases, skills, and limitations. The reason that a program fails to offer culturally congruent services should never be the lack of a person of color on staff. If the program does not have staff with the required skill base to work with diverse groups, then the program has to make a decision as to the population it is best equipped to serve and be honest about that. The field must begin to take steps to value this critical dimension of service provision or BIPs will continue to evidence minimal effectiveness. An enhanced cultural focus promises to increase the strength of services, widen the pool of persons being served, and create more opportunities for dialogue within diverse communities about domestic violence.

Ensuring That Services Are Coordinated and Comprehensive

The structure, the diversity of program services and offerings, and the consistency of service provision of BIPs must be critically examined. We need to develop better monitoring tools for BIPs to upgrade the quality and consistency of program delivery. Required program elements that meet minimum quality standards should be identified to provide greater guidance in the field. At the same time, innovative approaches are needed to engage batterers and to expand the capacity to offer a range of treatment plans geared to the different typologies of abusive behaviors. Prisoner reentry is one of a number of emerging issues that need more focused attention from BIPs. And determining the minimum length of treatment, basic program structure, and the methods to ensure compliance would be useful steps toward understanding the thought processes that support a perpetrator's decision to cease abuse.

It is important that any BIP model be integrated into the provider and community network, including agencies and systems for women and children and criminal justice personnel such as law enforcement, prosecution, judges and courts, and correctional and parole services. Each of those entities should be clear about what it can and cannot do to increase safety. BIPs work best as part of a larger comprehensive and coordinated community response approach to prevention. It is not realistic to expect BIPs to shoulder the entire responsibility of working with this population. Domestic violence advocates have helped advance understandings of how, for example, health care providers should screen and be able to refer women for assistance if domestic violence is detected. However, little is done outside of BIP services to screen and provide referrals for perpetrators of abuse. In addition to identifying victims of abuse, we need to find ways to engage men in stopping violence and to connect them to appropriate referral sources. This approach would convey a clear message across systems that violence is unacceptable. As men receive job training, employment, or housing support, there are opportunities to convey messages of violence prevention to them and connect them to services that address this issue. Although service providers would have to be trained to provide these services, doing so would greatly expand the opportunities to target men at risk of violence and send a unified message that violence is wrong, that there are other ways to address violence, and that there are supports available to help them stop their abusive behaviors.

Enhancing the Effectiveness and Evaluation of BIPs

As we consider strengthening both interventions and evaluations, it is important for BIPs to engage perpetrators in expanding awareness of their feelings, connecting those emotions to behaviors, and developing alternative sets of behaviors that are responsive to their emotions. Programs must also find better ways of tracking partner safety and ensuring that women understand that BIP services do not denote safety but are a first step toward addressing abusive behaviors. Programs must also find ways to integrate parallel issues, such as substance abuse and fatherhood, into treatment approaches and not postpone services until after the co-occurring problem has been addressed. Finding ways of connecting these diverse parallel areas is challenging, but it may open up new possibilities for identifying the factors that motivate change, as well as increasing opportunities for collaboration.

Need for More Effective and Rigorous Evaluations

The development of more effective and rigorous evaluations of BIP services is crucial (Hamberger, 2008). While BIP evaluations are increasing, the fragmentation of services, limited coordination, and poor congruity across systems and programs make it difficult to fully evaluate and compare the effectiveness of BIP models. Often program attrition is too high to attribute effectiveness to the intervention, small sample sizes limit more sophisticated analysis, the response rate is too low, co-occurring variables are not explored, or different outcomes measures are used across the studies (Bennett & Williams, 2001; Jackson et al., 2003). While there are increasing methodological approaches being used to address this problem (Carney, Buttell, & Muldoon, 2006; Schmidt et al., 2007), these kinds of issues discourage the field from advancing and offering more effective and proven services that can be offered and/or adapted across communities.

No specific approach has emerged as being better than another, but it is clear that it will take a comprehensive approach that is respectful of diverse experiences and capable of responding to the needs of different populations. The appropriate balance must be found between holding batterers accountable through punishment and strengthening their capacity and resources for stopping abusive thoughts and behaviors.

Engaging Communities and Men in Violence Prevention

Although women will continue to stand up against violence, men and boys must be engaged to stand with them and advocate for change. Reduction in domestic violence will not occur solely by working with individual perpetrators because batterers do not live in a vacuum. They are part of the life of a community that may condone violence in relationships. Communities, particularly nonviolent men in communities, play an integral role in preventing violence and finding solutions that are sustainable. When communities are engaged as part of BIP service provision, messages learned during group interventions can be sustained and reinforced outside the treatment center. Awareness campaigns build consciousness of how devastating domestic violence is to the life and well-being of entire communities and how violence reduction and healthy relationships benefit the entire community. Community institutions, such as faith-based groups, can define and reaffirm the qualities of healthy relationships and provide ongoing, informal support to help perpetrators of abuse maintain attitude and behavior change. In many ways, the success of BIPs rests in the supports provided within the community and by other men.

More Advocacy to End Abuse

Although the majority of this chapter has focused on individual and community level solutions, the issue will not be fully addressed, nor will genuine and lasting change occur, without increased advocacy to stop violence against women and girls. In the media, in the entertainment industry, and in our laws, abusive behaviors are often validated, deemed as provoked, or not unusual in a relationship. It is important to advocate for gender equality within social, cultural, and legal structures and address issues of gender inequality swiftly and strongly. Abuse against women and girls as reflected in music, television, movies, and other media must continue to be countered with new ideas and new measures that help to both stop these negative images and educate young people as to why they are harmful to advancing healthy relationships. There must be public campaigns that are both general and culturally specific to ensure that diverse voices and opinions are represented, valued, and leveraged to send the message that violence is wrong no matter the circumstance, no matter the person, no matter the situation, no matter what. The role of the community and the need for men to be more vocal in the antiviolence movement are crucial to finding solutions that better serve perpetrators of abuse and prevent others from following their path.

CONCLUSION

This chapter has examined what we know, how we know it, and where we need to go in the treatment for perpetrators of domestic violence. Although considerable progress has been made in this area, more must be done to create effective programs for those who perpetrate abuse. There must also be an emphasis on finding solutions that speak to the diverse needs of men across populations and acknowledgment of emerging issues that require attention. Ultimately, advancing nonviolent, nonabusive, healthy relationships is at the center of these efforts and will continue to fuel efforts that get us closer to ending domestic violence.

REFERENCES

Arean, J. C., & Davis, D. (2007). Working with fathers in batterer intervention programs: Lessons from the fathering after violence project. In J. L. Edleson & O. J. Williams (Eds.), *Parenting by men who batter: New directions for assessment and intervention* (pp. 19–44). New York, NY: Oxford University Press.

Aymer, S. (2008). Beyond power and control: Clinical interventions with men engaged in partner abuse. *Clinical Social Work Journal, 36,* 323–332. doi:10.1007/s10615-008-0167-z

Bancroft, L., & Silverman, J. (Eds.). (2002). *The batterer as parent: Addressing the impact of domestic violence on family dynamics*. Thousand Oaks, CA: Sage.

Bell, C. C., & Mattis, J. A. (2000). The importance of cultural competence in ministering to African American victims of domestic violence. *Violence Against Women, 6*, 515–532. doi:10.1177/10778010022182001

Bender, K., & Roberts, A. (2007). Battered women versus male batterer typologies: Same or different based on evidence based studies? *Aggression and Violent Behavior, 12*, 519–530. doi:10.1016/j.avb.2007.02.005

Bennett, L., & Williams, O. (2001, August). *Controversies and recent studies of batterer's intervention program effectiveness.* Retrieved from http://www.vawnet.org

Bennett, L., & Williams, O. (2003). Substance abuse and men who batter: Issues in theory and practice. *Violence Against Women, 9*, 558–575. doi:10.1177/1077 801202250453

Bent-Goodley, T. B. (2001). Eradicating domestic violence in the African American community. *Trauma, Violence & Abuse, 2*, 316–330. doi:10.1177/15248380010 02004003

Bent-Goodley, T. B. (2005a). An African centered approach to domestic violence. *Families in Society, 86*, 197–206.

Bent-Goodley, T. B. (2005b). Culture and domestic violence: Transforming knowledge development. *Journal of Interpersonal Violence, 20*, 195–203. doi:10.1177/ 0886260504269050

Bent-Goodley, T. B., & Brade, K. (2007). Domestic violence and kinship care: Connecting policy with practice. *Journal of Health & Social Policy, 22*, 65–83. doi:10. 1300/J045v22n03_05

Bent-Goodley, T. B., & Williams, O. J. (2008). *Community insights of domestic violence among African Americans: Conversations about domestic violence and other issues affecting their community—Detroit.* St. Paul, MN: Institute on Domestic Violence in the African American Community.

Campbell, M., Neil, J., Jaffe, P., & Kelly, T. (2010). Engaging abusive men in seeking community intervention: A critical research and practice priority. *Journal of Family Violence, 25*, 413–422. doi:10.1007/s10896-010-9302-z

Carney, M., Buttell, F., & Muldoon, J. (2006). Predictors of batterer intervention program attrition: Developing and implementing logistic regression models. *Journal of Offender Rehabilitation, 43*, 35–54. doi:10.1300/J076v43n02_02

Carrillo, R., & Tello, J. (Eds.). (2008). *Family violence and men of color: Healing the wounded male spirit* (2nd ed.). New York, NY: Springer.

Chiffriller, S. H., & Hennessy, J. (2007). Male batterer profiles: Support for an empirically generated typology. *Journal of Offender Rehabilitation, 44*, 117–131. doi:10. 1300/J076v44n02_05

Dutton, D. G., Bodnarchuk, M., Kropp, R., Hart, S., & Ogloff, J. (1997). Client personality disorders affecting wife assault post-treatment recidivism. *Violence and Victims, 12*, 37–50.

Gondolf, E. (1997). *Multi-site evaluation of batterer's intervention systems: A summary of preliminary findings.* Indiana, PA: Mid-Atlantic Addiction Training Institute.

Gondolf, E. (2002). *Batterer intervention systems*. Thousand Oaks, CA: Sage.

Gondolf, E. (2004). Evaluating batterer counseling programs: A difficult task showing some effects. *Aggression and Violent Behavior, 9*, 605–631. doi:10.1016/j.avb.2003. 06.001

Gondolf, E., & Williams, O. (2001). Culturally focused batterer counseling for African American men. *Trauma, Violence & Abuse, 2*, 283–295. doi:10.1177/152483800 1002004001

Hamberger, L. K. (2008). Twenty-five years of change in working with partner abusers: Part II: Observations from the trenches about changes in understanding of abusers and abuser treatment. *Journal of Aggression, Maltreatment & Trauma, 17*, 1–22. doi:10.1080/10926770802344810

Hancock, T., & Siu, K. (2009). A culturally sensitive intervention with domestically violent Latino immigrant men. *Journal of Family Violence, 24*, 123–132. doi:10. 1007/s10896-008-9217-0

Healey, K., Smith, C., & O'Sullivan, C. (1998). *Batterer's intervention: Program approaches and criminal justice strategies*. Washington, DC: U.S. Department of Justice, Office of Justice Programs.

Holtzworth-Munroe, A., & Stuart, G. (1994). Typologies of male batterers: Three subtypes and the differences among them. *Psychological Bulletin, 116*, 476–497. doi:10.1037/0033-2909.116.3.476

Jackson, S., Feder, L., Forde, D., Davis, R., Maxwell, C., & Taylor, B. (2003). *Batterer's intervention programs: Where do we go from here?* (NCJ 195079). Washington, DC: U.S. Department of Justice.

Levin, A., & Mills, L. (2003). Fighting for child custody when domestic violence is at issue: Survey of state laws. *Social Work, 48*, 463–470.

Lohr, J., Bonge, D., Witte, T., Hamberger, K., & Langhinrichsen-Rohling, J. (2005). Consistency and accuracy of batterer typology identification. *Journal of Family Violence, 20*, 253–258. doi:10.1007/s10896-005-5989-7

Oliver, W., & Hairston, C. (2008). Intimate partner violence during the transition from prison to the community: Perspectives of incarcerated African American men. *Journal of Aggression, Maltreatment & Trauma, 16*, 258–276. doi:10.1080/ 10926770801925577

Peled, E. (2000). Parenting by men who abuse women: Issues and dilemmas. *British Journal of Social Work, 30*, 25–36. doi:10.1093/bjsw/30.1.25

Powell, J. (2008). The impact of societal systems on Black male violence. *Journal of Aggression, Maltreatment & Trauma, 16*, 311–329. doi:10.1080/10926770801 925742

Salisbury, E. J., Henning, K., & Holdford, R. (2009). Fathering by partner-abusive men: Attitudes on children's exposure to interparental conflict and risk factors for child abuse. *Child Maltreatment, 14*, 232–242. doi:10.1177/1077559509 338407

Saunders, D. (1992). A typology of men who batter: Three types of derived of derived from cluster analysis. *American Journal of Orthopsychiatry, 62*, 264–275. doi:10.1037/h0079333

Schmidt, M., Kolodinsky, J., Carsten, G., Schmidt, F., Larson, M., & MacLachlan, C. (2007). Short term change in attitude and motivating factors to change abusive behavior of male batterers after participating in a group intervention program based on the pro-feminist and cognitive-behavioral approach. *Journal of Family Violence, 22*, 91–100. doi:10.1007/s10896-007-9064-4

Tubbs, C. Y., & Williams, O. J. (2007). Shared parenting after abuse: Battered mothers' perspectives on parenting after dissolution of a relationship. In J. L. Edleson & O. J. Williams (Eds.), *Parenting by men who batter: New directions for assessment and intervention* (pp. 19–44). New York, NY: Oxford University Press.

Williams, O. J. (1999). African American men who batter: Treatment considerations and community response. In R. Staples (Ed.), *The Black family: Essays and studies* (5th ed., pp. 265–279). Belmont, CA: Wadsworth.

Williams, O. J. (2008). Healing and confronting the African American male who batters. In R. Carrillo & J. Tello (Eds.). *Family violence and men of color: Healing the wounded male spirit* (pp. 85–116). New York, NY: Springer.

Williams, O. J., & Becker, L. (1994). Partner abuse programs and cultural competence: The results of a national study. *Violence and Victims, 9*, 287–296.

Williams, O. J., Boggess, J., & Carter, J. (2001). Fatherhood and domestic violence: Exploring the role of men who batter in the lives of their children. In J. Edleson & S. Graham-Bermann (Eds.), *Future directions for children exposed to domestic violence* (pp. 157–187). Washington, DC: American Psychological Association. doi:10.1037/10408-008

Williams, O. J., Oliver, W., & Pope, M. (2008). Domestic violence in the African American community. *Journal of Aggression, Maltreatment & Trauma, 16*, 229–237. doi:10.1080/10926770801925486

11

THE JUSTICE SYSTEM RESPONSE TO DOMESTIC VIOLENCE

LISA A. GOODMAN AND DEBORAH EPSTEIN

From the earliest days of the domestic violence movement in the early 1970s, activists sought to transform the public's perception of intimate partner violence (IPV) from a private problem to be kept behind closed doors to a public problem requiring public solutions. The justice system became a major focus of this effort, as activists pushed the legal system to treat domestic violence as seriously as any other crime, rather than as a family issue.

This effort was enormously successful. Over the past 30 years, the justice system has improved its response to domestic violence in three fundamental ways. First, in the criminal justice system, activists secured the adoption of mandatory arrest laws, which require police to arrest in domestic violence cases, and no-drop prosecution policies, pursuant to which the government proceeds with criminal charges against accused perpetrators regardless of whether the victim chooses to cooperate. Second, in the civil system, activists persuaded state legislatures to enact protection order laws, authorizing judges to award survivors a wide variety of protections that are specially tailored to meet their needs. Third, activists developed public–private collaborations, often referred to as *coordinated community responses*, designed to expand the scope of the justice system's response to victims of intimate abuse.

Together, these reforms have dramatically increased battered women's access to justice, as well as the practical options available to them. According to the National Violence Against Women Survey (Tjaden & Thoennes, 2000), a national study of 8,000 women in the United States, 27% of women assaulted by an intimate partner reported police involvement in response to the last incident of abuse. Another study found that among IPV survivors identified as those who seek help from public agencies, 77% called the police and 61% filed a complaint against the abuser (Anderson et al., 2003).

But despite these improvements, numerous obstacles to victim safety remain, and recent justice system reforms have created new and unanticipated challenges for battered women. These reforms, either explicitly or as applied in practice, tend to adopt a fairly rigid, one-size-fits-all approach that often marginalizes a woman's particular situation and perspective and sacrifices the contextualized, survivor-centered focus that existed in the early years of the domestic violence movement (Goodman & Epstein, 2008). As a result, the justice system frequently fails to effectively support battered women.

This chapter analyzes both the positive impact of recent justice system reforms and their problematic consequences.

WHAT DO WE KNOW? THE CRIMINAL JUSTICE SYSTEM

Historical Context and Current Status

Police: Mandatory Arrest Laws

Historically, police officers have failed to recognize intimate partner abuse as a criminal act, ignoring domestic violence calls or delaying responses. When officers did respond, they were trained to mediate and to avoid arrest, if possible (Eisenberg & Micklow, 1974). Arrests were rare; studies estimate that they occurred in only 3% to 14% of all IPV cases to which officers actually responded (Buzawa & Buzawa, 1992). Battered women were left with little access to the criminal justice system.

But all of this changed following the publication of a highly touted and well-publicized research effort, the Minneapolis Domestic Violence Experiment. The study, which concluded that arrest dramatically reduced the risk of reassault against the same victim during a 6-month period, had an enormous influence on public policy (Sherman & Berk, 1984). In 1984, the same year the study's results were published, the U.S. Attorney General's Task Force on Family Violence (Hart et al., 1984) issued a report recommending arrest as the standard response to all cases of misdemeanor domestic assault. In response to this pressure, states began to enact laws requiring arrest in domestic abuse cases. Oregon passed the first mandatory arrest statute in 1977, and other states soon followed suit. By 2005, twenty-six states and the District of Columbia either required arrest or had adopted a proarrest policy (Miccio, 2005). Mandatory arrest policies dramatically increased arrest rates for IPV and had a profound impact on survivors; those who sought access to the criminal justice system were far more likely to succeed with the advent of mandatory arrest.

Prosecution: No-Drop Policies

The police were not the only sector of the criminal justice community that historically had failed to take domestic violence seriously; prosecutors did as well, often actively discouraging victims from pursuing cases against perpetrators. Even when mandatory arrest laws increased the number of domestic violence incidents brought to their attention, prosecutors rarely pressed charges, and when they did, they rarely followed through and took the case to trial (e.g., Epstein, 1999). District Attorneys nationwide explained that "because victims simply do not follow through in domestic violence cases, there is no need to waste precious prosecutorial resources on them" (Cahn, 1992, p. 163).

This "automatic drop" policy ceded to perpetrators an enormous degree of control over the criminal justice process. All a batterer had to do was coerce his victim—through threats, violence, guilt, or apologies—into asking the prosecutor to drop the charges; once she did so, there was no longer a risk of jail time or a disincentive to batter. Although some prosecutors recognized that batterers might be pressuring victims into making the request to drop charges, they reported being unable to distinguish between a battered woman who was communicating her true feelings and one who had a literal or figurative gun to her head. So the government adopted a uniform approach and dropped charges in every case in which a woman requested it (Epstein, 1999). During the 1980s and 1990s, advocates began to make inroads in changing these policies. In a growing number of states, prosecutors have adopted *no-drop* policies. Once charges are brought, a case proceeds regardless of the victim's wishes, as long as sufficient evidence exists to prove criminal conduct beyond a reasonable doubt. Such evidence can include recorded calls to 911, photographs and hospital records documenting injuries, and testimony from eyewitnesses or police officers who responded to the crime scene. Even in cases where the victim refuses to cooperate with the government or recants her original story and testifies for the defense, prosecuting attorneys often persevere, relying on these alternative sources of evidence. As with mandatory arrest, no-drop prosecution strategies proved quite successful in improving victim access to justice.

In many ways, mandatory arrest laws and no-drop prosecution policies represent enormous progress for victims of IPV within the criminal justice system. Domestic abuse prosecutions are now in a position of rough parity with those of stranger violence; battered women seeking to escape abuse now have a far broader range of tools available to them. These policies also represent an important symbolic shift: a clear declaration by the state that it no longer condones domestic violence (Ford & Regoli, 1992). And some scholars and activists argue that no-drop prosecution is the most effective way to prevent a perpetrator from escaping punishment by threatening victims into dropping charges (Hanna, 1996). But what do we really know about how effective these policies are?

Effectiveness of Criminal Justice System Mandates

Several factors make research on the effectiveness of any justice system response to IPV difficult to evaluate. First, with few exceptions (e.g., the Minneapolis Domestic Violence Experiment and its replications), the research in this area is naturalistic and descriptive, rather than experimental. Second, studies vary widely along a range of critical dimensions, making them difficult to compare and synthesize. Third, it is difficult to generalize the results of studies that explore reform efforts whose specifics vary greatly across jurisdictions (e.g., coordinated community responses, described in a later section), since these projects often truly are apples and oranges.

Given these difficulties, no clear picture exists regarding the effectiveness of mandatory arrest and no-drop prosecution. But what we do know gives rise to some substantial concerns. Since the original Minneapolis Domestic Violence Experiment, numerous studies have analyzed the impact of arrest on recidivism rates. A relatively recent reanalysis of the pooled data from these studies showed that, at best, mandatory arrest has a mixed impact on reabuse, with effectiveness varying to some extent with the perpetrator's employment status (Maxwell, Garner, & Fagan, 1999). In the aftermath of a mandatory arrest, unemployed perpetrators are more likely to commit a subsequent assault resulting in rearrest than are those who are employed. Researchers theorize that the difference could stem from a lower "stake in conformity" on the part of unemployed batterers or from a lower likelihood that survivors will call the police when their partners are bringing income into the home (Wooldredge & Thistlethwaite, 2002).

Far fewer data exist in the area of no-drop prosecution, but, again, the available results appear problematic. The only experimental study to look directly at no-drop prosecution and reabuse rates found that victims who followed through with prosecution were less likely to experience violence within the subsequent 6 months only if they made a personal choice to participate and were not coerced into doing so (Ford & Regoli, 1992). Another study found that women who were given a choice about whether to drop charges reported an increased sense of the court's fairness over a 6-month period, whereas the greatest decreases in women's perceptions of the court's fairness over time were among those who had minimal contact with prosecutors and those who were subjected to coercive treatment by prosecutors (Finn, 2003).

Another set of studies has suggested that policies promoting prosecution in the vast majority of circumstances can themselves create risk for battered women. For example, several studies indicate that 20% to 30% of arrested offenders reassault their partners either before the court process has concluded or shortly afterward, often as retaliation for the victim's perceived role in their involvement with the court system (e.g., Finn, 2003; Goodman, Bennett, & Dutton, 1999). And a National Institute of Justice study found that increased prosecution rates for domestic assault were associated with increased levels of homicides among White married couples, as well as Black and White unmarried couples, even when controlling for other relevant variables (Dugan, Nagin, & Rosenfeld, 2001).

This research has dampened the enthusiasm with which many advocates for battered women initially embraced criminal justice mandates. Concern about the degree to which mandatory arrest and no-drop prosecution policies actually keep women safe is steadily growing (see, e.g., Mills, 1998; Weisz, 2002).

Unintended Negative Consequences

Why have mandatory criminal justice system interventions not been more effective? The problematic data can be explained in large part by the numerous unintended negative consequences arising from these policies. The crux of the problem is that given the enormous complexity of IPV, no single response can meet the needs of every woman, and many responses that are well suited to one situation can worsen another. But mandatory arrest laws and no-drop prosecution policies are designed to operate on a one-size-fits-all basis. By definition, they lack sufficient flexibility to permit effective responses to particularized situations and leave no room for a contextualized understanding of an individual battered woman's life circumstances. Pursuant to these mandates, once a woman, or her neighbor or friend, makes an initial call to the police, she is swept into a process over which she has little control. The survivor's own wishes and needs become largely irrelevant, even when she fears that prosecution will provoke the batterer into retaliatory abuse against her and her children, when she needs her partner's economic support to keep her family afloat, or when she fears that he will be deported as a result of the prosecution.

But consideration of these survivor concerns is essential to the goal of eradicating domestic violence. Because criminal justice system mandates fail to respond to individual battered women's safety concerns, they cannot be fully effective. A battered woman's fear of retaliatory violence, for example, is a realistic one. Substantial data show that separation from the batterer is the time of greatest risk of serious violence and homicide for battered women (see, e.g., Fleury, Sullivan, & Bybee, 2000). And, as discussed previously, prosecution itself can increase the risk of harm to battered women. All of these risks are compounded by the facts that convicted domestic violence perpetrators receive relatively lenient sentences (Erez & Tontodonato, 1990) and few are sentenced to serve any jail time (Hemmens, Strom, & Schlegel, 1998). Many victims take this risk of retaliatory violence seriously. In one study (Erez & Belknap, 1998), 498 domestic violence victims rated fear of the batterer as the most important reason they were unwilling to cooperate with the prosecution of their abusive partners. Despite this fact, prosecutors regularly subpoena victims and force them to testify (Epstein, Bell, & Goodman, 2003). And as survivors learn that their individual needs will not be taken into account, some of them choose to avoid police and prosecutors altogether, leaving them far more vulnerable to their partner's abuse.

Research also demonstrates that a victim's children also are at high risk of harm when separation occurs (Fleury, Sullivan, & Bybee, 2000). Victims who choose to remain in an abusive relationship may be making a choice to protect their children. Victims rank concern for their children's safety high on the list of factors that lead them to decline to cooperate with a prosecution (Erez & Belknap, 1998). But justice system officials often assume that a "good" mother would leave an abusive relationship. Many prosecutors threaten to refer "uncooperative" victims to child protective services, where action may be taken to remove their children (Epstein, 1999). Such practices create an antipathy between government officials and battered women that leaves some women deeply reluctant to use the justice system as a resource.

Criminal justice system mandates also fail to appropriately recognize the financial dependence of many battered women on their abusive partners. A victim may seek to have charges dropped so that the father of her children can continue to work, provide her with financial support, and prevent her family from sliding into homelessness. For these and other reasons, a lack of sufficient economic resources creates a significant obstacle to survivors' willingness to cooperate with prosecutors (Hare, 2006). But prosecutors typically refuse to drop charges in such situations, reasoning that dropping the case would not serve the interests of the state in deterring future batterers from harming women. After all, it sends a mixed message, at best, if charges can be dropped for batterers whose families need their income. Such reasoning may be theoretically sound, but in practice it results in the sacrifice of individual survivors' safety needs in favor of general deterrence of domestic violence.

As for the risk of deportation, federal law provides that an immigrant convicted of a domestic violence offense becomes deportable, even if he has previously obtained lawful permanent resident status (Omnibus Consolidated Appropriations Act, 1997, 1996, 8 U.S.C. § 1227(a)(2)(E)). Many women are reluctant to risk triggering the deportation of their partners and being ostracized from their cultural communities for doing so. This concern is particularly salient where the perpetrator might be subjected to political persecution if forced to return to his home country. Faced with rigid policy mandates, these women often choose to remain silent about abuse or refuse to cooperate with criminal justice agents (Loke, 1997).

Similarly, African American women often are reluctant to involve police and prosecutors in domestic disputes because this entails participating in a criminal justice system that historically has failed to provide equal justice to people of color. Referring to communities of color, Crenshaw (1991) wrote that there is a "generalized community ethic against public intervention, the product of a desire to create a private world free from the diverse assaults on the public lives of racially subordinated people" (p. 1257). Victims whose experience has led them to expect to encounter racism in the criminal justice system are far less likely to turn to the police for assistance (Websdale, 2001), and if calling 911 necessitates arrest, people of color may be even less likely to access emergency police assistance.

The fundamental failure of mandatory policies to respond to a woman's individual circumstances may leave her more trapped than ever in her violent home. In one study of women whose partners had been arrested for domestic violence, over half (57.5%) of the victims who disclosed that they were revictimized at some point over the next year did not report the new incident to the criminal justice system (Buzawa, Hotaling, & Byrne, 2006). Importantly, those who did not report were significantly more likely than the other participants to depict the criminal justice system as unresponsive to their preferences. Similarly, a second study of women whose partners had been arrested in Washington, DC, found that at follow-up, more empowering experiences in court predicted stronger intentions to use the system in the future if the need arose (Bennett Cattaneo & Goodman, 2010).

WHAT DO WE KNOW? THE CIVIL JUSTICE SYSTEM

Historical Context and Current Status

In the late 1960s and early 1970s, frustrated with the slow pace of reform among police and prosecutors, activists turned their attention to creating protections for battered women in the civil justice system. Their efforts resulted in the widespread adoption of protection order statutes, which authorize judges to create flexible, individually responsive solutions. Today, every state has a protection order statute, though eligibility criteria and the scope of available protections differ (DeJong & Burgess-Proctor, 2006).

Protection orders (also called *restraining orders, domestic violence orders,* and *peace bonds*) can direct a batterer to avoid all contact with a victim and to refrain from assaulting or threatening her. In addition, these orders may contain directives concerning custody, visitation arrangements, child support, and access to housing (Logan, Shannon, & Walker, 2005). The inclusion of these latter issues is critical. One of the primary reasons victims return to their abusive partners is the pressure created by the loss of economic support (Goodman et al., 2009). For a woman with children, a support award may be the key to freedom. Similarly, because the potential for renewed violence is particularly acute during visitation exchanges, carefully structured pick-up and drop-off provisions, designed to eliminate victim–perpetrator contact, also can significantly reduce the risk of future violence (Finn & Colson, 1990).

In contrast to the criminal justice approach, protection order laws were developed expressly to provide individually tailored legal remedies for battered women. A perpetrator might be ordered to attend parenting counseling, provide spousal support, reimburse the victim for injury-related medical bills, or refrain from contacting the victim's employer, among other situation-specific remedies. In most states, protection orders remain in effect for 1 to 3 years and may be extended upon demonstration of continued need. In addition, every state has adopted criminal enforcement mechanisms for protection orders (Epstein, 2002).

How Effective Are Civil Protection Orders?

A few studies have explored the impact of civil protection orders on victim safety (e.g., Holt, Kernic, Wolf, & Rivara, 2003; Keilitz, 1997; Klein, 1996; McFarlane et al., 2004). These studies use a variety of data sources, including victim follow-up, police reports, and new restraining order applications. Follow-up periods range from 4 months to 2 years. Overall, these studies indicate that between 23% and 70% of batterers violate protection orders, with victim report–based studies finding far higher violation rates than studies based on official records. Averaging across 32 studies, Spitzberg (2002) reported that batterers violate approximately 40% of protection orders. Several studies further suggest that a substantial portion of violations occur within the first 3 months after issuance of the order (Harrell & Smith, 1996; Keilitz, 1997; Klein, 1996).

Despite these sobering statistics, research comparing outcomes for women with and without protection orders suggest that orders do provide some protection. Although the data are mixed, several of the largest and most rigorous studies indicate that those women who obtained a permanent order reported considerably less reabuse over time, compared with those who reported an incident to the police but did not file for a protection order (Holt et al., 2003; Logan, Shannon, Walker, & Faragher, 2006). In addition, a number of studies suggest that a majority of women who obtain permanent orders report feeling both safer and better about themselves after doing so (Fischer & Rose, 1995; Keilitz, 1997).

One of the most significant obstacles to greater effectiveness of the protection order system stems from the failure to enforce these orders (Kane, 2000). Frequently, police still refuse to arrest a batterer who has violated a protection order. This practice can substantially undermine a woman's faith in the justice system, making her far less likely to rely on it in the future. Why should she risk her abusive partner's wrath when an order turns out to be "nothing but a piece of paper," just as he told her it was?

Unintended Negative Consequences of Civil Protection Orders

Although the civil protection order system is far more responsive to the individual needs of battered women than its criminal justice counterpart, it too has given rise to unanticipated challenges for survivors. And again, these challenges stem from officials' tendency to adopt a uniform, monolithic view of battered women. Perhaps the most significant problem here is that, in practice, the protection order system rests on the assumption that all survivors wish—or should wish—to exit their abusive relationships (Goodman & Epstein, 2008). But women may have numerous reasons for choosing to stay in such a relationship. As noted earlier, survivors may stay to avoid retaliatory violence against themselves and their children or because they rely on their abusive partners (for financial support, child care, or housing), and they may not be able to survive without continued contact. Accordingly, they may want the violence to stop but not yet be ready to end the relationship. These women need support in their efforts to become more economically self-reliant, but such assistance is not offered by the justice system or by most community programs (Logan et al., 2006). Immigrant women may be particularly unlikely to choose separation from their partners for reasons having to do with religion, tradition, economic dependence, or a desire to remain part of a community that would not condone such an action (Latta & Goodman, 2005). By assuming that all battered women should end their relationships, judges in civil cases often substitute their own judgment for that of a victim seeking assistance in their courtrooms. Some fine or even imprison battered women for initiating contact with an abusive partner during the effective period of a protection order (e.g., Goodmark, 2003). These actions demonstrate how little tolerance many judges in civil protection order cases have for women who do not conform to state expectations, as well as how willing judges are to use criminal sanctions to enforce officially "appropriate" behavior.

The pressure toward separation is particularly problematic when juxtaposed with evidence that many judges presiding over contested custody proceedings fail to credit or refuse to consider allegations of IPV. Instead, these judges emphasize the importance of dual parent involvement and award joint custody—thus forcing survivors to maintain unwanted close contact with abusive partners (Meier, 2003). Survivors thus find themselves on the receiving end of deeply inconsistent judicial messages—you must separate from your abusive partner, regardless of your preference, except if you have children, in which case you must remain in regular contact with him even if you wish to leave.

As is evident from both of these situations, civil judges, like their criminal justice counterparts, often use their considerable power to control the lives of victims. Even assuming that such judicial actions stem from the best intentions—an effort to do everything possible to keep battered women safe—this regular undermining of battered women's autonomy is deeply problematic and undermines the system's potential effectiveness.

WHAT DO WE KNOW? COORDINATED COMMUNITY RESPONSES

Historical Context and Current Status

As increasing resources and attention began to be devoted to the justice system's response to battered women, advocates began to search for ways to become involved in its routine operations. The most successful of these efforts has been the creation of coordinated community responses. As discussed next, coordination has come in the form of interagency communication, colocation of services for battered women, and unified domestic violence courts.

Interagency Communication

In 1980, advocates in Duluth, Minnesota, initiated the Domestic Abuse Intervention Project, the first formal, coordinated community response to domestic violence (Pence & Shepard, 1999). They brought police, prosecutors, judges, and other court personnel together with antidomestic-violence advocates and social service providers to cross-train and coordinate their responses to cases of partner abuse. As part of this process, advocates convinced officials throughout the criminal justice system to rethink their policies to enhance the safety of battered women. Advocates then led an intensive effort to foster interdisciplinary collaboration and design interagency procedures to further this goal. In the words of Ellen Pence (2001), one of the program's founders,

> We found opportunities to enhance women's safety in dispatch and patrol response procedures, booking procedures and bail hearings; when decisions were being made to prosecute, defer, or drop a case; during pretrial maneuvers, trial tactics, sentencing hearings, and revocations of probation. We proposed new legislation, new notions of practitioners' job duties, new department policies, new interagency protocols, and new administrative forms. (p. 338)

The coordinated community response model substantially reshaped the Duluth criminal justice system's approach to domestic violence crimes, and soon, jurisdictions throughout the country began to replicate the model (Pence, 2001).

Coordinated community responses succeeded in bringing together agencies that previously had rarely, if ever, communicated about their work. They provided opportunities for lawyers to talk with health care providers about how important properly documented medical records can be to a successful trial; for probation officers to talk with counselors about how to obtain a victim's perspective on her abusive partner's responsiveness to treatment; and for judges to hear from advocates about how better to understand the behavior of battered women in their courtrooms (Shepard & Pence, 1999). Coordinated community responses continue to be the centerpiece of domestic violence criminal justice system reform efforts nationwide.

Colocated Services

In addition to coordinating procedures, many communities have promoted comprehensive provision of services to battered women at a single site. These sites are designed to provide a wide range of criminal justice system, medical, counseling, and social services to battered women in a single, convenient location. Colocation of services can help to improve battered women's access to assistance, limit the number of times a victim must repeat her story to different service providers, and foster interdisciplinary collaboration with an eye toward increased safety (see Epstein, 1999).

Unified Domestic Violence Courts

A third major effort at coordination was the creation of unified domestic violence courts. Although such courts are structured in a variety of ways, they typically include a limited number of judicial officers who hear only domestic violence cases and receive specialized training, partnerships between the court and community agencies to improve service provision, in-court advocacy services, efforts to make the court system more accessible and less onerous for victims, and efforts to increase the consistency of court orders affecting a single family (Goodman & Epstein, 2008). Some unified domestic violence courts have brought together civil and criminal cases into a single unit, coordinating calendars so that victims need to appear less frequently and can better understand the judicial process. Others have brought together protection order and family law cases, such as divorce and custody, helping to improve access to both short- and long-term relief for families (Epstein, 1999).

Effectiveness of Coordinated Community Responses

Studies evaluating the effectiveness of coordinated community responses have focused on both victims' experiences with the process and rates of batterer recidivism. With regard to the first of these, survivors appear to experience coordinated community responses as empowering. One large-scale study of women in the justice system found that the more battered women perceived different agencies as working together, the more highly they rated them in terms of helpfulness and effectiveness, and the more satisfied they were both with the legal system in general and with their own individual case outcomes in particular (Zweig & Burt, 2006).

Studies investigating the impact of coordinated community responses on batterer recidivism are, however, far from clear. A number of researchers have investigated recidivism among men who have participated in coordinated community response systems composed of a wide variety of components (e.g. Murphy, Musser, & Maton, 1998; Shepard, Falk, & Elliot, 2002; Syers & Edleson, 1992). Syers and Edleson (1992), for example, found that although men who participated in more components of a coordinated response model in Minneapolis (i.e., they were arrested and under court order to receive treatment) had the lowest recidivism rates, these results were not statistically significant. In another quasi-experimental study, Murphy et al. (1998) used official data to determine that those men who participated in more components of the program model in Baltimore (prosecution, probation, and counseling) were less likely to become reinvolved in the justice system. But it is possible that the decrease in reinvolvement could be explained by the victims' decision to stop calling the police when the justice system proved ineffective in stopping their abusive partners' violence. More research is needed before the impact of coordinated community responses on rates of reabuse can be determined.

Unintended Negative Consequences

Despite a small body of positive findings related to coordinated community responses, the absence of attention to women's individual stories and needs thwarts the potential of such efforts. In most coordinated community response systems, victims are relegated to a peripheral status. Although their criminal cases are aggressively pursued, centralized access to a variety of resources is available, and case logistics are more likely to be coordinated, there still are few opportunities for victims to communicate their own goals, desires, material needs, and safety concerns to system actors with the power to dramatically affect their lives.

WHAT ARE THE NEXT STEPS?

Survivors of domestic violence have benefited enormously from recent reforms such as mandatory arrest, no-drop prosecution, civil protection order statutes, and coordinated community responses. The rapid pace and broad scope of these changes have been truly breathtaking. And yet, such responses still fail to reach many battered women, and recent reforms have themselves created new, unanticipated risks and challenges for numerous survivors. So where do we go from here? How do we continue to improve the justice system's response to IPV?

Renewed Focus on Women's Particular Voices

The justice system needs to undergo substantial change before it can meaningfully accommodate the needs of individual women. Although mandatory arrest laws and no-drop prosecution policies were adopted in large part to promote battered women's safety, they tend to be rigidly applied, even when doing so may expose women to more violence. The solution is greater flexibility. Starting with the criminal justice system, police and prosecutors should have limited authority to decide, in collaboration with a victim, whether in light of her particular circumstances arrest and prosecution make sense.

Prosecutors could take one step in this direction by considering the postponement of prosecution in some limited situations. Prosecutors could accumulate the evidence necessary to go forward but delay filing charges while the victim receives the advocacy services she needs to take action or to move beyond the batterer's psychological control and to assess her situation with greater clarity.

Increased communication is another important avenue toward greater flexibility within the criminal justice system. For prosecutors to choose a course that will best serve a battered woman, they need to have all pertinent information at their disposal at the initial, charging stage. In reality, however, they typically have limited time to devote to an individual case, especially at the outset, and thus tend to focus on the most recent incident of violence. By creating opportunities for advocates, attorneys, and survivors themselves to share more about the history and context of the most recent incident, prosecutors may be able to add charges that otherwise never would have been brought. These additional charges may increase the length of a jail sentence for the perpetrator, giving the victim additional time and space to create a new, safer life. Or, when appropriate, such discussions could result in a prosecutor agreeing to decline pursuit of certain charges, where doing so would increase the victim's sense of support and general willingness to cooperate (for an example of one such collaboration, see Epstein, Bell, & Goodman, 2003).

The civil justice system also could be substantially improved through increased flexibility and responsiveness to survivors' individual needs. One important step in this direction would be to eradicate the existing reflexive judicial bias in favor of partner separation. Judicial training might begin to alleviate this problem, but many judges are not particularly receptive to advocacy-based training programs (Epstein, 1999). Solid research comparing the psychological and physical security of battered women who choose to stay and those who are forced to leave against their will could be extraordinarily useful in any project designed to expand judicial perspectives. As noted previously, judges also tend to prefer joint custody awards in partner abuse cases; additional research and training on the risks battered women face when forced to maintain contact with abusive fathers is needed here as well.

To increase the voice of the victim in the context of coordinated community responses, coordination must be further developed to go beyond the coordinated initiation of cases (e.g., in a domestic violence intake center, where a victim can obtain "one-stop shopping" access to civil and criminal justice system advocates) and the coordinated logistics of cases (e.g., in a unified domestic violence court, where civil protection order and criminal prosecution cases may be scheduled for the same date, before the same judge). Meaningful coordination requires that all providers responding to a particular woman understand her specific needs and concerns. Service providers, including the prosecution, must routinely share case-specific information and even case-specific goals across agencies and providers to respond successfully to a client's needs. Lay advocates, who spend the most time in direct contact with survivors, often are best positioned to ensure that victims' voices are heard. But their meaningful participation in criminal justice system collaborations is currently curtailed by a cultural climate in which the views of legal professionals predominate. A new atmosphere, in which state actors understand and value advocates' perspectives, may not be realistic in the short term. One step toward reaching this goal, however, would be research demonstrating positive outcomes for such an approach in terms of victim safety and perpetrator accountability (Epstein, Bell, & Goodman, 2003).

Increased Opportunities for Economic Empowerment

Historically, there has been little connection between the justice system and the economic empowerment of litigants. In domestic violence cases, a victim may be informed about the possibility that she is eligible for a limited amount of state assistance through crime victims' compensation funds, and she may be referred to community agencies to assist her with welfare, food stamps, and housing. However, given the large numbers of victims who use the courts in their efforts to escape IPV, far more substantial links with antipoverty resources are needed.

Initial steps have been made in a handful of states to link civil protection order and longer term child support cases, thus increasing the likelihood that a parent–survivor will receive at least one form of relatively long-term economic assistance (Epstein, 1999). Additional justice system efforts might include the provision of sufficient resources to support a survivor's interactions with the court, including funds for transportation, quality child care, and compensation for workdays missed for attendance at court hearings.

Alternatives to the Justice System

Even with substantial improvements, however, the justice system may still fail, or even create real risks for, some battered women. As a result, it is crucial that we explore viable alternatives that could enhance women's choices and control. One of the most promising—and controversial—of these potential alternatives is *restorative justice*. Restorative justice has been defined as "a broad range of informal practices designed to meet the needs of victims, offenders, and communities in the wake of crime" (Ptacek & Frederick, 2009). Hearing, restoring, and empowering individuals and their larger communities, consistent with the survivor's culture and context, is the central goal (Stubbs, 2004; Zehr, 2004). Conceptually, such an approach could fit the needs of many survivors who are not sufficiently supported by the justice system.

At a more concrete level, restorative justice approaches deemphasize the role of the state, focusing instead on structured dialogues within families and communities, with the goal of finding a way for the offender to make up for his wrongdoing, including apologizing and making some sort of reparations (Coker, 2004; Curtis-Fawley & Daly, 2005; Grauwiler & Mills, 2004; Stubbs, 2004; Zehr, 2004). Typically, meeting participants include the victim, family and community members, and a facilitator; some models also include the accused. This process may occur in conjunction with or independent of the criminal justice system.

To date, restorative justice practices have occurred primarily in juvenile justice situations; in the context of intimate partner abuse, restorative justice has been tried only on a small scale, and virtually no reliable evaluation data exist. Feminist critics and battered women's advocates have expressed a range of concerns about using the approach in the context of domestic violence. First, by moving the response to domestic violence outside the reach of the criminal justice system—as some restorative justice models do—we may unwittingly create "a second rate justice that offers little protection for battered women" (Coker, 2002, p. 149). Second, current restorative justice processes rarely incorporate an understanding of the particular dynamics of abusive partnerships (specifically, the imbalance of power between victim and perpetrator) or of the broader social context that serves to reinforce abusive behavior (Curtis-Fawley & Daly, 2005). Third, restorative justice models prioritize communication between the survivor and those closest to her, but it may be that these are the very people who were unwilling or unable to support or protect her. Indeed, as Coker (2002) noted, "family and community are often the primary supports for male control of women" (p. 129). Despite these real concerns, restorative justice concepts hold some promise for survivors whose primary needs cannot be addressed through the justice system—particularly women who wish to remain a part of their communities, or who choose to stay with their partners but hope to increase their safety. Coker, for example, suggested the exploration of "transformative justice" models, which would "address the structural inequalities that frame the battering experience for men and women in subordinated communities, provide material and social support for battered women, and hold men who batter responsible for their violence" (p. 150).

The promise of restorative justice remedies for survivors of IPV remains relatively unexplored. Although the scope and seriousness of advocacy concerns dictate that such work must proceed with real caution, a variety of carefully structured demonstration projects should be encouraged as a potential complement to justice system remedies.

CONCLUSION

Over the past several decades, the justice system has made enormous strides toward taking IPV seriously and responding more forcefully to the needs of victims. But until the justice system is able to respond directly to the particular obstacles, needs, and goals of diverse battered women, the justice system will remain inaccessible or even harmful to many survivors of IPV.

REFERENCES

Anderson, M., Gillig, P., Sitaker, M., McCloskey, K., Malloy, K., & Grigsby, N. (2003). "Why doesn't she just leave?" A descriptive study of victim reported impediments to her safety. *Journal of Family Violence, 18,* 151–155. doi:10.1023/A:1023564404773

Bennett Cattaneo, L., & Goodman, L. A. (2010). Through the lens of therapeutic jurisprudence: The relationship between empowerment in the court system and wellbeing for intimate partner violence victims. *Journal of Interpersonal Violence, 25,* 481–502. doi:10.1177/0886260509334282

Buzawa, E., Hotaling, G. T., & Byrne, J. (2006). Understanding the impact of prior abuse and prior victimization on the decision to forgo criminal justice assistance in domestic violence incidents: A life-course perspective. *Brief Treatment and Crisis Intervention, 7,* 55–76. doi: 10.1093/brief-treatment/mhl020.

Buzawa, E. S., & Buzawa, C. G. (1992). The scientific evidence is not conclusive: Arrest is no panacea. In R. J. Gelles & D. R. Loseke (Eds.), *Current controversies in family violence* (pp. 337–341). Thousand Oaks, CA: Sage.

Cahn, D. D. (1992). *Conflict in intimate relationships.* New York, NY: Guilford Press.

Coker, D. (2002). Transformative justice: Anti-subordination processes in cases of domestic violence. In J. Braithwaite & H. Strand (Eds.), *Restorative justice and family violence* (pp. 128–152). Cambridge, England: Cambridge University Press.

Coker, D. (2004). Race, poverty, and the crime centered response to domestic violence. *Violence Against Women, 10,* 1331–1353.

Crenshaw, K. (1991). Mapping the margins: Intersectionality, identity politics, and violence against women of color. *Stanford Law Review, 43,* 1241–1299. doi:10.2307/1229039

Curtis-Fawley, S., & Daly, K. (2005). Gendered violence and restorative justice: The views of victim advocates. *Violence Against Women, 11,* 603–638. doi:10.1177/1077801205274488

DeJong, C., & Burgess-Proctor, A. (2006). A summary of personal protection order statutes in the United States. *Violence Against Women, 12,* 68–88. doi:10.1177/1077801205277720

Dugan, L., Nagin, D., & Rosenfeld, R. (2001). *Exposure reduction or backlash? The effects of domestic violence resources on intimate partner homicide: Final report.* Washington, DC: U.S. Department of Justice.

Eisenberg, S., & Micklow, P. (1974). *The assaulted wife: "Catch 22" revisited.* Unpublished manuscript.

Epstein, D. (1999). Effective intervention in domestic violence cases: Rethinking the role of prosecutors, judges, and the court system. *Yale Journal of Law and Feminism, 11,* 3–50.

Epstein, D. (2002). Procedural justice: Tempering the state's response to domestic violence, *William and Mary Law Review, 43* 1843–1905.

Epstein, D., Bell, M. E., & Goodman, L. A. (2003). Transforming aggressive prosecution policies: Prioritizing victims' long-term safety in the prosecution of domestic violence cases. *Journal of Gender, Social Policy and the Law, 11*, 465–498.

Erez, E., & Belknap, J. (1998). In their own words: Battered women's assessment of the criminal processing system's responses. *Violence and Victims, 13*, 251–268.

Erez, E., & Tontodonato, P. (1990). The effect of victim participation in sentencing on sentence outcomes. *Criminology, 28*, 451–474. doi:10.1111/j.1745-9125.1990.tb01334.x

Finn, M. A. (2003). *Effects of victims' experiences with prosecutors on victim empowerment and re-occurrence of intimate partner violence, final report.* Washington, DC: National Institute of Justice.

Finn, P., & Colson, S. (1990). *Civil protection orders: Legislation, current court practice, and enforcement.* Washington, DC: National Institute of Justice.

Fischer, K., & Rose, M. (1995). When "enough is enough": Battered women's decision making around court orders of protection. *Crime and Delinquency, 41*, 414–429. doi:10.1177/0011128795041004003

Fleury, R. E., Sullivan, C. M., & Bybee, D. I. (2000). When ending the relationship doesn't end the violence: Women's experiences of violence by former partners. *Violence Against Women, 6*, 1363–1383. doi:10.1177/10778010022183695

Ford, D. A., & Regoli, M. J. (1992). The preventive impacts of policies for prosecuting wife batterers. In E. S. Buzawa & C. G. Buzawa (Eds.), *Domestic violence: The changing criminal justice response* (pp. 181–207). Westport, CT: Auburn House.

Goodman, L., Bennett, L., & Dutton, M. A. (1999). Obstacles to domestic violence victims' cooperation with the criminal prosecution of their abusers: The role of social support. *Violence and Victims, 14*, 427–444.

Goodman, L. A., & Epstein, D. (2008). *Listening to battered women: A survivor-centered approach to advocacy, mental health, and justice.* Washington, DC: American Psychological Association. doi:10.1037/11651-000

Goodman, L. A., Smyth, K. F., Borges, A. M., & Singer, R. (2009). When crises collide: How intimate partner violence and poverty intersect to shape women's mental health and coping. *Trauma, Violence & Abuse, 10*, 306–329. doi:10.1177/1524838009339754

Goodmark, L. (2003). Law is the answer? Do we know that for sure? *Saint Louis University Public Law Review, 23*, 7–48.

Grauwiler, P., & Mills, L.G. (2004). Moving beyond the criminal justice paradigm. A radical restorative justice approach to intimate abuse. *Journal of Sociology & Social Welfare, 31*, 46–69.

Hanna, C. (1996). No right to choose: Mandated victim participation in domestic violence prosecution. *Harvard Law Review, 109*, 1849–1910. doi:10.2307/1342079

Hare, S. C. (2006). What do battered women want? Victims' opinions on prosecution. *Violence and Victims, 21*, 611–628. doi:10.1891/vivi.21.5.611

Harrell, A., & Smith, B. (1996). Effects of restraining orders on domestic violence victims. In E. S. Buzawa, & C. G. Buzawa (Eds.), *Do arrests and restraining orders work?* (pp. 214–242). Thousand Oaks, CA: Sage.

Hart, W. L., Ashcroft, J., Burgess, A., Flanagan, N., Meese, U., Milton, C. . . . Seward, F. (1984). *Family violence: Attorney General's Task Force final report* (ERIC# ED251762). Washington, DC: U.S. Department of Justice.

Hemmens, C., Strom, K., & Schlegel, E. (1998). Gender bias in the courts: A review of the literature. *Sociological Imagination, 35,* 22–42.

Holt, V. L., Kernic, M., Wolf, M., & Rivara, F. (2003). Do protection orders affect the likelihood of future partner violence and injury? *American Journal of Preventive Medicine, 24,* 16–21. doi:10.1016/S0749-3797(02)00576-7

Kane, R. J. (2000). Police responses to restraining orders in domestic violence incidents: Identifying the custody-threshold thesis. *Criminal Justice and Behavior, 27,* 561–580.

Keilitz, S. L. (1997). *National Center for State Courts, civil protection orders: The benefits and limitations for victims of domestic violence.* Williamsburg, VA: National Center for State Courts.

Klein, A. R. (1996). Re-abuse in a population of court-restrained male batterers: Why restraining orders don't work. In E. S. Buzawa & C. G. Buzawa (Eds.), *Do arrests and restraining orders work?* (pp. 192–213). Thousand Oaks, CA: Sage.

Latta, R. E., & Goodman, L. A. (2005). Considering the interplay of cultural context and service provision in intimate partner violence. *Violence Against Women, 11,* 1441–1464. doi:10.1177/1077801205280273

Logan, T. K., Shannon, L., & Walker, R. (2005). Protective orders in rural and urban areas: A multiple perspective study. *Violence Against Women, 11,* 876–911. doi:10.1177/1077801205276985

Logan, T. K., Shannon, L., Walker, R., & Faragher, T. M. (2006). Protective orders: Questions and conundrums. *Trauma, 7,* 175–205.

Loke, T. (1997). Trapped in domestic violence: The impact of United States immigration laws on battered immigrant women. *The Boston University Public Interest Law Journal, 6,* 589–628.

Maxwell, C. D., Garner, J. H., & Fagan, J. A. (1999, June). *The impact of arrest on domestic violence: Results from five policy experiments.* Paper presented at the Research in Progress Seminar, Washington, DC.

McFarlane, J., Malecha, A., Gist, J., Watson, K., Batten, E., Hall, I., & Smith, S. (2004). Protection orders and intimate partner violence: An 18-month study of 150 black, Hispanic, and white women. *American Journal of Public Health, 94,* 613–618. doi:10.2105/AJPH.94.4.613

Meier, J. (2003). Domestic violence, child custody, and child protection: Understanding judicial resistance and imagining the solutions. *Journal of Gender, Social Policy and the Law, 11,* 657–725.

Miccio, G. K. (2005). A house divided: Mandatory arrest, domestic violence, and the conservatization of the battered women's movement. *Houston Law Review, 42,* 237–323.

Mills, L. G. (1998). Mandatory arrest and prosecution policies for domestic violence: A critical literature review and the case for more research to test victim empowerment approaches. *Criminal Justice and Behavior, 25,* 306–318. doi:10.1177/009 3854898025003002

Murphy, C. M., Musser, P. H., & Maton, K. I. (1998). Coordinated community intervention for domestic abusers: Intervention system involvement and criminal recidivism. *Journal of Family Violence, 13,* 263–284. doi:10.1023/A:1022841 022524

Omnibus Consolidated Appropriations Act of 1997, 104 Pub. L. 208, § 350 (1996), codified at 8 U.S.C. § 1227(a)(2)(E)(2006).

Pence, E. (2001). Advocacy on behalf of battered women. In C. Renzetti, J. Edleson, & R. Bergen (Eds.), *Sourcebook on VAW* (pp. 329–344). Thousand Oaks, CA: Sage.

Pence, E. L., & Shepard, M. L. (1999). An introduction: Developing a coordinated community response. In M. F. Shepard & E. L. Pence (Eds.), *Coordinating community responses to domestic violence: Lessons from Duluth and beyond* (pp. 3–23). Thousand Oaks, CA: Sage.

Ptacek, J., & Frederick, L. (2009). *Restorative justice and intimate partner violence.* Retrieved from http://new.vawnet.org/category/Main_Doc.php?docid=1656

Shepard, M. E., Falk, D. R., & Elliot, B. A. (2002). Enhancing coordinated community responses to reduce recidivism in cases of domestic violence. *Journal of Interpersonal Violence, 17,* 551–569. doi:10.1177/0886260502017005005

Shepard, M. F., & Pence, E. L. (Eds.). (1999). *Coordinating community responses to domestic violence: Lessons from Duluth and beyond.* Thousand Oaks, CA: Sage.

Sherman, L. W., & Berk, R. A. (1984). The specific deterrent effects of arrest for domestic assault. *American Sociological Review, 49,* 261–272. doi:10.2307/2095575

Spitzberg, B. H. (2002). The tactical topography of stalking victimization and management. *Trauma, 3,* 261–288.

Stubbs, J. (2004). *Restorative justice, domestic violence and family violence* (Issues Paper No. 9). Sydney, Australia: Australian Domestic and Family Violence Clearinghouse.

Syers, M., & Edleson, J. L. (1992). The combined effects of coordinated criminal justice intervention in woman abuse. *Journal of Interpersonal Violence, 7,* 490–502. doi:10.1177/088626092007004005

Tjaden, P., & Thoennes, N. (2000). *Extent, nature and consequences of intimate partner violence* (NCJ 181867). Washington, DC: U.S. Department of Justice, Office of Justice Programs, National Institute of Justice.

Websdale, N. (2001). *Policing the poor: From slave plantation to public housing.* Boston, MA: Northeastern University Press.

Weisz, A. N. (2002). Prosecution of batterers: Views of African American battered women. *Violence and Victims, 17*(1), 19–34. doi:10.1891/vivi.17.1.19.33642

Wooldredge, J., & Thistlethwaite, A. (2002). Reconsidering domestic violence recidivism: Conditioned effects of legal controls by individual and aggregate levels of stake in conformity. *Journal of Quantitative Criminology, 18*, 45–70. doi:10.1023/A:1013292812895

Zehr, H. (2004). *Critical issues in restorative justice.* Monsey, NY: Criminal Justice Press.

Zweig, J. M., & Burt, M. R. (2006). Predicting case outcomes and women's perceptions of the legal system's response to domestic violence and sexual assault: Does interaction between community agencies matter? *Criminal Justice Policy Review, 17*, 202–233. doi:10.1177/0887403405280944

12

PRIMARY PREVENTION OF DOMESTIC VIOLENCE

SUSAN L. STAGGS AND PAUL A. SCHEWE

In general, scholars are in agreement that this is an exciting time for the primary prevention of domestic violence (DV). The field has taken quantum leaps forward since its recent inception (e.g., Hammond, Whitaker, Lutzker, Mercy, & Chin, 2006; Mihalic, Irwin, Elliott, Fagan, & Hansen, 2001). However, scholars also concur that difficult work is just beginning. Critical near-term priorities include implementing interventions that target multiple factors at multiple ecological levels across the life span, accounting for multiple forms of prevention activities and implementation processes and settings, and increasing the methodological rigor of evaluations.

These priorities illustrate the developmental aspect of DV prevention science in that they reflect a discipline in flux. The first DV prevention efforts began about 20 years ago, fueled by a still-influential feminist approach. As the field matured, a family violence perspective on DV emerged. This perspective viewed DV as a form of familial dysfunction, linking it to other forms of family violence, such as child abuse (Stith, 2006). More recently, scholars have put forth a new generation of theories that integrate feminist, family violence, developmental, and ecological perspectives (e.g., Bronfenbrenner, 1979; Edelson, 2000; Kelly, 1966; Heise, 1998; Whitaker, Hall, & Coker, 2009). These theoretical advances drove changes in the way DV prevention initiatives were designed and implemented. Over time, as researchers learned more about DV and the science of prevention evolved, DV prevention initiatives became more sophisticated and interdisciplinary, targeting multiple risk and protective factors simultaneously. Separate prevention subfields of primary, secondary (conducted with at-risk populations), and tertiary (conducted with victims and perpetrators) prevention emerged. Thus, there are at present many forms of DV prevention. *Primary prevention* initiatives aim to better educate the public at large and to intervene before the onset of violence. *Secondary prevention* aims to address populations with elevated risk and few protective factors such as children exposed to violence, child victims or perpetrators of bullying, or couples with high levels of stress or conflict. A third set of initiatives, often referred to as *tertiary prevention* or treatment, .is designed to prevent revictimization or to reduce rates of future perpetration (Stith, 2006).

This chapter reviews the state of DV prevention research and practice. We discuss what is known about DV prevention, provide a critical analysis of existing findings, and delineate gaps in research and practice. We close with a series of recommendations for enhancing the primary prevention of DV. This review focuses on primary prevention: initiatives designed to prevent DV before it happens. Primary prevention of DV means preventing first instances of victimization and perpetration of psychological and physical violence between intimate opposite-sex and same-sex partners in dating or marital relationships. In contrast to secondary and tertiary prevention efforts that target individuals across the life span, primary prevention often targets children, as its aim is to prevent (rather than reduce the negative impact of) maladaptive developmental trajectories. One of the difficulties in discussing preventive interventions is that existing conceptual frameworks are inadequate to capture the complexity of the work and bridge the research–practice gap. The focus up to now in DV prevention science has been on the development and evaluation of programs such as school-based prevention curricula. Programs were implemented and postprogram changes in target populations were documented. Evaluations did not take the complex process of implementation into account.

Such a heavy focus on programs led scholars to insufficiently examine the support and delivery mechanisms through which the programs reached their target audiences and the process of disseminating best practices information in a format accessible to practitioners. A good program might not be implemented as planned because the implementers lacked the time, resources, or money to implement the program properly or were unaware of how to incorporate the latest research findings (Saul et al., 2008). Rather than asking the question, "How effective is this program?" scholars have begun asking, "How effective is this particular implementation of the program?" and taking into account implementation processes as well as programmatic outcomes in their evaluations of DV prevention efforts.

In the midst of the larger shift in prevention science toward a consideration of implementation processes, there has been a growing realization that many existing prevention programs are not based on sound science, in part because the academic community has not been engaged in synthesizing and translating research for consumption by practitioners (Saul et al., 2008). To address this issue, the Centers for Disease Control and Prevention (CDC) has funded organizations such as the National Online Resource Center on Violence Against Women and the National Resource Center on Domestic Violence to promote use of research findings among practitioners and the public. The CDC has itself also been active in translating research for practitioners, publishing the excellent *Best Practices in Youth Violence Prevention—A Sourcebook for Community Action* (Thornton, Craft, Dahlberg, Lynch, & Baer, 2002), which includes accessible guidelines on choosing, implementing, and evaluating violence prevention programs.

In a major recent initiative, the CDC Division of Violence Prevention gathered violence scholars and practitioners together in a series of planning sessions to create a new way of thinking about DV prevention. One outcome of this process is the Interactive Systems Framework for Dissemination and Implementation (Wandersman et al., 2008), a conceptual model that integrates and overcomes limitations of existing prevention frameworks by more fully accounting for the context in which prevention initiatives occur. This model was developed through a special effort to reduce the gap between research and practice in violence prevention, and it is adapted here to frame DV prevention efforts.

WHAT DO WE KNOW?

Sequence and Structure of DV Prevention

The Interactive Systems Framework for Dissemination and Implementation is a dynamic, nonlinear model in which prevention activities are shown to be influenced by four external factors: existing research, available funding, climate, and policy. Here, concepts from the original model are modified to relate what the authors of this chapter believe is the typical linear sequence of events in DV prevention. In the *Research System*, researchers review evaluation results published in journals or on websites, synthesize what is known about prevention, prepare the results in a format accessible to the relevant audience (usually practitioners), and then disseminate information. According to Wandersman and colleagues (2008), prevention works by introducing new ideas, or *innovations*, into settings where prevention might occur, such as at-risk families, schools, judicial systems, or social service agencies. Innovations are categorized as principles, policies, processes, or programs (the 4 Ps), rather than being narrowly conceived of as programs. *Principles* are qualities of innovations that make them more effective, such as timing interventions for the earliest possible developmental stage. *Policies* are legal, formal, and informal governmental or organizational rules for behavior, such as mandated reporting of suspected child abuse in emergency rooms. *Processes* are activities performed by individuals or organizations charged with preventing domestic violence, such as data sharing protocols. In DV primary prevention, the principles, policies, and process innovations normally attempt to increase the use of best practices and build the capacity of organizations that implement prevention activities.

Programs are specific curricula, interventions, and other sets of strategies or actions designed to reduce violence. DV prevention programs can operate at the individual, family or peer group, community, and/or societal levels of the social ecology. Individual level interventions include *educational programs* designed to address knowledge, attitudes, and skills to promote healthy relationships (e.g., Cornelius & Resseguie, 2007; Ferguson, San Miguel, Kilburn, & Sanchez, 2007; Hickman, Jaycox, & Aronoff, 2004). Some of the most effective and oldest prevention innovations are *family and relationship strengthening programs*, which ordinarily attempt to create more positive, healthy environments in families that are at risk of experiencing violence, by increasing communication skills among couples, parenting skills among caregivers, and addressing young children's exposure to DV among families (e.g., Graham-Bermann & Hughes, 2003; Kumpfer & Alvarado, 2003). At the community level, *public awareness campaigns* attempt to change harmful cultural or community norms and attitudes (Campbell & Manganello, 2006). Finally, some programs in the prevention community *promote nonviolent cultures* or healthy conflict resolution at the societal level as a way of reducing violent norms and behaviors (e.g., Erickson, Mattaini, & McGuire, 2004; Mattaini & McGuire, 2006).

Implementation Systems receive innovations from the Research System (Wandersman et al., 2008). Implementation Systems have general and innovation-specific capacity to successfully support and deliver promising practices. Supporting innovations involves handling the administrative aspects of implementation, such as providing technical assistance, developing education and media materials, tracking implementation progress, and managing budgets. Delivering innovations means targeting audiences or executives who implement policies. This delivery is often performed by instructors, health professionals, DV advocates, and practitioners. Innovations are ultimately delivered to universal or at-risk populations, often students within schools or families residing in low-income, high-crime communities. Principle, policy, and process innovations are normally implemented in communities or public health systems. Programs are implemented in a variety of settings. Public awareness campaigns are introduced into community and home settings via public service announcements, billboards, or posters. Innovations directed to countering children's exposure to violence, bullying, and teen dating violence are usually delivered in school and family settings. Nonviolence promotion and violence prevention curricula are often a part of preschool, elementary, and secondary school socioemotional learning initiatives. More intensive programmatic innovations may occur in social service settings, where professionals attempt to strengthen at-risk families through parenting, communications, and conflict-resolution training (Mihalic et al., 2001). *Evaluation Results* are released that document the effectiveness of implemented innovations. These results are received by the Research System and used to improve programs and increase their impact.

Prevention Innovations Specific to DV

Principles, Processes, and Policies

There are no known formal prevention activities that have solely sought to infuse existing or future efforts with principles, or best practices, although such interventions may hold promise for the future, as research indicates that they can make the difference between success and failure (Mercy & Hammond, 2001). Funding agencies may stipulate adherence to a set of principles, and implementers may seek to infuse their innovations with as many good prevention principles as possible. Best practice principles may and in fact often are not solely targeted at improving programs; they may be concerned with building the capacity of the Research and Implementation Systems.

DV Prevention Programs

A number of programs exist that are intended to impact DV. Common types of DV prevention programs include public awareness campaigns, programs designed to address children's exposure to violence, bullying, teen dating violence programs, nonviolence and conflict resolution programs, and family-strengthening programs. Public awareness programs aimed at changing harmful cultural and peer group norms associated with acceptance of DV are one type of prevention innovation aimed at the societal or community level. An example of this type of program is the There's No Excuse campaign, which used television/print media and bumper stickers to change people's attitudes toward DV (Klein, Campbell, Soler, & Ghez, 1997). Some interventions are directed at the level of the family or the individual and aim to prevent future adult DV by reducing the impact of children's exposure to violence, addressing bullying, and preventing teen dating violence, as these are strongly linked to involvement in DV in adulthood (Edleson, 2000; Mihalic et al., 2001). Others are designed to create healthy communication and conflict resolution skills. These interventions often attempt to change behavior by changing how people cognitively and emotionally react to stressors and interact with their families, peers, and partners. The Safe Dates program is an example of a primary program for prevention of teen dating violence. Safe Dates is a school-based intervention for eighth-graders that includes a student theatrical production, 7.5 hr of psychosocial education delivered in health and physical education classes, and a poster contest (Foshee et al., 2004). An example of a program focused on children's exposure to violence is The Learning Club, in which children of abused women received an average of 9 hr per week of mentoring and 10 weeks of psychosocial education (Sullivan, Bybee, & Allen, 2002). Nonviolence and conflict resolution programs are usually implemented within communities or schools and attempt to change the social climate by providing individuals in these settings with nonviolent ways of resolving conflict and creating a positive environment. An example is the PeaceBuilders program, implemented in schools. This program uses teacher, parent, and child education coupled with community media campaigns to create PeaceBuilders, people who frequently praise others and engage in proactive efforts to resolve conflict peacefully (Embry, Flannery, Vazsonyi, Powell, & Athna, 1996).

Increasingly, multiple types of preventive innovations are introduced. The Chicago Safe Start initiative to address child exposure to violence included a public awareness campaign, training for health care professionals, individual, group, and family therapy for caregivers and children exposed to violence, and a systems change component designed to change policies and processes to include screening and referral for violence exposure in child-serving systems such as schools, police departments, and social service agencies (Staggs, Schewe, White, Davis, & Dill, 2007). Best practices in each of the prevention systems, as well as information on what works in prevention programming, are discussed below.

General Types of Prevention Innovations

General Prevention Principles, Policies, and Processes

Examining the principles and characteristics of prevention innovations for substance abuse, violence, risky sexual behavior, and academic failure in 35 published evaluations, Nation and colleagues (2003) found nine principles associated with program success. Effective prevention programs are comprehensive; they introduce multiple innovations into multiple settings. Programs that include educational components should include interactive, hands-on activities that use diverse methods of instruction and aim to develop skills as well as increase knowledge. Furthermore, it is necessary to expose target populations to a sufficient dosage of the intervention (Nation et al., 2003, p. 452). Although no specific recommendations in terms of exposure length are given, participants in effective programs are exposed to enough of the innovation to produce an effect and are also provided with follow-up sessions to ensure maintenance of initial effects. Programs should be based on empirically validated theory and build positive relationships among participants and their families. Successful programs are introduced as early as possible in the life span and are socioculturally relevant. Such programs are delivered by well-trained staff and carefully evaluated (Nation et al., 2003).

Programs Not Specific to DV Prevention

Surprisingly, based on the evidence available now, most of the effective programs are not those designed specifically to prevent DV. Such programs are too new to have a sufficient evidentiary base, although they may in time prove effective. Instead, scholars, for the present, should think about good DV prevention as programs that intervene very early in an at-risk child's life to increase individual and familial prosocial behavior and reduce aggressive responses to environmental stimuli.

HOW DO WE KNOW IT?

Although there are many reviews of DV prevention programs (e.g., Cornelius & Resseguie, 2007; Edleson, 2000; Ferguson, San Miguel, Kilburn, & Sanchez, 2007; Graham-Bermann & Hughes, 2003; Kerns & Prinz, 2002; Kumpfer & Alvarado, 2003; Tolan, Gorman-Smith, & Henry, 2006; Whitaker et al., 2006), it is difficult to definitively determine program effectiveness because the evidentiary criteria used by reviewers vary in terms of comprehensiveness and inclusion of critical data such as cost–benefit information (Mihalic et al., 2001). To address this issue, in 2001 the Blueprints for Violence Prevention initiative was launched by the Office of Juvenile Justice and Delinquency Prevention of the U.S. Department of Justice. This initiative brought together prominent violence scholars, who conducted an exhaustive, multitiered review of 500 violence prevention programs. Criteria that were used to determine effectiveness included adequate power, low attrition, robust outcome measures, replication, analysis of mediating factors, and cost–benefit analysis (Mihalic et al., 2001).

Of the 500 programs reviewed, only 11 met these strict standards. Of those, only five were designed as primary violence prevention programs.

These programs are described later in this section. There are other programs with promising results, such as the Safe Dates program for teen dating violence prevention (Foshee et al., 2004), but they have not been in existence long enough to have been widely replicated or to have measured long-term behavior change. They are therefore designated as *promising* rather than *proven* in this review. Most of the proven programs focus primarily on family strengthening, although they may intervene in multiple ways and in multiple settings such as in schools, peer groups, families, and communities.

Proven Programs

Because of the longevity, replication, and rigorous evaluations performed on family-strengthening programs, they comprise the major proven approach to DV prevention. A family-strengthening intervention, the Prenatal and Infancy Home Visitation by Nurses program, works to prevent adult DV. This program intervenes with low-income, at-risk first-time mothers in their homes (Olds et al., 1998). Trained nurses visit families once or twice a week in an intensive intervention to promote maternal, child, and environmental health. Participation in this program reduces, by up to 79%, exposure to child neglect and domestic violence in the homes. Fifteen years after program implementation, participating children were 80% less likely than control group children to have been convicted of a crime and over 50% less likely to have engaged in antisocial behavior (Olds et al., 1998). Program costs are recovered by the time the children reach 4 years of age. By the time they reach the age of 15, cost savings are estimated to be 4 times the original investment due in part to reductions in crime and welfare expenditures and increases in contributions to the tax base.

The Incredible Years Series is a program that combines parent, teacher, and child interventions to promote social competence and prevent conduct problems in youth (Webster-Stratton & Hammond, 1997). The program trains parents in parenting skills and addresses family risk factors for DV. Teacher training focuses on promoting prosocial behavior in the classroom, whereas child training develops emotional intelligence, perspective-taking, conflict resolution, and anger management. This program results in reduced aggression in over 66% of child participants and requires only a minimal initial cost investment (in materials and group leader training) that is quickly recouped.

Big Brothers and Big Sisters of America is a well-known and time-tested program that results in a 32% reduction in physical violence among participants when compared with a control group. It is cost-effective as well, with a taxpayer and crime-victim cost savings per participant of $2,143. In this program, adult mentors meet with children three to five times per month to engage in prosocial activities tailored to the needs of individual children (Mihalic et al., 2001).

Functional Family Therapy (FFT) is a family program with three phases: engagement and motivation, which focuses on teaching cognitive reframing techniques; behavior change, which focuses on culturally appropriate changes in behavior; and generalization, which concentrates on preventing relapse and generalizing good behavior to multiple contexts. Length of participation is determined by the extent of familial dysfunction; most families receive a 12-hr dose of the program over a 3-month period. After 1 year, 36% of control group participants were convicted of crimes, compared to 20% of those in the program. Although the program is relatively expensive, costing an average of $2,068 per participant, it pays off in taxpayer and victim cost savings of $22,739 per participant (Mihalic et al., 2001).

Like FFT, Multisystemic Therapy, or MST, is an intensive home, school, and community approach that has proven effective in reducing DV. MST improves parenting and child social skills by pairing therapists with parents to collaborate in formulating and implementing customized intervention plans. MST includes parenting, peer, and school interventions at a dosage of 60 hr over 4 months. MST results in a reduction of up to 70% in rates of rearrest by juvenile offenders 4 years after program implementation. It is intensive and costly to implement, with an average cost per participant of $4,540, but, like FFT, results in significant cost savings over time—$61,068 per participant (Henggeler, 1997).

One bullying prevention program has also proven its effectiveness. The Olweus Bullying Prevention Program has delivery staff work with schools, classrooms, parents, and at-risk children to reduce the incidence and harmful effects of bullying. Schools administer surveys to document the prevalence of bullying and implement classroom and individual interventions for those who bully or are bullied. In classrooms, teachers set out antibullying rules and meet with students and parents to reduce bullying. Staff also intervene individually with parents, bullies, and bullying victims. This program reduces bullying by up to 50%, and effects are maintained up to 2 years after program implementation. The program also produces improvements in school climate and reductions in antisocial behavior (Olweus, 1993), although the program's cost-effectiveness is unknown.

Promising Programs

Although the programs described in this section have not been implemented or evaluated enough to meet the strict criteria that proven programs have met, they nevertheless show strong promise. Two such programs were identified in a 2005 review of 11 primary DV prevention programs (Whitaker et al., 2006). The Safe Dates program (Foshee et al., 2004) and the Youth Relationships Project (Wolfe et al., 2003) have both shown the ability to change long-term behavior. Safe Dates is designed to improve prosocial skills and change harmful norms regarding dating violence. It is implemented in eighth- and ninth-grade classrooms (7.5 hr of programming) and in the communities in which students reside. Strategies include training community health providers in dating violence prevention, holding poster contests and theatrical productions in schools, and teaching students about the right and wrong ways to interact with romantic partners. Safe Dates produced reductions in physical and sexual violence among participants that, when compared with a control group, were maintained after 4 years. The Youth Relationships Project promotes healthy, nonviolent interpersonal problem solving and discourages rigid gender role stereotyping by intervening with 14- to 16-year-old victims of child maltreatment. This program provides 36 hr of programming in classroom and community settings. Activities include guest speakers, role playing, and videos in the classroom and fundraising and community awareness in the community. This program produced reductions in physical violence that were greater for participants than for a control group.

The Prevention and Relationship Enhancement Program (PREP) is a primary prevention program that focuses on enhancing couples' communication and conflict resolution skills (Markman, Stanley, & Blumberg, 2001). PREP is designed for couples who are planning marriage, with the aim of inoculating the marriage from future distress. PREP addresses risk factors for marital violence that include poor communication, negative reciprocity, and deficits in conflict management. PREP is a 12-hr program that teaches couples communication skills designed to promote focused and noncritical discussions, problem-solving skills, and self-regulation of affect (Markman, Floyd, Stanley, & Storaasli, 1988). Couples using the skills taught in PREP workshops report greater satisfaction with conflict discussions, greater relationship satisfaction, and lower levels of conflict escalation. Follow-up research has also shown that couples receiving PREP training were less likely to engage in physical aggression up to four years after learning PREP skills (Markman, Renick, Floyd, Stanley, & Clements, 1993).

Programs With Insufficient Evidence

There is no compelling evidence that public awareness campaigns change behavior, although there do appear to be small effects for attitude change (Campbell & Manganello, 2006). Most antibullying programs do not produce reductions in violent behavior, although the Olweus program mentioned earlier is an exception (Clayton, Baliff-Spanvill, & Hunsaker, 2001; Ferguson et al., 2007). Although some show promise, most programs directed at children's exposure to violence and teen dating violence have not amassed enough evidence to be considered effective for general adoption (Cornelius & Resseguie, 2007; Graham-Bermann & Hughes, 2003; Hickman et al., 2004). However, three violence exposure programs—The Learning Club, Project Support, and the Kids Club—were cited as promising in a recent review (Graham-Bermann & Hughes, 2003), even though they have not been widely replicated. These programs intervene with children of mothers when the families leave DV shelters or with children who have been exposed to parental violence.

Finally, innovations that seek to promote nonviolent cultures and peaceful conflict resolution have not yet reached a point at which their effectiveness can be adequately determined. However, preliminary evidence for many of these programs, although not meeting the stringent standards used by the Blueprints for Violence Prevention evaluators, is strong and bodes well. Specifically, Aggression Replacement Training, Anger Coping, BrainPower, Child Development Project, Good Behavior Game, I Can Problem Solve, and Positive Action have been cited as exemplars (Clayton, Baliff-Spanvill, & Hunsaker, 2001; Mattaini & McGuire, 2006).

WHERE ARE THE GAPS AND WEAKNESSES IN EXISTING KNOWLEDGE?

Numerous innovations for the primary prevention of DV have been developed, but only a handful show robust evidence of success. There are many reasons for this, but the overarching factor appears to be the newness of prevention science in general and DV primary prevention in particular. Simply put, we do not yet have sufficient information to determine how effective most DV prevention programs are. Researchers have documented a set of remarkably similar shortcomings across the different types of innovations and their corresponding bodies of evaluation results. This and subsequent sections use the modified Interactive Systems Framework for Dissemination and Implementation to critically analyze what is known about prevention, delineate gaps between what we know and what we need to know, and make recommendations for future research and practice.

Prevention Research System

The Prevention Research System, which is responsible for taking evaluation results of DV prevention programs, synthesizing and evaluating them, and disseminating information about effective innovations to implementers, has been cited as the point at which a breakdown occurs, leading to the current research–practice gap in violence prevention (Wandersman et al., 2008).

Researchers have cited two main challenges for violence prevention in this system: the lack of funding for projects that make research accessible to those responsible for implementing and delivering innovations and the lack of guidance for implementers on how to access information on innovation effectiveness (Saul et al., 2008). Often, information about innovations is disseminated by researchers in journal articles using language that is not accessible to implementers. These researchers do not have funding for communicating their research to implementers; therefore, they do not do so. This may discourage implementers from using evidence-based innovations (Clancy & Cronin, 2005). The recent emphasis on translational research by the National Institutes of Health and others suggests that bridging the research–practice gap is increasingly becoming a national priority.

Implementation System

The Implementation System is in the background of innovation delivery and so has not received sufficient attention from evaluators. We have not reached the point of having evaluation information on support and delivery activities. But to fully understand why some innovations are ineffective, or why the same innovations may be evaluated as effective in one context and not in another, we must understand how innovations are implemented. There is consensus among researchers that high-quality evaluations of innovation support and delivery activities, and not just of program outcomes, are necessary to further our understanding of how to increase successful implementation (Wandersman et al., 2008). What is currently known is that implementers may perceive that prevention support is unavailable to them because they do not know how to access such support. For example, a recent study of implementer use of technical assistance found that those who most needed it most were the least likely to access it (Mitchell, Stone-Wiggins, Stevenson, & Florin, 2004). Implementers, often practitioners, may not be aware of how to access the prevention support that is available at national, state, and local levels. A second issue is that although support may be available, it is of varying quality and may not be grounded in best practices (Saul et al., 2008).

Regarding innovation delivery, Implementation Systems may lack adequate infrastructure and grounding in research on effective implementation practices (Saul et al., 2008). Further, we do not know much about how innovations should be delivered. Unresolved issues include whether innovations should be delivered to universal or at-risk populations, how attendance, program fidelity (whether programs were delivered as intended), and facilitator skill impact delivery effectiveness, and whether innovations are delivered in a cost-effective manner (Hamby, 2006). A recent review of DV primary prevention programs found that information about how delivery staff were trained and fidelity monitored was not reported in many published evaluations (Whitaker et al., 2006). Clearly, we need more information on the systems that support innovation implementation before we are able to confidently evaluate the effectiveness of DV primary prevention innovations.

Evaluation Design and Reporting of Results

By far the most information on innovations is obtained from reported evaluation results. Yet researchers concentrating on evaluations of programs have emphasized the incomplete nature of these evaluations and criticized the lack of experimental designs in evaluations of DV prevention innovations (e.g., Clements, Oxtoby, & Ogle, 2008; DeVoe & Kaufman Kantor, 2002; Murray & Graybeal, 2007; Whitaker et al., 2006). Other researchers argue that emphasizing the virtues of experimental designs (increased internal validity) at the expense of the advantages of methods that examine innovations under more real-world conditions in community and organizational settings (increased external validity) is not an appropriate goal for prevention research. These scholars champion methodological appropriateness rather than experimental design as the gold standard for evaluation studies (Patton, 2008; Trochim, 2006).

Definitional, Design, and Measurement Issues

Prevention scholars have noted a lack of standardized ways of defining and operationalizing the constructs of children's exposure to violence, teen dating violence, and DV. The key issue here is that some studies define violence as psychological, sexual, and physical while other studies define violence only as physical. This inhibits cross-study comparisons (Hickman, Jaycox, & Aronoff, 2004; Murray & Graybeal, 2007). Scholars also note a lack of randomized experimental designs, overuse of retrospective designs, lack of articulated parameters for excluding participants from studies, and lack of longitudinal designs in evaluations of DV prevention innovations. Problems with representativeness in sampling have also been noted. In a recent review of nine interpersonal violence prevention innovations, only one used an experimental design, none used random assignment, and only one published the exclusion criteria they used during recruitment (Murray & Graybeal, 2007). Funding and time constraints may combine with attrition to decrease the chances that evaluators will conduct longitudinal studies (Guterman, 2004).

Another design issue is that, currently, many primary prevention programs are designed for general audiences. Therefore, research on what works for diverse groups is lacking. Programs targeting members of specific cultural, educational, or socioeconomic backgrounds are only beginning to appear, and many of those are secondary and tertiary rather than primary prevention programs (Kasturirangan, Krishnan, & Riger, 2004). This is perhaps because research is scant on how different risk factors manifest over time and affect responses to prevention efforts among members of diverse subgroups (Aber, Brown, & Jones, 2003). However, a number of promising culturally anchored interventions are currently being implemented and evaluated, both in the United States and internationally, and best practices information on interventions with diverse groups is available in Guerra and Phillips Smith's book *Preventing Youth Violence in a Multicultural Society* (2005).

Problems with inappropriate measurement also have been documented for violence prevention programs (Devoe & Kaufman Kantor, 2002; Waltermaurer, 2010). Devoe and Kaufman Kantor (2002) listed most of the major instruments used in violence prevention research, reported their psychometric properties, and recommended uses for each measure; the reader is referred to their work for detailed evaluation of the effectiveness of measures used in DV prevention innovations. Too many innovation outcomes are measured only by self-reports, which may be influenced by social desirability, and many measure attitudes rather than behavior (Murray & Graybeal, 2007), hampering attempts to determine which innovations actually reduce violence. Further, individual outcomes are the most frequently measured, whereas measurement of important contextual factors known to be associated with successful DV prevention is virtually absent from published literature, although this is beginning to change (Lindhorst & Tajima, 2008). These shortcomings are to be expected in a discipline as new as DV primary prevention.

WHAT ARE THE NEXT STEPS?

Prevention Research Systems

One gap that must be closed before we begin to see more successful efforts to prevent DV is the research–practice gap, which as discussed earlier is primarily a function of failures in the Research System. To overcome the lack of support for this system's activities, Saul et al. (2008) recommend distribution of information about innovation effectiveness, best practices in building capacity for innovation implementation, and necessary core elements of effective innovations to implementers (practitioners) in an accessible, user-friendly format. Likewise, more study is needed of the most effective means to communicate scientific concepts and studies to practitioners that both increases their valuing of research as an activity that enhances practice and increases the likelihood that they will use evidence-based practices. In one example of this type of research, the American Psychological Foundation recently funded Schewe and Mattaini to develop and evaluate the relative efficacy of in-person versus online dissemination of kernels of knowledge, or promising practices, to prevention educators via their association with state coalitions (Packard, 2007).

Prevention Implementation System

Factors related to innovation success in implementation include appropriate innovation-setting fit, adequate site preparation, robust recruitment and retention procedures, accessible and ongoing technical assistance, and key stakeholders who champion the innovation (Wandersman et al., 2008). Future DV prevention efforts should seek to incorporate these factors into innovations. To overcome the lack of access to existing support and the lack of evidence-based support activities, incentives for improving the capability to support implementation are recommended. Funders could provide incentives to implementers to increase the use of best practices for providing accessible and appropriate technical assistance, for example. Attention to defining and measuring capacity-building and other support activities so that such measurement becomes an integral part of all prevention innovation evaluations is also needed (Saul et al., 2008). Activities and research on how innovations are delivered is also recommended. Problems here include lack of understanding of the implementation process, lack of information on what innovation components are disposable or adaptable and which must be implemented with fidelity, and lack of local strategic planning for delivery. Recommendations include promoting prevention delivery in treatment-oriented implementers, conducting qualitative studies on how and why innovations are not delivered with fidelity, developing guidelines for innovation delivery, and providing funding incentives for strengthening the delivery of prevention innovations.

Evaluation Design and Reporting of Results

Many researchers have bemoaned the lack of evaluation specifics reported in published articles (e.g., Ferguson et al., 2007; Clements, Oxtoby, & Ogle, 2008; Devoe & Kaufman Kantor, 2002; Whitaker et al., 2006), citing this failure as one reason that so many prevention innovations fail to meet standards for recommendation. To address this gap, Murray and Graybeal (2007) recommended that implementers use and report on 15 design aspects to increase the chances that their innovation evaluations will yield meaningful data. In contrast, many prevention advocates extol the virtues of a participatory, community-based approach and advocate a move away from randomized clinical trials (RCTs) in prevention (Staggs et al., 2007). RCTs have been criticized on ethical grounds, as they often withhold or delay access to effective programs. However, RCTs do appear to produce the most scientifically robust evaluation results in the absence of well-articulated, time-tested alternatives. Thus, the authors recommend that representative sampling, random assignment of participants to groups, use of alternate-treatment control groups, and clearly documented exclusion criteria be used to prevent sampling and selection bias. Evaluators are also encouraged to analyze sociodemographic differences and similarities between intervention and control groups to control for their impact on innovation effectiveness. Evaluators should also take care to report details of how innovations were implemented, including specific details on, for example, the activities conducted, materials used, and number of hours devoted to each activity. Such specifications are also necessary to document for no-treatment or alternate-treatment control groups. Appropriate process and outcome measures, follow-up assessments, and statistical analyses should also be used and reported in evaluation outcome articles. Devoe and Kaufman Kantor (2002) recommended the following regarding measuring the effectiveness of DV prevention innovations:

> In selecting an appropriate package of measures, the following specific questions serve as useful guidelines: (a) Has the intervention been sufficiently intense to achieve measurable change in relevant domains? (b) Does the measure assess relevant areas of client functioning? (c) Is the measure regarded as scientifically valid and reliable? and (d) Is the measure appropriate to the population being assessed? The integrity of measurement is also influenced by the manner in which the measures are completed and collected, the attitude of practitioners toward the measures, and the willingness of clients to complete the measures. Thus, factors other than the scientific properties need to be considered, including the following: (a) time to administer, (b) clarity of directions, (c) language of instrument, (d) sensitivity of questions, and (e) scoring ease. (p. 32)

In addition to design and measurement recommendations, prevention researchers should seek to conduct more longitudinal, prospective studies to overcome the limitations of cross-sectional designs. And given that environmental factors are known to be associated with DV and to influence the effectiveness of prevention innovations, evaluators should seek to systematically vary or at least measure extraindividual factors to overcome the limitations of existing innovations, which focus mainly on individual-level variables (Guterman, 2004; Mattaini & McGuire, 2006). Social support, community resources, the impact of experiencing multiple forms of violence, and community norms have all been implicated as risk factors for DV, and their inclusion in innovation strategies may lead to more effective outcomes

(Budde & Schene, 2004; Daro, Edleson, & Pinderhughes, 2004; Mattaini & McGuire, 2006).

The art and science of DV prevention is in its infancy. It is difficult to assess, at this early stage, which of the innovations specifically targeted at DV prevention are effective. Sufficient information is lacking for assessing the effects of programs directed at children who have been exposed to violence, bullying, teen dating violence, and DV and other interventions that promote healthy, nonviolent relationships. There is little evidence that public awareness innovations have an appreciable impact on behavior, although there is a strong body of evidence supporting family-strengthening innovations as both effective and cost-effective. Critical near-term priorities for primary prevention include (a) implementing developmentally appropriate interventions across the life span that target multiple risk factors at multiple ecological levels, (b) accounting for multiple forms of prevention activities and implementation processes and settings, (c) increasing the methodological rigor of evaluations, (d) funding researcher–practitioner collaboration, (e) creating mechanisms to support development of innovative programs to the point at which they are amenable to strong evaluation designs, and (f) developing culturally anchored innovations to improve our knowledge of what works with diverse subpopulations.

REFERENCES

Aber, J. L., Brown, J. L., & Jones, S. M. (2003). Developmental trajectories toward violence in middle childhood: Course, demographic differences, and response to school-based intervention. *Developmental Psychology, 39*, 324–348. doi:10.1037/0012-1649.39.2.324

Bronfenbrenner, U. (1979). *The ecology of human development: Experiments by nature and design.* Cambridge, MA: Harvard University Press.

Budde, S., & Schene, P. (2004). Informal social support interventions and their role in violence prevention: An agenda for future evaluation. *Journal of Interpersonal Violence, 19*, 341–355. doi:10.1177/0886260503261157

Campbell, J. C., & Manganello, J. (2006). Changing public attitudes as a prevention strategy to reduce intimate partner violence. *Journal of Aggression, Maltreatment & Trauma, 13*(3), 13–39. doi:10.1300/J146v13n03_02

Clancy, C. M., & Cronin, C. (2005). Evidence-based decision making: Global evidence, local decisions. *Health Affairs, 24*(1), 151–162. doi:10.1377/hlthaff.24.1.151

Clayton, C. J., Baliff-Spanvill, B., & Hunsaker, M. D. (2001). Preventing violence and teaching peace: A review of promising and effective antiviolence, conflict resolution, and peace programs for elementary-school children. *Applied & Preventive Psychology, 10*(1), 1–35. doi:10.1016/S0962-1849(05)80030-7

Clements, C. M., Oxtoby, C., & Ogle, R. L. (2008). Methodological issues in assessing psychological adjustment in child witnesses of intimate partner violence. *Trauma, Violence & Abuse, 9*, 114–127. doi:10.1177/1524838008315870

Cornelius, T. L., & Resseguie, N. (2007). Primary and secondary prevention programs for dating violence: A review of the literature. *Aggression and Violent Behavior, 12*, 364–375. doi:10.1016/j.avb.2006.09.006

Daro, D., Edleson, J. L., & Pinderhughes, H. (2004). Finding common ground in the study of child maltreatment, youth violence, and adult domestic violence. *Journal of Interpersonal Violence, 19*, 282–298. doi:10.1177/0886260503261151

DeVoe, E. R., & Kaufman Kantor, G. K. (2002). Measurement issues in child maltreatment and family violence prevention programs. *Trauma, Violence & Abuse, 3*, 15–39. doi:10.1177/15248380020031002

Edleson, J. L. (2000). *Primary prevention and adult domestic violence.* Paper presented at the meeting of the Collaborative Violence Prevention Initiative, San Francisco, CA.

Erickson, C., Mattaini, M. A., & McGuire, M. S. (2004). Constructing nonviolent cultures in schools: The state of the science. *Children and Schools, 26*, 102–116.

Ferguson, C. J., San Miguel, C., Kilburn, J., & Sanchez, P. (2007). The effectiveness of school-based anti-bullying programs: A meta-analytic review. *Criminal Justice Review, 32*, 401–414. doi:10.1177/0734016807311712

Foshee, V. A., Bauman, K. E., Ennett, S. T., Linder, G. F., Benefield, T., & Suchindran, C. (2004). Assessing the long-term effects of the Safe Dates program and a booster in preventing and reducing adolescent dating violence victimization and perpetration. *American Journal of Public Health, 94*, 619–624. doi:10.2105/AJPH.94.4.619

Graham-Bermann, S. A., & Hughes, H. M. (2003). Intervention for children exposed to interparental violence: Assessment of needs and research priorities. *Clinical Child and Family Psychology Review, 6*, 189–204. doi:10.1023/A:1024962400234

Guterman, N. B. (2004). Advancing prevention research on child abuse, youth violence, and domestic violence: Emerging strategies and issues. *Journal of Interpersonal Violence, 19*, 299–321. doi:10.1177/0886260503261153

Hamby, S. L. (2006). The who, what, when, where, and how of partner violence prevention research. *Journal of Aggression, Maltreatment & Trauma, 13*, 179–201. doi:10.1300/J146v13n03_07

Hammond, W. R., Whitaker, D. J., Lutzker, J. R., Mercy, J., & Chin, P. (2006). Setting a violence prevention agenda at the Centers for Disease Control and Prevention. *Aggression and Violent Behavior, 11*, 112–119.

Heise, L. L. (1998). Violence against women: An integrated, ecological framework. *Violence Against Women, 4*, 262–290. doi:10.1177/1077801298004003002

Henggeler, S. W. (1997, May). Treating serious anti-social behavior in youth: The MST approach. *Juvenile Justice Bulletin.* Washington, DC: U.S. Department of

Justice, Office of Justice Programs, Office of Juvenile Justice and Delinquency Prevention.

Hickman, L. J., Jaycox, L. H., & Aronoff, J. (2004). Dating violence among adolescents: Prevalence, gender distribution, and prevention program effectiveness. *Trauma, Violence & Abuse, 5,* 123–142. doi:10.1177/15248380032 62332

Kasturirangan, A., Krishnan, S., & Riger, S. (2004). The impact of culture and minority status on women's experience of domestic violence. *Trauma, Violence & Abuse, 5,* 318–332. doi:10.1177/1524838004269487

Kelly, J. G. (1966). Ecological constraints on mental health services. *American Psychologist, 21,* 535–539. doi:10.1037/h0023598

Kerns, S. E. U., & Prinz, R. J. (2002). Critical issues in the prevention of violent behavior in youth. *Clinical Child and Family Psychology Review, 5,* 133–160. doi:10.1023/A:1015411320113

Klein, E., Campbell, J., Soler, E., & Ghez, M. (1997). *Ending domestic violence: Changing public perceptions/halting the epidemic.* Thousand Oaks, CA: Sage.

Kumpfer, K. L., & Alvarado, R. (2003). Family-strengthening approaches for the prevention of youth problem behaviors. *American Psychologist, 58,* 457–465. doi:10.1037/0003-066X.58.6-7.457

Lindhorst, T., & Tajima, E. (2008). Reconceptualizing and operationalizing context in survey research on intimate partner violence. *Journal of Interpersonal Violence, 23,* 362–388. doi:10.1177/0886260507312293

Markman, H. J., Floyd, F., Stanley, S. M., & Storaasli, R. (1988). The prevention of marital distress: A longitudinal investigation. *Journal of Consulting and Clinical Psychology, 56,* 210–217. doi:10.1037/0022-006X.56.2.210

Markman, H. J., Renick, M. J., Floyd, F. J., Stanley, S. M., & Clements, M. (1993). Preventing marital distress through communication and conflict management training: A 4- and 5-year follow-up. *Journal of Consulting and Clinical Psychology, 61,* 70–77. doi:10.1037/0022-006X.61.1.70

Markman, H. J., Stanley, S., & Blumberg, S. L. (2001). *Fighting for your marriage: Positive steps for preventing divorce and preserving a lasting love.* San Francisco, CA: Jossey-Bass.

Mattaini, M. A., & McGuire, M. C. (2006). Behavioral strategies for constructing nonviolence cultures with youth: A review. *Behavior Modification, 30,* 184–224. doi:10.1177/0145445503259390

Mercy, J. A., & Hammond, W. R. (2001). Learning to do violence prevention well. *American Journal of Preventive Medicine, 20*(1, Suppl. 1), 1–2. doi:10.1016/S0749-3797(00)00267-1

Mihalic, S., Irwin, K., Elliott, D., Fagan, A., & Hansen, D. (2001, July). Blueprints for violence prevention. *Juvenile Justice Bulletin.* Washington, DC: U.S. Department of Justice, Office of Juvenile Justice and Delinquency Prevention.

Mitchell, R. E., Stone-Wiggins, B., Stevenson, J. F., & Florin, P. (2004). Cultivating capacity: Outcomes of a statewide support system for prevention coalitions. *Journal of Prevention & Intervention in the Community. 27*, 67–87.

Murray, C. E., & Graybeal, J. (2007). Methodological review of intimate partner violence prevention research. *Journal of Interpersonal Violence, 22*, 1250–1269. doi:10.1177/0886260507304293

Nation, M., Crusto, C., Wandersman, A., Kumpfer, K.L., Seybolt, D., Morrissey-Kane, E., & Davino, K. (2003). What works in prevention: Principles of effective prevention programs. *American Psychologist Special Issue: Prevention that Works for Children and Youth, 58*, 449–456.

Olds, D., Henderson, C. R., Cole, R., Eckenrode, J., Kitzman, H., Luckey, D., . . . Powers, J. (1998). Long-term effects of nurse home visitation on children's criminal and antisocial behavior: 15-year follow-up to a randomized trial. *JAMA, 280*, 1238–1244. doi:10.1001/jama.280.14.1238

Olweus, D. (1993). *Bullying at school: What we know and what we can do.* Cambridge, England: Blackwell.

Packard, E. (2007). American Psychological Foundation $20,000 grant awarded to fight sexual violence. *Monitor on Psychology, 38*(3), 68–69.

Patton, M. Q. (2008). The paradigms debate and utilization-focused synthesis. In *Utilization-focused evaluation* (pp. 419–470). Thousand Oaks, CA: Sage.

Saul, J., Duffy, J., Noonan, R., Lubell, K., Wandersman, A., Flaspohler, P., . . . Dunville, R. (2008). Bridging science and practice in violence prevention: Addressing ten key challenges. *American Journal of Community Psychology, 41*, 197–205. doi:10.1007/s10464-008-9171-2

Staggs, S. L., Schewe, P., White, M., Davis, E., & Dill, E. (2007). Changing systems by changing individuals: The incubation approach to systems change. *American Journal of Community Psychology, 39*, 365–379. doi:10.1007/s10464-007-9103-6

Stith, S. M. (2006). Future directions in intimate partner violence prevention research. *Journal of Aggression, Maltreatment & Trauma, 13*, 229–244. doi:10.1300/J146v13n03_09

Sullivan, C. M., Bybee, D. L., & Allen, N. E. (2002). Findings from a community-based program for battered women and their children. *Journal of Interpersonal Violence, 17*, 915–936. doi:10.1177/0886260502017009001

Thornton, T. N., Craft, C. A., Dahlberg, L. L., Lynch, B. S., & Baer, K. (Eds.). (2002). *Best practices of youth violence prevention—A sourcebook for community action.* Retrieved from http://www.cdc.gov/violenceprevention/pub/YV_bestpractices.html

Tolan, P. H., Gorman-Smith, D., & Henry, D. B. (2006). Family violence. In S. T. Fiske, A. E. Kazdin, & D. Schacter (Eds.), *Annual Review of Psychology, 57*, 550–583. doi:10.1146/annurev.psych.57.102904.190110

Trochim, W. M. K. (2006). *Experimental design.* Retrieved from the Social Research Methods Knowledge Database at http://www.socialresearchmethods.net/kb/desexper.php

Wandersman, A., Duffy, J., Flaspohler, P., Noonan, R., Lubell, K., Stillman, L., . . . Saul, J. (2008). Bridging the gap between research and practice: The interactive systems framework for dissemination and implementation. *American Journal of Community Psychology, 41*, 171–181. doi:10.1007/s10464-008-9174-z

Waltermaurer, E. (2010). Measuring intimate partner violence: You may only get what you ask for. In H. Lune, E. S. Pumar, & Koppel, R. (Eds.), *Perspectives in social research methods and analysis: A reader for sociology* (pp. 220–224). Thousand Oaks, CA: Sage.

Webster-Stratton, C., & Hammond, M. (1997). Treating children with early-onset conduct problems: A comparison of child and parent training interventions. *Journal of Consulting and Clinical Psychology, 65*, 93–109. doi:10.1037/0022-006X.65.1.93

Whitaker, D. J., Hall, D. M., & Coker, A. L. (2009). Primary prevention of intimate partner violence: Toward a developmental, social-ecological model. In C. Mitchell & D. Anglin (Eds.), *Intimate partner violence: A health perspective* (pp. 289–305). New York, NY: Oxford University Press.

Whitaker, D. J., Morrison, S., Lindquist, C., Hawkins, S. R., O'Neil, J. A., Nesius, A. M., . . . Reese, L-R. (2006). A critical review of interventions for the primary prevention of perpetration of partner violence. *Journal of Adolescent Health, 11*, 151–166.

Wolfe, D. A., Wekerle, C., Scott, K., Straatman, A., Grasley, C., & Reitzel-Jaffe, D. (2003). Dating violence prevention with at-risk youth: A controlled outcome evaluation. *Journal of Consulting and Clinical Psychology, 71*, 279–291. doi:10.1037/0022-006X.71.2.279

IV

CONCLUSION

13

VIOLENCE AGAINST WOMEN AND CHILDREN: PERSPECTIVES AND NEXT STEPS

MARY P. KOSS, JACQUELYN W. WHITE, AND ALAN E. KAZDIN

Across all areas of interpersonal violence, women and children experience a disproportionate amount of violence in their day-to-day lives at the hands of those who are assumed to love and protect them. The Violence against Women Act (VAWA), originally enacted by the United States Congress in 1994 and reauthorized in 2000 and 2008, as well as the National Center for Injury Prevention and Control's *CDC Injury Research Agenda, 2009–2018* (2009) and the article "Child Maltreatment Prevention Priorities at the Centers for Disease Control and Prevention" (Whitaker, Lutzker, & Shelly, 2005), attest to the priority and concern for responding to and reducing victimization of women and children. The two volumes in this series were conceived to systematize scientific information on child abuse and maltreatment, domestic violence, and sexual violence. Our goal in this chapter is to synthesize the material to identify commonalities and gaps in existing knowledge from which we could draw conclusions on next steps to further the research and services agenda.

To ensure high-quality, timely information, contributors were recruited to prepare chapters within their expertise; they reflect the range of professions and diverse perspectives demanded to encompass the breadth of issues. Each author was asked to focus on broad consensus or to outline areas of contro-

versy, avoiding professional jargon as much as possible, and to resist the temp-
tation to exhaustively catalog relevant work but rather to select representative
recent documents or scientific studies that the reader interested in more depth
may consult. Whenever possible, contributors were asked to adopt a common
organizational scheme to their presentation, beginning with a summary of
what we know, then critically examining how we (think) we know it by cri-
tiquing the scientific methods used to generate the information, and finally
concluding with their distillation of the next steps that would advance scientific understanding, inform advocacy efforts, and improve policy, services, and
prevention. This scheme facilitated identifying common themes across child
abuse and maltreatment, domestic violence, and sexual violence that have
typically been pursued as separate and distinct specialty areas. Table 13.1
presents a detailed summary of conclusions reached by each author in this
volume (and a companion table is included for this purpose in the conclusion
to *Violence Against Women and Children, Volume 1: Mapping the Terrain*; White
Koss, & Kazdin, 2011). These tables provide enough detail to establish that
there has been remarkable progress in understanding violence against women
and children and to mark the line beyond which many gaps remain to be filled.

Emerging from these chapters are consensus themes and recommendations on future directions. In this concluding chapter, we identify commonalities on the basis of what we know, how we know it, and gaps in knowledge,
and we offer practical suggestions for where to go in epidemiology, study of
causes and impact, training, policy, interventions, prevention, and, most of all,
initiatives that fall within what disciplines have done in the past and perhaps
could do better with collaboration. In the following three sections, we address
major common themes and shared methodological issues, and we conclude
with consensus recommendations.

COMMONALITIES AMONG AREAS OF VIOLENCE

Contributors all issued a call for more consistency and uniformity in
many areas. These included harmonizing definitions both for legal and
research purposes, using common assessment strategies to facilitate comparison of studies, and creating conceptual models that adequately capture the
substantial overlap in risk, protective, and causal factors identified for each
separate form of violence. All reiterated the importance of services and treatment and recognized the urgency of focusing on prevention as a long-term
strategy. Contributors warned that without emphasis on prevention, we risk
remaining forever stuck in a circular process by which the need for services never
diminishes because new victims and perpetrators continue to emerge from what
is now a well-known set of adverse individual and societal characteristics that

TABLE 13.1
Summary of Conclusions

Area	What do we know?
	Victim services

Child abuse	• Two paradigms dominate: rescue and rehabilitation.
	  • Rescuing children from harmful home environments results in many investigations and few removals.
	  • Out-of-home placements are traumatizing and inequitable by race.
	  • Rehabilitation raises the question of who is the real target of service in child maltreatment, the parent or the child.
	• The array of popular programs for family support is *assumed* to be helpful.

Sexual violence	• Services often focus on rape, excluding other forms of sexual violence. Typical services: emergency medical care and presumably longer term care about which little is known, mental health (short- or long-term counseling), and advocacy services to obtain care and negotiate justice.
	• Care is inequitable by race; White women are better served than Black.
	• Although Sexual Assault Nurse Examiner programs have improved services, medical care remains traumatizing.
	• Documented levels of posttraumatic stress disorder are high, but
	  • most care is provided by community-based providers outside the formal mental health system and often does not involve empirically supported therapies;
	  • even newly trained professional psychologists combine methods and therapeutic models rather than delivering treatment programs that have been empirically validated; and
	  • White women utilize community services most, and no evaluations of the services' impact meet minimum scientific standards.
	• Sexual assault response teams aim for comprehensive medical, mental health, and justice system response; they are growing rapidly with virtually no evaluation.

Domestic violence	• Informal supports are frequently used, but they often fail to help. • Community-based services include crisis-oriented (shelter and first response teams) and long-term services. • Evaluation of first response teams shows no effect on overall abuse, but victims were more willing to call police. • Battered women report that shelter programs are one of the most supportive and effective services, but the number of beds falls below needs. • Longer term services, including transitional housing, are few; women in transitional housing say they would have returned to assailants otherwise. • Counseling for domestic violence shows promise. • Empowerment model is typical and supported by promising but limited evidence of effectiveness.

(continues)

TABLE 13.1
Summary of Conclusions *(Continued)*

Area	What do we know?
	• Evaluations of support groups using experimental designs showed more improvement in reducing distress and better social resources among participants, compared with those assigned to control conditions. • Advocacy services aim to improve victim experience and change public policy or institutionalized practices. • Legal advocacy on civil and criminal matters assists victims to get protection orders or accompanies them to court; one quasi-experiment showed decreased risk of abuse at 6 weeks and marginally higher emotional well-being. • Services advocacy refers to assistance in accessing needed services; one experimental evaluation suggested positive impact compared with standard care, with a quarter of victims reporting no further physical abuse for 2 years. • Child and family advocacy includes counseling, safety planning, support, and education, as well as supervised child visitation and exchange by divorced parents. • Children's counseling evaluations lack comparison or control groups; findings suggest improved improvements in behavior as perceived by mothers.

Offender services

Area	What do we know?
Child abuse	• Currently, primary emphasis is on parents as abusers and secondarily on parent as in need of individual help and community integration. • Services emphasize forensic investigation, child removal, foster care, and adoption as opposed to support for struggling families. • Foster care has poor outcomes, including children's failure to complete high school (1 in 3 foster children), elevated rates of homelessness, unemployment, and serious mental health issues. • Home visiting for family support has mixed evidence of success. • Racial bias exists: • Children of color are overrepresented, and they are more likely than White children to be placed with relatives. • In-kin placement is associated with greater behavioral and mental health issues, fewer state support resources, and less chance of permanent adoption compared with non-kin placement. • Consensus has emerged that reducing and eliminating maltreatment must have a focus broader than offender services, to include parent, family, and community levels and to emphasize prevention. • Building community for isolated parents is encouraged by feminist, youth, cultural, faith, and consumer groups.

TABLE 13.1
Summary of Conclusions *(Continued)*

Area	What do we know?
	• An innovative family group decision-making model has been evaluated using a longitudinal, quasi-experimental design and has demonstrated absence of negative impact on endangerment, reduced indicators of child maltreatment and less racialized bias, accelerated gains in child development, strengthened social networks, reengaged fathers on the parental side of the family, increased sense of family togetherness and greater pride in their own efficacy, improved relationships with the social welfare system, more kinship placement, and growth in the cultural competence of providers. • Not every state is meeting national performance goals. • Remaining problems include heavy-handed treatment of low-risk families, underinclusion of some higher risk families, lack of service provider capacity, fragmented services, and unresolved tensions between the dual mandates of protecting children while keeping families together.

Sexual violence	• Treatment is not widely available in prisons.
	• 20 states have civil commitment allowing for indeterminate confinement of sexually violent persons after completing their sentences.
	• The U.S. Supreme Court has ordered states with civil commitment to provide adequate mental health treatment.
	• Whether in prison or in civil commitment, in regard to most sex offender treatment:
	  • prisoners are captive and enter therapy without a desire to change;
	  • treatment has the primary goal of reducing the likelihood of re-offending and assisting with management upon release; and
	  • the therapeutic techniques of sex-offender and non-sex-offender therapy are similar, but conditions of therapy differ and minimal requirements for therapeutic success are not met.
	• Despite the limitations, in-prison treatment has modest success; meta-analyses report a 6% reduction in recidivism.

Domestic violence	• Batterers' intervention programs:
	  • More than 80% are court mandated; 50% drop out.
	  • Programs are typically in groups; they emphasize holding the perpetrator accountable, keeping victims safe, challenging rigid sex-role perceptions, developing the necessary skills to be nonviolent, and the individual influences for violence.
	  • No specific approach has emerged as superior to others.
	  • Typologies of perpetrators have been developed to inform treatment decisions, but they have not yet been shown to increase effectiveness through matching.

(continues)

TABLE 13.1
Summary of Conclusions *(Continued)*

Area	What do we know?
	• The system response to domestic violence is fragmented and geared to women and children; services for batterers could be more proactive.
	• Services often do not address fatherhood, yet many men who batter remain in the lives of their partners and children.
	• Many men released from prison have histories of domestic violence but are rarely provided in-prison services.
	• Many experts call for more attention to culture in serving men of color in batterers' intervention programs (BIPs). A *blended perspective* emphasizes the core elements of BIPs, and includes attention to themes of concern to men of color. There are multiple challenges when trying to evaluate the extent to which BIP programs actually keep women safe.
	• Long-term follow-up may be complicated if the relationship ends or the perpetrator shifts to nonphysical tactics of abuse.

Justice responses

Area	What do we know?
Child abuse	• Justice response includes the child welfare, criminal justice, medical, and educational systems; all systems are known to be biased against nonmajority racial groups, those who live in poverty, and nonheterosexual parents.
	• Policies are primarily developed and regulated state by state, leading to widespread disparities in application of federal mandates.
	• Criminal justice:
	• Victimization constitutes harm against the state. States have power to incapacitate, place moral blame, and impose punishment, including mandated drug treatment for parents/guardians.
	• New methods of testimony reduce courtroom trauma on children, but they also reduce credibility and juror empathy.
	• Despite effective methods to increase truthfulness of disclosure, forensic investigators evidently gain little from either intensive or brief training.
	• Offenders against children are subject to civil commitment, which requires clinical judgment to predict dangerousness; however, clinicians' accuracy is worse than chance.
	• Community notification, monitoring, and supervision have little empirical support, nor are they enforced; some data show negative outcome.
	• Juvenile justice
	• Deals with crimes and status offenses; juveniles are a major source of maltreatment against children including sex offenses and peer harassment

TABLE 13.1
Summary of Conclusions   *(Continued)*

Area	What do we know?
	• Defines its mission as benevolent and rehabilitative but in reality, it combines the functions of child welfare and criminal justice
	• Juvenile judges can remove children from homes.
	• Child advocacy centers are proliferating rapidly; they are not perceived by children as more friendly, and they may not lead to more prosecutions.
	• Medical systems
	• Parental failure to provide medical care is a form of abuse, and providers are subject to mandatory reporting.
	• Failure to substantiate the majority of reported cases undermines the motivation to report; massive under-reporting exists.
	• Despite parents' legal responsibility to provide medical care for their children, it is not a right unless they relinquish custody to the state, which is then mandated to meet medical needs.
	• Educational systems
	• Educational neglect is a form of maltreatment.
	• Schools are an important place to recognize abuse.
Sexual violence	• Criminal justice
	• Rights of the accused carry more legal weight than the rights of the victims.
	• Legislative change attempted to increase victims' rights through shield statutes, privilege protection to mental health and counseling records, limited inclusion of marital rape, and repeal of evidentiary corroboration requirements.
	• Evidence suggests these reforms have failed. Rape is under-reported and under prosecuted—15 of 16 victims can expect no accountability from the criminal justice system.
	• Criminal justice decisions continue to hold antiquated views.
	• Major obstacles include:
	(a) Consent: Law requires victims to show proof of lack of consent and assailants' use of force, resulting in a trial in which victims' credibility is measured against that of the offender.
	(b) Intoxication: The majority of sexual assaults involve consumption of alcohol, supporting widespread, prejudicial beliefs that conduct was consensual and victim's memory is impaired; women's drinking is viewed as more morally objectionable than drinking by men.
	(c) Unconsciousness or severe intoxication is recognized as lack of consent, but some states require that the offender have administered the alcohol/drug and exclude victims who voluntarily drank.

(continues)

TABLE 13.1
Summary of Conclusions   *(Continued)*

Area	What do we know?

	(d) Rape shield: Trials still focus heavily on victim conduct; shield laws do not prevent all attacks on character. Some mental health and counseling records may be ruled admissible. Information may be publicly released or discovered by media.
	(e) Marital rape: Many states still endorse restrictions on spouse prosecutions for rape.
	(f) Disturbing patterns of racial bias: Reported rapes involving Black men are more likely to be investigated and prosecuted than those committed by other races.
	• Civil justice
	  • Prevalence of tort cases for rape has significantly increased.
	  • Although civil process has certain advantages over criminal justice, the same barriers exist, and new avenues of victim trauma are opened, such as more loss of privacy and comparative fault that allows third-party defendants to argue that victim was wholly or partly responsible for the rape because of her own behavior.
	  • Civil processes other than tort exist to assist rape victims:
	    (a) protection orders theoretically exist but are not uniformly available to rape victims;
	    (b) reasonable accommodations under disability law;
	    (c) family and medical leave and job protections under employment law;
	    (d) protection from employer retaliation and state antidiscrimination under civil rights legislation; and
	    (e) challenges to loss of employment or student visas under immigration law.
	  • Sexual assault may constitute sexual harassment, allowing additional forms of redress.
	• Education: Institutions have a duty to protect and to effectively respond. However, many have largely failed to address sexual assault.
	• Restorative justice
	  • Creates a process of accountability aimed in part to reduce retraumatization; it is nonadversarial and in its best implementations it is a victim-driven process.
	  • A variety of restorative approaches exist, but there is resistance that has multiple roots: feminist jurist critique, comfort with the status quo, and stasis of institutionalized bureaucracies; emotionally based resistance among potential partners—including the justice system and community-based sexual assault service providers.
	  • Resistance impacts policy because federal and state policymakers respond to advocacy from the justice community and the antiviolence movement.

TABLE 13.1
Summary of Conclusions   *(Continued)*

Area	What do we know?

Domestic violence	• Advocacy agenda: Existing scholarship supports revisioning and revitalization of legislative, statutory, and policy goals.
	• Advocacy over 30 years has secured mandatory arrest, no-drop prosecution, civil protection order laws, and coordinated community responses.
	• Criminal justice impact of advocacy:
	  • Arrest rates have dramatically increased—27% of domestic violence victims now report to police.
	  • The only experiment testing mandatory arrest found that it reduced reabuse only if victims, contrary to legal intent, were not coerced to participate.
	  • Domestic violence perpetrators receive lenient sentences, few involving any jail time; the value of prosecution may be outweighed by the increased level of homicide associated with it.
	  • Reporting and cooperation with prosecution are hindered because children are also placed at risk of harm.
	  • Domestic violence conviction is a deportable offense impacting victims' ability to access protection.
	• Civil justice
	  • Every state has protection orders available that in theory promote safety and allow rapid resolution of child support and access to housing.
	  • Protection orders are not effective in protecting victims; on average, 40% of batterers violate orders, and police often refuse to arrest the violator of an order.
	  • Nevertheless, women report that they *feel* safer.
	• Coordinated community responses
	  • Interdisciplinary collaboration in service delivery should be fostered.
	  • Colocated services increase access.
	  • Some (unified) domestic violence courts coordinate civil and criminal actions. In one study, victims who participated in unified courts viewed them as more empowering, helpful, and effective than standard court; in another jurisdiction, there was decreased reinvolvement of batterer in reported abuse.
	• Numerous justice obstacles remain that inform a change agenda.
	  • Responses are rigid and marginalize women's individual context and perspective; victims have little opportunity to express their own desires, material needs, or safety concerns.
	  • Needed services are infrequently or inadequately provided.
	  • Civil responses are more flexible but rest on the assumption that victims wish to leave the batterer.
	  • Restorative justice responses are receiving attention but suffer from the same resistance as in sexual violence.
	(continues)

TABLE 13.1

Summary of Conclusions *(Continued)*

Area	What do we know?
	Prevention
Child abuse	• Home visitation is child maltreatment primary prevention. • Aim is to reduce risk factors for maltreatment and promote competent care. In one study it was effective in reducing verified cases of maltreatment over 15 years. • Home visitation was most likely to be effective if it focused on higher risk parents with low to moderate levels of domestic violence, began during pregnancy, used nurses or other professionals, involved frequent visits (30 or more), used a variety of strategies (teaching, modeling, behavioral rehearsal, and referrals), and addressed support of both parents and children. • Other parenting programs, such as Healthy Families America, have found mixed results. • Hawaii Healthy Start reported no effects for confirmed child maltreatment reports, parents' reports of abusive or neglectful caregiving, or observational data in homes. • Alaska Healthy Families also reported null effects except that some mothers reported using less mild physical and psychological punishment. • Healthy Families America New York found no effect on substantiated child protection reports through age 2, but parents' self-reports suggested fewer acts of serious physical abuse. • School readiness programs, such as Parents as Teachers Born to Learn Curriculum, has components targeted at risk factors for maltreatment. Three experimental, randomized trials in diverse settings reported no impact except for a noncorroborated effect for teen parents. • School-based programs, such as Body Safety Training, Talking About Touching, and Good-Touch/Bad-Touch, include printed matter, videos, and instruction by adults, and some programs involve parents in meetings or send materials home. Meta-analysis reports significant improvements in children's knowledge but no retention beyond 12 months, some positive effects on protective behaviors in simulated risk situations, and stronger effects for 8- to 13-year-olds than for younger children. • Early Head Start in a randomized trial involving 17 programs showed a number of gains in cognitive and language development, supportive and safe home environments, and increased reading and decreased spanking. • Comprehensive programs, such as Chicago Child-Parent Centers, offer multiple modalities to improve the home environment, including home visits, child care, case management, parenting education, health care and referrals, and family support. Internationally, an experimental test of the Triple P program in Australia, which has five levels of intervention, revealed positive outcomes at the population

TABLE 13.1
Summary of Conclusions *(Continued)*

Area	What do we know?
	level in program counties, including lower rates of substantiated child maltreatment, out-of-home placements, and emergency department visits for maltreatment.
	• Media campaigns; one such is the Shaken Baby Syndrome campaign, which involved a brief educational program using print and video in 16 New York hospitals. It showed a 47% reduction in abusive head trauma in the following years compared with years before the campaign.
Sexual violence	• The most effective sexual violence prevention programs are interactive, multimedia, multimethod (role playing or other methods of modeling, practicing, and rehearsing skills) and culturally relevant; lecture formats are less effective.
	• Programs that emphasize central route processing, where the message is personally relevant and provocative of issue-relevant thinking, create more stable and long-term attitude change.
	• Children: Programs aim to protect by raising awareness of what constitutes coercion and providing skills and attitudes for violence-free relationships. Meta-analysis of more than 40 studies of elementary school children involving quasi-experimental or experimental design with random assignment suggested modest changes in knowledge, and acquisition of skills, such as saying "no."
	• Middle school children: The largest evaluation involved Safe Dates, which is a violence prevention curriculum created in 1996. A 2005 analysis of 4 follow-up assessments of over 3,000 original participants reported small but enduring effects without clear systematic trends.
	• College students: These programs emphasize gender role socialization, sexual violence definitions, prevalence, consent, resistance tactics and safety, aftereffects, and resources.
	• The major types of primary prevention programs are
	(a) mixed sex;
	(b) women only, particularly focused on assessing risk situations, self-protective behavior, assertive communication, verbal and physical resistance, and aftereffects and resources;
	(c) men only, focused on empathy, asking men to learn communication, anger management, and consent negotiation skills, and male socialization; and
	(d) bystander intervention.
	• Although inexpensive and easy to present, these programs have not been evaluated carefully enough for potential harm that could result from discussion of victim resistance strategies before potential. perpetrators or the possibility of backlash among male participants.

(continues)

TABLE 13.1
Summary of Conclusions   *(Continued)*

Area	What do we know?
	• Literature suggests that of these programs the most impactful are rape resistance programs for women, which result in greater assertiveness, self-esteem, perceived control, use of self-protective dating behavior, and competence in self-defense, and decreased risk-taking and fear of sexual violence.
	• Little credible evidence suggests that men's programs reduce perpetration.
	• There have been no systemic evaluations of societal-based prevention efforts and none of community-level prevention.
Domestic violence	• Most of the programs effective in preventing domestic violence are not those designed specifically to prevent domestic violence.
	• Contemporary thought is that domestic violence is a familial dysfunction, linked to other forms of family violence, such as child abuse.
	• A strong case can be made for the proposition that to prevent domestic violence, primary prevention must target young children and aim to interrupt the negative impact of maladaptive developmental trajectories.
	• Many programs targeting children are not based on sound science.
	• Effective programs are comprehensive, based on empirically validated theory, introduced as early as possible in the life span, and are socioculturally relevant; involve multiple innovations in multiple settings; employ interactive, hands-on education using diverse methods of instruction; build skills as well as increase knowledge; last long enough to have an impact; involve follow-up sessions over time to ensure maintenance; build positive relationships among participants and their families; and are delivered by well-trained staff and carefully evaluated.
	• A research–practice gap is recognized. Evaluations have not taken the complexities of implementation into account.
	• Constraints within support and delivery systems have been insufficiently examined.
	• The process of disseminating best practices in accessible formats for practitioners has been insufficiently studied.
	• Many barriers to implementing good programs, exist including lack of awareness of how to incorporate latest research and lack of time, resources, or money to implement properly.
	• Recent activity has focused on developing and building the infrastructure that is essential to making prevention work.

foster violence against women and children. In the material that follows, we highlight six key commonalities.

Scope of the Consequences of Victimization

Each type of abuse has numerous untoward system-produced consequences—that is, trauma introduced by actions intended to help. Removing a child from the home in the case of child abuse or moving a woman and child to a shelter to protect them from further domestic violence inevitably stresses them further. The processes involved in adjudication also present victims with significant psychological, family, and economic burdens. Throughout such processes, victims relive the experience of abuse and are shamed and blamed, and they often report that resources that might facilitate their recovery are inadequate. We are not implying that actions to intervene and protect should be reduced. Instead, the common concerns in the fields related to the study and prevention of violence pertain to how such remedial actions are implemented. And such concerns are not merely a matter of victim rights, which can often seem to receive less attention than do the rights of alleged perpetrators. Rather, the chief concern is for responders and helpers to recognize what victimization means and what it does to a person. Given the problems we have highlighted, the victim is found in a very physically and emotionally precarious position that is easily exacerbated. An emergent theme is the need not only to address the consequences of the experience of violence but also to continue efforts to shape services, rehabilitative efforts, and justice responses to meet the needs of victims in ways that strengthen and support them and do so sensitively.

Multisystem Response to Violence

Abuse and victimization are not single events but are embedded in social conditions that, along with the violence, decrease opportunity and quality of life across the course of development. Thus, multiple systems and services are required to respond. However, models that derive from usual medical or psychological practice are too narrowly focused. More is needed than practices based in a biomedical model of service delivery where a primary agent addresses a specific problem such as by treating depression. What has emerged from the prior chapters is the need for integrated care to see victims and perpetrators through a set of service needs and obstacles that can contribute to better postvictimization outcomes and reduction of reoffending. Social, legal, medical, and psychological services may be required to handle the multiple needs of the moment and the changing needs that may unfold over time. For a victim of domestic violence, services may involve tangible resources, counseling, health care, attention to children's needs, education, and assistance with housing and employment, sometimes requiring legal services. While this is taking place, ongoing legal issues may emerge for the perpetrator leading to mandated rehabilitation services. All require coordination of multiple services to collectively achieve their aims.

Often the services for victims (or perpetrators) should, but do not, work together, and often they actually work against each other. Passing children or women from one service to another is likely to let them slip through the cracks. When a perpetrator is given a restraining order or put on probation, with inadequate monitoring, the efforts of other providers to increase victim safety are defeated. People get victimized in part because they lack resources; they are "safe" targets for motivated offenders. A service system is needed that addresses the value of augmenting victims' social, financial, and emotional strengths. Numerous contributors to this volume noted the insignificant attention paid to a strengthening approach, whether for an individual battered woman, a couple or family with maltreated children, or perpetrators at risk of repeat offending.

Novel models of intervening are needed to address critical themes that emerged in the chapters. We have learned that most people in need of services are not receiving them. New ways of delivering interventions need to be explored to take advantage of technology to reach larger numbers, in light both of the prevalence of violence against women and children and of the victims' significant hesitation to present themselves openly to police, hospitals, and social services. In addition, many people live in rural areas, such as Indian reservations, where specialized direct services, even if available, may be too far away to be useful. Online interventions are currently being used and advocated as one way to redress disparities in health care access and to reach groups that otherwise would go without psychosocial interventions (Muñoz, 2009). These include groups varying in ethnicity and socioeconomic disadvantage. Online interventions have been used to treat a wide range of social, emotional, behavioral, and psychiatric problems among adults (e.g., Barak, Hen, Boniel-Nissim, & Shapira, 2008; Carlbring & Anderson, 2006). Trauma, depression, and substance use and abuse are among the problems, often experienced by victims of violence, that have been treated online. Many such online interventions are evidence based. Models delivered on the Internet need not replace current interventions but are intended, rather, to expand them. Even so, there will be many individuals who still are not reached. Nevertheless, a broader portfolio of ways of delivering intervention and prevention in different languages and over longer distances could play an important role.

Intervention Research

A common theme was the importance of and need for evidence-based services and prevention. The chapters in this volume identified 500 programs that focus on the prevention of violence. Of these, only a small number (11) meet criteria designed to select programs with strong methodology for establishing efficacy and cost-effectiveness. No doubt different criteria would change the number, but the general trend is clear: Most programs, including treatment, prevention, and other services, are not adequately evaluated. Contributors also identified several specific psychological interventions and prevention approaches that have an established evidence base. It was frequently noted, however, that these programs are inadequately applied across communities, and when they are translated from ideal conditions to communities, they often lack fidelity to the procedures that were used in the evaluation. The concern is that some elements that contributed significantly to effectiveness in the research context are not administered when the methods are translated to the community setting. The integrated, coordinated, multilevel services that contributors identify as next steps will be difficult to evaluate with the formal scientific procedures that characterize the controlled experiments used to establish interventions as evidence based. Numerous obstacles contribute to the lack of evaluation of community-based approaches. What is needed are, for example, better infrastructure for technical assistance at the community level and a general upgrade in capacity for community-based service provision and participation in evaluation. Furthermore, higher funding ceilings are needed to support feasible evaluation designs that are scientifically sound and provide sufficient follow-up time periods to assess long-term as well as intermediate outcomes, and in particular to assess impact at a community level.

Cultural Context and Inequalities

Neglect of the cultural backdrop of interpersonal violence was noted by many authors. Too often, interpersonal violence occurs in groups in which prevailing norms at the societal level legitimize violence between men and women and parent and child. Following from these norms are policies that codify power differentials, inadequately censure physical and sexual violence, or ignore these matters entirely because they are within the family sphere. Victimization of women and children too often intersects with poverty, increasing not only the risk of violence, abuse, and maltreatment but also the likelihood that the available service providers will offer inappropriate treatment or none. Likewise, some research and intervention programs either ignore race, ethnicity, class, and gender issues or focus on certain groups to the exclusion of others. And, too often, cultural fit and community input, which should perhaps be the first step, appear at a later point, after programs have advanced in their development. Contributors observed the tension between the need for cultural competence and the important advances in the field that would arise from broader scale implementation of standard approaches. In some cases, innovative programs were described that successfully combined both elements.

METHODOLOGICAL CONCERNS AND THE WAY FORWARD

After cataloguing what we know across fields, contributors took a close look at how the knowledge base has been established. Many concerns were expressed that informed where the next steps should begin. Several methodological issues were discussed in the conclusion to *Violence Against Women and Children, Volume 1: Mapping the Terrain* (White et al., 2011) and are not repeated here. Rather, our discussion focuses primarily on responses to violence and evaluation of intervention and prevention schemes in three select areas. We balance an overview of the concerns with discussion of some strategies to overcome them. Table 13.2 summarizes the full set of issues raised by the contributors to Volumes 1 and 2 in this series.

Role of Risk in Understanding Causality and Change

Too often risk factors are assumed to be directly causal. However, risk factors may be a proxy for some other influence and not causal in and of themselves (Kraemer et al., 1997). Some risk factors do not necessarily cause the onset of a problem, so altering or reducing them may not produce the desired prevention or treatment outcome. The conceptual basis of prevention interventions needs to address not only empirically supported risk factors that are malleable but also, most important, those that are also causal. Certain assumptions about risk and protective factors are deeply embedded. One is that theories of causation and theories of change are very similar or indeed identical. For example, in the area of sexual violence, we know that alcohol consumption is a risk factor for victimization. Changing that risk by telling women to not drink may lower the numbers of individual women being assaulted, but it will do little or nothing to alter perpetrator behavior; her drinking may affect some of the perpetrator's actions, but it is not a cause of his behavior, nor will it stop him from moving on to someone he perceives as more vulnerable.

In contrast to causal theories, theories of change describe how to produce results in treatment or prevention. They do not invariably require knowledge of causality. For example, in the area of child abuse, we can reduce future abuse by removing the child from the home without understanding the causes of the abuser's behavior. Not an argument for ignoring etiology, theories of change merely caution that a successful intervention or prevention program does not necessarily depend on understanding causality. It may be a trap to cling to categorical conclusions that intervention and pre-

TABLE 13.2
Methodological Issues

Issue	Specific problems and dilemmas
Challenges on the front line	• Little recognition of dilemmas associated with work on inter-personal violence that distinguish the field from all others • Inadequate attention to connecting university-based and community-engaged action research • Inadequate communication between stakeholders during planning phases • Underappreciation of the constraints on ideal designs in real-world settings • Dilemma of overreliance on self-report when it may be the only method of assessment • Misunderstandings in the community on the worth and components of sound evaluation
Definitions	• Lack of consensus on standardized definitions and means to increase their use • Lack of criteria for when to use narrow to broad definitions
Incidence and prevalence	• Too little explanation of what is being measured: incidence or prevalence, for lifetime or shorter periods, an experience or event? • Discrepancies between data sources need further analysis: large-scale surveys, convenience samples, criminal justice statistics, health care statistics, other agency sources, annual national and state level data
Measurement	• Underestimation of the extent to which self-report contributes to all data sources; seemingly objective data are underestimates because many cases of victimization and perpetration go unreported or uninvestigated and thus cannot be substantiated. • Line-based random-digit dialing data collection needs to be replaced due to increased sole use of mobile phones that challenge traditional representative sampling. • Few standard measures, of varying length and specificity, with little reliability/validity data • Insufficient qualitative data to illuminate nuanced questions • Unclear distinctions between proxy measures and the actual outcome of interest • Inadequate training for those who extract data from criminal and health records • Variability in the estimation models for economic costs • Inadequate assessment of contextual factors surrounding victimization • Unrealistic community-based staff and respondent burden; need to streamline assessment

Sampling	• Not clear on who is selected and why:
	  • Random, representative, or convenience samples?
	  • Arbitrary age ranges
	  • Inclusion/exclusion criteria vary across studies
	• Missing or inappropriate comparison groups
	• Little effort to get input from consumers of services about their ideas for proposed studies or their thoughts on how to recruit and disseminate information

(*continues*)

TABLE 13.2
Methodological Issues *(Continued)*

Issue	Specific problems and dilemmas
Theoretical models	• Most work is descriptive. • Etiology and causal mechanisms are too often inferred from correlations. • Lack of recognition of the interconnectedness of various types of abuse, their interactions, and the interactions among outcomes • Too few multilevel models that include mediators and moderators and that address roles of multiple systems • Little work on pathways to victimization and perpetration, as well as to outcomes • Lack of translational work to use etiologic models to improve treatment/intervention • Inadequate attention to protective factors • Overemphasis on theorizing at individual as opposed to system level
Designs	• Mismatches between designs used and questions asked • Too much focus on the cons of cross-sectional studies in the face of advances in strengthening inferences that can be drawn from them • Too few multilevel, longitudinal designs to separate cause and effect • Underuse of innovative quasi-experimental or mixed methods • Overvaluation of randomized clinical trials with insufficient attention to their feasibility, appropriateness, ethics, and weaknesses • Too few evidence-based evaluations
Analyses	• The available data often violate the criteria for validity of the most commonly used statistical approaches. • Unreported confidence intervals, especially with small sample sizes • Inadequate use of advances in analytic techniques
Culture	• Unexamined racial biases • Underrepresentation of ethnic and cultural population groups • Inadequate attention to culturally appropriate assessment; language barriers are not always appreciated
Collaboration	• Too little interaction among those with different types of expertise • Lack of mechanisms and support for large-scale, interdisciplinary work
Funding	• Inadequate funding for the level of research and evaluation that needs to be done
Dissemination	• Insufficient use of burgeoning new technologies for dissemination of stories, descriptive data, and user-friendly synopses of studies

Note. Assumptions: All parties (researchers, service providers, policymakers, advocates) recognize the value of research-generated knowledge for moving the field forward, which would include continuous quality improvement in interventions, prevention programs, and advocacy for policy change. Each problem has various responses/solutions that depend on context. Responses to a problem may include improving current practice and/or developing new practices.

vention must be theoretically driven or based on empirically supported risk factors. There are potentially more immediate gains to be made from working with models of change, although it is not an either/or choice.

Conceptual Models of Intervention

Conceptual models of intervention represent ideas about the processes that explain how change comes about. They attempt to sketch in the contents of the black box within which something happens that translates inputs into outcomes. These processes that occur within the black box are called *mediators* and can then become the immediate target for intervention (see Kazdin, 2007; Rodgers, 2010). Mediation analyses require that investigators not only assess the outcomes of interest but also measure the variables that are assumed to create them. Study of mediators proposes possible bases for the change, such as cognitive processes, stress reduction, or improved parenting skills, and then tests whether changes in outcomes at a later point can be specifically traced to these influences. For example, a recent evaluation tested the mediating effects of social support on survivors of interpersonal violence (Beeble, Bybee, Sullivan, & Adams, 2009). Social support mediated quality of life over time and provided a strong case for bolstering support as part of any intervention.

Research Design and Data Analyses

Many contributors recognized randomized controlled trials (RCTs) as the gold standard for evaluating the impact of interventions or prevention programs while also acknowledging the difficulty in conducting them. Although RCTs are feasible and useful in many contexts, they are not perfect. Randomization does not necessarily make groups equivalent prior to intervention (Hsu, 1989). Also, when results from randomized and nonrandomized studies are compared, the differences in the findings often are small (Shadish & Ragsdale, 1996). And such evidence-based interventions as exist are not likely to be in widespread use. We note these points not to dismiss RCTs but to foster greater receptivity to other options, especially when RCTs cannot be used.

When the intervention under study is treatment or services, one cannot randomly assign rape victims or battered women to control conditions for ethical reasons. If a high-risk group is included in a prevention evaluation, the concerns are the same. RCTs are not likely to be feasible when no-treatment or waiting-list control conditions are part of the design. Moreover, even if an RCT were feasible in principle and participants might be assigned to different conditions, often the design is not doable in practice. Accumulating enough cases in a given setting or conducting a preventive intervention across multiple sites to accrue sufficient cases is difficult and costly. Most services and interventions reviewed in the prior chapters of this volume were not evaluated and many barriers were documented. We suggest that there are design options and statistical tools that could greatly expand the horizon for scientifically strong, systematic, and rigorous evaluation. Consider three research traditions—quantitative, single-case, and qualitative research—that could improve and increase evaluation of intervention programs.

Quantitative Research

Within the quantitative tradition, there are many underused alternatives. First, quasi-experimental designs are useful when random assignment of participants or random allocation of the intervention is not possible. Strong inferences can still be drawn, but the strength comes from adding comparison groups to the design. A group can be identified that is very similar to the group that receives the intervention but did not receive the program. The comparison group receives assessments at the same time points that would be equivalent to assessments pre- and postintervention and on follow-up. These measurements help evaluate changes that may occur naturally over time without the intervention or are stimulated by thinking about the topics raised in the evaluation measures. The interested reader could see Evans and Ildstad (2001) for an in-depth discussion of alternative designs (see also Ellsburg and Heise, 2005, for methods feasible in underresourced settings). As a separate or complementary strategy, the strength of evaluation designs can be improved by the use of sophisticated statistical techniques. When cases cannot be assigned randomly to groups, such as prevention versus no prevention, people can be matched in various other ways such as according to their risk levels. Matching can greatly strengthen the inferences that can be drawn between groups (e.g., Hong & Yu, 2008; Stuart & Green, 2008). Prevention programs, and service and treatment programs as well, can be much more readily evaluated now than ever before in light of such advances, and thus the insistence on the superiority of RCTs has become a hindrance to progress.

In studies of violence it is often difficult to find sufficiently large numbers to permit allocation of individuals to different groups, whether random or not. Within the quantitative tradition, there is increased recognition that small samples are often the rule and place limitations on statistical power, that is, the likelihood of detecting truly significant differences. Examples of research in which large samples are unlikely include the study of people with unique experiences, such as multiple types of abuse, and evaluations of services provided by agencies outside of the megacities. There are many design alternatives that have been articulated for such situations to extract causal relations and to clarify the relations among multiple variables of interest (Rodgers, 2010).

Single-Case Designs

Apart from the quantitative tradition, single-case experimental research designs represent another viable alternative to RCTs. The designs use ongoing assessment on multiple occasions over time. Quantitative research is characterized by broad samples and relatively few measurement points. Single-case research is characterized by a small number of people from whom information is obtained frequently. Although there are many exceptions to this characterization, it conveys the main difference. Many community-based services are unlikely to be evaluated from the standpoint of a design that requires comparing groups and using a control group that does not receive the intervention. Single-case designs are readily available in these contexts. Interventions can be evaluated with several options, such as implementing the intervention for all cases but starting it at different times. Ongoing assessment can help to determine whether the intervention had the desired impact and permits causal inferences to be drawn about the role of the intervention by examining when the changes have occurred in relation to the ongoing assessment data. No control groups or withholding of the intervention is needed. If large numbers of cases are included, that is all the better, but if a program focuses on a limited number of cases a year or one program in one service setting, evaluation is still possible. The designs permit valid inferences to be drawn about causal relations with an individual or a single group and also with multiple groups (Kazdin, 2011).

Qualitative Research

Qualitative research was mentioned as an option for describing samples and for generating theory in the conclusion of *Violence Against Women and Children, Volume 1: Mapping the Terrain* (White et al., 2011). Qualitative research can evaluate change as well. The methodology provides in-depth description and evaluation of an individual's experience (Berg, 2001; Denzin & Lincoln, 2005). How individuals subjectively view, perceive, and react to situations and contexts are the central foci. For example, qualitative research can look at the experience of individuals who have been assaulted or who are the ones doing the assaulting and the ways in which their lives are influenced. The in-depth focus moves well beyond questionnaires and standardized interviews. The rigors of qualitative research can demonstrate change as well as inform us regarding how change comes about and different paths of change induced by the same intervention. We mentioned previously the scope of dysfunction caused by violence, and the breadth of its causes has important implications for assessing change. One must look broadly at the impact of interventions. Qualitative research allows emergent themes and domains to be revealed as part of the change process. Qualitative approaches also are well suited for the study of ethnic minority groups, immigrant populations, and other understudied groups for whom standardized measures might be intimidating or inappropriate. For example, among some Native American tribes, storytelling provides an effective vehicle for understanding victimization experiences.

Beyond variations in designs, novel or at least underused methods of statistical evaluation could contribute greatly to our understanding of interpersonal violence. Within the different areas of violence, a common concern was the importance of identifying mechanisms through which variables operate and moving from correlational to causal analyses (Rodgers, 2010). Statistical methods exist to provide options to advance analysis from looking at statistical probability to examining mechanisms of action and deeper explanations among relations involving several variables and variables at multiple levels (for descriptions and illustrations, see Foster & Kalil, 2008). Collaborations across disciplines are needed to promote these novel methods of study and to use advances in statistics and mathematics to increase the quantity and quality of application-relevant research.

CONSENSUS RECOMMENDATIONS

The introductory chapters to *Violence Against Women and Children, Volume 1: Mapping the Terrain* (White et al., 2011) and to this volume briefly discussed an analysis that Koss and White (2008) conducted of 11 national and international agendas aimed at providing recommendations to reduce and ultimately eliminate violence against women and children. They noted that these agenda recommendations were often expressed in broad language that had not changed much over time, thus creating the erroneous impression that little progress has been made. To achieve language that accommodated the growth of knowledge, they called for an accessible compendium of current science-based knowledge accompanied by expert opinions about the next steps in basic research, services, and prevention. These two volumes represent that careful study and the accumulated knowledge of the recent past. Contributors were asked for concrete recommendations—specifically, the substantive, methodological, and infrastructure changes that are needed to have a palpable impact.

There is remarkable synergy among the agenda items just released by the Centers for Disease Control and Prevention (CDC) as their 2018 aims (National Center for Injury Prevention and Violence, 2009) and the next steps suggested by contributors, which in many cases nudge the dialogue toward concrete action plans. Table 13.3 collects the next steps that emerged from the contributors. We have qualitatively sorted and listed them according to the agenda themes identified by Koss and White (2008), which were data, design, and measurement; medical responses; psychotherapy and support;

TABLE 13.3
Next Steps in Consensus Recommendations of 11 Existing Agendas

Recommendation[a]	Next steps
Data, design, and measurement	

Improve database.	• Encourage continued and expanded surveillance:
	  • Identify poly-victims.
	  • Improve surveillance of SV-related deaths and DV pregnancy-related deaths.
	• Include data on families involved in multiple systems.
	• Improve measurement of SV and DV in crime surveys.

Collect ongoing representative prevalence statistics.	• Develop a public health surveillance system (part of the Centers for Disease Control and Prevention's Injury Research Agenda). • Provide annual national and state-level figures. • Address sampling biases. • Increase application of qualitative methods to reflect the victimization experience across various diverse populations.
Improve and standardize measurement.	• Use alternative communication technologies for data collection. • Elaborate data presentation and clarify data: lifetime vs. past year; incidence vs. prevalence; narrow vs. broad definitions; survey context, question format, and sample. • Mitigate context effects from how questions are presented (e.g., as crime, health, relationship, problems). • Diversify research designs and match them to the questions. • Distinguish the condition of victimization from the event.
Develop standard terminology.	• Define key terms going beyond the basic forms of violence. • Incentivize standardized definitions and screening tools. • Delineate and provide choice in measurement: narrow and broad definitions; short and long formats; age appropriateness.
Include special populations.	• Assess social context of victimization and perpetration. • Move beyond reliance on college populations, expanding study of diverse groups (e.g., those of different races, socioeconomic groups, ethnicities, sexual orientations, global areas [e.g., conflict areas], age groups). • Oversample minority groups and look at subpopulations (avoid panethnic analysis without justification for merging data).

(continues)

TABLE 13.3
Next Steps in Consensus Recommendations of 11 Existing Agendas
(Continued)

Recommendation[a]	Next steps
	• Increase qualitative research to assess language barriers, cultural barriers to disclosure, and barriers to recruitment.
	• Link monitoring to improved program quality and consistency.
Assess life-span experiences and interrelatedness of forms of violence against women.	• Address the distinct cohorts served by child welfare systems: infants, school-age children, and adolescents.
	• Clarify that sexual violence can be one form of DV and that different forms often co-occur.
	• Collect longitudinal or temporally bounded data to quantify risk of prior victimization on revictimization.
Examine cultural supports for violence.	• Study development of and models of change for cultural norms.
	• Include economic, legal, religious, and social institutional practices that support and perpetuate violence.
Strengthen government coordination of database.	• Envision how to link law enforcement, health care provider, employer, college, and emergency department data.

	Medical responses
Train medical professionals to provide victim-sensitive, nonstigmatizing health care.	• Increase emphasis on psychological first aid.
	• Improve effectiveness of professional training to recognize signs of abuse.
	• Avoid revictimization; monitor responsiveness.
	• Incentivize professional mental health providers to continue upgrading skills of those with most contact with victims through participation/ information exchange in diverse settings such as emergency rooms, Sexual Assault Nurse Examiner programs, police departments, and community-based service agencies.
Improve emergency response.	• Enhance training in medically documenting context of injury.
	• Design studies to implement victim support services in health settings and examine their cost-effectiveness.
Research mental and physical health impact.	• Innovate approaches to encouraging participation in research, especially soon after assault.
	• Assess directionality of relationship between victimization and health effects in longitudinal research.
	• Use larger samples to make clear associations with specific health outcomes.
	• Examine how mental and physical outcomes interact; avoid overly narrow conceptualization of mental health such as posttraumatic stress disorder.
	• Research mediators and moderators of health impact.
	• Examine impact on reproductive decision making.

TABLE 13.3
Next Steps in Consensus Recommendations of
11 Existing Agendas   *(Continued)*

Recommendation[a]	Next steps
Integrate violence care into existing medical settings.	• Assess DV comprehensively to better understand impact of overlapping experiences. • Modify forms and train health care providers to code for violence. • Seek opportunities to integrate care for victimized women and children into emergency, reproductive, antenatal, family planning, postabortion, mental health, HIV/AIDS, and adolescent medicine services. • Consider how medical service providers may also facilitate referral of the men who are victimizing the women and children under their care.

Psychotherapy and support

Develop culturally and linguistically informed interventions.	• Infuse culture and inclusiveness throughout; encourage staff to recognize their limitations in the populations that they can serve well; locate services in areas of greatest need. • Research clinically based decision making to understand how values and beliefs impact treatment implementation. • Increase diversity of participants in efficacy studies to make research more applicable from community perspectives. • Incorporate broader social context into interventions to reduce disconnection between empirically evaluated treatments and the advocacy community's empowerment focus. • Examine whether community-based treatment methods might be effective to avoid overvaluing empirically validated treatments developed in academic settings. • Prioritize better responses to victimization for women with mental health problems, cognitive disabilities, substance abuse disorders, criminal records, and limited use of English. • Promote policy change in how in-prison therapy is offered.
Target high-risk groups of offenders and victims, especially youth.	• Balance research priorities to recognize that neglect is the most common form of child maltreatment. • Find ways to integrate parallel issues, such as violence, substance abuse, and fatherhood. • Find ways to engage men in the community in stopping violence because the success of treatment programs rests in the support of antiviolence efforts in the community and by other men.

(continues)

TABLE 13.3
Next Steps in Consensus Recommendations of
11 Existing Agendas   *(Continued)*

Recommendation[a]	Next steps
Strengthen formal and informal support systems for women living with violence.	• Prioritize comprehensive family support for parents in need and community building for isolated parents. • Offer holistic services because victimized women and children and violence-impacted families have many needs.
Document and evaluate community-based services.	• Develop national data on victims' experiences with community-based services and their impact, using longitudinal designs. • Identify required program elements that meet minimum quality standards to provide greater guidance in the field. • Determine the minimum length of treatment, basic program structure, and compliance monitoring for any offender service. • Find better ways of tracking partner safety.
Foster coordination of medical, mental health, and justice.	• Build interdisciplinary practice and research to protect children and strengthen families and communities. • Utilize innovative venues to provide male-targeted violence-prevention messages, including job training, employment, or housing support programs. • Define and reaffirm the qualities of healthy relationships, especially within religious minority groups, and utilize the capacity of faith-based communities for ongoing, informal support.
Improve evaluation of treatment effectiveness in reducing future violence.	• Align research efforts with the data on where most mental health services are delivered and by whom. • Evaluation and acceptance of evidence-based treatments have prerequisite conditions: training, funding, and mutual buy-in.

	Justice responses
Increase effectiveness of retributive responses.	• Approach measurement of justice system performance from a longitudinal perspective, tracing cases through reporting, investigation, prosecution, plea agreements, guilty verdicts, sentences, and recidivism rates to adequately assess the extent to which retributive responses are predictably and effectively applied. • Assess the risk of stigma and potential punishment that boys and men believe would result if they perpetrated various forms of violence against women and children. • Increase involvement of experts in applying sociopsychologically based, effective methods to change stereotypes in the minds of justice personnel and jury members.

TABLE 13.3

Recommendation[a]	Next steps

	• Influence the openness of the legal system to knowledge-based input.
	• Rebalance disproportionate use of prosecutorial resources on drugs or immigration to better address violence against women and children.
	• Avoid hierarchy rule in crime statistics so that all crimes, not just the most serious, are counted.
	• Address anomalies, such as low percentage of prosecutions for crimes against children and civil laws that permit parents' religious and cultural exceptions to child maltreatment and medical treatment laws.
	• Incorporate treatment for domestically abusive men into prisoner reentry programs.
	• Reenvision sexual assault change agenda:
	  • Change passive-consent standard to require active consent.
	  • Revise proof requirements associated with nonconsent and burden of proof of force in sexual assaults.
	  • Recognize alcohol as a weapon when used to rape.
	  • Create legal right or standing to challenge the revelation of private records and communications.
	  • Allow independent representation for victims in trial.

Identify justice barriers and initiatives to increase justice options.	• Address conflicts between state and federal mandates.
	• Accord victims greater flexibility; promote victim input into criminal justice decisions such as postponing prosecution, delaying charges while victim receives advocacy services, or declining to prosecute some charges if victims cooperate on others.
	• Extend coordination to hold offenders in treatment to their support obligations without coercing or threatening victim.
	• Develop family-focused solutions and alternatives that focus on building resources.
	• Focus reform at the broader system level; move outside the justice system to offer assistance and resources to victims and those who are at risk of doing harm.
	• Implement and evaluate
	  • alternative, victim-centered remedies;
	  • holistic approach to offender accountability, victim remedies, and community healing; and
	  • community-based prevention rather than justice responses after the fact.

(continues)

TABLE 13.3
Next Steps in Consensus Recommendations of
11 Existing Agendas *(Continued)*

Recommendation[a]	Next steps
	Prevention
Develop and evaluate theoretically based interventions to change social norms.	• Conceptualize empirically and theoretically based risk factors more broadly, prioritizing societal level causes over individual. • Develop more gender-specific programs. • Distinguish associated risks from causes and recognize that behavior *can* be changed without direct focus on cause. • Create approaches that involve multiple targets (risks, people, and communities) and use multiple change methods designed to alter several risk behaviors at once. • Promote dialogue to negotiate the tension between those who prioritize participatory, community-based approaches and those identified with randomized clinical trial (RCT) methodology. • Do formative research including pilot testing of methods and research on feasibility. • Maintain flexibility to implement quantitative and qualitative methods that may be better suited than formal experiments and may increase the overall level of community-based research • When possible, address threats to integrity of RCTs to assess prevention efficacy, including eligibility requirements that make the sample unlike the real world, biased assignment, lack of statistical power, and diffusion of treatment into control group. • Include near-term goals to increase chances of meaningful data. • Adopt appropriate measurement that detects change and is reliable and valid, as well as acceptable to clients and practitioners in terms of time, clarity, language, sensitivity, and usefulness. • Create a primer on modern, robust statistical approaches that addresses innovative designs and the multilevel complexity presented by ecological, life span, and diversity ideals. • Foster a culture of knowledge generation and knowledge use. • Report implementation information to increase chances that innovative programs will be adopted. • Research delivery systems to improve understanding of implementation; study how and why innovations are not delivered with fidelity. • Identify obstacles encountered in implementation of evidence-based programs, including tension

TABLE 13.3

Recommendation[a]	Next steps
	over implementing as designed, which is more effective, or adopting it to community needs, which results in higher cultural competence, recruitment, retention, and provider acceptance.
	• Nurture key stakeholders who champion innovation and provide technical assistance, capacity building, and other support activities.
Research risks for victimization, focusing on features that are amenable to change.	• Mount multivariate evaluations of risk factors at all levels of social ecology and within various ethnic and cultural groups.
	• Place more emphasis on effects of exposure to violence and the pathways that mediate their influence.
	• Integrate developmental psychopathology, trauma theory, and family systems theory.
	• Focus prevention on causes but recognize that behavior *can* sometimes be changed without direct focus on them.
	• Target for risk reduction those most at risk, which may be potentially more cost effective.
	• Monitor effects of individual or universal prevention, as some initiatives may be harmful.
	• Develop culturally competent programming and programming tailored to high-risk groups.
Research risks for perpetration.	• Research conditions that channel individual motivation into violent action.
	• Study decision making and factors that foster maintenance, escalation, reduction, or desistence.
	• Translate what is known about risk factors into effective and large-scale prevention efforts.
Create multisectoral, multimethod action plan.	• Overcome isolation of disciplines and potential partners, including medical, justice, and public health systems and family, friends, community organizations, business, military, unions, and the faith community.
	• Reduce isolation of mental health, substance use, and DV scholars, programs, services, advocacy, and policy.
	• Incentivize submission of joint planning and funding proposals across federal and state agencies responsible for child welfare, mental health, substance abuse, maternal and child health, justice, and public health to encourage multisector research and service provision.
Collect systematic data on injuries and a biomechanical profile of characteristic injuries.	• Consider interface with a national surveillance system.

(continues)

TABLE 13.3
Next Steps in Consensus Recommendations of
11 Existing Agendas   *(Continued)*

Recommendation[a]	Next steps
Emphasize primary prevention.	• Recognize the expense and limitations of in-prison treatment; invest in and build primary prevention so that the need for imprisonment is reduced.
Prioritize prevention with children.	• Target prevalent risk or protective factors with the strongest associations with maltreatment that are shown to be modifiable with reasonably priced interventions. • Maintain attention to mitigating child victims' vulnerability to abuse later in life.
Identify and intervene in high-risk families.	• Aim for long-term goals of reducing revictimization and intergenerational transmission with specified intermediate goals. • Provide support for families through community action programs to strengthen parent–child relations. • Focus on broad social forces instead of over-emphasis on individual children, parents, and families. • Coordinate social service delivery with prevention. Poverty is an established risk factor, but prevention programs often fail to connect with available emergency cash assistance. • Enhance Early Head Start with Nurse Family Partnership model of home visiting so future evaluations are a better test of its potential.
Create sustained, long-term antiviolence curricula in schools.	• Target high-risk children as they enter school and develop comprehensive, age-appropriate school-based programs designed to promote general developmental competencies; actively involve parents and teachers. • Include initiatives for neediest schools, whose students share multiple risk factors. • Balance mixed-sex and same-sex programs. • Collaborate with other health promotion initiatives, such as alcohol abuse prevention.
Make physical environments and schools safer. Use media for prevention.	• Teach about safe relationships in the schools. • Use youths themselves as change agents. • Teach people who work with children to recognize the signs of abuse. • Educate young people about how media images are unrealistic, faulty, harmful, and should not be believed. • Address depictions of abuse against women and girls in entertainment media through efforts to stop negative imagery. • Infuse public campaigns with both general and culturally specific information.

TABLE 13.3
Next Steps in Consensus Recommendations of
11 Existing Agendas *(Continued)*

Recommendation[a]	Next steps
Share assessable, evidence-based summaries of research.	• Offer technical assistance to build a prevention infrastructure. • Study the implementation process as conceptualized by the Centers for Disease Control and Prevention's Prevention Synthesis and Translation System or SAMHSA's Strategic Prevention Framework.

Advocacy

Use knowledge-based advocacy and public speaking out.	• Increase the usefulness and accessibility of scientific knowledge. • Dialogue with service sectors to determine information needs and preferred methods of delivery.
Strengthen national commitment and strategic planning.	• Augment the social will for a coordinated multi-sectoral strategy to support programs for parenthood, children, and the social safety net. • Remediate VAWA legislation to increase funding for research and academic-community partnerships. • Reincentivize VAWA funding to support meaningful collaboration rather that dividing funds into identified "pots" set aside for existing systems to use independently. • Communicate findings: Current research can inform priorities and policies regarding funding. • Advocate for a National Institute as an expression of national commitment and a vehicle for strategic planning, coordination, and collaboration.
Promote human rights and gender and socioeconomic equality.	• Increase resources for poor families, and connect families to informal supports and formal services appropriate to setting and culture. • Move beyond continuing focus on values of middle-class Anglo women to provide competent services for more women. • Analyze socioeconomic differences. • Broaden prevention beyond the individual level to engender community and societal change.

Funding

Increase funds for prevention.	• Increase funding for child abuse research. • Increase funding through advocacy for sound science. • Remediate VAWA legislation that currently fails to direct sufficient funds toward supporting research and academic-community partnerships.

(continues)

TABLE 13.3
Next Steps in Consensus Recommendations of
11 Existing Agendas *(Continued)*

Recommendation[a]	Next steps
Raise funds for service provision and shelters.	• Provide funding incentives for strengthening prevention delivery systems. • Raise funding to implement evidence-based community services, including support to accommodate training, achieving mutual buy-in, and resolving value incongruence.
Increase research and evaluation funding and use it strategically.	• Shift from a "what doesn't work" to a "what does work" model to drive research. • Increase funding and raise ceilings on funds per study to permit rigor. • Create support mechanisms to develop innovative programs to the point that they are culturally anchored and capable of strong evaluation design. • Conceptualize academic and community partnerships as bidirectional, starting at the conceptualization stage of research. • Increase funding for research on risk and protective factors.

Note. DV = domestic violence; SAMHSA = Substance Abuse and Mental Health Services Administration; VAWA = Violence Against Women Act.
[a]See Koss and White (2008) for the qualitative policy analysis on which the consensus recommendations are based. The next steps were identified by the expert contributors to these volumes.

justice responses; prevention; advocacy; and funding. Readers are reminded that when considering implementation of these recommendations, we remain cognizant of the numerous dilemmas associated with work on interpersonal violence that distinguish the field from others. As noted in the concluding chapter to *Violence Against Women and Children, Volume 1: Mapping the Terrain* (White et al., 2011), standard operating procedures do not always work. In the following sections we emphasize seven overarching themes within the recommended next steps.

Improving Assessment

We already know from current assessments that violence is a costly public health problem both in terms of direct economic costs and in lowered life quality, which points to the urgency for data that will lend itself to systematic national tracking of prevalence, incidence, impact on morbidity and mortality, and societal costs across diverse groups and encompassing the life span. The prospect of large-scale preventive strategies and local, state, and national efforts to intervene at multiple levels will require a much better database than we currently have. An improved database can serve as a natural laboratory to track the impact of local policies. Several next steps pertaining to measurement are fundamental to progress. The first issue begins with defining different types of interpersonal violence and the need for agreed-upon definitions. Standard, formally stated definitions are central and a starting point for developing assessment instruments, whether for screening, risk-factor identification, or program evaluation. National and international health and justice organizations have articulated definitions, but the incentives to adopt them uniformly have been lacking. They could be uniform in grant proposals for funding, in contract reporting requirements, and in the publication standards of scientific journals regarding what constitutes state-of-the-art measurement. Consistency is needed so that data can be integrated, combined and compared and the knowledge base augmented by studies of specialized topics and samples too small to be present in adequate numbers for analysis in national surveillance data but too important to ignore. Consistency across studies is also a viable strategy for maximizing scarce research dollars. Maintaining the ability to aggregate that database would allow more small-scale and specialized endeavors to be funded, rather than focusing disproportionate resources on large, multisite trials that, for all the information they contribute, are not strategic to obtaining quantitative and qualitative information across diverse groups and ages.

Building on uniform definitions, the standard measure was identified as a crucial step to progress. Contributors encouraged supplementing self-reported information with other modalities of assessment whenever possible. However, self-report has perhaps inappropriately become synonymous with paper-and-pencil or telephone surveys. It is important to recognize that many sources of seemingly independent quantitative data, such as police reports, depend heavily on disclosure by the victim and are thus a proxy for self-report. And although there may be witnesses to maltreatment, they often are other family members, who may choose not to fully reveal what they know or have ulterior motives that drive what they share. Unrelated third-party observers, when they exist for intimate crimes and abuse, may not have the contextual information to interpret what they see. Qualitative data potentially enlarge understanding because their adaptability to linguistic and content analysis may reveal deeper meanings about what was said and not said.

Assessment needs in the area of interpersonal violence are broad because violence influences multiple aspects of an individual's functioning at a given point in time and over time. A related assessment challenge is addressing the multiple contexts in which violence occurs. These too need to be assessed because they relate to future risk of revictimization or reperpetration, individual recovery, family and community support, and societal norms. Understanding victimization and perpetration of violence and intervening for prevention or treatment purposes will require evaluation at individual, family, and societal levels and considering how these influences interact with policy and contextual factors to promote or reduce violence. A broad ecological model is routinely advocated to conceptualize the scope of violence. For research and evaluation, the model also conveys the assessment challenge. The central issues going forward are what influences need to be assessed and what measures we lack to assess them reliably and validly. Much of the focus to date has been on measurement at the individual level and much less at the broader levels, especially community-wide change. Within individual assessment, scales have proliferated around single aspects of risk and cause, such as attitudes. Finally, contributors emphasized the strengths of prospective measurement when feasible because of its greater contribution to assigning causality. However, as we previously discussed, these types of studies are resource intensive and difficult in community settings. More widespread use of novel designs and contemporary statistical approaches have made great strides in increasing what can be learned from retrospective information obtained on a single occasion where conditions constrain other approaches.

The objective that could be realized by improving and standardizing assessment would be the ability of individual studies to contribute to a comprehensive, national database on violence victimization and perpetration, based on agreed-upon definitions and assessment tools. The synergetic relations between common terminology, assessment tools, and improved databases cannot be overstated. Any research endeavor, treatment provision, system response, and prevention program ultimately rests on the accumulation of information and the ability to reach conclusions based on a broader database using techniques such as meta-analysis.

Diversifying Our Focus

Recommendations for next steps include the need to sample more broadly across our population. Here, too, special challenges are raised by the subject matter. Interpersonal violence spans the entire age range. In these two volumes, we have not focused specifically on infants and older adults, but child abuse, sexual violence, and domestic violence involves these groups. Research on assessment, services, and intervention is taxed by the challenge to attend to the full age range and the different needs at given points in the life span. The first task is to better document given types of violence longitudinally and to evaluate them developmentally—specifically, how age and development influence risk factors, recovery, trajectory, and deterrence or prevention of violence. We are accountable to a population that is diverse ethnically, culturally, socially, sexually, religiously, and in their abilities. Correlates of violence can vary as a function of group characteristics. Frequency of victimization, reactions to victimization, and long-term course are influenced by how the culture responds, expected reactions of the victim, and the presence, absence, and type of social supports available. Services are often not available to all, and when they are available, individuals may be treated quite differently as a function of ethnicity, socioeconomic status, and culture, as well as other social indicators including gender, sexual orientation, and disability status. Reporting patterns also are likely to vary as a function of beliefs about victimization but also from fear of differential treatment through health care and legal systems. Justice accountability and child protection decisions are also widely recognized as influenced, frequently inappropriately, by these characteristics.

Accumulating national databases that incorporate studies focused on specific populations will begin to provide more systematic descriptive data and help those in practice, prevention, and policy to focus their work. This initial point dovetails with our comments about assessment challenges. Documenting violence will not be accomplished by a single measure that can be applied across the developmental spectrum, but standard measures covering various life epochs are feasible. One could envision a comprehensive screening for adults that devoted equal but brief attention to the various manifestations of violence across life. Balancing measurement precision with feasibility is central to the success of this aim. Companion brief modules are needed to assess children and adolescents, and third-party reporting may be needed in the case of younger children and some disabled persons. An agreed-upon core and incentives for its adoption would permit investigators to amplify their measurement within the study focus, yet still contribute to the greater good by collecting information suitable for inclusion in national databases. As is true with many other criminal justice and public statistical resources, the contributions of many widely dispersed individual practitioners and scientists could be guided by federal leadership. Likewise, a common core would create far more opportunity than currently exists to use approaches such as meta-analysis to empirically evaluate existing knowledge and inform the agenda going forward.

Ethnicity and culture raise many opportunities to intervene to prevent violence and mitigate its effects. There may be culturally specific support opportunities that draw on strengths of a given community. These strengths might be found in peer groups, supportive roles that religion and spirituality may play, or in the leadership of community elders. An ideal model of services, treatment, and prevention would profit from an understanding how culture may moderate onset, course, and consequences of the experience of violence. Socioeconomic status also raises sampling issues. Ethnicity and culture in the United States are often closely tied to socioeconomic status, but they are not the same. Different strata need to be studied, because the levels of violence, needs, services, detection, and interventions are likely to vary depending on the educational, economic, and social resources upon which individuals can draw. Our call for qualitative studies is a case in point, where the intensive study of small numbers of individuals could generate as well as test hypotheses about ethnicity and culture that increase the inclusiveness of larger scale quantitative studies. A coordinated series of studies of this nature would be of great help in achieving CDC's aim to focus resources where they are most needed to build and strengthen safe, secure, nurturing relationships and, we might add, environments, policies, and broader social norms that reduce violence proclivity and violence-supportive norms.

Enhancing Services and Treatment

Quite clear from the chapters is that victims and perpetrators of violence require a broad range of supports and types of care. There are simply too few services available to address the medical, psychological, and legal issues that routinely emerge. The standard reply is that providing such services would be very costly. Yet, the estimates of the economic costs provided by the contributors in *Violence Against Women and Children, Volume 1: Mapping the Terrain* (White et al., 2011) suggest that the cost of not providing services is exorbitant, as reflected in morbidity, mortality, and transmission of victimization and perpetuation across generations. Thorough evaluation of the costs of victimization and perpetuation may be critical in relation to policies that decide where to allocate resources. In light of what we have learned about the scope of the impact of violence on individuals, we need to consider anew what services are needed, how are they sequenced, and on what basis we decide that they have met their goals.

A consensus recommendation was the need to coordinate services. Victims of violence are not at their peak moments in life to negotiate the many services that constitute a holistic response. Indeed, there are likely to be obstacles and delays in procuring services, discriminatory practices, a deficit-based and punitive-values model as opposed to a strengths approach, and over-emphasis on prescribed professional interventions in a context of lack of empowerment of individuals, families, and communities. Access to services is a critical topic, and it includes real and perceived barriers to services and how they can be overcome. It is worthwhile to distinguish the components of services—procedures, interventions, supports, education, and assistance— from the way in which the service is delivered. Victims of violence are already vulnerable, stressed, and understandably likely to just opt out of any service that confronts them with red tape, delay, excessive time demands, shame, blame, and other challenges. Likewise, perpetrators of violence are likely to be defensive and vulnerable to frustration with interventions that are perceived as obstacles. We need to know about those characteristics that make services acceptable and accessible, used or not used, and ultimately effective or ineffective as viewed from the perspective of their recipients and measured by their impact on community-level indicators. It is of little use to have evidence-based procedures if we cannot make them widely available and bring individuals to them. That requires better understanding of why prospective clients may resist interventions and why those who desire help may be prevented from getting it. These points are also quite apt for perpetrators of violence. For them, entry into a system is typically through the criminal justice system, which, despite its enormous costs, is ill-equipped to deal with the perpetrators' myriad other problems, which, if left unaddressed, increase the risk of reperpetration; also, their reintegration into the community may be made more difficult by supervisory conditions placed on offenders. Many services for perpetrators are court mandated. More work is needed to find interventions that are effective under such constraints, as is a policy analysis to examine how institutional practices could be modified to better meet the minimum conditions required for therapeutic effectiveness.

Finally, given the scope of services needed for victims and perpetrators, more sophisticated strategies than merely adding more of the same will be required. That is, simply providing more funding for more services as they are currently provided will not address core needs of victims and perpetrators. If there is a single model in use now, it is a fragmented and inconsistent one. There might be different models for accomplishing integration, and they may well be suited to different settings and locales, such as community health centers, shelters for the homeless, social services, schools, or prisons. One model suggested would be better integration of responses to violence into other services. Conceptual work is needed on the nature of the services that are likely to help. In addition, modeling of how these services are to be provided would be useful to determine the best way to reach more people, given the distribution of violence and the variables that influence that distribution, such as geography, culture, age, gender, physical ability, and ethnicity. Conceptual modeling can identify what needs there are and how we might have overlapping ways of meeting them so that more people receive services. Mathematical modeling can be useful in identifying the most efficient way of getting services to the people in the greatest need and what the benefits of different models of delivering services will be. Math sounds like a cold way to address the poignant and wrenching problems in violence against women and children. The opposite is true. We need our very best tools to deploy existing resources and to decide the most effective ways of bringing new resources online.

Growing Prevention

There is consensus on the centrality of prevention. Violence has consequences that fan out and lead to broad physical and mental health problems, for both victims and perpetrators, which have been well documented in prior chapters. The sheer scale of violence adds to the priority of prevention and deterrence by public health and criminal justice systems. Prevention is a stage at which the very best and most rigorous science is needed to ensure effective application. First, we need conceptual models related not only to onset of violence but theories of change. What are the different paths to prevention, and can we test these paths to be sure we understand them? Basic work on how to tailor prevention and to change behavior, including identifying the mediators of change, is pivotal. Contributors have provided a set of next steps that could be viewed as the intermediate actions needed to achieve the CDC agenda that aspires to evaluate the effectiveness, efficacy, and cost-to-benefit ratio of programs, strategies, and policies designed to reduce violence. Although we do not want to suggest moving prevention work to the lab with basic science, we ought to do more basic science to help move prevention forward. It is still common to identify risk factors, select those thought to be malleable, and design a prevention program around them. That approach can be successful, but it also can fail because risk factors and their change are not necessarily the only way to reduce violence. A public-health perspective also benefits from the search for risk factors that are causal. Once risk factors are taken into account, the next steps are to test how they might operate in a causal sequence. A universal intervention aiming at a certain familiar and understandable set of risk factors could equalize them to the point that it would be impossible to know which ones to emphasize, in what dose, when, and for whom.

We need to outline an integrated portfolio of viable preventive interventions that address diverse points of intervening over the course of life. By necessity this will involve primary, secondary, and tertiary methods, levels of foci ranging from individual-based to societal, degrees of effort and cost that vary from brief, educational, and informational to more intensive clinical services, and models and means of delivery. Related but less well conceptualized or studied are the synergistic effects of coordinated multilevel approaches. For prevention of violence, interventions that are focused on specific at-risk groups are likely to be more effective against a larger backdrop of efforts to influence social norms and public policy. We mention an effective media approach (Entertainment Education) that has been used to have impact on large-scale public health and social problems, including family planning, and applied across many cultures on different continents. Interestingly, the model is also being adopted and adapted to exert influence on behaviors that promote a sustainable environment and mitigate climate change (Charles, 2009). No less an effort is needed to change the cultural climate in relation to violence against women and children.

There is much to be learned from public health prevention successes such as the reduction of smoking, lowered incidence of shaken baby syndrome, and increased use of seat belts and infant seats. All of these successes depended on a multilevel approach beginning with individual-level education and services— strategic activities intended to change norms across the society, often utilizing communication through public media and advocacy in public policy. In this context, universal preventive interventions that are not necessarily designed to reach specific groups play a role but are best viewed in the context of more finely honed interventions focusing on situations, contexts, and settings where we find the individuals who are more likely to be victims and perpetrators of violence. Thus, multilevels of preventive interventions, including universal interventions, are essential not only because of the potential synergistic effects of such interventions but also because of the imperfections in identifying those who warrant specific interventions. Among the challenges are identifying what proportion within the at-risk sample is likely to be a victim or perpetrator of violence and the extent to which that proportion can be decreased by preventive interventions.

It is difficult to demonstrate changes in the proportion that are victimized or perpetrate because their relative numbers are low. How can that be when the cumulative proportion of women and children with histories of violence is so high? At any given measurement point, the numbers of recent victims or perpetrators are low in the context of groups of 1,000 or 100,000 people. Very large samples are required to achieve numbers of recent victims or perpetrators sufficient for analysis, and currently we are not notably capable of predicting the occurrence or nonoccurrence of low-incidence acts. This is a limitation that is true across other forms of injury research, as well as other topics in mental health, medicine, social welfare, and criminal justice. This challenge may circle back to the earlier recommendation of a cumulative database because only very large numbers of people, consisting of diverse samples that have been the focus of intentional outreach, will yield sufficient cases that can be identified to respond to many of the scientific challenges we have raised.

Building Infrastructure

Contributors identified several specific areas in which the infrastructure is inadequate. Among them are delivery and coordination of services, facilitation of efforts to translate basic research into community application, support and technical assistance to move approaches developed under ideal academic conditions to the real world, implementation of programs with fidelity and evaluating effectiveness in real-world settings, and fostering basic research as well as community-engaged action research. Contributors across the board called for more funding and training in relation to the infrastructure that supports effective research, services, and prevention. Piecemeal funding and training increases, however, will not make the advances needed. Interpersonal violence is inherently a multidisciplinary topic, and simply creating more slots for training in areas such as family law, medicine and nursing, psychology, public health, or social work alone is not optimally helpful.

Currently the violence portfolio is dispersed across numerous federal agencies and nominally follows a structure for interagency communication and coordination recommended by the National Academy of Sciences in 1996 (Crowell & Burgess, 1996). It could be argued that this recommendation was not fully implemented or the approach taken has not achieved the intended aim. To the extent that a lead agency has emerged, it is the CDC, which has made phenomenal progress in advancing the injury prevention agenda, addressing violence that is self-inflicted, interpersonal, or supported by the community's culture. Contributors identified a much broader group of players whose activities should be integrated into a national agenda. Piecemeal funding injects a stimulant dose but does not make a structural change; more resources used in the same way are not what is needed. It is possible for various agencies or organizations to hold a conference on interpersonal violence or have requests for grant proposals. An isolated article, consensus panel, and blue ribbon committee may have some impact. However, to keep violence against women and children at the forefront requires organizations dedicated to that purpose. Such organizations, moreover, cannot be expected to have a longer term perspective without support from the major funding agencies. The funders have tended to indicate the will to address the complex issues associated with the intimate forms of violence against women and children, but the dollars have not followed. Nor can individual investigators be expected to focus on the overall goals, as each identifies and carves an area in which "more research is needed." A formula to realize a large, interwoven, coordinated, and multipronged agenda to respond to and prevent violence against women and children cannot be achieved given current operating procedures, which include the following: requests for proposals, responses from investigators or service providers, and intense competition for a minimal number of funded projects; small resource centers that maintain the artificial and counterproductive separation of the forms of violence against women and children; scattered prevention centers where these forms of violence are frequently marginalized; symbolic gestures toward providing culturally competent responses; and initiatives by individual states that allocate funds according to fixed formulas that channel money into independent streams for criminal justice, public health, and social service.

Novel thinking about the use of funds and about training models, and how these fall in line with long-term goals, is needed at a structural level that is permanent. Multiple disciplines and the workforce that performs an array of tasks within the field need to be brought together to address the issues raised in these volumes. A strategic approach is needed to prioritize questions that ought to be addressed first and identify the best way to accomplish them. A national clearinghouse is needed for evidence in relation to interpersonal violence. A model exists in the National Criminal Justice Resource Service, but this information does not include material from other systems that contribute knowledge and experience in addressing violence. Information resources are difficult to locate because they are dispersed across federal and state agencies, small-scale federally supported nongovernmental organizations, privately funded single-focus advocacy groups, and the disseminations arms of large professional organizations. Furthermore, these resources typically are crafted to meet specific objectives rather than to coalesce into a comprehensive information archive. More centralized and authoritative information ranging in sophistication from research studies, statistical databases, and policy documents to materials aimed at the general public can be broadly useful to all. Apart from conveying that our government is working for us, the information itself can be concretely useful in providing the national heft to maintain the public's sensitivity to violence against women and children.

Promoting Equity

The critical issues in violence, including the scope of its consequences, impact, and costs to our society, have been recognized for decades and nonetheless persist despite gains in the sophistication of the knowledge. Victimization of women and children is widely considered to be based in part on gender. The *World Report on Violence Against Children* (Pinheiro, 2006) concluded that girls' "greater vulnerability to violence in many settings is in large part a product of the influence of gender-based power relations within society" (p. 7) and that "violence against children is a major obstacle to gender equality" (p. xi). The promotion of human rights was identified by contributors to this volume as essential to address interpersonal violence. There are many international treaties and efforts to ban violence. Among the most visible efforts is the United Nations Conventions on the Rights of the Child (United Nations High Commissioner for Human Rights, 1990) with stipulations (Article 19) to prohibit all forms of physical or mental violence, abuse, injury, and neglect of children, including corporal punishment. The goal was to have all 192 member nations of the United Nations legislate the ban by 2009. Only the United States and Somalia refused to ratify the treaty. As of this writing, 25 nations have banned all violence against children; another

20 or so countries are debating the matter within their national governing bodies. Again, the United States is not one of the latter countries. Within the United States, child abuse is defined by the states. Twenty-eight states and the District of Columbia have banned corporal punishment in the schools, but none have reclassified it as abuse when it occurs in the home. Clearly, there is work to be done to eliminate corporal punishment in homes when almost three quarters of the state legislatures have not even seen fit to prohibit it in public educational institutions. Similarly, the United Nations Convention for the Elimination of All Forms of Discrimination Against Women (CEDAW), first adopted September 18, 1979, has been ratified by 185 countries, the United States again not among them (see Division for the Advancement of Women, 2000). This is a national disgrace and tragedy inasmuch as the World Health Organization (2009) has acknowledged that there is a synergistic relation between the elimination of gender-based violence, the achievement of gender equality, and the achievement of various economic goals. Given the United States' current rapprochement with the United Nations and its intent to improve America's world image, there could be no more critical time than now for Congress to pass legislation ratifying CEDAW.

Realizing Collaboration

We are not the first to suggest the need for a national organization or structure to take a broad integrative perspective on interpersonal violence. It is one matter to note the importance of collaboration, but another to have a suitable and effective centralized policy center or agency organized to accomplish these goals. We would like to highlight the National Partnership to End Interpersonal Violence Across the Lifespan (NPEIV). The NPEIV is a national network of over 150 organizations, agencies, and coalitions that deal with various aspects of interpersonal violence. Its mission is to increase public awareness and education; contribute to training and mentoring; disseminate translation research; promote best practices in research, practice, policy, and grass-roots organizing; and inform public policy through user-friendly electronic informational resources and advocacy work by action teams. The network has working groups dedicated to 11 areas: public awareness, training and mentoring, practice, research, funding development, public policy, community action/capacity building, technology, dissemination/translation, outreach/networking, and publicity/public relations. This network has the potential to move the field beyond the platitudes that have been heard since the 1990s and to offer an independent structure where conversations can take place, fences begin to fall, and a reinforced voice for change take root.

CONCLUSION

These two volumes accomplished our original goals of bringing together the highest level of scholarship from multiple disciplines. We sought to convey the latest advances among areas of child abuse, sexual violence, and domestic violence that relate to each other and to an overall problem for society and for individuals and to suggest the next steps that can guide researchers, practitioners, legislators, and policymakers. We identified the progress in research, practice, and policy and focused on many areas where research is not very widely available.

Women and children are the victims of violence, yet in many cases (a) women are blamed for the violence because "bad mothering" started an intergenerational cycle of abuse even when the mother was not the perpetrator and (b) most of the early prevention programs expected women to shoulder the burden of preventing violence. Programs focusing on men and identifying high-risk men, as well as those that are universal and give every citizen something to do to prevent violence, are positive developments. However, what we are doing with men has virtually no demonstrated effectiveness. It is not a matter of poor design; the simple fact is that few programs are even evaluable. There is also the important issue of the repressive culture of U.S. public schools and its hypersensitivity toward offending *any* segment of the community, to say nothing of a policy emphasis on achieving academic standards that has pushed critical developmental educational activities (e.g., education about social and relationship skills) out of school curricula. We are seeing the impact of these constraints in the proliferation and exacerbation of physically violent bullying and gender, racial, and sexual orientation–based harassment and hateful acts. All our writers emphasized the urgency of starting prevention much earlier than the current norm and shifting in adulthood toward family strengthening and citizen roles in responding to violence and previolent acts. Finally, as discussed earlier, the evidence-based requirements that both the CDC (National Center for Injury Prevention and Control, 2009) and the World Health Organization (2009) have endorsed are important, but their standards are so rigorous that few studies are considered to measure up. When scientists and funders enforce narrow views of what constitutes informative knowledge, the field figuratively shoots itself in the foot. We hope we have persuasively argued that there are design options that are equally valuable in applied settings and that we are missing opportunities for knowledge development in our attempts to always emulate the methods of other sciences.

Violence against women and children is one of the most heart-wrenching of all forms of human suffering. It is that fact that makes our work and the work of our colleagues in these volumes much more than an abstract exercise. Each instance of abuse is a human tragedy. But regardless of whether one is moved by empathy for personal suffering, by practicalities such as monetary costs, or by some combination of both, action cannot wait.

REFERENCES

Barak, A., Hen, L., Boniel-Nissim, M., & Shapira, N. (2008). A comprehensive review and a meta-analysis of the effectiveness of Internet-based psychotherapeutic interventions. *Journal of Technology in Human Services, 26,* 109–160.

Beeble, M. L., Bybee, D., Sullivan, C. M., & Adams, A. E. (2009). Main, mediating, and moderating effects of social support on the well-being of survivors of intimate partner violence across 2 years. *Journal of Consulting and Clinical Psychology, 77,* 718–729. doi:10.1037/a0016140

Berg, B. L. (2001). *Qualitative research methods for the social sciences* (4th ed.). Needham Heights, MA: Allyn & Bacon.

Carlbring, P., & Andersson, G. (2006). Internet and psychological treatment: How well can they be combined? *Computers in Human Behavior, 22,* 254–553.

Charles, D. (2009, August 14). Soap operas to save energy. *Science, 325,* 807. doi:10.1126/science.325_807a

Crowell, N.A., & Burgess, A.W. (1996). *Understanding violence against women.* Washington, DC: National Academies Press.

Denzin, N. K., & Lincoln, Y. S. (Eds.). (2005). *The Sage handbook of qualitative research* (3rd ed.). Thousand Oaks, CA: Sage.

Division for the Advancement of Women. (2000). *The optimal protocol to the Convention on the Elimination of All Forms of Discrimination Against Women: Text and materials.* Geneva, Switzerland: United Nations.

Ellsburg, M.C. & Heise, L. (2005). *Researching violence against women: A practical guide for researchers and activists.* Washington, DC: World Health Organization, PATH.

Evans, C. H., Jr., & Ildstad, S. T. (Eds.). (2001). *Small clinical trials: Issues and challenges.* Washington, DC: National Academies Press.

Foster, E. M., & Kalil, A. (Eds.). (2008). New methods for new questions in developmental psychology [Special section]. *Developmental Psychology, 44,* 301–495.

Hong, G., & Yu, B. (2008). Effects of kindergarten retention on children's social-emotional development: An application of propensity score method to multivariate, multilevel data. *Developmental Psychology, 44,* 407–421. doi:10.1037/0012-1649.44.2.407

Hsu, L. M. (1989). Random sampling, randomization, and equivalence of contrasted groups in psychotherapy outcome research. *Journal of Consulting and Clinical Psychology, 57,* 131–137. doi:10.1037/0022-006X.57.1.131

Kazdin, A. E. (2007). Mediators and mechanisms of change in psychotherapy research. In S. Nolen-Hoeksema, T. D. Cannon, & T. Widiger (Eds.), *Annual review of*

clinical psychology (Vol. 3, pp. 1–27). doi:10.1146/annurev.clinpsy.3.022806.
0191432

Kazdin, A.E. (2011). *Single-case research designs: Methods for clinical and applied settings* (2nd ed.). New York, NY: Oxford University Press.

Koss, M. P., & White, J. W. (2008). National and global agendas on violence against women: Historical perspective and consensus. *American Journal of Orthopsychiatry, 78,* 386–393. doi:10.1037/a0014347

Kraemer, H. C., Kazdin, A. E., Offord, D. R., Kessler, R. C., Jensen, P. S., & Kupfer, D. J. (1997). Coming to terms with the terms of risk. *Archives of General Psychiatry, 54,* 337–343.

Muñoz, R. F. (2009, October). *Using psychology to reduce the global burden of disease.* Presented at the First International E-mental Health Summit, Amsterdam, the Netherlands.

National Center for Injury Prevention and Control. (2009). *CDC injury research agenda, 2009–2018.* Atlanta, GA: U.S. Department of Health and Human Services, Centers for Disease Control and Prevention. Retrieved from http://www.cdc.gov/ncipc

Pinheiro, P. S. (2006). *World report on violence against children.* Geneva, Switzerland: United Nations.

Rodgers, J. L. (2010). The epistemology of mathematical and statistical modeling: A quiet methodological revolution. *American Psychologist, 65,* 1–12. doi:10.1037/a0018326

Shadish, W. R., & Ragsdale, K. (1996). Random versus nonrandom assignment in controlled experiments. Do you get the same answer? *Journal of Consulting and Clinical Psychology, 64,* 1290–1305. doi:10.1037/0022-006X.64.6.1290

Stuart, E. A., & Green, K. M. (2008). Using full matching to estimate causal effects in nonexperimental studies: Examining the relationship between adolescent marijuana use and adult outcomes. *Developmental Psychology, 44,* 395–406. doi:10.1037/0012-1649.44.2.395

United Nations High Commissioner for Human Rights. (1990). *Convention on the rights of the child* (adopted November 20, 1989, and effective September 2, 1990). Retrieved from http://www2.ohchr.org/english/law/crc.htm

Whitaker, D. J., Lutzker, J. R., & Shelly, G. A. (2005). Child maltreatment prevention priorities at the Centers for Disease Control and Prevention. *Child Maltreatment, 10,* 245–259. doi:10.1177/1077559505274674

White, J. W., Koss, M. P., & Kazdin, A. E. (Eds.). (2011). *Violence against women and children, Vol. 1: Mapping the terrain.* Washington, DC: American Psychological Association.

World Health Organization (WHO). (2009). *Violence prevention: The evidence.* Geneva, Switzerland: World Health Organization.

INDEX

Closed support groups, 188
Coats, S., 99
Coerced treatment, 129
Cognitive behavioral therapy, 17–18, 100, 101, 117
Cohen, J. A., 17
Cohen, M., 58
Coker, D., 230
Cole, J., 99, 105
Collaboration of services
    among legal systems, 62–63
    methodological issues with, 278
    for violence against women and children, 302–303
Collaborative Outcome Data Project on the Effectiveness of Psychological Treatment for Sex Offenders, 119
College students, 149, 166–170, 271–272
Colocated services, 225
Communication, 224–225, 227–228, 300
Communities
    African American. See African American communities
    help seeking in, 103
    Native American, 151–152
    privacy of sexual assault victims in, 150–151
    protection of, 58–59
    representation in research, 193–194
    response to sexual assault in, 105–106
Community Advocacy Project, 189
Community-based services
    for domestic violence victims/ survivors, 184, 263
    evaluation of, 286
    for postassault mental health, 100, 101
    single-case research on, 281
Community building, 33–36
Community-level interventions. See also Coordinated community responses
    for batterers' intervention programs, 209
    for change in social norms, 174, 288–289
    for child abuse prevention, 78

for domestic violence prevention, 241–242
for domestic violence services, 224–227
family engagement strategies, 35–36
public awareness campaigns. See Public awareness campaigns
for released sex offenders, 129–130
research–practice gap with, 275
Community Programming Initiative, 171
Comparative fault, 147
Comprehensive programs, 270–271
Conceptual models (intervention/ prevention), 279, 297, 298
Conduct offenses, 51
Conferencing, 152
Confidentiality, 122–123, 129
Conflict resolution, 247
Consensus recommendations, 283–292
Consent, 140–141, 267
Consistency, 262, 293
Constitutional protections, 53, 146
Contested custody, 224
Contraception, 97, 99
Coordinated community responses
    to domestic violence perpetrators, 207–208
    effectiveness of, 226
    historical context of, 224–226
    in justice system responses to domestic violence, 215, 224–229, 269
    for sexual assault victims, 104–105
    unintended negative consequences of, 226–227
Coordinated multilevel approaches, 298–299
Coordination, interagency, 300
Corporal punishment, 302
Counseling services, 105, 187–188, 203
Couples interventions, 246
Court-mandated treatment, 57–58, 117–118
Craft, C. A., 239
Craig, C., 101
Crandall, C., 99
Credibility, 140–142
Crenshaw, K., 221
Criminal justice system
    barriers for sexual assault victims, 146
    communication in, 227–228

Homebuilders, 15
Home visitation, 30–31, 73–75, 270.
    See also In-home interventions
Hospital emergency departments. *See*
    Emergency response
Housing, 148, 186–187, 193
Human immunodeficiency virus (HIV),
    97, 99
Human rights, 291, 301–302

Ildstad, S. T., 280
Immigration status, 150
Implementation process
    of child maltreatment prevention
        programs, 85–86
    of domestic violence prevention
        programs, 238–239
    program evaluation of, 248–249
Implementation System, 240–241, 248
Incarcerated men, 205. *See also* Prison-
    based treatment programs
Incidence, 277
Incredible Years Series, 244
Indicated interventions, 72
Indigenous practices, 109
Individual-level programs
    advocacy services for domestic
        violence, 188–189
    assessment of, 294
    for domestic violence prevention,
        240
    for sexual violence prevention, 173
Individual-level research, 281
Individual needs, 227–228
Infants, 39
Informal support systems, 184, 286
Information resources, 301
Infrastructure services, 299–301
In-home interventions
    effectiveness of, 18
    Healthy Start, 15
    Homebuilders, 15
    multisystemic therapy, 17
    parent–child interaction therapy,
        16–17
Injuries, 289
Innovations, 239–243, 247
In Re Gault, 52–53
Integration models, 85, 297
Intensive Family Preservation, 14–15

Interactive Systems Framework for Dis-
    semination and Implementation,
    85–86, 239–241
Interagency communication, 224–225,
    300
International agendas, 282–292
Interventions
    based on theoretical models,
        288–289
    for child abuse victims, 12
    conceptual models of, 279
    cultural ethics against, 221
    online, 274
    for physical abuse, 14
    research on, 274–275
    for sexual abuse, 14
Interviews, of children, 56
Intimate partner violence (IPV).
    See Domestic violence
Intoxication, 141–142
Investigative interviews, 56
IPV (intimate partner violence).
    See Domestic violence
Isolated parents, 33–36

Jeglic, E. L., 58
Joint custody, 224
Jones Harden, B., 32, 37
Judicial training, 228
Jurisdiction, 52
Jurors, 140–141
Justice system. *See also specific headings*
    alternatives to, 229–230
    barriers/obstacles in, 269, 287
    coordination with other systems, 286
Justice system responses to child
        maltreatment, 47–66
    and child welfare systems, 48–50
    in criminal justice systems, 50–52
    and educational systems, 54, 267
    juvenile justice systems, 52–53,
        266–267
    key decision points in, 54–59
    legal issues with, 59–65
    and medical/mental health care
        systems, 53–54, 267
    recommendations for improvement
        of, 266–267
Justice system responses to domestic
        violence, 215–230

Perpetrators of sexual violence, 169–170. *See also* Sex offender treatment programs

Person-centered interventions, 39–40

PFA (psychological first aid), 106–107

Phillips Smith, E., 250

Physical abuse, 14, 17–19

Physical evidence, 140

Physical health, 284

Physical safety, 106

Plante, E. G., 165

Play therapy, 16

Policy(-ies)
for domestic violence prevention, 241
on family services for child maltreatment, 37–40
as innovation category, 240
offender registration, 58–59
for prosecution of domestic violence, 217–219

Political will, 128

Population-based interventions, 79

Postassault medical care, 96–99

Postassault mental health care, 100–102

Posttraumatic stress disorder (PTSD)
mental health services for, 100, 101
psychological first aid for, 106
recommendations for victim services, 263
short-term, trauma-focused counseling for, 187–188
and victim blaming, 98

Poverty, 275–276, 291, 295–296

Pregnancy services, 97

Premarriage interventions, 246

Prenatal and Infancy Home Visitation by Nurses, 244

Prentky, R. A., 116, 125, 130

PREP (Prevention and Relationship Enhancement), 246

Preschool programs, 77

Presidential Summit on Violence and Abuse in Relationships, xiv–xv

Prevalence, 277

Prevalence statistics, 283

Preventing Youth Violence in a Multicultural Society (N. G. Guerra & E. Phillips Smith), 250

Prevention. *See also* Prevention programs
of child abuse. *See* Child abuse

of domestic violence. *See* Domestic violence prevention
emphasis on, 262, 273
evidence-based practices for, 274–275
funding for, 291–292
large-scale, 292–293
primary. *See* Primary prevention
prioritization of children in, 290
recommendations for improvement of, 288–291, 297–299
secondary, 201, 238
steps in research on, 85–86
of violence, x–xi

Prevention and Relationship Enhancement Program (PREP), 246

Prevention Delivery System, 86

Prevention Implementation System, 251

Prevention programs
accessibility to support for, 248
for child maltreatment. *See* Child maltreatment prevention programs
general types for domestic violence, 242–243
implementation of, 238–239
with insufficient evidence of effectiveness, 246–247
integration of, 85
media-based. *See* Media-based interventions
not specific to domestic violence, 243
for sexual violence. *See* Sexual violence prevention programs

Prevention Research System, 247–248, 250–251

Prevention science. *See* Science of prevention

Prevention Support System, 86

Prevention Synthesis and Translation System, 86

Primary prevention
defined, 238
of domestic violence, 272
for domestic violence perpetrators, 201
emphasis on, 290
of sexual violence, 159, 160

Principles, 240, 241

Prison-based treatment programs
confidentiality in, 122–123

dual role of therapists, 124
efficacy of, 126–127
evidence-based practices in,
    125–126, 128–129
as mandated interventions, 128–129
for sex offenders, 118
treatment goals for, 129
values in, 124–125
willingness to participate in, 122
Prisoner reentry, 205, 207–208
Privacy violations, 142–143, 150–151
Private charities, 62
Privileged information, 143
Problematic parenting, 79
Procedural restraints, 51
Processes, 240, 241
Program development
    for childhood sexual abuse
        prevention, 163
    of dual-pronged programs, 167
    evaluation methodology in, 170–171
Program evaluation, 275
    batterers' intervention programs,
        205–206, 208–209
    children's domestic violence services,
        190–191
    community-based services, 275, 286
    domestic violence, 187–188, 192,
        248–249
    methodological rigor of, 80–81,
        173–174
Project Safecare, 73
Project Support, 247
Proof, burden of, 146
Prophylaxis, 97
Prosecution
    and child safety in domestic violence
        cases, 220
    for crimes against children, 60–61
    of domestic violence cases, 217–219,
        227–228
    of rape perpetrators, 139–140
    rates for rape of minority women,
        143–145
    of sexual assault, 137–138
Prosecutors, 139–140, 144
Prospective studies, 252
Protection of communities, 58–59
Protection orders, 148, 222–224
Protective factors, 83–84, 276, 279

Psycholegal issues, 126
Psychological first aid (PFA), 106–107
Psychological safety, 106
Psychology of Violence, xv
Psychotherapy, 115–116, 285–286
PTSD. *See* Posttraumatic stress disorder
Public awareness campaigns
    for child abuse prevention, 77–78, 271
    community-level programs, 240
    for domestic violence prevention,
        241, 242
    recommendations for improvement
        of, 299
Public child welfare, 28–30
Public health model, x, 72, 172
Public health systems
    child maltreatment interventions,
        77–79
    priority of prevention and deterrence
        by, 298
    and violence against women and
        children, ix–xi

Qualitative research, 281–282
Quantitative research, 280
Quasi-experimental designs, 280

Racialized populations, 32, 61–62.
    See also specific headings
RAD (reactive attachment disorder), 15
Raja, S., 101
Randomized clinical trials (RCTs)
    for domestic violence prevention
        evaluation, 252
    feasibility/usefulness of, 279–280
    integrity of, 84
    of sex offender treatment programs,
        119–120
Rape. *See also* Sexual assault; Sexual
    violence
    attitudes that support, 169
    criminal justice system responses to,
        268
    crisis centers for, 98, 99, 102, 108
    defined, 95
    legal system conceptualization of, 147
    marital, 143, 153
    normative narrative of, 144
    prosecution of, 139–140, 143–145
    stereotypes about, 144

Rape in America, 103
Rape kit, 96
Rape law reform
 in civil law, 147–151
 consent and force in, 140–141, 267
 effectiveness of, 138–139
 intoxication/drug use in, 141–142
 marital rape, 153
 privacy violations, 142–143
 racial biases, 143–145
 rape shield statutes, 138, 142, 147
 recommendations for improvement
  of, 153
 tort remedies, 145–147
RCTs. *See* Randomized clinical trials
Reactive attachment disorder (RAD),
 15
Rebirthing therapy, 15
Recidivism
 of domestic violence perpetrators,
  218–219
 impact of coordinated community
  responses on, 226
 of sex offenders, 118–121
Rehabilitation, 14–18, 263
Relapse prevention (RP), 121–122
Relative placement, 13
Relevance, 192–193
Reporters, mandated, 13
Representative prevalence statistics, 283
Rescue, 12–14, 263
Research
 on child maltreatment prevention
  programs, 79–85
 on domestic violence prevention,
  250–253
 on family services for child
  maltreatment, 36–40
 funding for, 292
 individual-level, 281
 on interventions, 274–275
 qualitative, 281–282
 quantitative, 280
 representation of communities of
  color in, 193–194
 on risk factors, 289
 sharing of, 291
 on victim services, 18–20, 102–105,
  191–194
 on violence, xv–xvi

on violence against women and
  children, 276–282, 302–303
Research design
 experimental, 249, 280
 methodology in, 278–282
 for program evaluation, 249–252,
  280
 quasi-experimental, 280
 recommendations for improvement
  of, 283–284
 retrospective, 104
 single-case, 281
 validity of, 170
Research methodologies
 in child abuse program evaluations,
  80–81
 for cultural context, 275–276, 278
 for data analysis, 279–282
 for evaluation, 170–171
 for measurement, 277
 recommendations for improvement
  of, 277–278
 in research design, 278–282
 rigor of, 80–81, 173–174
 in sexual violence program evaluations, 173–174
 in victim services research, 103–104
Research–practice gap
 in community settings, 275
 in domestic violence prevention,
  238–239, 250–251, 272
 in violence prevention, 247–248
Research subjects, 100
Research System, 239–240
Resnick, H. S., 107
Responsivity, 126
Restorative justice
 for domestic violence, 229–230
 responses to sexual assault, 147–148,
  151–152
 responses to sexual violence, 268
RESTORE, 152
Restraining orders, 222–224
Restraints, 51
Results reporting, 249, 251–252
Retaliatory abuse, 219–220
Retraumatization, 151
Retributive responses, 286–287
Retrospective research designs, 104
Rights, 61–65

Risk factors
    and causality/change, 276, 279
    for child maltreatment, 83–84
    for domestic violence perpetrators,
        289
    research on, 289
Risk/Need/Responsivity (R/N/R),
    125–126
Risk-reduction programs, 167–168
R/N/R (Risk/Need/Responsivity),
    125–126
Roberts, D., 35
Rothery, M. A., 188
Rozee, P. D., 167
RP (relapse prevention), 121–122
Ruzek, J. I., 106

Safe Dates, 164, 242, 244, 246
Safe Families Act, 30, 38, 49
Safety
    of abused women and children,
        219–220
    in child welfare services, 38
    immediate, 184
    justice system responses, 148
    psychological, 106
Sampling issues, 192, 277, 280
SANE (Sexual Assault Nurse Examiner),
    98–99
SARTs (sexual assault response teams),
    104–105
Saul, J., 250
School-age children, 39
School-based programs
    for bullying prevention, 245
    for child maltreatment prevention,
        76–77, 270
    medical and mental health services,
        54
    recommendations for improvement
        of, 290
    for sexual violence prevention,
        271–272
School personnel, 163
Schuerman, J., 18
Schulhofer, S. J., 141
Schwartz, B. K., 130
Science of prevention
    advances in, 84
    child maltreatment, 83

domestic violence, 238–239
    innovations in, 239–240
    recommendations for improvements
        of, 298
Secondary prevention, 201, 238
"Second rape," 138, 151
Sefl, T., 101
Selective interventions, 72
Self-defense programs, 168
Self-reports
    of child maltreatment, 55
    in domestic violence prevention,
        250
    of sexual violence prevention pro-
        gram participants, 171
Sentencing circles, 152
Service systems
    coordination of, 286, 296–297
    delivery of. See Delivery of services
    economic costs of not providing, 296
    evidence-based practices for, 274–275
    for infrastructure, 299–301
    for maltreating families, 57–58
Sex offender treatment programs,
    115–130
    evidence-based practice for, 125–128
    legal context for, 116–117
    mental health treatment, 265
    models for, 121–125
    rationale for, 117–118
    recidivism research on, 118–121
    recommendations for improvement
        of, 128–130
Sex-role perceptions, 200, 201
Sexual abuse. See also Sexual violence
    empirical support for interventions,
        18–19
    prevention strategies with children,
        162–163
    rehabilitation for, 14
    school-based prevention programs
        for, 76
    successful treatment of perpetrators,
        58
Sexual assault, 137. See also Justice system
        responses to sexual assault;
        Sex offender treatment programs;
        Victim services for sexual assault
Sexual Assault Nurse Examiner
        (SANE), 98–99

specific problems of, 278
used in rape crisis centers, 102
Theories of change, 276, 279
Theory-driven programs, 173
Therapists, 123–124
Third-party lawsuits, 146
Thornton, T. N., 239
Title IX, 149
Tort litigation, 145–147
Tough Guise, 169
Tracy, E., 39–40
Training, 107–108
Transitional housing services, 186–187
Trauma-focused cognitive behavioral
    therapy for child traumatic grief
    (TG-CBT), 17–19
Trauma-focused play therapy, 16
Traumatic experiences, 104
Treatment goals, 129
Treatment modalities, 126, 200
Trial procedures, 51
Triple P Program, 79
Turay v. Seling et al., 116
Tutty, L. M., 188
Typologies, 200

Ullman, S. E., 98, 108
Unconsciousness, 142
Unified domestic violence courts,
    225–226
Uniformity, 262, 293
Unintended negative consequences
    of civil protection orders/restraining
        orders, 223–224
    of coordinated community responses,
        226–227
    of criminal justice responses to
        domestic violence, 219–221
    of mandated reporting, 55
    in models of crisis intervention, 107
    of victim services, 273
United Nations, 301–302
United Nations Convention for the
    Elimination of All Forms of
    Discrimination Against Women
    (CEDAW), 302
United States, x, 301–302
Universal interventions
    child abuse public awareness
        programs, 77–78

defined, 72
in public health model, 172
recommendations for improvement
    of, 299
Usefulness, 279–280

Validity, 170
Values, 124–125
VAWA. *See* Violence Against Women
    Act
Victim(s)
    blame of, 97–98
    character of, 142
    dialogue with offender, 152
    diversity of, 294–296
    impact statements from, 145
    use of term, 95
Victim-centered model, 104
Victim-centered protection, 138
Victimization, 273, 294–295
Victim Rights Law Center, 153
Victim services (in general)
    crisis-oriented, 185–186
    multisystem response to, 273–274
    psychotherapy and support, 285
    recommendations for improvement
        of, 296–297, 299–303
    sensitive, nonstigmatizing health
        care, 284
    for sexual violence, 263
    unintended negative consequences
        of, 273
Victim services for child abuse, 11–22
    in child welfare systems, 60–61
    knowledge gaps, 20–21
    rehabilitation, 14–18
    rescue, 12–14, 263
    research on, 18–20
    resources for, 21–22
    service delivery gaps, 20–21
Victim services for domestic violence,
    183–194
    accessibility and relevance of,
        192–193
    advocacy and legal advocacy services,
        188–190
    children's services, 190–191
    counseling services and support
        groups, 187–188
    recommendations for improvement
        of, 263–264

ABOUT THE EDITORS

Jacquelyn W. White, PhD, is a professor of psychology and associate for research in the College of Arts and Sciences at the University of North Carolina at Greensboro. Her research focuses on gender issues, aggression, and intimate partner violence. Dr. White has conducted research in the area of aggression and violence for more than 30 years. She is a past editor of the *Psychology of Women Quarterly* and is on the board of editors for the journal *Aggressive Behavior*. She was the 2008 recipient of the Carolyn Wood Sherif Award, given by the Society for the Psychology of Women. She currently cochairs the National Partnership to End Interpersonal Violence.

Mary P. Koss, PhD, is a Regents' professor in the Mel and Enid Zuckerman Arizona College of Public Health at the University of Arizona, Tucson. She has served on the National Academy of Sciences Panel on Violence Against Women and currently sits on the Coordinating Committee of the Sexual Violence Research Initiative, funded by the Global Forum and the Ford Foundation, based in Johannesburg, South Africa. She is a member of the Department of Defense Rapid Research Response Team on children, youth, and families. She consults nationally with the Gallup Organization on sexual assault prevalence and response in the military justice system. She recently served as *rapporteur* on gender-based violence at the fourth Milestones of a Global Campaign for Violence Prevention in Geneva, Switzerland. She received the Award for Distinguished Contributions to Research in Public Policy in 2000, the Committee on Women in Psychology Leadership Award in 2003, and a presidential citation in 2008 from the American Psychological Association. In 2010, she was the eighth recipient of the Visionary Award from Ending Violence Against Women International (Vice President Joe Biden was the first).

Alan E. Kazdin, PhD, is the John M. Musser Professor of Psychology and Child Psychiatry at Yale University, New Haven, Connecticut, and Director of the Yale Parenting Center and Child Conduct Clinic, an outpatient treatment service for children and families. Before coming to Yale, he was on the faculty of The Pennsylvania State University, State College, and the University of Pittsburgh School of Medicine, Pittsburgh, Pennsylvania. At Yale, he has been chairman of the Psychology Department, director of the Yale Child Study Center at the School of Medicine, and director of Child Psychiatric Services, Yale–New Haven Hospital. In 2008, he was President of the American Psychological Association. He has authored or edited more than 650 articles, chapters, and books. His 45 books focus on child and adolescent psychotherapy, parenting, and aggressive and antisocial behavior. His work has been featured on television (e.g., *Good Morning America, Primetime, 20/20,* and PBS) as well as in articles on parenting challenges in *Slate.com.*